OUR KIND

ALSO BY MARVIN HARRIS

Town and Country in Brazil

Minorities in the New World
(with Charles Wagley)

Patterns of Race in the Americas

The Nature of Cultural Things

War: The Anthropology of Armed Conflict and Aggression
(with M. Fried and R. Murphy)

The Rise of Anthropological Theory

Culture, People, Nature

Cows, Pigs, Wars and Witches

Cannibals and Kings

America Now

Cultural Anthropology

Good to Eat

Death, Sex and Fertility
(with Eric Ross)

Food and Evolution
(with Eric Ross)

OUR KIND

WHO WE ARE
WHERE WE CAME FROM
WHERE WE ARE GOING

MARVIN HARRIS

HARPER & ROW, PUBLISHERS, NEW YORK

Grand Rapids, Philadelphia, St. Louis, San Francisco

1817 London, Singapore, Sydney, Tokyo, Toronto

FIRST EDITION

Designed by Karen Savary

Library of Congress Cataloging-in-Publication Data

Harris, Marvin, 1927–
    Our kind : who we are, where we came from, where we are going / Marvin Harris — 1st ed.
      p.   cm.
    Bibliography: p.
    Includes index.
    ISBN 0-06-015776-3
    1. Anthropology. 2. Human evolution. 3. Social evolution. I. Title.
GN31.2.H37   1989
573.2—dc20   88-45514
                                                     CIP

89 90 91 92 93 DT/HC 10 9 8 7 6 5 4 3 2 1

CONTENTS

favor is to draw up definitive lists of names, places, events, and literary works guaranteed to lift the uneducated out of their stygian ignorance. As an anthropologist, I worry as much about the promulgation of such lists as I do about the vacuum they are intended to fill. Produced mainly by historians and literary celebrities, they focus on the events and achievements of Western societies. Moreover they are silent about the great biological transformations that led to the appearance of our ancestors on earth and that endowed our species with a unique capacity for culturally constructed adaptations. And they are equally silent about the evolutionary principles that shaped the social life of our species after our ancestors achieved "cultural takeoff." Indeed, as lists they are intrinsically incapable of educating people concerning anything about the biological and cultural processes that constrain our lives and mold our destiny. Or to speak more positively, as an anthropologist I believe that the minimal task of any modern educational reform lies in imparting a comparative, global, and evolutionary perspective about who we are as a species and what we can and cannot expect our cultures to do for us.

In advocating a pan-human, biosocial, and evolutionary perspective, I do not wish to detract from the importance of traditional local and particular knowledge. We live and act in local and particular contexts and have no choice but to begin to learn about the world from the inside out. But too much of the particular, a failure to see the world from the outside in, is a form of ignorance that can be as as dangerous as not knowing the boundaries of the United States. Does it make sense to know the history of a few states and yet know nothing about the origin of all states? Should we study the wars of a few countries and yet know nothing of war in all countries?

Now that I have registered my protest against list makers, let me confess that I have had something similar in mind while writing this book. For I have asked myself what I as an anthropologist have learned about our kind that I think all the members of our species ought to know. And I have tried to present the result of this autointerrogation—surely not as a list but as a rapid-moving, compact narrative.

And now it is time for another warning. Please judge this book by what it covers, not by what it leaves out. I want to tell you

PREFACE

ARE YOU AS INTERESTED as I am in knowing how, when, and where human life arose, what the first human societies and languages were like, why cultures have evolved along diverse but often remarkably convergent pathways, why distinctions of rank came into being, and how small bands and villages gave way to chiefdoms and chiefdoms to mighty states and empires? And do you wonder as much as I what part of the human condition is in our genes and what part in our cultural heritage, whether jealousy, war, poverty, and sexism are inevitable, and whether our species has a chance to survive? Then read on.

To judge from the universal telling of myths that explain how the world was created and how the ancient ones acquired powers of speech and mastery of the useful arts, people everywhere want to know the answers to such questions. But be forewarned. The story I have to tell is not meant for a particular group or culture but for human beings everywhere. Are you ready to look beyond the smoke of your own chimney? Are you ready to view the world first as a member of the species to which we all belong and only second as a member of a particular human tribe, nation, religion, sex, class, race, kind, or crowd? Yes? Then read on.

The discovery that large numbers of college students cannot recognize the outlines of their own country on unlabeled maps or identify on whose side the Russians fought during World War II has provoked heated debates about what it is that anybody must know in order to be considered an educated person. One remedy much in about what I have learned. Unfortunately I have not learned all that I would like to learn and so there are many gaps in my story. I would especially have liked to be able to say more about the evolution of music and the arts, but these are aspects of human experience that are difficult to understand in terms of evolutionary processes. I have not the foggiest notion, for example, why some artistic traditions stress realistic representations while others stress abstract or geometric designs, or why African rhythms are generally more complex than those of Native Americans. Perhaps some day we will understand more about the emotional, aesthetic, and expressive dimensions of human life, or it may turn out that there are things that can be known only from inside and only in the particular, never in the general. Meanwhile there are worlds enough to explore. So let me begin.

ACKNOWLEDGMENTS

I AM GRATEFUL to Marjorie Shostak and Melvin Konner for
believing that I could write a book that in their words "put it all
together." Just knowing that someone thought that such a book was
possible and that I could write it kept me going through some
difficult times. I am also grateful to many colleagues and friends
who provided information, references, and good wishes, especially
Barbara Miller, Linda Wolfe, Leslie Lieberman, Otto von Mering,
Shirley von Mering, Maxine Margolis, Jerry Milanich, Gerald
Murray, Carol Bernard, Russ Bernard, Charles Wagley, Cecilia
Wagley, Murdo Macleod, Sheena Macleod, Ronald Cohen, and Bill
Keegan.

I also want to thank David Price for his work on the
bibliography and his substantive suggestions, Phyllis Durell for
producing the typescript, and Ray Jones and Delores Jenkins for
being such generous and intrepid librarians.

It has been a pleasure working with Harper & Row on this
project, especially with Carol Cohen and Eric Wirth. I have also had
the pleasure of being represented by Murray Curtin, who is both a
fine literary agent and a loyal and devoted friend. Finally, I thank
Madeline Harris for helping me make one more impossible dream
come true.

IN THE
BEGINNING

IN THE BEGINNING was the foot. Four million years ago, before speech or consciousness, our ancestors already walked erect on two feet. Other apes kept the handlike foot of our common tree-climbing, tree-dwelling past. They remained, in effect, four-handed, with big toes like thumbs that could touch any of the other toes, good for hooking around limbs and branches while reaching for fruits high above the forest floor, but not good for bearing the full weight of the body. When they came down to earth, to move from grove to grove of fruiting trees, they mostly walked on all fours, possibly like modern gorillas and chimpanzees who get about on short, stubby legs, flat-footed, big toe spread wide, and long arms locked in line straight from shoulders to the knuckles of their hands. Or perhaps they used their hands like modern orangutans, to walk on the side of their fists. Like the modern great apes, they could stand or walk on two legs, but only briefly and for short distances. Not only were their feet ill-suited for standing or walking upright, but their legs and buttocks lacked the muscles that keep human beings upright. Also, their spines curved in a simple arc without the stabilizing forward turn that humans have in the small of the back. On two legs they staggered more than walked, their arms held high for balance, useless for carrying anything except for short distances.

Our own ancestral apes were different. They had our feet, feet whose toes could not curl together to grasp or pick up objects and which were good mainly for standing, running, jumping, or kicking. Everything else was the responsibility of the hands.

As long as hands had to do the work of feet, their virtuosity as hands remained impaired. The thumb had to be short and stubby in the great apes to keep it out of the way while walking on knuckles or fists. As the thumb grew longer and more robust, our ancestor apes came to possess the most powerful and tenacious and yet the most delicate and precise manipulatory forelimbs in the animal kingdom.

Why did nature fashion an ape that walked on two legs? The answer must lie in the ability of such a creature to prosper on the ground. No large animal walks upright on tree limbs, much less jumps on two legs from branch to branch. But mere ground-dwelling cannot account for our upright posture. Living on the ground is exactly what most mammals do best. And from elephants to cats, horses, and baboons, they get about on all fours. A two-footed, two-handed ape makes evolutionary sense only because it could do something on the ground that no other creature had ever done so much of or done so well: use hands to make and carry tools, and use tools to satisfy daily needs.

Part of the evidence is in our teeth. All modern apes possess protruding canines—"fangs"—useful for opening tough-skinned fruits and for shredding bamboo as well as for weapons, bared in threat or relied on in combat against predators or sexual rivals. But our earliest two-footed, two-handed ancestors had no fangs. Their front teeth were already small, their molars broad and flat, their jaws hinged more for grinding and milling than for cutting and slashing. Were these fangless forebears harmless, then? I rather doubt it. Human dentition carries a different and more ominous message. We understand it all too well. Those who brandish the biggest sticks are more to be feared than those who snarl with the biggest teeth.

THE BIRTH
OF A
CHIMERA

CHARLES DARWIN first addressed the question of human evolution in a book called *The Descent of Man,* published in 1871, twelve years after he wrote *Origin of Species.* It was there that he stated for the first time that "man like every other species is descended from some pre-existing form," that natural selection accounts for human origins to the same extent that it accounts for the origins of any other species, and that this includes not merely our bodies, but our "highest" cognitive, aesthetic, and moral capabilities, which exist to a rudimentary degree even among creatures as humble as cats and dogs. The impression of a sharp break between them and us was a misapprehension caused by the fact that the protohumans who possessed intermediate powers of mind and body were losers in the struggle for survival and reproductive success, and long ago became extinct.

The great apes weighed heavily in favor of an evolutionary origin for human beings. They showed that the human form did not exist in splendid isolation from the rest of the biological world. In their skeletons, physiology, and behavior, chimpanzees, gorillas, and orangutans were uncannily reminiscent of human beings. They looked like family members, albeit poor and mentally retarded. In fact, long before Darwin, the great Swedish taxonomist, Carolus Linnaeus, had placed apes and humans in the same taxonomic family. Even biologists who were opposed to evolutionism had to admit that they could not find any purely anatomical reasons against considering the great apes as so many different kinds of human beings or humans as just one more kind of ape. So Darwin and his followers never hesitated after deciding that humans did descend from a "pre-existing form" that it must have been some kind of ape.

These conjectures led to the search for what came to be called "the missing link" (an inept concept from the start because evolution implies that there are many links, not just one, between related species). In trying to picture what this half-ape, half-human must have looked like, Darwin's followers fell into a trap. They constructed a chimerical beast out of the features most associated in the popular mind with ape status and human status, respectively. They pictured it as having a large human brain and an ape jaw with big canines. Darwin himself inadvertently contributed to this imaginary creation by predicting that among the "early progenitors of man . . . the males had great canine teeth, which served them as formidable weapons." Darwin was actually trying to picture a different "missing link"—a species that could serve as the common ancestor of both apes and humans. But this distinction got blurred in the ensuing rush to find *the* "missing link" between humans and apes.

The first victim of this chimera was a Dutch physician by the name of Eugène Dubois. On assignment in the Dutch East Indies during the early 1890s, Dubois was searching for fossils along the banks of the Solo River in Java, when he came across a flat, heavy-browed, primitive-looking skull cap. Nearby he found a thigh bone that was very much like a human thigh bone. He called his find *Pithecanthropus erectus*—"the humanlike ape with erect posture"—and announced that it was "the precursor of man." But back in Europe, the experts were not impressed: The skull was too low-browed to contain a brain with human affinities; it was nothing but an ape. As for the thigh bone, it belonged to a modern human whose remains had somehow gotten misplaced. Dubois himself later decided that his find was not a missing link but an extinct giant gibbon. He did not live to see *Pithecanthropus* reclassified as an early member of the species known today as *Homo erectus*. For he had in fact discovered an important missing link between *Homo sapiens* and our more apelike ancestors. Although its brain was bigger than Dubois's critics allowed, and although it made sophisticated stone tools, erectus, as I'll call it from now on, was not yet fully at the human level. But that is getting ahead of the story.

At last the glad tidings came. The real missing link had been found; and not in far-off Java but right at home, in Sussex, England.

THE RISE
AND FALL OF
DAWSON'S
DAWN MAN

SPEAKING TO THE GEOLOGICAL SOCIETY in 1912, Charles Dawson, an amateur antiquarian, explained how he had dug up several skull fragments and half of a broken lower jaw, mixed in with the bones of extinct mammals, in the Pleistocene gravels near Piltdown Commons in Sussex. Smith Woodward, a brilliant anatomist and curator at the British Museum of Natural History, rose to corroborate Dawson's account. He presented the audience with a plaster reconstruction of what he thought the extinct creature must have looked like, and suggested that it be known from then on as *Eoanthropus Dawsoni*— "Dawson's Dawn Man." This missing link had a proper modern-looking voluminous, globular, high-browed skull, but a chinless, apelike lower jaw. The canines were missing, but Woodward invoked Darwin. He predicted that when they found the canines they would be suitably fanglike. Within a year, the French scientist-priest Teilhard de Chardin, who had volunteered to help with the excavations at Piltdown (the Catholic Church having by then accepted the physical facts of evolution), found a canine tooth that looked exactly as Woodward had predicted: "pointed; projecting, and shaped as in anthropoid apes."

Small wonder. It *was* an ape's canine, and Dawn Man's jaw was an ape's jaw. Someone—identity still not known—had devised a clever hoax. He had obtained a modern human skull with unusually thick bones, broken it into small pieces, stained the pieces brown to look like fossils, and salted them into the Piltdown site along with some real and some fake fossils of extinct Pleistocene mammals. He had also gotten hold of half of a modern orangutan's lower jaw with its canine missing, broken off the nobby upper rear portion so that no one could see that it could not have fitted together with the human skull, filed down the jaw's molar teeth to imitate the kind of wear that human chewing produces, stained the whole thing fossil brown, and buried it near the pieces of the skull. The hoaxer knew that the final bit of evidence needed to confirm his creation as the real missing link would be the discovery of the fanglike canine that Darwin had prepared everyone to expect. After Woodward fell into the trap and made his prediction about the missing canine, the hoaxer completed his masterpiece by partially filing down a chimpanzee canine, coloring it with the usual brown stain, and placing it in a spot where it was sure to be found by a completely trustworthy man of the cloth.

A few scholars expressed disbelief. There was just too much of a difference between Dawn Man's brain and Dawn Man's jaw. But the majority found the big head irresistible. The brain, after all, is the organ that most distinguishes us from the beasts. How could the hand be artful unless the human brain was there to guide it? Surely the brain must have evolved first as a precondition for unleashing the cunning of the hand. And what could be more appropriate than that the first human inhabitant of the British Isles should be more high-browed and intelligent and therefore better fit to rule the world than low-browed, retarded erectus of Java?

Dawn Man became a new kind of British crown jewel. They put it under lock and key in the Museum of Natural History, and scientists who wanted to examine the precious remains of the first Englishman had to be content with working on plaster casts. This explains why the hoax remained undetected for so many years. Not until 1953 were the bones themselves given close scrutiny. As part of a routine program to test the age of fossils in the British Museum, the originals were subjected to the newly developed fluorine dating method. The test indicated that neither the skull nor jaw possessed any great antiquity. Out from their case came the miscreant bones, and into the laboratory of the disbelieving Oxford anthropologist, J. S. Weiner. An ordinary microscope sufficed to reveal the file marks on the teeth, while small holes drilled into the teeth and jaw quickly exposed the difference between their fresh white interiors and their artificially discolored surfaces. As the chimera that had haunted paleontology for eighty years melted into thin air, the way was cleared at last to stand human evolution on its feet.

LUCY IN THE
SKY WITH
DIAMONDS

*N*OT EVERYONE WAS DISAPPOINTED by Weiner's revelations. In fact, a small group of scientists who had been searching for missing links in South Africa was positively delighted. Since 1924, they had been pondering the fossil remains of a juvenile primate retrieved from a limestone quarry by Raymond Dart of the University of Witwatersrand. This creature possessed an apelike face and a brain whose volume was only slightly larger than a chimpanzee's, but its jaw and teeth, including its canines, were of human shape and dimension. Furthermore, the opening in the base of the skull where the head and vertebral column join together was located much farther forward than in any known ape, indicating that the creature maintained an upright position while standing or moving about. Dart lost no time in declaring that it was he, not Dubois or Dawson, who had found the earliest hominid, the true "man-ape," to which he gave the name *Australopithecus africanus*—"southern ape from Africa." But with Piltdown still in the cabinet at the British Museum, few scientists paid heed.

By 1950, the evidence in favor of Dart's contention had become much stronger. In various caves and limeworks in the Transvaal region, Robert Broom of the Transvaal Museum had found additional australopithecine remains, including a well-preserved skull belonging to the adult form of Dart's juvenile "southern ape." Broom also discovered a second species of australopithecus, characterized by large front teeth and large molars, a massive face, widely flaring cheekbones, and a sharp keel or crest that ran from the front to the back of the top of the skull and to which in life huge chewing muscles had been anchored. Today this second species generally goes by the name *Australopithecus robustus,* setting it apart from the smaller and more gracile africanus.

With Dawn Man's fall, Dart's and Broom's discoveries took center stage and Africa became the place to look for more missing links. Eastern Africa, especially, where the great tectonic feature known as the Rift Valley, extending from Tanzania in the south to Ethiopia in the north, contains some of the world's richest deposits of exposed fossils. We know today from a profusion of skulls, teeth, jaws, legs, pelves, and many other skeletal parts excavated from Rift Valley sites that Africa was once inhabited by at least two species of humanlike apes—one, robust and with large molars possibly specialized for cracking nuts and grinding up high-fiber plant foods, the other, gracile and with teeth suitable for a more omnivorous diet. Both stood and moved about on two feet, neither had a brain much larger than a chimpanzee's or a gorilla's, and neither had protruding canines. Thanks to a number of dating techniques based on such principles as the reversal of the earth's magnetic field and the shifting ratio of radioactive potassium to radioactive argon in volcanic deposits, the life and times of these two species can be bracketed to between 3 million and 1.3 million years ago. But more spectacular discoveries were soon to come.

In 1973, Donald Johanson discovered a still more ancient australopithecine in the Afar region in Ethiopia. It lived some 3.25 million years ago. Among the remains was the skeleton, miraculously 40 percent complete, of a diminutive adult female hominid, only three-and-a-half feet tall. To capture the effect of the surreal reunion between this ancient creature and some of its twentieth-century descendants, Johanson named her Lucy, evoking the then popular Beatles song "Lucy in the Sky with Diamonds," itself a cryptogram for mind-altering L.S.D. In a more prosaic mood, Johanson named his find *Australopithecus afarensis.* I'll take the liberty of calling it afarensis.

Other afarensis remains found near Lucy were considerably taller. Presumably they were the males (although they might represent the presence of another species). A year after Johanson discovered Lucy, Mary Leakey and her associates found additional afarensis remains at Laetoli, near the Serengeti Plain in northern Tanzania. Johanson's and Leakey's afarensis flourished between three and four million years ago, but an afarensis jaw discovered by Steven Ward and Andrew Hill near Lake Baringa, Kenya, indicates that the hominids first arose five million years ago. Afarensis possessed features that would have served it well if it had to climb trees in an emergency. The bones of its fingers and toes were somewhat curved as if to grasp tree trunks and boughs with hands and feet. Moreover, to be less than four feet tall is a good thing if you have to scramble up a tree in a hurry. Finally, the length of its upper arm was 95 percent of the length of its upper leg—very much like chimpanzees, whose upper leg and arm are the same length. In contrast, the human upper arm is only 70 percent as long as the upper leg. Long arms and short legs are also assets in tree climbing.

None of these features compromised afarensis's erect posture. Like all members of the hominid family, afarensis's main adaptation was to move about on the ground on two legs. As if to remove all doubt that it was a true hominid, afarensis bequeathed the world a unique memorial to upright posture. Three of them went for a walk one day 3.5 million years ago just after the volcano Sadiman, which rises near Laetoli, had blanketed the area with a layer of fine ash. As they strolled along, their feet sank in, leaving a well-defined trail of footprints. Shortly after they moved on, Sadiman obligingly covered the area with another blanket of ash, sealing and preserving the footprints. In the last few thousand years, the protective covering has worn away, revealing several portions of the trail, the longest of which extends for about seventy-five feet. Careful study of these footprints shows that they closely resemble the prints that a modern human foot would make on a similar type of surface. The heel is well marked, and the big toe is aligned parallel to the other toes rather than spreading to the side as in our familiar "four-handed" modern apes. Given its great antiquity, its humanlike foot, and its human-like dentition, afarensis was probably the ancestor of all the later australopithecines as well as of the first members of the genus *Homo*.

THE TREE
OF LIFE

*T*HERE REMAINS THE QUESTION of where and when afarensis originated. Between four million and eight million years ago, the fossil record pertaining to hominid origins is largely blank. All that we know is that eight million years ago a variety of now long-extinct apes, some large, others small, characterized by many different kinds of jaws and teeth, lived in Africa. Specialists in the evolution of the nonhuman primates from time to time have put forward one or another of these creatures as the ancestors of the hominids. But none of these claims has been verified. Witness the recent dethronement of the nine-million-year-old genus of apes called *Ramapithecus,* once thought to be ancestral to afarensis, but, on the basis of new evidence, now believed to be the ancestor of the orangutan.

In the absence of fossils, several biochemical methods can be used to catch a glimpse of afarensis's ancestors. One group of techniques is based on the analysis of the chains of amino acids in proteins such as hemoglobin. The greater the resemblance between the chains, the closer the relationship between the species. More precise measurements of the genetic differences between two species can be obtained by recombinant techniques that identify the actual sequence of base pairs in their genes. Another technique measures the relative strength of immunological reactions created by the introduction of a particular foreign substance into the blood of two different species. The more similar the strength of the reaction, the more closely the species are related. As expected from anatomical evidence, all of these techniques show that humans and the living African apes—chimps and gorillas—are more closely related to each other than to any other species.

The immunological techniques can also be used to estimate the time that has elapsed since two related species began to diverge from each other, provided that immunological differences accumulate at approximately the same rate over a long period of time. On the basis of this assumption, Vincent Sarich of the University of California at Berkeley estimates that modern-day gorillas, chimpanzees, and humans had a common ancestor no more than six million years ago, which means that afarensis puts us within one or two million years of the common ancestor of the great apes and the hominids.

The tree of life has been growing, branching, and putting out twigs and buds for over three billion years. Among the limbs that belong to the primate order, there is a thirty-million-year-old branch that belongs to the apes. On buds at the end of a twig on this branch are the living African great apes. Nearby, at a point obscured at present by the foliage, the ape branch gives rise to the branch occupied by our zoological family, the hominids. Our kind, genus *Homo,* species *sapiens—Homo sapiens—*is a bud on a little twig at the end of that branch.

THE ENIGMA
OF THE
LITTLE
HANDY MAN

*T*HE NEXT QUESTION is how were the australopithecines related to the earliest members of the genus *Homo.* Teams of scientists working at sites along the Rift Valley have made the most important discoveries bearing on this question. They found first of all that erectus—Dubois's *Pithecanthropus*—lived in Africa as well as in other parts of the Old World. More crucially, they found that erectus lived in Africa as long ago as 1.6 million years, far earlier than anywhere else.

In addition, they established the existence of another hominid species that could have been the link between afarensis and erectus. Identified first at Olduvai Gorge, Tanzania, by Louis Leakey, Richard Leakey's father and Mary Leakey's husband, this species flourished from 2 million to 1.8 million years ago. It had a brain whose volume ranged between 650 and 775 cubic centimeters as compared with a range of between 450 and 500 cubic centimeters for the australopithecines and between 900 and 1,000 cubic centimeters for erectus. Close to this new hominid's cranial remains, Louis Leakey encountered a deposit of crude stone tools, most of which fall into the category of choppers and flakes, made by chipping off one end of fist-sized nodules of lava rock. Convinced that an australopithecine would be incapable of making stone tools, Leakey decided that his new find, and not erectus, should have the honor of being the first member of the genus *Homo,* and forthwith gave it the name *Homo habilis,* "the human who was handy at making things." I'll call it habilis for short.

Since habilis's cranial capacity was intermediate between that of afarensis and erectus, everyone assumed its bodily dimensions would also be intermediate. Discovery of the limb bones of a female habilis in Olduvai Gorge in 1986 destroyed this assumption and is forcing a reexamination of the whole question of whether stone tool-making is an adequate basis for identifying members of the genus *Homo.* Habilis turns out to have been only a little over three feet tall

—just like the diminutive afarensis named Lucy. And it still had somewhat curved toes and fingers, long arms, and short legs, indicative of a life in which tree-climbing continued to play some kind of role. Except for its bigger brain and its association with stone tools, habilis is virtually indistinguishable from the earliest australopithecines. This raises doubts about whether habilis should be regarded as a member of the genus *Homo*. Only a geologically scant 200,000 years separate habilis from erectus, whose height ranged to over six feet in males and to well over five feet in females. Despite their somewhat smaller brains, the gracile australopithecines (*A. africanus*), contemporaries of habilis, cannot be ruled out as plausible direct ancestors of erectus. Leakey gave habilis center stage essentially because it was associated with simple stone tools. While stone tools have never been found in close association with a gracile australopithecine, there is a compelling reason to conclude that at least some of the australopithecines did make such tools (and they have, in fact, been found at robustus sites). The earliest simple stone choppers and flakes are from Ethiopian sites in the Omo Valley and at Gona in the Hadar region. Using the potassium-argon method, researchers have established a firm date of 2.5 million years for the Omo tools and a provisional date of 3.1 million years for the Gona tools. The first date precedes habilis by half a million years; the second by over a million years. In either case, the only hominids alive at that time were australopithecines, which means that one or all of them must have made some tools. But what did they use these tools for? And if they made stone tools, they were surely capable of making tools from more perishable kinds of materials. What were these like, and what were they used for?

THE DAWN OF
TECHNOLOGY

*A*NIMALS DO NOT NEED big brains to use tools. Even insects use tools. For example, the wasp *Amophila urnaria* tamps down the sides of its burrow with a pebble held in its mandible. Ant lion larvae lie half-buried at the bottom of their funnel-shaped pit- falls and with a snap of their heads send a shower of sand against hapless bugs that try to escape up the steep walls. Myrmicene ants dip bits of wood and leaves into soft foods such as honey, fruit pulp, and the body fluids of prey, wait for the substance to adhere or soak in, and then carry it back to their nest.

Several species of birds use stones to open the hard-shelled eggs of ostriches, emus, and giant cranes. The Egyptian vulture, for example, picks up a stone in its beak, stands about three feet away from an ostrich egg, bends its neck backward and then hurls the stone with considerable accuracy. Finches pick up twigs, cactus spines, or leaf stalks in their beaks and use them as probes to impale or dislodge insects from hiding places in the bark of trees. While eating, they hold the tool down with their feet, then fly with it to the next tree. Even fish use a kind of tool, witness the archer of Southeast Asia, which knocks down flies and mosquitoes by squirting water at them.

Paradoxically, spontaneous tool use is not more elaborate or common among animals that possess bigger brains and that depend more on learning than on instinct. Few mammals are habitual tool-users in the wild. Elephants occasionally break off branches of trees to scratch themselves, dislodge leeches, and fan away flies. Polar bears, say the Eskimo, sometimes kill or wound seals or walruses by hurling blocks of ice at them from above. One of the most habitual mammalian tool-users is the California sea otter. Lacking any bodily structure capable of opening mussel shells, it swims to the bottom, picks up a flat rock weighing as much as half a pound, tucks the rock under a loose flap of flesh between forelimb and chest, swims to a mussel bed, and wrenches off a single big mussel. Then it rises to the surface, flips over on its back, and holding the mussel with both front feet pounds it against the rock until it opens.

Despite their marked intelligence and highly manipulative hands, free-ranging great apes and monkeys also have only a small repertory of tool-using behavior. It consists mainly of repelling intruders with a barrage of nuts, pinecones, branches, fruits, feces, or stones. Baboons additionally use stones to pound and hammer tough-skinned fruit and to kill scorpions (before eating them), and they use sticks to widen the entrances of subterranean insect nests.

Aside from humans, chimpanzees are the most accomplished extant tool-users in the animal kingdom. Over a period of many years, Jane Van Lawick-Goodall and her associates studied the behavior of a single population of free-ranging chimpanzees in the Gombe National Park in Tanzania. One of their discoveries was that chimpanzees use tools to "fish" or "dip" for ants and termites. To fish for termites, they select a twig and strip away the leaves. The termite nest is as hard as concrete and impenetrable except for certain thinly covered tunnel entrances. They scratch off this thin covering and insert the twig. The termites inside bite the end of the twig, and the chimpanzees pull it out and lick off the termites clinging to it. Having exhausted the supply at one nest, they put the twig in their mouth and carry it about while searching for another nest with suitable tunnel entrances.

The Gombe chimps "dip" for a species of aggressive nomadic driver ant that can inflict a painful bite. On finding the temporary subterranean nest of these ants, the chimps make a tool out of a green twig and insert it into the nest entrance. Hundreds of fierce ants swarm up the twig to repel the invader. "The chimpanzee watches their progress and when the ants have almost reached its hand, the tool is quickly withdrawn. In a split second the opposite hand rapidly sweeps the length of the tool . . . catching the ants in a jumbled mass between thumb and forefinger. These are then popped into the open waiting mouth in one bite and chewed furiously."

Chimpanzees also manufacture "sponges" for sopping up water from an inaccessible hollow in a tree. They strip a handful of leaves from a twig, put the leaves in their mouth, chew briefly, put the mass of leaves in the water, let them soak, put the leaves to their mouths, and suck the water off. They use a similar sponge to dry their fur, to wipe off sticky substances, and to clean the bottoms of chimpanzee babies. Gombe chimpanzees also use sticks as levers and digging tools to pry ant nests off trees and to widen entrances of subterranean beehives.

Observers in other parts of Africa report similar types of behavior, including variants of fishing for ants, dipping for termites, and digging up insect nests or prying them loose. Chimpanzees in the Kasakati Forest of Tanzania collect the honey of a stingless species of bee by inserting a stick into the nest and licking off the honey that adheres to it. Elsewhere, observers have watched chimpanzees pound or hammer tough-skinned fruits, seeds, and nuts with sticks and stones. One of the most sophisticated examples of this kind of behavior occurred in the Tai Forest of the Ivory Coast. To open the hard shells of the panda nut, the chimpanzees searched the forest floor for rocks to serve as hammers. The rocks weighed between one and forty pounds and, depending on the weight, the chimpanzees carried them up to a distance of 600 feet in the crook of one arm while hobbling on three limbs. They used the roots of trees or pieces of exposed rock as anvils. Another instance of sophisticated tool use among Ivory Coast chimpanzees occurred when a group of chimps was unable to climb a large, fruiting fig tree because its bark was too smooth and slippery. Climbing to the top of an adjacent tree, they still found themselves a few feet short of being able to grasp the fig tree's lowest limbs. So they made hooks out of branches from the tree they were on, stripping them of leaves and holding them up with one hand as high as they could reach. At last one of them hooked a branch and pulled it down far enough to grab it and get into the fig tree.

Chimpanzees appear to go further than other primates in using weapons and projectiles. They hurl stones, feces, and sticks with considerable accuracy. One Gombe chimp threw a large stone at an adult bush pig, hitting it and driving it off long enough for another chimp to rush in and capture the piglet that the pig had been guarding.

All the animals I have been discussing display much greater tool-making and tool-using virtuosity in captivity in zoos and laboratories than in the wild. This is especially true of chimpanzees. I am not thinking of the deliberate training of chimpanzee movie and television stars by human handlers to do everything from washing dishes to driving the family car. Even rats can be *trained* to climb ladders, build bridges, ring bells, and turn lights on or off. Rather, I mean spontaneous tool-making and tool-using behavior that chimpanzees learn by themselves with objects deliberately or accidentally made available to them. For example, provided with boxes on which to stand, sticks that fit together, and bananas out of reach, they quickly learn to push the box under the bananas, put the sticks together, stand on the box, and knock down the bananas. Likewise, they quickly learn to use small sticks to pull in bigger sticks to pull in still bigger sticks to pull food into their cage. When it comes to gaining their freedom, captive chimpanzees display the same kind of desperate ingenuity that humans display in trying to get out of jail. They use sticks as levers to pry open doors and to break the wire mesh on their cages. At the Delta Regional Primate Center near Atlanta, they broke big sticks into small ones and jammed the small ones into the crevices of a twenty-foot-high fence. Then they stood on the small sticks, much as mountaineers stand on pitons to scale cliffs, and escaped over the top. In other escape attempts they piled sticks and branches against the wall of their enclosures, forming a kind of ladder. My favorite example is that of chimpanzees who develop the habit of shining a flashlight into their mouth in order to clean their teeth and throat with their fingers while watching what they are doing in a mirror.

Under quasi-laboratory conditions, chimpanzees wield clubs with deadly effect. One investigator built a stuffed leopard whose head and tail could be moved mechanically. He set the leopard down in open country inhabited by chimpanzees, and when the chimpanzees came into view he animated the leopard's parts. The chimpanzees attacked the leopard with clubs that were placed nearby, tore it apart, and dragged the remnants off into the bush.

The elaborate tool-using behavior of captive chimpanzees has important implications for understanding tool use among our proto-human ancestors. It shows that when the need arises, chimpanzees are capable of expanding their tool-making and tool-using skills. The relatively small inventory of tool behavior observed in the wild does not reflect a lack of intelligence so much as a lack of motivation. In the wild, they are normally able to satisfy their everyday needs in a cost-effective manner simply by using their naturally endowed bodily equipment.

Let me explain what I mean by cost-effectiveness. The ancestors of today's chimpanzees never had to cope with wire mesh cages or twenty-foot-high fences. Thanks to natural selection, their arms and legs were able to get them out of all the confined spaces they were ever likely to encounter. For the same reason, being superb climbers, they seldom benefitted in the wild from using long sticks to knock down fruit suspended from hard-to-reach places (although they could do it if the occasion demanded, as in the Ivory Coast fig tree problem). Rather than making and using such sticks to get at the few morsels at the end of branches that couldn't support their weight, they were usually much better off moving on to another tree. The other side of this reckoning is that since chimpanzees need all four limbs for climbing, walking, and running, they cannot carry heavy tools around with them for any length of time without risking a dangerous loss of mobility. So when they do use tools in the wild, they rely mostly on materials close at hand such as branches, twigs, leaves, and stones—objects that can be instantly discarded without any great loss because there is very little effort invested in them and because replacements are available wherever they go. This explains why dropping and throwing dead branches and leaves are the most common forms of tool use among the great apes and monkeys. It is doubly cost-effective. It dispels intruders more effectively and with less risk than direct combat; and yet it does not interfere for more than a split second with their ability to use their hands to climb to safety.

This is why I believe that the australopithecines could have greatly expanded their tool-using behavior while remaining on the intellectual level of a modern chimpanzee. Upright posture changed the cost-effectiveness of picking up, carrying, and using tools to do things that the body could not do. Our earliest ancestors must have used tools the way modern chimpanzees use them when captive in zoos and laboratories—not occasionally nor out of desperation, but every day as an essential part of their way of life.

TOOLS FOR WHAT?

OOL USE AND UPRIGHT POSTURE evolved in tandem. The more the australopithecines relied on tools, the more their hands differed from their feet. And the more their hands differed from their feet, the more they relied on tools. But for what? How did this advantage them? The answer almost certainly has to be that the tools enabled them to consume nutritious foods found on the ground that four-handed, tree-dwelling apes could not exploit as effectively.

As these terrestrial food sources replaced arboreal fruits in their diet, natural selection favored individuals who traded off the losses associated with diminished tree-climbing ability for the gains of the new diet. But what was on the ground that was so attractive to apes that they would invest in making and carrying tools to obtain it? Let the chimpanzees be our guide. We know that they invest most heavily in tool-making and tool-using in pursuit of insects hidden inside of mounds or burrows. Twigs and sticks are their favored tools in these pursuits. And observers report that Gombe chimps carry well-made termiting tools from one nest to another for as long as an hour, covering a total distance of one kilometer. Ant and termite nests are bigger and easier to spot in open, tree-dotted savannas than in the forest itself. We can picture the ancestors of the australopithecines venturing forth seasonally from the forest in pursuit of the highly nutritious packages of fats and proteins imbedded within these insect fortresses. With nests separated from sources of appropriate fishing, dipping, probing, and digging instruments, the tools or the raw materials for making them would have to be carried over longer distances than in the forest. Individuals who manufactured the best sticks and who used them most skillfully would enjoy diets richer in fats and proteins, be bigger and healthier, and leave more progeny. As the frequency and duration of travel into open country increased, the ancestors of the australopithecines would soon begin to exploit additional food resources available in this new habitat. At certain seasons the seeds of grasses could be stripped off and eaten. And in their digging for subterranean insects, they would inevitably discover calorie-rich edible bulbs, tubers, and roots that to this day remain an important resource for human foragers in Africa. Getting at this buried treasure would have led to attempts to improve their digging stick—perhaps by biting one end to make it more pointy, or perhaps by rubbing it against rocks to smooth and sharpen it.

And so had we been present where the forest meets the savanna one morning five million years ago, we would have caught a glimpse of our ancestors. Still in shadow, they stood peering anxiously across the bright panorama. It would have been easy at a distance to mistake them for a family of chimpanzees. Except that as they started forward through the grass, they kept erect. Each of the adults held a pointed stick in one hand. All of history was there that morning—all that we were to become and still might be.

MEAT

HE OPEN COUNTRY beckoned with another resource. In the forest, animals tend to be small, furtive, difficult to see. But the savanna teemed with visible herds. From time to time a stick-carrying group of australopithecines would encounter an infant gazelle or antelope that had strayed from the protection of its mother and they would surround, seize, and eat it. Occasionally they would also stumble upon the remains of a larger animal that had died from natural causes or had been killed by the feline predators that lived off the herds. Hooting and howling and waving their sticks, they would drive away the vultures and jackals, rush in and tear off bits of decaying meat, and run to the nearest clump of trees, ready to drop everything and seek safety in the branches if one of the felines returned and interrupted their meal.

I confess that there is no archaeological evidence that such events ever happened. But the behavior of chimpanzees and other primates, as well as our kind's dietary preferences, leave little doubt that the australopithecines had a special fondness for meat. And as savanna-dwelling, tool-using animals, they had a developed capacity and plenty of opportunity to scavenge and hunt. As for seeking the safety of trees, we do have the fossil evidence of curved fingers and toes and the chimpanzeelike long arms and short legs.

Not so long ago scientists believed that monkeys and apes were strict vegetarians. After meticulous observation in the wild, most primates turned out to be omnivores. Like humans, they eat both plant and animal foods. Being rather small creatures, monkeys necessarily prey mostly on insects rather than on game. And a significant amount of their insect eating is simply a natural by-product of the consumption of leaves and fruit. When they encounter a leaf with a weevil wrapped in it, or a fig with a worm in it, they do not spit out the intruder. If anything, they spit out the leaf or fruit, a practice that produces a steady rain of half-chewed plant food as the troop progresses from tree to tree.

As among most human populations, monkeys usually eat only relatively small amounts of animal food compared to plant food. This is not a matter of choice, but simply of the difficulties monkeys confront in obtaining a steady supply of animal flesh. Studies in Namibia and Botswana show that baboons will stop eating virtually everything else when insects swarm. They prefer animal matter first; roots, seeds, fruits, and flowers second; and leaves and grass third. At certain seasons of the year, they spend as much as 75 percent of their eating time on insects. Several species of large monkeys not only consume insects but actually hunt small game. My reconstruction of the australopithecine way of life gains plausibility from the fact that the most accomplished hunters among monkeys appear to be ground-dwelling baboons that live in open country. During a year of observation near Gelgil, Kenya, Robert Harding observed forty-seven small vertebrates being killed and eaten by baboons. The most common prey were infant gazelles and antelopes. If mere baboons are capable of capturing infant gazelles and antelopes, the early australopithecines cannot have been less capable.

Among extant nonhuman primates, chimpanzees are the most ardent meat eaters. The time and effort expended in termiting and anting alone suggest the degree of their fondness for animal flesh. And let us not forget the painful bites and stings that they risk in order to get at these tidbits. Nor do chimpanzees confine their pursuit of animal flesh to anting and termiting. They actively hunt and eat at least twenty-three species of mammals, including several kinds of monkeys and baboons, galagos, bush bucks, bush pigs, duikers, mice, rats, squirrels, shrews, mongooses, and hyraxes. They also kill and eat chimpanzee and even human babies if they get a chance. At Gombe, over the course of a decade, observers witnessed the consumption of ninety-five small animals—mostly infant baboons, monkeys, and bush pigs. This is only a partial accounting because the chimpanzees consumed additional animals out of sight of the observers. Altogether, Gombe chimpanzees devoted about 10 percent of their time spent on feeding to the pursuit and consumption of game.

Chimpanzees usually hunt cooperatively and share their

quarry with each other. In fact, if a chimpanzee is unable to get others to join in, it will abandon the hunt. Throughout the entire process of killing, distributing, and consuming prey animals, they display an unusual level of social interaction and excitement. During the hunt, anywhere from three to nine chimpanzees try to surround the prey animal. They keep positioning and repositioning themselves for as long as an hour, trying to cut off potential escape routes.

Both males and females hunt and consume meat. During an eight-year period, from 1974 to 1981, females captured or stole, and then ate, at least part of forty-four prey animals, not counting another twenty-one prey animals that they attacked or seized but were unable to hold on to. Males hunted more than females and consumed more meat. Chimpanzees occasionally share plant foods, but they always share meat unless the prey is captured by a solitary chimpanzee in the forest. Meat-sharing often results from persistent "begging." The supplicant holds an outstretched hand under the meat possessor's mouth, or parts the lips of a meat-chewing companion. If these tactics fail, the supplicant may begin to whimper and to express rage and frustration. Van Lawick-Goodall describes how a young chimp named Mr. Worzle threw a tantrum when Goliath, a dominant male, refused to share the body of a baby baboon with him. Mr. Worzle followed Goliath from branch to branch, hand outstretched and whimpering. "When Goliath pushed Worzle's hand away for the eleventh time, the lower-ranking male . . . hurled himself backward off the branch, screaming and hitting wildly at the surrounding vegetation. Goliath looked at him and then, with a great effort (using hands, teeth, and one foot), tore his prey in two and handed the entire hindquarters to Worzle."

AFRICAN
GENESIS
REVISITED

CHIMPANZEES HUNT more often than they scavenge. The reason is obvious. In the forest, there are fewer carcasses of large animals and they are harder to find. Given the great herds that grazed on the savanna, the early australopithecines probably scavenged more than they hunted. Their digging sticks were not sharp or strong enough to pierce the skin of wildebeests, antelopes, zebras, or gazelles. Fangless and bereft of cutting implements, they had no way of breaking through tough hides to get at the meat, even if they somehow succeeded in killing an adult. Scavenging solved these problems. Lions and other predators did the killing and obligingly ripped open the carcass, exposing the meat. Once the predators had eaten their fill, they departed to a shady spot and took a nap. The principal problem for our ancestors then became how to get rid of other scavengers. Vultures and jackals could be driven off by swinging and jabbing the digging sticks. They also undoubtedly threw stones if any were available in the immediate vicinity of the carcass. Hyenas, with their powerful bone-crushing jaws, would present a more formidable problem to a group of three- or four-foot-tall primates. The australopithecines were well advised to keep their distance if hyenas got to the carcass first; or to leave promptly if hyenas showed up after they had begun to dine. In any event, it was a good idea not to linger but tear and break off as much as they could and get to a safer place as quickly as possible. Predator cats might return to the scene of the kill for dessert; or if the carcass had been created by a natural death, the cats might soon be by to investigate—most predators have no qualms about doing a little scavenging on the side. The safer place was a grove of trees where, if danger threatened, the australopithecines could drop their sticks, grasp the bark with their curved toes, and scamper into the upper branches.

I don't want to overestimate the timorousness of the australopithecines. Japanese observers report that they have seen groups of chimpanzees at Mahale National Park in Tanzania occasionally confront and intimidate one or two big cats and sometimes succeed in taking meat away from them. The australopithecines with their sticks and stones might have done even better. Yet I doubt that they were like the fierce "killer apes" from whom we allegedly derive our "instinct to kill with a weapon," as depicted in Robert Ardrey's popular book, *African Genesis*. The idea that the australopithecines were mighty hunters grew out of Raymond Dart's belief that the fossil bones, horns, and tusks found at several australopithecine fossil sites in southern Africa were used by them as weapons. But I cannot see how these objects could have inflicted major wounds on large, tough-skinned animals. Even if they could have had lethal effects, how could the australopithecines have gotten close enough to use them against full-grown prey animals without being kicked or gored to death? A more likely explanation of the association between australopithecine fossils and the bones, horns, and tusks of other animals is that the caves where they occur together were hyena dens and that they were collected and deposited together by hyenas.

While the australopithecines never became mighty hunters, they did eventually improve their ability to compete as scavengers. The barrier to their success was that they had to wait for the teeth of better-endowed natural hunters or scavengers to penetrate the hides before they could approach a carcass. But sometime between 3 million and 2.5 million years ago, long before Louis Leakey's handy person was on the scene, the australopithecines achieved a technological breakthrough—as great as any that was ever to occur in human history. They began to make cutting, slicing, and chopping implements out of pieces of rock. Hide, muscle, sinew, and bone yielded to the new devices as readily as to the sharpest tooth and claw, and a bolder way of life beckoned.

KNAPPER,
BUTCHER,
SCAVENGER,
HUNTER

*T*HE EARLIEST AUSTRALOPITHECINES must have used stones at least to the same extent as do modern chimpanzees—as missiles to repel intruders and as hammers to break open nuts. This throwing and hammering would occasionally split off stone fragments whose edges were sharp enough to cut through hides. But such incidents occurred in the context of activities that could not be made more efficient by using sharp-edged implements and so their potential was not utilized. Sharp flakes created by ricocheting stones hurled to drive away vultures and jackals would have a better chance of being recognized as a way of cutting through tough hides, slicing off hunks of meat, and removing limb bones. The next step was to pick up a rock and bash it against another on the ground and then to search in the debris for the sharpest flakes. Finally, a rock was held in each hand and a carefully aimed blow was delivered to the edge of one rock by using the other as a hammer. Repeated hammering not only yielded useful flakes, but the core from which they were detached would itself begin to acquire edges useful for cutting and chopping.

The earliest stone tools—those found at Gona and Omo, in Ethiopia—already reveal a trained facility for selecting the best available materials to serve as cores and hammers and for delivering well-aimed blows to detach razor-sharp flakes. Experiments by archaeologists who have taught themselves to produce replicas of these earliest stone tools show that cores and flakes were equally valuable. Hammerstone blows delivered to one side of the end of a core produced a heavy chopping tool that is effective in severing tendons and sinews and in breaking joints apart. The flakes are best for cutting through hides and slicing through meat. Heavy cores are good for smashing bones to get at the marrow and for breaking open skulls to get at the brains. Nicholas Toth of Indiana University has duplicated these simple tools and used them to butcher elephants and other large, tough-skinned animals. The australopithecines undoubtedly applied their stone tool kit to tasks other than butchering carcasses. Toth found that heavy chopper cores were good for severing straight branches from a tree and that with small flakes he could whittle down and shape the points of digging sticks into spears. Other flakes were useful for scraping meat, fat, and hair from hides.

Some kind of container for carrying things was also probably essential for the australopithecine way of life after they began to use stone tools. Analysis of stone artifacts at sites in Tanzania that date to about two million years ago reveals that there are more flakes than can be accounted for by the number of scars on the cores found with them. This suggests that whoever did the knapping carried a supply of prestruck flakes and perhaps a small core and hammerstone or two from one butchering site to another. A small bag made out of scraped hide and secured by bits of sinew around the waist or over the shoulder would have made an appropriate container.

With the manufacture of core and flake stone tools, sharpened digging sticks, thongs, and skin bags, and the carrying and storing of tools and materials, the limit of the ape brain was reached. While none of these artifacts or behaviors in isolation would have taxed the capabilities of a chimpanzee, to operate them all as part of an increasingly complex scavenging, hunting, gathering, and digging system of production called for cognitive abilities that were beyond those of the early australopithecines. Natural selection favored the individuals who learned most quickly to make the best tools, who made the cleverest decisions concerning when to use them, and who could optimize production in relation to daily and seasonal changes in the abundance and availability of plant and animal foods. Selection for these capabilities may account for the 40 percent to 50 percent increment in the size of habilis's brain over that of the australopithecines.

But despite the more elaborate tool kit and bigger brains, there is no evidence that habilis was any closer to being a hunter of large game. Its diminutive stature and its curved fingers and toes—still indicative of tree climbing as a means of avoiding predators—do not bespeak of boldness in the hunt. And its tools, however useful in butchering large animals, show no sign of being useful in hunting them.

Our ancestors must have remained primarily scavengers, at least until the appearance of the first erectus, 1.6 million years ago.

Everything about erectus suggests that it was filling an ecological niche based on a new mode of subsistence. It was a conspicuously taller species than habilis, and its fingers and toes had lost all vestiges of arboreal agility. Its tools consisted of sharp flakes and new kinds of cores that were worked on both sides and shaped into large ovate, pointed "hand axes," cleavers, and picks. Experimental trials with these "bifaces" show that they are useful aids in the butchering of large animals. Moreover, microscopic striations interpreted as "cut marks" on animal bones associated with erectus tools provide direct evidence that they were used for dismembering and defleshing animals. Erectus was also probably skilled in using both core and flake tools to whittle, shave, and scrape sharp-pointed wooden spears.

Yet butchers need not be hunters. Moreover, there is something missing from erectus's bag of tools (and from habilis's tool kit as well). None of the cores or flakes are of the sort that could be inserted or hafted as points for spears or other projectiles. Perhaps they threw their wooden spears at small animals with deadly effect, but without stone or bone points they were unlikely, at a distance, to pierce the hides and penetrate to the vital organs of larger prey. The absence of stone projectile points lends support to the view that erectus was simply a more efficient scavenger than earlier hominids, and that if some of them occasionally did hunt, it was only for small animals.

I personally doubt that erectus settled for being a scavenger first and a hunter second. The readily visible herds of large animals would have acted as a constant temptation to take direct action in order to assure a supply of its favorite food. After all, the development of stone technology was largely a consequence of the australopithecine's attempt to exploit the nutritional advantages of meat. Having gone so far as to invent knives, hammers, axes, and containers primarily to facilitate the butchery of animals, the failure of erectus to invent stone-tipped projectiles need not indicate that they were not habitual hunters. Rather, it may simply indicate that they did not hunt by hurling spears at a distance but by thrusting them into their quarry at close quarters. Archaeology does not provide the evidence for this line of reasoning. We must turn instead to certain peculiarities of the human form—to our lack of body hair, to our sweat-gland-packed skins, and to our ability to run marathons. But first I shall have to say some unflattering things about erectus's brain.

46

THE ENIGMA
OF *H. ERECTUS*

*P*OSITIVE FEEDBACK between brains and tools carries us plausibly from afarensis to habilis. Does the same feedback, tool to brain, brain to tool, explain the transition from habilis to erectus? The archaeological evidence inclines me to say no. Erectus had a brain that is 33 percent larger than that of habilis, but I can see nothing in the erectus tool kit whose manufacture or use would require a brain that is 33 percent larger than that of habilis. Hand axes, cleavers, and picks manufactured by erectus served different functions from the tools used by habilis and the australopithecines. They were large implements suited for heavy-duty tasks such as butchering large animals or hacking off tree limbs. True, some erectus tools were better made than habilis tools. More symmetrical, with flakes detached on both sides and around the entire circumference of the core, they conform to higher standards of workmanship. Yet they do not imply the kind of quantum leap that brought the australopithecines into the Stone Age.

The most curious thing about the erectus tool kit is that it remained essentially unchanged for an immense stretch of time. Hand axes and other bifacial cores manufactured by the 1.6-million-year-old erectus at Koobi Fora, Kenya, were still being made essentially unchanged by late erectus populations in Africa and Eurasia 300,000 years ago. The pace of technological change throughout this vast span of prehistory was as slow as it had been during australopithecine times. And it was completely unlike the pace achieved by erectus's successor, *H. sapiens*. If erectus was much smarter than habilis, one would never know it from its contribution to technology.

Some evidence exists that early erectus had acquired a degree of control over fire. If true, this would certainly be a notable achievement. But the evidence is far from convincing. It consists of concentrated patches of discolored soils found at Koobi Fora and other East

African sites. The discoloration is reminiscent of baked clay such as might have been produced by prolonged and intense heat from camp fires. But natural fires started by lightning and burning more intensely in some places than others—near stands of trees under which erectus would be likely to camp, for example—could have produced the same effect. Similar problems exist with the association between fire and erectus based on 300,000-year-old layers of charcoal found in Choukoudien Cave near Beijing, China. Some anthropologists regard these deposits of charcoal to be the accumulated product of cave-dwelling erectus "hearths." Others, led by Lewis Binford of the University of New Mexico, cast doubt on this interpretation. Instead of being concentrated in a few places within the cave, as would be the case if it had been produced by cooking or warming fires, the charcoal is spread in thick layers that alternate with other layers of ordinary soils. So all that one can say with certainty is that fires from time to time occurred within the cave or close to its entrance. It is a long leap from this information to the conclusion that erectus regularly warmed itself and cooked with these fires or could ignite and extinguish them at will.

Should further studies confirm that our erectus forebears did learn to control fire to some degree, we are still left with the mystery of why they failed to make similar improvements in other branches of technology. Starting from a Stone Age base, our own species took fewer than 100,000 years to pass from a hunting, gathering mode of life to today's hyperindustrial societies. This is a mere 8 percent of the time our erectus ancestors had at their disposal. If our kind manages to endure for as long as erectus, we have another 1.2 million years ahead of us. My head spins when I try to think of all the changes that so much time could bring. All one can say about that unthinkably distant future is that it will be unimaginably different. By the same token, and with an equal sense of vertigo, all one can say about the 1,300 millennia from the beginning to the end of erectus's days on earth is that its way of life remained unimaginably the same.

Our erectus ancestors were extremely clever creatures compared with chimpanzees. But the archaeological record strongly suggests that they lacked the mental capacities that enabled our kind to apply the collective experience of each generation to the fabrication of an expanding, evolving repertory of social and technological traditions. Their means of communicating with each other must have surpassed the calls and signs emitted by chimpanzees and other apes. Yet they could not have possessed in full measure the linguistic and cognitive capacities of modern humans or else they would not have disappeared from the world, leaving nothing but little heaps of stone tools as reminders of their immensely long sojourn. For better or worse, if they had brains that were qualitatively different from the brains of habilis, they would long ago have changed the face of the earth.

Now brains are expensive organs to operate. Big brains make big demands on the body's supply of energy and blood. In a resting human, the brain accounts for about 20 percent of metabolic costs. So extra brain cells would be selected against if they did not make some important contribution to survival and reproductive success. If the brain of erectus was not good for making inventions and changing the face of the earth, what was it good for? Konrad Fialkowski, a member of the Committee for Evolutionary and Theoretical Biology of the Polish Academy of Sciences, has come up with an ingenious suggestion. It was good for running.

HEAT, HAIR, SWEAT, AND MARATHONS

BIGGER BRAIN made it possible for erectus to run in the midday sun, at a time of day when most predators seek shade and water and refrain from the pursuit of game. Fialkowski bases this theory on the assumption that by having extra brain cells, the brain of erectus was less likely to break down while experiencing heat stress during long-distance running. Individual brain cells are more susceptible to heat stress than are the cells of other organs. Their breakdown leads to cognitive disorientation, convulsions, stroke, then death. A basic principle of information theory holds that in an information system that has elements prone to breakdown (such as the human brain), the reliability of the system can be increased by increasing the number of elements that perform the same function and by increasing the number of connections among them. The brain of erectus may therefore have contained a large amount of neural redundancy selected as a means of achieving fail-safe operation under heat stress, which is generated during the pursuit of game over long distances.

Modern humans are far from being the swiftest runners in the animal kingdom. For short distances we are capable of top speeds of about twenty miles an hour, mere plodding when compared with forty-five miles an hour for the horse or seventy miles per hour for the cheetah. But when it comes to covering long distances, humans have the capacity to outrun every other animal.

Native peoples studied by anthropologists used this capability to capture prey species by running them down relentlessly, sometimes for several days. Among the Tarahumara Indians of northern Mexico, for example, "hunting deer consists of chasing the deer for two days—never less than one day. The Tarahumara keeps the deer constantly on the move. Only occasionally does he get a glimpse of his quarry, but follows it unerringly through his own uncanny ability to read tracks. The Indian chases the deer until the creature falls from exhaustion, often with its hoofs completely worn away. It is then throttled by the man or killed by the dogs." Humans can not only keep up a steady pace for hours at a time, but we are also capable of sudden bursts of speed at the end of a long run—with deadly effects, as recounted in this description of reindeer hunting among the Nganasan of Siberia: "A wild reindeer pursued by a hunter runs at a fast trot, stopping from time to time to look back. The hunter pursues it, hiding behind bushes, heaps of rock, and other natural cover, trying to get in front of it. The speed at which the Nganasan can run is amazing. Some hunters can overtake a young wild reindeer and seize it by a hind leg. Sometimes a runner will run after a reindeer for 10 kilometers. Female reindeer run faster than the bucks and do not tire so quickly, so it is considerably more difficult to overtake them. The hunter who pursues a wounded rein- deer must really exert himself." The Aché of Paraguay still use the run-down method to hunt deer, and the Agta of the Philippines run down wild pigs. I am not saying that this method of hunting is common among indigenous peoples. Since all contemporary foraging groups possess stone or bone projectile points, spear throwers, or bows and arrows, they seldom find it necessary to rely on their ability to outrun prey species. But long-distance running does continue to play an important role in relation to tracking animals that have been wounded by projectiles. Even with their poison-tipped arrows, the San of the Kalahari Desert, for example, are sometimes called upon to jog rapidly after wounded game animals under a broiling sun for hours at a stretch. Haste is necessary to prevent lions or vultures from getting to the quarry first after it drops from the combined effect of exhaustion and the poison. While not as strenuous as pursu- ing an unwounded animal, this mode of hunting still exposes the hunter to considerable heat stress. Fialkowski's theory does not imply that our erectus ancestors always engaged in running down unwounded animals. Under favorable conditions they might have gotten close enough to the quarry to wound it with their wooden spears; then they could have run after the animal until it became weak enough for them to approach and thrust more spears into its body. Selection would favor males and females who were capable of running the longest distances under the most severe conditions in pursuit of lightly wounded or unharmed animals.

Fialkowski's focus on heat stress as an explanation for the

enlargement of the erectus brain dovetails with the presence of several other heat-regulating features that are peculiar to humans. Most mammals that are subject to heat stress cool themselves by evaporating moisture from the nasal mucosa and mouth and tongue surfaces. The human refrigeration system is based on a completely different principle. We cool ourselves by wetting our skin with moisture exuded by our eccrine sweat glands. Humans have as many as five million of these glands—far more than any other mammal. As air moves across our sweaty skin, the moisture evaporates, lowering the temperature of the capillary blood that circulates close to the surface. Evaporation of sweat accounts for the dissipation of 95 percent of the heat generated by the human body in excess of our normal operating temperature. In order for moisture to evaporate from the skin and produce its cooling effect, the air must move across it; the drier the air and the more rapidly it moves, the greater the cooling effect. Running assures just such a rapid flow of air over the skin. And the dry air of the East African savannas would have provided ideal conditions for evaporation to take place.

Evaporative cooling in turn places definite limits on the hairy covering that can grow on our bodies. Forest-dwelling apes do not engage in the intense physical effort that prolonged running requires. Their principal thermodynamic challenge is not to dissipate excess heat but to avoid being chilled, especially at night, by exposure to high humidity and heavy rainfall. Hence the luxuriant, slightly oily, and downward-pointing hairy coats of the great apes. The development of erectus as a long-distance runner and the evolution of the evaporative cooling system were incompatible with the preservation of this coat. Air had to pass unobstructed over the film of moisture exuded by the eccrine glands. Hence the peculiar "nakedness" of the human body. Although we actually have as many hair follicles as the great apes, the hairs that emerge are too thin and short to form a coat. But vestiges of the water-shedding function of the fur are preserved in the downward pointing orientation of the hairs on our arms and legs.

Another detail that fits in with Fialkowski's theory is the recently revised picture of erectus's body build. Previously believed to be short and stocky, erectus males turn out to have been more than six feet tall. A simple principle known as Bergman's rule predicts that animals selected to withstand cold stress will have stocky, spherical bodies, while those selected to withstand heat stress will have tall, cylindrical bodies. This occurs because in a sphere the ratio of surface area to body mass is smaller than the ratio of surface area to body mass in a cylinder. Stocky, squat human bodies conserve heat because they have a proportionately small area of skin from which heat can radiate. Tall, thin human bodies dissipate heat because they have a proportionately large area of skin from which heat can radiate.

During the day, the nudity of erectus would not have created any need for artificial protection against the cold. But at night, things would be different. Temperatures in African savanna habitats can fall to as low as 40° Fahrenheit just before dawn. Modern-day hunters and gatherers who live in similar climates cover themselves with blankets made from animal skins. In Australia, the Aborigines of the central desert who went nude during the day possessed kangaroo skins under which people and dogs huddled together to ward off the early morning chill.

Since the australopithecines and habilis probably already knew how to make carrying bags out of animal skins, erectus would have had no difficulty in cutting and scraping hides to use as blankets as protection against the cold. Like the stone tools needed for butchering, erectus would have carried these skins from camp to camp or hidden them in some secure spot to be retrieved when needed.

Running upright on two legs, erectus presented an oblique target for the sun's rays except for the top of the head. While this minimized the heat load for the body in general as compared with that of animals that ran on all fours, it posed a special threat to the brain. Bald men, even Englishmen, are well advised not to go out in the noonday sun. And if we are doomed to earn our keep by the sweat of our brows, it is because our brows have a dense concentration of sweat glands and no hair.

Other questions about the distribution of human hair lie outside of Fialkowski's theory, but I had better attend to them while I'm on the subject. Men and women have about equal amounts of hair on their heads, but men have far more luxuriant moustaches and beards. Presumably this difference reflects a tendency for human males with hairy faces to scare off sexual competitors and/or to attract and mate with more females (more about this later). A third line of reasoning may be needed to account for the dense patches of hair under the arms and in the pubic area. These places are richly endowed not only with eccrine sweat glands but with a second type of skin gland, known as an apocrine gland. Apocrine glands do not contribute to evaporative cooling. Their function is to secrete the odoriferous substances that support the industry devoted to underarm deodorants. The apocrines are scent glands that signal an individual's state of excitement during intense physical exertion, sexual arousal, and stressful situations.

Erectus campmates probably stimulated each other to high levels of mutual excitement by emitting these odors. The vestigial patches of hair that occur, together with the apocrine glands, conserve and concentrate the glands' secretions, a function that has apparently outlived its usefulness in a world where many other involuntary signals about personal bodily states—such as blushing and weeping—are best hidden from view.

THE BRAIN
BEGINS TO
THINK

ETURNING TO THE MAIN THRUST of Fialkowski's theory, the transition from erectus to sapiens comes to the fore. Having reached a critical mass of brain cells as a result of selection for fail-safe operations under heat stress, erectus's neural circuits were ready to undergo a rapid and fundamental reorganization. I cannot describe the exact nature of this reorganization because scientists as yet know too little about how the human brain works. But analogies can be drawn between recent improvements in computer design and the changes in the post-erectus brain. Initially, computer engineers designed circuits that handled information in a linear fashion. The machines were given problems that were broken down into a sequence of steps that had to be taken one at a time. The whole machine worked on each of these steps as they arose in sequence. By building bigger machines with more transistors, memory units, and shorter distances between components to increase the speed of operations, more complex problems could be solved. But computer designers came to realize that certain kinds of problems like the recognition of faces, translation of languages, and guidance of teachable robots lie beyond the capabilities of linear processing. Their efforts now center, in effect, on linking many small computers and letting each seek a solution to a different aspect of the same problem at the same time. This new form of computer design is called parallel processing. It would be premature to say that the shift from the erectus brain to the sapiens brain was a shift from linear to parallel processing, but the analogy is apt because it was not until machines were built that had a capacity for linear processing that the human designers could begin to build machines based on parallel processing. In nature, selection often operates in a similar fashion, using structures that were selected for one function as the basis for the selection of structures that have an entirely different function. Lungs, for example, evolved from air sacs that fish used not for breathing but for flotation. Similarly, birds' wings evolved from front feet that bipedal reptiles used not for flying but for grasping. It would not be without precedent, therefore, if the brain we use to think evolved out of the brain erectus used for running.

Incidentally, Fialkowski's theory sheds an interesting sidelight on the pinnipeds, an order of sea-dwelling mammals that includes seals, porpoises, and dolphins and that are also renowned for their oversized brains and intense sociality. The problem these extremely active creatures confront is not thermal stress—the water takes care of that—but oxygen depletion during prolonged underwater swimming. Like long-distance runners on land, pinnipeds benefitted from having fail-safe networks of duplicate brain cells and circuits. The U.S. Navy has been training pinnipeds to retrieve missile parts that fall to the bottom of the sea and to attach explosives to the hulls of enemy vessels. Six dolphins were sent from San Diego to serve in the Persian Gulf during the Iran-Iraq war. But lacking any natural need to use tools or manipulate objects, the pinniped brain never underwent the reorganization that took place in the transition from erectus to sapiens. A good thing for them, it turns out, or now they would all be in boot camp, learning how to kill each other at the bottom of the sea.

RUDIMENTARY
CULTURES

*F*ROM THE BEGINNING, the members of the hominid family learned how to feed and protect themselves by following the example of their campmates, especially their elders. They possessed what I call rudimentary cultures. I mean they had a small repertory of simple traditions that got passed down from one generation to the next, not through the inheritance of their parents' genes, but through learning their parents' and their companions' ways of doing things. Since the distinction between genetic and cultural programming will come up again several times later on, let me try to be as precise as I can right now. Nothing that an animal does can be said to be free of genetic influence. The capacity to learn, store, and transmit information depends on specific genetically determined capabilities. Barnacles and oysters are not likely to acquire even rudimentary cultures. But it would be folly to deny that some organisms depend far more on learning as a means of coping with life's problems. Among these, some depend more on learning from each other. And among these, some depend more on learning what others have learned and passed on from one generation to the next.

In their zeal to promote genetic interpretations of human life, some biologists fail to pay due attention to the enormous differences that exist among organisms with respect to their ability to use information that is encoded in neural circuitry rather than in the genes. The genes account for the neural circuits, but something else accounts for what's in these circuits.

For example, there is no specific genetic information that is responsible for chimpanzee termiting and anting. True, in order for this behavior to occur, genetically determined capacities for learning, for manipulating objects, and for omnivorous eating must be present in the young chimpanzee. But these general biological capacities and predispositions cannot explain termiting and anting. The missing ingredient is the information about termiting and anting that is stored in the brains of adult chimpanzees. This information is passed on to young chimpanzees by their mothers. Young Gombe chimpanzees do not begin termiting until they are eighteen to twenty-two months old, and their behavior does not become proficient until they are about three years old. Infants watch intently as the adults termite. Novices often retrieve discarded termiting sticks and attempt to use them. Anting, with its risk of being bitten, takes longer to learn. The youngest chimp to achieve proficiency was about four years old. The fact that different groups of chimps do not exploit driver ants even though the species is widely distributed through Africa also suggests that anting is a rudimentary cultural trait. At the same time, other groups of chimps do exploit different species of ants and in ways that differ from the Gombe tradition. Chimps in the Mahale Mountains, 170 kilometers south of Gombe, insert twigs and bark into the nests of tree-dwelling ants, which the Gombe chimps ignore.

Apes are not the only nonhuman primates that possess rudimentary cultures. Primatologists of the Primate Research Institute of Kyoto University report that Japanese macaques have a variety of customs and institutions based on social learning. The males of certain troops, for example, take turns looking after the infants while the infants' mothers are feeding. Such baby-sitting is characteristic only of the troops at Takasaki-yama and Takhashi. Other cultural differences have been noted, too. When the monkeys of Takasaki-yama eat the fruit of the *muku* tree, they either throw away the hard stone inside or swallow it and excrete it in their feces. But the monkeys of Arashi-yama break the stone with their teeth and eat the pulpy interior. Some troops eat shellfish; others do not. Cultural differences have also been noted with respect to the characteristic distance that the animals maintain among themselves during feeding and with respect to the order of males, females, and juveniles when troops move through the forest.

Scientists at the Primate Research Institute actually observed behavioral innovations being spread from individual to individual and become part of a troop's rudimentary culture. To attract monkeys near the shore for easier observation, the scientists set sweet potatoes on the beach. One day a young female began to wash the sand from the sweet potatoes by plunging them into a small brook that cut through the beach. This washing behavior spread throughout the group and gradually replaced the former rubbing habit. Nine years later, 80 percent to 90 percent of the animals were washing their sweet potatoes, some in the brook, others in the sea. When the scientists spread wheat on the beach, the monkeys of Koshima at first had a hard time separating the kernels from the sand. One of them soon invented a process for removing sand from the wheat, and this behavior was taken over by others. (The solution was to plunge the wheat into the water. The wheat floats and the sand drops to the bottom.)

The fundamental difference between rudimentary and fully developed cultures is quantitative. Apes and monkeys have a few traditions, but humans have uncountable numbers of them. Cultural artifacts, practices, rules, and relationships constitute the largest part of our environment. Humans cannot eat, breathe, defecate, mate, reproduce, sit, move about, sleep, or lie down without following or expressing some aspect of their society's culture. Our cultures grow, expand, evolve. It's their nature. Cultural reality comes from, but rises above, ordinary organic reality, just as organic reality comes from, but rises above, its chemical and physical substrates. When our ancestors crossed the threshold of cultural takeoff, they achieved a breakthrough as fateful as the transition from energy to matter or from amino acids to living protein.

LINGUISTIC
TAKEOFF

ET ME DWELL a bit on the connection between cultural takeoff and the way humans communicate. In effect, cultural takeoff is also linguistic takeoff. A rapid and cumulative rate of change in traditions implies a breakthrough in the amount of information socially acquired, stored, retrieved, and shared. It is impossible to celebrate the one without celebrating the other. Human language is the medium by which memories outlive individuals and generations. But it is no mere passive palimpsest. It is also an active instrumental force in the creation of the increasingly complex social activity that cultural evolution imposes on everyday life. Linguistic competence makes it possible to formulate rules for appropriate behavior for situations that are remote in space and time. Without ever having seen a driver ant or a driver ant's nest, dull, normal humans, unlike the smartest chimpanzees, can instruct each other on what to do to go anting. Practice will still be needed (and will always improve the performances) but the ability to formulate a verbal rule for anting or termiting facilitates the replication of these activities by different individuals within and across generations. Human social life consists in great measure (but not exclusively) of thoughts and behavior that are coordinated and governed by such rules. As people invent new patterns of social activity, they invent corresponding rules to fit the new practices and they store these rules in their brains (unlike the instructions for biological innovations, which are stored in the genes). With verbal, rule-governed behavior in the ascendancy, humans easily surpass all other species in the complexity and diversity of social roles and in the formation of cooperative groups.

Is our linguistic virtuosity merely a by-product of expanded and reorganized circuitry of the hominid brain, or is it based on a definite species-specific neural program that enables us to acquire linguistic competence as we pass from infancy into childhood? No one suggests that children will learn to speak a language if they are brought up in total isolation. But children do seem to learn their linguistic competence much the way they learn to walk. Very little formal teaching suffices to get a child to pass from crawling to walking because most of the instructions about how to coordinate our feet, legs, arms, and torso in a bipedal gait are programmed into us. Although the programming for language may not be quite as strong and definite as for walking, it is strong enough to manifest itself with only a minimum of teaching by parents and other members of a speech community. Linguists have found evidence to support this view in the history of certain languages that arose as a consequence of the massive uprooting of people under the impact of colonialism and imperialism.

During the past few centuries, the demand for cheap plantation labor compelled or induced large numbers of people who spoke different native languages to live close together on isolated coasts and islands such as Haiti, Jamaica, Guyana, and Hawaii. In order to talk to each other, the members of these polyglot communities developed forms of communication known as pidgins. When the diversity of native languages with input into a pidgin was very great and there were only a few speakers of the plantation owner's languages, the pidgin constituted in effect a natural experiment in the formation of a new language. The first generation of pidgin speakers could not rely on their parents to teach them to speak this new language. Parents always know more about their community's language than their children do, but not in this case. In order for children to have full linguistic competence in pidgin, they must speedily outstrip the feeble form of pidgin that their parents speak. First-generation pidgins are genuinely rudimentary languages that may offer insights into pre-takeoff forms of speech. They conspicuously lack rules for word order such as subject-verb-object, articles like "a" and "the" that mark nonspecific and specific nouns, and regular ways of marking tense. Sentences are short and consist for the most part of disconnected strings of verbs and nouns. Derek Bickerton of the University of Hawaii gives these two examples from first-generation Hawaiian pidgin, which was developed by English, Japanese, Philippine, Korean, Portuguese, and native Hawaiian speakers in the late nineteenth century:

aena tu macha churen, samawl churen, haus mani pei
and too much children, small children, house money pay

bilhoa mil no moa hilipino no nating
before mill no more Filipino no nothing

Pidgins in several different parts of the world rapidly gave rise to new and completely adequate languages known as creoles. In Hawaii this happened in one generation, meaning in effect that children as they grew up had to adopt a whole series of grammatical rules that their parents could not have taught them and which, therefore, the children themselves must have in some sense "invented." What is most remarkable is that the grammar of Hawaiian creole turns out to be almost identical to the grammars of all other creoles that have emerged from pidgins in one generation, regardless of the combination of native languages represented in each case. For example, they all have a basic word order in which subject comes first, verb next, and object last, and they also have definite rules for changing this order to focus on one particular constituent of a sentence, as in Hawaiian creole:

Ai si daet wan	(I saw that one.)
Ai no si daet wan	(I didn't see that one.)
O, daet wan ai si	(Oh, that one I saw.)

How was it possible for pidgin-speaking children to change Hawaiian pidgin into Hawaiian creole in such a short time? According to Bickerton, they were able to do it because the modern human brain contains a biologically programmed blueprint for acquiring grammatically adequate language. This program is activated during a child's maturation and unfolds in the same manner that our programming for walking unfolds. Children could never invent a language without being exposed to the language of their parents. But with a minimum of exposure to other people's linguistic behavior, they stop "crawling." Once they're up on their two legs, no one needs to teach them the linguistic equivalent of running.

Clearly, the biological programming that makes it possible for modern human beings to acquire linguistic competency did not spring full-grown from the head of habilis or erectus. As with our ability to walk or to manipulate objects with an opposable thumb, there must have been a step-by-step process whereby natural selection laid the basis for increasingly efficient modes of concept formation and their linguistic expression. What were the first steps? I think our ape cousins have a lot to say to us on this subject. But before I draw them into the discussion, let me clear up a common misunderstanding about the status of contemporary languages.

PRIMITIVE LANGUAGES?

*L*INGUISTS THOUGHT THAT LANGUAGES spoken by contemporary "primitive" peoples were, in fact, intermediate between animal languages and civilized languages. They were forced to abandon this idea when they discovered that grammatical rules varied in complexity quite independent of levels of technological and political development. The obscure North American Indian language Kwakiutl, for example, has twice as many case endings as Latin. Other proposed diagnostics of "primitive" languages, such as the presence of appropriately general or specific words, proved to be equally unreliable indicators of evolutionary grades. For example, the Agta of the Philippines have thirty-one different verbs meaning "to fish," each word referring to a particular type of fishing. Yet they lack a simple generic word meaning "to fish." In the Tupi languages spoken by Native Americans in Brazil, there are numerous words that designate separate species of parrots, but no general word for parrot. Other languages lack words for specifics. They have separate words for numbers one through five; thereafter, they simply rely on a word that means "many." Today linguists realize that the failure of a language to have a general or specific word has nothing to do with its evolutionary standing. It simply reflects culturally defined needs to be specific or general. The Agta, who depend on fish for much of their subsistence, never have any need to refer to fishing as a general activity; what is important to them are the specific ways fish can be obtained. Similarly, speakers of the language of preliterate societies need to know about the distinctive properties of plants. On average, they can name and identify 500 to 1,000 separate plant species, while the ordinary speakers of the languages of urban industrial societies can name only 50 to 100 such species. Not surprisingly, the urbanites do more lumping and get along with vague concepts like grass, tree, shrub, bush, or vine. Speakers of languages that lack specific numbers beyond five also get along very well because they seldom have to be precise about large quantities. If an occasion arises when they have to be precise, they cope by repeating the largest term an appropriate number of times.

Speakers in preliterate societies also often lack specific words for colors. Lacking control over dyes and paints, they seldom need to be color-conscious. But if the need arises, they can always adapt to the occasion by referring to "the color of the sky," "the color of milk," or "the color of blood." Even parts of the body get named in conformity with the cultural need to refer to them. In the tropics, where people don't wear much clothing, they tend to speak languages that lump "hand" and "arm" under one term and "leg" and "foot" under another. People who live in colder climates and who wear special garments (gloves, boots, sleeves, pants, etc.) for different parts of the body, more often have separate words for "hand" versus "arm" and for "foot" versus "leg." None of these differences therefore can be interpreted as evidence of a more primitive or intermediate phase of linguistic evolution. All of the three thousand or so different languages spoken in the world today possess a common fundamental structure and need only minor changes in vocabulary to be equally efficient in storing, retrieving, and transmitting information and in organizing social behavior. So the conclusion of the great anthropological linguist Edward Sapir stands unchallenged: "When it comes to linguistic form, Plato walks with the Macedonian swineherd, Confucius with the head-hunting savages of Assam."

And now, back to the apes.

APE-SIGNS

APES IN THE WILD do not show themselves to be exceptionally gifted communicators. A large portion of their communication behavior consists of instinctive facial expressions and body language. They sneer when threatened, pout when in distress, and grin widely when there is danger. To show submission, they present their rump, extend their hand, crouch, and bob; to frighten each other, they fluff up their hairs, jump up and down, shake trees, hurl rocks, wave their arms, and swagger on four feet. Some even drag leafy branches behind them to attract attention and initiate group movement in a particular direction. They use instinctual vocal sounds to convey a broader but still unimpressive range of meanings: "aha" says they have found food, "wrah" communicates fear, "auk" expresses puzzlement, a soft bark or cough shows annoyance. They cry, whimper, or scream to show distress. They greet each other with pant-hoots, express excitement with barks, and grunt to show satisfaction with their nest mates or when they are enjoying a good meal. They laugh, pant, smack their lips, and clack their teeth when they make friendly body contact. And they pant and squeal while copulating. But they do not have names for each other; nor can they tell each other what they did when they were out of sight; nor can they ask each other for specific objects, such as a stick, a nut, a stone, or a banana (unless such objects are being held by someone close by).

This sums up the communicative capacities chimpanzees exhibit in their native habitats. But, as in the case of tool use, chimps placed in zoos and laboratories can outdo themselves. Scientists were slow to realize this because they initially concentrated on teaching chimps to talk. That is what Keith and Cathy Hayes tried to do with a chimp named Viki, whom they adopted as an infant and reared as if she were a human baby. After six years of intensive effort, Viki was able to say only "mama," "papa," "cup," and "up," and none too clearly at that. But the fault was in Viki's throat and not in her head. The sounds of human speech and song originate in the larynx, the upper portion of the breathing tube that contains the vocal cords. The sounds then pass through a flexible resonating chamber called the pharynx, which is located between the larynx and the mouth, and finally exit through the mouth and nose.

Interruptions in the flow of air by tongue, teeth, and lips produce most of the consonant sounds in human speech. The vowel sounds "oh" and "ah" can be made in the larynx: but the vowel sounds "ee," "ay" (as in bay), and "ooo," which occur in every known human language, are produced in the pharynx. They cannot be produced in the larynx. Chimpanzees (as well as other nonhuman primates) do not possess a pharynx, and it is this physiological fact that accounts for Viki's inability to learn to utter no more than four words.

Beginning in 1966, with Allen and Beatrice Gardner's attempt to teach a female chimpanzee named Washoe how to con- verse in American sign language, experimenters concentrated on using visual rather than auditory channels to teach apes to communi- cate. In four or five years, Washoe acquired a repertory of 160 sign- words that she used in many different novel combinations. She first learned the sign "open" as part of a request to open a particular door. Then she signed to open other kinds of doors such as the refrigerator door and the closet door. Later she generalized her use of "open" to requests to open any kind of closed container, such as desk drawers, briefcases, boxes, and jars.

Once Susan, a research assistant, stepped on Washoe's doll. Washoe had many ways to tell her what was on her mind: "Up Susan," "Susan up," "mine please up," "give me baby," "please shoe," "more mine," "up please," "please up," "more up," "baby down," "shoe up," "baby up," "please move up." Soon another researcher, David Premack, used a set of plastic chips to teach a chimpanzee named Sarah the meaning of a set of 150 symbols with which they could communicate with each other. Premack asked Sarah rather abstract questions, such as "What is an apple the same as?" Sarah responded by selecting the chips that stood for "red," "round," "stem," and "less desirable than grapes." Premack incor- porated rudimentary grammatical rules into his human-chimp language. Sarah learned to respond appropriately to the word- order dependent plastic chip command: "Sarah, put the banana in the pail and the apple in the dish." Sarah herself, however, did not make such grammar-dependent demands of Premack.

Both Washoe and Lucy, a chimpanzee raised by Roger Fouts, learned to generalize the signs for "dirty" from the sign for "feces." Lucy applied it to Fouts when he refused her requests! Lucy also invented the combinations "cry hurt food" to name radishes and "candy fruit" for watermelon.

Another approach, with a three-and-a-half-year-old chimpanzee named Lana, utilized a keyboard controlled by a computer and a written language known as Yerkish. Lana could read and write such sentences as "Please machine make the window open," correctly distinguishing between sentences that begin appropriately and inappropriately and that have permitted and prohibited combinations of Yerkish words in permitted and prohibited sequence.

The most dramatic achievement of these studies is that they have demonstrated that signing chimpanzees can pass on their signing skills to nonsigning chimpanzees without direct human mediation. Loulis, a ten-month-old chimp, was presented to Washoe, who adopted the infant and promptly began to sign to him. By thirty-six months, Loulis was using twenty-eight signs that he had learned from Washoe. After about five years of learning to sign from Washoe and two other signing chimps, but not from humans, Loulis had acquired the use of fifty-five signs. Washoe, Loulis, and other signing chimps regularly use their sign language to communicate with each other even when humans are not present. These "conversations," as recorded by remote cameras on videotape, occurred from 118 to 649 times a month.

According to some researchers, these experiments demonstrate that chimpanzees can acquire the rudiments of human linguistic competence. Others see only a travesty of human linguistic competence. In my opinion, the experiments prove that apes have more talent for communicating abstract ideas than most scientists previously thought possible. But ape competence does not rise beyond that of a three-year-old human child. Their discourse consists mostly of requests for specific objects and of expressions of emotional states. They seldom use their knowledge of signing to communicate about past or future events unless asked; and they do not use it to plan for contingencies, coordinate cooperative ventures, or formulate social rules of behavior. The fact that Washoe taught Loulis fifty-five signs without human intervention has a double-edged significance. I am impressed that Loulis learned any signs at all. Yet that he learned fewer signs than his mother shows that, left to their own devices, chimps would use fewer and fewer signs, and that the habit of using any at all would be lost after a few generations.

But I think we are asking the wrong question about ape language. The question is not whether their signing behavior resembles human signing behavior, but whether their rudimentary ability to use sign language could have served as the starting point for the evolution of greater linguistic competence. I think the answer has to be yes. At some stage in the evolution of human linguistic skills, the messages our ancestors sent and received must have strongly resembled the messages that now pass between the signing chimps and their trainers. These messages consist almost entirely of requests on the part of chimps and humans to get each other to do something: "give me the doll," "put the banana in the pail," "open the window." Videotape studies that my students and I carried out on the everyday speech of New York families show that messages exchanged among humans also consist largely of requests of one sort or another: "sit here," "give me the money," "shut up," "please get me a Coke," "put it down," "take the garbage out." The more we surround ourselves with or become dependent on culturally created goods and services, the more we experience a need to make requests to others to help us obtain those goods and services. As our ancestors came to depend more and more on tool-making, tool-using, and cultural traditions, their genetically controlled repertory of grunts, grimaces, and tantrums no longer sufficed to convey the expanding range of requests that they needed to make. Culturally invented gestures and sounds would have increased proportionately. What the ape-signing experiments show, therefore, is that afarensis could easily have possessed a repertory of 100 or 200 socially acquired gestures or sounds that they employed in making simple requests to each other. This was not language as we know it, but it was certainly a beginning from which language as we know it could have evolved.

THE TRIUMPH
OF SOUND

ALTHOUGH OUR ANCESTORS used both visual and auditory signals to express emotions and make simple requests, sight and sound had markedly different potentials for the evolution of more complex systems of communication. By erectus times, our forebears were too busy making and using tools, and carrying food, babies, and the weapons of the hunt to commit their arms, hands, and fingers to the task of conveying complex messages. The vocal-auditory channel suffered no equivalent conflicts of interests—at least, not at the beginning. Air coming from the lungs was a waste product; it had to be expelled anyway. Furthermore, sounds conveyed messages at night as readily as in the day; they could be made while walking or running; and they were effective over long distances even when the line of sight was obstructed by trees or hills.

As the use of larger and more precise repertories of meaningful sounds began to pay off in enhanced reproductive success, the portion of our ancestors' respiratory tract known as the pharynx became uniquely flexible and elongated. In all other mammals the pharynx is small because the larynx, or upper trachea, is positioned close to the base of the skull, leads almost directly to the rear of the nasal cavity, and gets shut off from the mouth during breathing. Because of lengthening of the pharynx in humans, the food passage and the air passage cross each other, with the strange consequence noted by Charles Darwin that "every particle of food and drink which we swallow has to pass over the orifice of the trachea, with some risk of falling into the lungs." Indeed, "swallowing the wrong way," which can be fatal for us but is impossible in other mammals, is a cost we pay for having deep throats. But as I've already indicated, the benefits of this arrangement outweigh its dangers, for possession of an enlarged pharynx is what makes it possible for us to form the vowel sounds "ee," "ay," and "ooo," which are essential components of all human languages. Exactly when the pharynx achieved its modern dimensions is difficult to say because the soft parts of our hominid ancestors never got fossilized. But Philip Lieberman of Brown University has attempted to reconstruct the architecture of the mouth and throat from a knowledge of the shape of the bottom of the skull and on this basis believes that the hominid vocal tract acquired its modern dimensions roughly coincident with the appearance of anatomically modern sapiens. If Lieberman is correct, neither erectus nor Neandertal engaged in fully evolved human speech.

Nothing runs deeper in human nature than our tendency as infants to babble and gurgle. While each human language uses fewer than fifty distinct sounds to build its words and sentences, human infants spontaneously produce a much greater variety of vocalizations. Parents and other members of the speech community gradually reinforce the linguistically appropriate noises and ignore or repress those which will not be needed to produce the sounds of their language.

These sounds result from the most complex motor control maneuvers that human beings carry out and are possible only because they become completely automated. Lieberman believes that the neural circuitry that enables us to automate human speech evolved in tandem with the ability to make vowel sounds in the pharynx. Presapiens, in other words, not only lacked a vowel-producing pharynx, but they also lacked the neural circuitry for achieving rapid-fire emissions of whatever distinctive sounds they were able to make. Lieberman has an even more intriguing suggestion: namely, that the neural circuitry that was responsible for the automation of the production of speech sounds could have served equally well as the substrate for the automation of the higher-order rules that govern word order and other grammatical and syntactic aspects of human speech.

Virtuosity in talking implies virtuosity in listening. It is as much in our nature to hear the difference between sounds as to be prolific in making them. Is it merely coincidental, then, that it is also in our nature to make music? Whether we so love music because it is in essence a form of speech, or we so love speech because it is in essence a form of music cannot be decided. The rising and falling tones and the rhythms of speech and song appeal to the same sensibilities and by extension so do all similar acoustic effects made with horns, drums, strings, or electric synthesizers. Is this the reason that music has the power to make people dance, armies march, and lovers swoon? Does every musical performance, from the plaintive plucking of a single bow to the soaring frenzy of rock, celebrate in its own way the evolution of signals heard over signals seen, the birth of language, and the beginning of the transcendent flight of human cultures?

ON BEING
NEANDERTAL

WAS OUR KIND the first and only species on earth ever to achieve cultural and linguistic takeoff? I cannot answer with certainty. Between 400,000 and 200,000 years ago, erectus was gradually replaced by somewhat more sapiens-looking species in Africa and Asia known collectively as "archaic *Homo sapiens.*" Although their heads were rounder and less rugged compared to erectus, their tool kits contained essentially the same array of simple core and flake implements that erectus had been using for over a million years. Little about them suggests that they had passed beyond the phase of protoculture and protolanguage.

If there is any contender for cultural takeoff other than our kind, it is the Neandertals, an extinct species of near-humans who appeared in Europe and the Middle East about 100,000 years ago. Named after the river valley in Germany where they were first discovered, the Neandertals had bigger brains—as big, in fact, as our own—than the archaic sapiens from whom they presumably descended. But they also had huge, forward-jutting jaws, massive front teeth, heavy browridges, sloping brows, elliptical heads with a peculiar bony bun at the rear, short necks, and extra thick arm and leg bones—a combination of traits that would make them stand out on the line of scrimmage in a big-league football game, even when suited up with regulation helmets and uniforms.

A plausible explanation for Neandertal anatomy comes readily to mind. The erectus and archaic sapiens who preceded the Neandertals lived in Europe only when the continental glaciers were in retreat and the climate was temperate or even subtropical. But the appearance of the Neandertals in the fossil record about 100,000 years ago coincides with the onset of one of the last great continental glaciations. The Neandertals were probably the first hominids to survive for an extended period in an extremely cold climate. Several of the Neandertals' anatomical features may represent adaptations to life in their outdoor refrigerator. First of all, their bodies were thick and squat just as predicted by Bergman's rule. Second, their huge front teeth may have been selected as a means of softening animal skins to satisfy their need for fur blankets and warm clothing—even the front teeth on juvenile Neandertals were worn down from constant chewing, a condition that occurs as well among modern Eskimo women, who spend a good deal of time softening hides and boots with their teeth. Selection for forceful chewing may also explain the heavy browridges, which serve to buttress the face against the upward thrust of the Neandertals' powerful jaws. Unlike their warm-climate contemporaries, the Neandertals had few plants to eat, and therefore were obliged to rely almost exclusively on the hunt.

Many archaeologists attribute advanced forms of symbolic behavior and thought to the Neandertals. Alexander Marshack of Harvard's Peabody Museum interprets pendantlike objects made from antlers, bone, and the canine teeth of a fox, found in association with other Neandertal remains, as personal adornments. Bones engraved with fine zigzag lines found in France and Bulgaria and a polished section of a mammoth's tooth from Tata, Hungary, may also be evidence for Neandertal rituals. Many archaeologists also believe that Neandertals deliberately buried their dead, laying them to rest with knees drawn up to chests in a fetal position. Stone tools and parts of cave bears and other mammal skeletons found alongside or on top of the Neandertal remains have inspired the theory that the Neandertals conducted mortuary rituals and believed in an afterlife. Traces of red ochre, a dye that modern-day Aboriginals often place on the bodies of the dead to ward off evil, have been detected near the skeletons. Ralph Solecki of Columbia University added a final, poignant touch to the supposed funerary rituals with his interpretation of the pollen grains that covered the skeleton of a Neandertal male who died 60,000 years ago in Shanidar Cave, Iraq. According to Solecki, the pollen is all that is left of massive bouquets of bachelor buttons, hollyhocks, and other wild flowers that someone had brought into the cave and lovingly heaped on the deceased.

Unfortunately, most of these alleged tokens of cultural competence could have been produced by natural accidents rather than by Neandertal design. The burials could have been the result of cave-ins; the flexed postures of the skeletons might merely mean that the cave-ins occurred at night, while the victims were sleeping; the animal bones and stone tools might be due to chance association with the remains of a meal; the traces of red ochre could simply indicate the occurrence of ochre-bearing soils. The "ornaments" could have been nothing more than a kind of "doodle" made out of bone and teeth. And the flowers of Shanidar? Perhaps it was the wind and not the mourners that deposited the pollen on the grave site.

But let us suppose that Neandertals were indeed the active agents of all of the disputed customs. Would this warrant the conclusion that the Neandertals possessed advanced linguistic power and had crossed the threshold of cultural takeoff? Not necessarily. Personal adornments fashioned from bones or antlers do not necessarily imply any quantum leap in consciousness. Males and females may simply have discovered that by wearing finely crafted objects they became more alluring to each other, no more than that. As for the hypothesized rituals, none of them is so complex or arcane that it could not have become established in the absence of verbalized beliefs. For example, application of a red dye to a lifeless body might merely reflect an association of red with blood, and of blood with life, as a result of common behavioral experiences rather than a conscious theory of how the dead should be treated. Likewise, food set aside for the deceased might simply continue a pattern of food sharing previously established among group members and have nothing to do with shared conceptualization about journeys to an afterlife. What about deliberate burials? These also follow behaviorally, if one takes note that cave sites were habitation sites. Burial then becomes the only way of disposing of a decaying body while keeping it close to its lifelong companions. As for the fetal position, Neandertal grave diggers, lacking shovels and pickaxes, naturally preferred to dig small holes, which therefore could accommodate only a body with legs drawn up under the chin. And this leads to the heaps of wild flowers. If the graves were shallow, odors from the decomposing remains could have motivated those who continued to sleep and eat nearby to scent the air with the only perfume available. The point is that when the behavior in question occurs among our kind, we automatically assume it is accompanied by rules for explaining and justifying it. But in Neandertal we have another species, about which we can't automatically assume anything.

There are other grounds for being skeptical about the Neandertals' ability to create the conscious symbolic and verbal components of cultural life. First of all, measurements of the base of skulls indicate that the vocal tract in Neandertals resembles the vocal tract in chimpanzees. The pharynx, especially, was much less developed than in modern sapiens, probably because of the Neandertals' shortened neck and forward-jutting face. So there is a good chance that Neandertals lacked the sound-making virtuosity that distinguishes our kind, and that their powers of thought and consciousness were correspondingly immature. Can this be the explanation for why the Neandertals became extinct shortly after modern sapiens entered Europe and achieved cultural takeoff 45,000–35,000 years ago?

NEANDERTAL'S FATE AND THE ORIGIN OF OUR KIND

*W*HERE DID ANATOMICALLY modern human beings first appear? It may have been in Africa, to judge from fossils recovered in caves near the southern tip of that continent at a site known as Klasies River Mouth. The dating, dependent on geological markers, is far from precise, having an upper limit of 115,000 and a lower limit of 85,000 years ago. Anatomically the Klasies River hominids are fully modern in appearance, but the tools they used are not very different from those associated with more archaic types of sapiens in Africa and Neandertals in Europe. Very early remains of anatomically modern sapiens have also been found at Qafzeh Cave near Nazareth in Israel. There the dating is more precise, 92,000 ± 5,000 years, based on the emission of electrons trapped in stone tools that had once been exposed to fire. Again, most of the tools themselves were not much different from those employed by archaic sapiens. In contrast to these early African and Middle Eastern dates, anatomically modern sapiens did not appear in Europe and Asia until after 45,000 years ago. But by that time, they were using tools that were quite different from tools possessed by archaic sapiens and were already at the point of cultural and linguistic takeoff.

One interpretation of these finds is that modern sapiens originated in Africa and then spread to Europe and Asia via the Middle East. But given the lower estimate of Klasies River, at 85,000 years, it is possible that modern sapiens appeared first in the Middle East and then subsequently dispersed to Africa, Europe, and Asia. Whether the migration went from the Middle East to Africa or from Africa to the Middle East, it is hard to understand why the spread to Europe and Asia seems to have taken 50,000 years while the spread between the Middle East and Africa required an interval of only about 5,000 years. Perhaps with the northern latitudes in the grip of the Ice Age, modern sapiens lacked a motivation for leaving their homelands.

The alternative interpretation of the Qafzeh and Klasies River cave materials is that the transition from archaic to modern sapiens took place not in one but in several world regions. In this view, which is defended by Mildreth Wolpoff of the University of Michigan and James Spuhler of the University of New Mexico, Neandertals were not a separate species of hominid but the direct progenitors of modern humans who lingered on in Europe and the Middle East as racial variants and who had their counterparts in other transitional archaic races in Africa and Asia. Both sides in this dispute have turned to the analysis of DNA obtained from different modern races to bolster their positions. Theoretically, one should be able to tell from the number of changes that have accumulated in the DNA of the cellular organelles known as mitochondria in what order the major regional populations diverged from a common female ancestor, and how long ago. Unfortunately, this work is still in an experimental stage, and one should remain skeptical of a widely publicized claim made by Rebecca Cann and her associates at the University of Hawaii that our kind's "Eve" was a woman who lived in Africa 140,000 to 290,000 years ago.

Another part of the puzzle is the coexistence of Neandertals and modern sapiens in the Middle East. At Mount Carmel not far from Qafzeh, archaeologists found bones and tools belonging to Neandertals that date to 60,000 years before the present. This means that in the Middle East, unlike in Europe, Neandertals and modern sapiens may have coexisted for 30,000 years (from 65,000 to 35,000 years ago). And not only did they coexist for all those millennia, but they manufactured and used the same kinds of tools for the whole period.

I am prompted therefore to raise the question of just how "human" the anatomically modern sapiens of Klasies River and Qafzeh really were. Did they possess the program for human linguistic competence? My hunch is that prior to 45,000–35,000 years ago the linguistic and cultural capacities of anatomically modern sapiens were not yet fully formed and were no more advanced than the Neandertals'. This would explain why the tools associated with early African and Middle Eastern modern sapiens are very similar to tools used by Neandertals in Europe and the Middle East and why it was possible for Neandertals and modern sapiens to exist in close proximity for at least 30,000 years in the Middle East while their coexistence in Europe did not last more than 5,000 years.

When modern sapiens suddenly appeared in Europe, their technology was a quantum jump ahead of the Neandertals'. The basis of stonework was no longer cores and flakes but long, thin, razor-sharp blades detached with great precision and economy from carefully selected flint nodules. At the same time, they had become masters of cutting, carving, and drilling in materials such as bone, ivory, and antler. They had invented needles and were probably sewing garments to fit the shape of their bodies. They were using throwing boards that extended the range they could hurl spears and darts, and their projectiles could be equipped with a dazzling choice of ingenious barbed and tanged points.

Aside from one or two isolated sites in France, Neandertal remains have never been found in association with these advanced tools and weapons, implying that our kind had become much faster learners than the Neandertals and that the Neandertals were never able to achieve cultural and linguistic takeoff.

I don't want to say that direct armed confrontations caused their demise. Both the invaders and the Neandertals lived in small, mobile bands, and neither possessed the political organization necessary to wage wars of extermination. But it would have taken only an occasional skirmish with the newcomers to make the Neandertals retreat into areas that offered diminished opportunities for hunting. This would have led to undernutrition, elevated mortality rates, and an accelerated decline in what was at the outset an already sparse population. I cannot help thinking that a very different kind of scenario would have unfolded had the Neandertals been the equals of our kind in their capacity for language and culture.

CULTURE
OVERSHADOWING

*N*OW ALL PROLOGUES are at an end. Our ancestors of 30,000 years ago reveal themselves in full control of tongue, hand, eye, and ear. Culture, "overshadowing," lunges ahead, while human nature creeps at a petty pace or stands still. In a geological instant—5,000 years—every form of art is born and religions flourish.

On the walls and ceilings of subterranean galleries, far from the light of day, lifelike animals, recognizable across 30,000 intervening years, suddenly appear. Painted over one another, some larger than life, in glorious colors, there are horses, bison, reindeer, ibex, boars, wild cattle, woolly rhinoceros, and hairy mammoths. Occasionally, the artists painted a human figure wearing a mask; and there are vulva- and penislike symbols and mysterious disembodied hands. Sculpture begins at the same time. First with small ivory animals and crude human figurines found near Vogelhard, Germany. Later, statuettes of fat women with enlarged buttocks and huge breasts catch the fancy of the times. Artists from France to Siberia rendered these "Venus" figurines in stone, bone, ivory, and even unbaked clay, possibly for ritual use in ceremonies aimed at increasing the fertility of animals or people, or possibly simply because they wanted women to be fat. Cave sites also contain stone tablets engraved with pictures of animals. Out of thousands, a handful bear the earliest human portraits of specific human beings—adult males, each in profile, with long noses, and hair covering their ears. Jewelry becomes abundant, not simple pendants but whole necklaces of matched bones, teeth, shells, and tusks, plus bracelets and pins all decorated with fine, incised designs. Out on the Russian plains where people lived in huts made of mammoth ribs covered with skins and where there were no caves to paint, jewelry became a kind of obsession. In a single 24,000-year-old grave containing the remains of an adult and two children, Russian archaeologists counted over 10,000 bone-and-ivory beads.

But let us return to the caves of Western Europe, for they tell the most about the burgeoning of art and religion. The fact that the murals occur in remote and inaccessible subterranean galleries, where the artists had to use oil lamps to see what they were doing, proves to my satisfaction that the paintings were part of a religious ceremony. So does the fact that the artists painted new pictures over earlier paintings even though unused surfaces were available. Appropriately enough, near some of the paintings archaeologists have found small, hollow bird bones, perforated on one side, fragments of flutes 25,000 years older than the pipes of Pan. So there was music, too. And if music, then song and poetry. Nor is it possible to stop there, since the paintings themselves show dancing figures wearing masks and costumes. And in some caves the sand floors still hold the imprints left by dancing feet.

The wall paintings, therefore, were not the kind of pictures that hang on the walls of museums, preserved for viewing, never to be changed. Rather, they were moments in multimedia ceremonial performances that affirmed and renewed relationships between people and animals and people and people. I do not know if the paintings were specifically intended to increase the future supply of meat or to express reverence for animals already killed, or both. The fact that the species depicted were generally the largest of the animals that were actually hunted although not necessarily the most abundant in the region suggests that the paintings may have been a wish list. But the ceremony as a whole must have had multiple social and psychological functions. Perhaps it affirmed and intensified the participants' sense of identity as members of a community; or perhaps it educated children about their duties and their place in the world. In any event, the whole complex invites comparison with rituals performed by hunting peoples who have survived into modern times. I have in mind, for example, the annual Australian Aborigines' "intichiuma" festivals, at which people paint their bodies, wear feathers, chant the story of the creation, dance in imitation of their witchetty grub or emu ancestors, and visit the remote cliffs and rock shelters to gaze upon and to add to galleries of paintings that depict the history of the dream-time when the world was young.

As our kind struggled to understand and control their dream-time world, their minds laid down the beginnings of science as well as of art and religion. They grappled with time and its markers and learned the changes that the seasons brought. Details from paintings and engravings show not just horses, but horses in summer or winter coats; not just reindeer but males with fully grown antlers, heads up, mouths open, braying during the autumn rut. It is winter when the males are shown without their antlers; it is springtime when the female reindeer have antlers of their own to protect their newborn calves. Bison appear with full coats in winter and molting coats in summer, each kind facing in a different direction. Is it to show the direction of their annual migration, northward in the summer, southward in the winter?

A consciousness of seasons supports Alexander Marshack's idea that the hunters of the upper Paleolithic made astronomical observations to record the passage of time. They marked the passage of time on bone plaques that were also used to retouch the edges of worn-out cutting tools, or on antlers that bore engraved pictures of horses and animals. There Marshack found neat rows of tiny, punched or scratched wedge-shaped lines and holes, grouped into sets, which other archaeologists saw as tallies of animals caught by hunters. But Marshack sees the holes and scratches as days and lunar months.

A plaque found near Blanchard in southwestern France is the earliest. Like the first cave paintings and the first sculpture, it, too, is about 30,000 years old. Under the microscope one can see sixty-nine marks divided into twenty-four sets, ranging from one to seven units each. The marks have a distinctly lunate shape; some are fully rounded, others are crescentic, curving now to the left, now to the right. They begin in the center of the notational area, and follow a serpentine pattern that bends twice on the left and twice on the right. Marshack claims that by using the serpentine form, the sky-watchers preserved the continuity of the lunar changes, positioning the bends or turns so that they corresponded to the major bends or turns in the moon's phases. Crucial to this interpretation is that adjacent marks seem slightly different from each other, as if as the days passed, different tools were used to make them. Randall White of New York University doesn't see it that way. They look different, he contends, because the stone punches and burins used to make the "notations" became dull and chipped and changed shape during what was actually only a single creative episode. Although White may be right, I for one do not doubt that the creators of the great galleries of anatomically and seasonably accurate paintings of animals could have made a picture of the phases of the moon if they thought it would be worth their while.

ANCESTORS

*E*LWYN SIMONS, a paleontologist, famous for his discovery of early apelike creatures in Egypt, once explained to me how he became interested in digging up old bones. His father, an amateur genealogist, was always talking about their family ties to the original Dutch settlers of the Hudson River valley. If it was ancestors people wanted, he'd show them some real ancestors—thirty-million-year-old ones.

Despite a shared curiosity about ancestry, genealogists and paleontologists operate with different concepts of descent. The ancestors who interest genealogists have to be particular named individuals, preferably distinguished ones, linked by particular forebears. (Genealogists are definitely not interested in finding a monkey uncle!) This confines their reckoning of descent to a tiny fraction of the time during which humans have begat humans. The longest pedigrees based on secure documentary evidence are those that connect living individuals with Pepin of Laudan, one of the founders of the Carolingian Empire, who lived in the seventh century A.D. At twenty-five years per generation, the Carolingian pedigrees cover a span of about fifty-six generations. But if the first modern sapiens appeared 150,000 years ago, each of our family trees goes back for 5,600 generations, leaving 99 percent of everybody's ancestry genealogical *terra incognita*.

Mormons (members of the Church of Jesus Christ of Latter-Day Saints) are the world's most devoted genealogists. They have stored the names and vital statistics of about a billion and a half dead individuals on computer tapes in a climate-controlled, underground, nuclear-bombproof vault not far from the church's Salt Lake City headquarters and they are adding new names at the rate of several million a year, until, it is hoped, everyone who has ever been born is identified by name. Belief about the afterlife provides the rationale for this effort. The dead cannot enjoy paradise unless they are named and baptized in absentia during ceremonies that only Mormons are authorized to perform. Mormons believe that they will reign as gods after they die and enter paradise, and that the number of spirits over whom they will reign depends on the number of people they can posthumously bring into the Mormon fold. One Mormon genealogist, Thomas Tinney, claims to be able to trace his ancestry directly to Adam, for a total of 156 generations, but few of his coreligionists take him seriously. A shade more credible is another Mormon genealogist's use of Norse sagas and myths to reach ancestors who lived in A.D. 260. But when all is said and done, European ancestors fade into nameless obscurity when the Dark Ages are reached—at most only about fifty generations ago.

To achieve maximum genealogical depth, genealogists resort to a questionable strategy. They trace descent from only one direct lineal ancestor—usually a male—thereby neglecting hundreds if not thousands of other equally direct lineal ancestors. Alex Haley pursued this strategy in his best-selling book and extremely popular television miniseries *Roots*. He started with his mother, switched to her father, and thereafter concentrated exclusively on males, reaching Kunta Kinte, an African captured by British slavers and sold to a Maryland plantation in 1767. But in that year, Haley could have had 255 direct lineal ancestors in addition to Kunta Kinte. Haley himself inadvertently revealed the importance of some of the "roots" he neglected when he says he felt "impure" because of his light complexion while visiting a village in Gambia.

Beyond the mere sixty or so generations that mark the flawed and contrived outer limit of genealogical accounts, other ways of reckoning descent await those who yearn for deeper roots. Abandoning the pursuit of our unbroken succession of named progenitors, one can invoke the principle of descent that charters tribes and ethnic communities—Scots, Germans, Aztecs, Cambodians, Vietnamese, Tamils, Ashanti—you name it—around the world. To validate these deeper roots, all that needs to be done is to show that parents and grandparents were acknowledged members of the same ethnic or tribal entity. From then on, history, myth, and linguistic affinities magically waft us back through the corridors of time to a remote tribal or ethnic dawn. But a key assumption of ethnic or tribal descent is that Scots have always only mated with Scots, Germans only with Germans, Aztecs only with Aztecs, and so on—a dubious assumption given their strife-ridden histories and the well-known propensity of victors to count women among the spoils of war.

The Basques and the Jews are two of the oldest surviving ethnic groups. Basques, whose homeland lies on both sides of the northern Pyrenees, in Spain and France, speak a language that is unrelated to any other spoken in Europe. Their ethnicity has roots that extend back long before Roman times, into the beginnings of the European Bronze Age. As for Jews, on the scriptural authority that Abraham was born in Ur of the Chaldees, they claim an antiquity of about 4,000 years. But neither Basques nor Jews can lay claim to purity of descent produced by rigorous endogamy. In both cases, the canons of common descent can be satisfied only by disregarding large numbers of foreign ancestral lines. Using blood groups and other immunological markers, researchers have repeatedly shown that in any given region, Jews are genetically more like their neighbors than they are like Jews in other regions.

If we ignore these imperfections, we are still left with an outside limit for ethnic descent that takes us back no more than 4,000 years, or 160 generations. Beyond that point, there is only one remaining recourse for those who crave remote ancestors. They can claim to be descended from the founding ancestors of one of the divisions of our kind popularly known as races: caucasoids from caucasoid ancestors; negroids from negroid ancestors; mongoloids from mongoloid ancestors, and so on. But how old are these divisions, and does each really have an exclusive set of ancestors?

HOW OLD ARE THE RACES?

REGRET THAT I must begin by making excuses. This is a tricky question to answer because the features that we depend on to identify whether a person is caucasoid, negroid, or mongoloid, etc., are the superficial soft parts of the body. Lips, noses, hair, eyes, and skin do not fossilize. At the same time, the hard parts that do get preserved are not reliable as racial markers because almost all of the skeletal dimensions of all the races overlap. But there is a more profound problem with trying to say how long the contemporary races have been in existence. Genes that determine features used for defining contemporary races need not form permanently associated hereditary bundles of traits. Variants of skin color, hair form, lip size, nose width, eye folds, and so on can be assorted and inherited independently of each other. This means that the traits that go together today did not necessarily go together in the past, or indeed even existed in the past, among the populations that were ancestral to today's racial groupings.

Even today, there are so many different combinations of racial traits around the world that no simple scheme of four or five major racial types can do justice to them. Millions of people with thin lips, thin noses, and wavy hair, but dark brown to black skin, live in North Africa. Native inhabitants of southern Africa, such as the San, have epicanthic eye folds (like most Asians), light brown to dark brown skin, and tightly spiraled hair. India has people with straight or wavy hair, dark brown to black skin, and thin lips and thin noses. On the steppes of central Asia, epicanthic eye folds combine with wavy hair, light eyes, considerable body and facial hair, and pale skins. Indonesians have a high frequency of epicanthic eye folds, light to dark brown skin, wavy hair, thick noses, and thick lips. Inhabitants of the islands of Oceania present combinations of brown to black skin, with contrastive forms and quantities of hair and facial features. An interesting bundle of traits occurs among the Ainu of northern Japan, who have light skin and thick browridges, and are the hairiest people in the world. In Australia, pale to dark brown skin color and wavy blond to brown hair are common.

Ignorance or denial of the separability of traits used for racial identity can lead people to create strange biological categories. The distinction between blacks and whites in the United States, for example, ignores the obvious fact that individual blacks can have eyes, nose, hair, and lips that are indistinguishable from these features among whites. The reverse is also true of whites, among whom some individuals look more negroid than some blacks. These anomalies occur because Americans do not mean by race what people actually look like as determined by their genes but by how their parents were classified. According to this conception of race, if one parent is "black" and the other is "white," their child is "black," despite the fact that by the laws of genetics, half of a child's genes are from the black parent and half from the white. The practice of cramming people into these racial pigeonholes becomes absurd when black ancestry consists of only a single grandparent or great-grandparent. This produces the phenomenon of the white who is socially classified as "black." Most American blacks have received a significant portion of their genes from recent European ancestors. When samples of American blacks are studied, the assumption that they genetically represent Africans is incorrect. Perhaps we would do well to emulate the Brazilians, who identify racial types not by three or four terms but by 300 to 400, in proper deference to the fact that people whose parents and grandparents were a mixture of Europeans, Africans, and American Indians cannot be said to be either Europeans, Africans, or American Indians.

Traits that we can see don't stick together with those we can't. Take the ABO blood groups. Between 70 percent and 80 percent of light-skinned Scots, black-skinned central Africans, and brown-skinned Aborigines of Australia all have type O. If we could see type O blood groups the way we see skin color, would we put the Scots and the Africans in the same race? Type A is equally unmindful of skin-deep distinctions. Africans, East Indians, and Chinese all have 10 percent to 20 percent frequencies of type A. Should we put them all in the same race?

Another example of an invisible trait that blithely ignores conventional racial boundaries is the ability to taste PTC (phenylthiocarbamide). In 1931, a laboratory researcher accidentally dropped a sample of this substance. Fellow workers complained about the bitter taste that it produced in their mouths; others said they tasted nothing. Anthropologists now know that the world is divided into PTC-tasters and non-PTC-tasters. In Asia, nontasters range from 15 percent to 40 percent. There are twice as many nontasters in Japan as in China, and three times as many in Malaysia. Does this mean that each of these groups belongs to a separate race? If tasters could see nontasters, would they make fun of them and refuse to let them into their neighborhoods or their schools?

New combinations and frequencies of genes have kept the species' racial types in a state of flux ever since populations of modern sapiens began to spread throughout Africa and Eurasia. Some of these changes reflect the workings of chance. During migrations by small groups into new regions, the settlers by accident may happen to have had a high frequency for a gene that was rare in their ancestral population. Thenceforth, the new population had a high frequency of the variant. Such a scenario could account for the distinctive shovel shape of the incisors of Asian peoples.

An accelerated flow of genes when migrants encounter genetically distinct populations is another essentially random process contributing to the evanescence of racial types. During earlier times, nothing quite so massive as the blending of races in the United States and Brazil could have happened, yet some degree of race mixture would have been unavoidable at the shifting boundaries between genetically distinct populations in remotest antiquity.

Finally, as is generally true of all biological evolution, a major cause of the shifting distribution and frequency of genes conventionally used to identify racial divisions is natural selection. As populations move into different habitats or as environments change, selection for reproductive success leads to the appearance of new bundles of hereditary traits.

Anthropologists have made a number of plausible suggestions relating racial differences to temperature, humidity, and other climatological factors. For example, long, narrow noses of Europeans may have been selected to warm extremely cold, damp air to body temperature before it reached the lungs. The generally rounded, squat bodies of Eskimo may also represent adaptation to cold—Bergman's rule again. A tall, thin body, in contrast, leads to maximum heat loss. And this may explain the tall, thin bodies of Nilotic Africans, who inhabit regions of intense arid heat and whose descendants make some of the world's greatest basketball players.

Ironically, traits whose frequencies are determined by natural selection are not very good markers for the purpose of reconstructing the history and antiquity of today's racial divisions. Suppose, for example, that people with short noses migrate from a tropical to a cold climate. Within a few-score generations, natural selection will increase the frequency of long noses among them. An observer noting the similarity between them and their long-nosed neighbors might readily conclude that they were descended from a long-nosed cold-climate race rather than a short-nosed hot-climate one. So the best markers of racial ancestry are traits that are accidental or nonadaptive, like the shovel-shaped incisors I mentioned a moment ago.

Unfortunately, many of the traits that anthropologists once thought were the best markers of racial ancestry have turned out to have adaptive value in certain contexts. Blood groups were a particularly keen disappointment, for it turns out that the ABO series is linked to resistance to diseases that may affect reproductive success, such as smallpox, bubonic plague, and food poisoning by toxic bacteria. So the explanations for blood-type frequencies probably lie as much in the history of transient exposures of different populations to different diseases as in racial ancestry. Even a trait as cryptic and seemingly useless as the ability to taste PTC may not indicate common descent as much as similar adaptive responses by ancestrally separate populations. Chemically, PTC resembles certain substances that have adverse effects on the functioning of the thyroid gland. A common consequence of thyroid malfunction is goiter, a crippling, life-shortening disease. In populations at risk for goiter, the ability to taste foods containing the PTC-like thyroid-inhibiting substances would be selected for, rendering the distinction between taster and nontaster unreliable for reconstructing racial ancestry.

Despite all of these reservations, it still remains possible to distinguish human populations on the basis of a large number of invisible genetic traits whose average frequencies cluster together to a statistically significant extent. The percentage of genes that these populations have in common can then be used to measure the genetic "distance" between them. Furthermore, on the assumption that the rate of genetic change has been uniform for all such populations, one can estimate the point in time when any two of them began to diverge and thereby construct a probable genetic tree that shows the sequence of their branchings through time. Anthropologist Luigi Cavalli-Sforza has used these techniques to identify seven contemporary major populations: Africans, Europeans, Northeast Asians, Southeast Asians, Pacific Islanders, Australians, and New Guineans. The most probable genetic tree shows the first branching from a common African root stock at about 90,000 years ago. The two major branches became three about 60,000 years ago; between 45,000 and 35,000 years ago three became five, including the split between Europeans and North Asians. The most recent divergences involved the separation of North Asians from Amerindians and Southeast Asians from the Pacific Islanders.

Only time will tell if Cavalli-Sforza's genetic tree will survive the gale of criticism that it has provoked. But bear in mind that the bundle of traits used to establish the tree does not include skin color, hair form, or any other conventional "racial" trait and that the more remote the time period, the less likely we are to be talking about groups that look like the races as we know them today.

HOW OUR
SKINS GOT
THEIR COLOR

OST HUMAN BEINGS are neither very fair nor very dark, but brown. The extremely fair skin of northern Europeans and their descendants, and the very black skins of central Africans and their descendants, are probably special adaptations. Brown-skinned ancestors may have been shared by modern-day blacks and whites as recently as 10,000 years ago.

Human skin owes its color to the presence of particles known as melanin. The primary function of melanin is to protect the upper levels of the skin from being damaged by the sun's ultraviolet rays. This radiation poses a critical problem for our kind because we lack the dense coat of hair that acts as a sunscreen for most mammals for reasons I discussed a while back. Hairlessness exposes us to two kinds of radiation hazards: ordinary sunburn, with its blisters, rashes, and risk of infection; and skin cancers, including malignant melanoma, one of the deadliest diseases known. Melanin is the body's first line of defense against these afflictions. The more melanin particles, the darker the skin, and the lower the risk of sunburn and all forms of skin cancer. This explains why the highest rates for skin cancer are found in sun-drenched lands such as Australia, where light-skinned people of European descent spend a good part of their lives outdoors wearing scanty attire. Very dark-skinned people such as heavily pigmented Africans of Zaire seldom get skin cancer, but when they do, they get it on depigmented parts of their bodies—palms and lips.

If exposure to solar radiation had nothing but harmful effects, natural selection would have favored inky black as the color for all human populations. But the sun's rays do not present an unmitigated threat. As it falls on the skin, sunshine converts a fatty substance in the epidermis into vitamin D. The blood carries vitamin D from the skin to the intestines (technically making it a hormone rather than a vitamin), where it plays a vital role in the absorption of calcium. In turn, calcium is vital for strong bones. Without it, people fall victim to the crippling diseases rickets and osteomalacia. In women, calcium deficiencies can result in a deformed birth canal, which makes childbirth lethal for both mother and fetus.

Vitamin D can be obtained from a few foods, primarily the oils and livers of marine fish. But inland populations must rely on the sun's rays and their own skins for the supply of this crucial substance. The particular color of a human population's skin, therefore, represents in large degree a trade-off between the hazards of too much versus too little solar radiation: acute sunburn and skin cancer on the one hand, and rickets and osteomalacia on the other. It is this trade-off that largely accounts for the preponderance of brown people in the world and for the general tendency for skin color to be darkest among equatorial populations and lightest among populations dwelling at higher latitudes.

At middle latitudes, the skin follows a strategy of changing colors with the seasons. Around the Mediterranean basin, for example, exposure to the summer sun brings high risk of cancer but low risk for rickets; the body produces more melanin and people grow darker (i.e., they get suntans). Winter reduces the risk of sunburn and cancer; the body produces less melanin, and the tan wears off.

The correlation between skin color and latitude is not perfect because other factors—such as the availability of foods containing vitamin D and calcium, regional cloud cover during the winter, amount of clothing worn, and cultural preferences—may work for or against the predicted relationship. Arctic-dwelling Eskimo, for example, are not as light-skinned as expected, but their habitat and economy afford them a diet that is exceptionally rich in both vitamin D and calcium.

Northern Europeans, obliged to wear heavy garments for protection against the long, cold, cloudy winters, were always at risk for rickets and osteomalacia from too little vitamin D and calcium. This risk increased sometime after 6000 B.C., when pioneer cattle herders who did not exploit marine resources began to appear in northern Europe. The risk would have been especially great for the brown-skinned Mediterranean peoples who migrated northward along with the crops and farm animals. Samples of Caucasian skin (infant penile foreskin obtained at the time of circumcision) exposed to sunlight on cloudless days in Boston (42°N) from November through February produced no vitamin D. In Edmonton (52°N) this period extended from October to March. But further south (34°N) sunlight was effective in producing vitamin D in the middle of the winter. Almost all of Europe lies north of 42°N. Fair-skinned, nontanning individuals who could utilize the weakest and briefest doses of sunlight to synthesize vitamin D were strongly favored by natural selection. During the frigid winters, only a small circle of a child's face could be left to peek out at the sun through the heavy clothing, thereby favoring the survival of individuals with translucent patches of pink on their cheeks characteristic of many northern Europeans. (People who could get calcium by drinking cow's milk would also be favored by natural selection, but that's a story I'll go into later on.)

If light-skinned individuals on the average had only 2 percent more children survive per generation, the changeover in their skin color could have begun 5,000 years ago and reached present levels well before the beginning of the Christian era. But natural selection need not have acted alone. Cultural selection may also have played a role. It seems likely that whenever people consciously or unconsciously had to decide which infants to nourish and which to neglect, the advantage would go to those with lighter skin, experience having shown that such individuals tended to grow up to be taller, stronger, and healthier than their darker siblings. White was beautiful because white was healthy.

To account for the evolution of black skin in equatorial latitudes, one has merely to reverse the combined effects of natural and cultural selection. With the sun directly overhead most of the year, and clothing a hindrance to work and survival, vitamin D was never in short supply (and calcium was easily obtained from vegetables). Rickets and osteomalacia were rare. Skin cancer was the main problem, and what nature started, culture amplified. Darker infants were favored by parents because experience showed that they grew up to be freer of disfiguring and lethal malignancies. Black was beautiful because black was healthy.

WHY
AFRICA
LAGS

A CENTURY AGO, every biologist and anthropologist believed that our kind's races were endowed with unequal aptitudes for achieving industrial civilization. Thomas Huxley (Darwin's bulldog), one of the most learned scientists of his time, avowed:

> It may be quite true that some Negroes are better than some white men; but no rational man, cognisant of the facts, believes that the average Negro is the equal, still less the superior of the average white man. And if this be true, it is simply incredible that, when all his [social] disabilities are removed, and our prognathic relative has a fair field and no favour, as well as no oppressor, he will be able to compete successfully with his bigger-brained and smaller-jawed rival, in a contest which is to be carried on by thoughts and not by bites.

Huxley's facts were not facts at all, for subsequent research shows them to be based on unrepresentative samples, faulty measuring techniques, and ethnocentric stereotyping. But for many people of Huxley's generation, the seemingly incontrovertible evidence for racial superiority lay in the failure of blacks and other races to compete successfully against whites in manufacturing, commerce, and war. Whites from Europe and their American counterparts had gained political and economic control over almost the entire human species. Wasn't the technological and industrial backwardness of native Asians, Africans, and Americans proof enough that whites were the superior race? Eager to justify their imperial hegemony, Europeans and North Americans failed to see the hollowness of this argument. They conveniently forgot the great upendings of history such as the destruction of Rome by "backward" Germanic tribes and the end of 2,000 years of Chinese imperial rule brought on by long-nosed, hairy, red-faced sailors who lived on the other side of the globe in tiny, backward kingdoms.

Alfred Kroeber, founder of the Department of Anthropology at the University of California at Berkeley, succinctly conveyed the irony of Rome's collapse at the hands of despised barbarian races in these words:

> Had Julius Caesar or one of his contemporaries been asked whether by any sane stretch of fantasy he could imagine the Britons and the Germans as inherently the equals of Romans and Greeks, he would probably have replied that if these northerners possessed the ability of the Mediterraneans they would long since have given vent to it, instead of continuing to live in disorganization, poverty, ignorance, rudeness, and without great men or products of the spirit.

As for China's racial hubris, nothing tells it better than Emperor Ch'ien-Lung's 1791 rejection of a "red-faced barbarian" delegation's request to open up trading relationships. England, the Emperor said, had nothing China wanted. "As your ambassador can see for himself, we possess all things." There was a lot of truth in Ch'ien-Lung's observation. Almost to the end of the eighteenth century, China's technology was as advanced as England's. The Chinese excelled at making porcelain ("chinaware"), silk cloth, and bronze castings. They had invented gunpowder, the first computer (the abacus), the canal lock gate, the iron-chain suspension bridge, the first true mechanical crank, the stern-post rudder, the man-lifting kite, and the escapement, a vital forerunner of European clockwork. In transport, agricultural productivity, and population, the tiny nations of Europe scarcely merited comparison. Ch'ien-Lung's empire stretched from the Arctic Circle to the Indian Ocean and 3,000 miles inland. It had a population of 300 million, all under the control of a single, centralized bureaucracy. It was the biggest and most powerful empire the world had ever seen. Yet in fewer than fifty years after Ch'ien-Lung's arrogant verdict, Chinese imperial power was destroyed, its armies humiliated by a handful of European troops, its seaports controlled by English, French, German, and American merchants, its peasant masses gripped by famine and pestilence.

The burden of racism falls heaviest on those who suffer the

scorn of their would-be superiors. But there are costs for the snobs as well as for the snubbed. When people start to believe that the color of their skin or the shape of their nose guarantees their future ascendency, they are usually helping to dig their own graves. I wonder, for example, how much of the humiliation suffered by U.S. industry and commerce at the hands of Japanese competitors stems from racial hubris. In the 1930s, Americans knew the Japanese only as makers of cheap toys, paper fans, and watches with mainsprings that broke at the first winding. American engineers soberly declaimed that no matter how hard the Japanese might try, they could never catch up with the industrial superpowers, especially with the United States. They didn't have that special inborn quality that Americans called "Yankee ingenuity." How earnestly the Julius Caesars of American industry argued that Japan could only imitate! By no "sane stretch of fantasy" could they imagine that in fifty years Japanese auto imports would bring Detroit to its knees and that Japanese microscopes, cameras, digital watches, calculators, television sets, videorecorders, and dozens of other made-in-Japan consumer products would dominate America's market.

Undaunted by these upendings, many people believe that black Africa is an exception, doomed by its genetic heritage to be a perpetual laggard. Ironically, the Japanese, whose prime minister once publicly attributed America's decline to the presence of too many people of African descent, espouse a similar view. Are the genetic aptitudes for creating a United States or a Japan somehow in short supply in Africa south of the Sahara? In view of the frequency with which those who lag farthest behind in one period move farthest ahead in the next, I do not think racial factors merit serious consideration as an explanation of Africa's predicament. Not at least until the historical reasons for Africa's lagging pace of development have been throughly explored.

In A.D. 500, the feudal kingdoms in West Africa—Ghana, Mali, Sanghay—strongly resembled the feudal kingdoms of Europe except for the fact that the Africans were cut off by the Sahara from the heritage of technology and engineering that Rome had bequeathed to Europe. Subsequently, the great desert inhibited the southward flow of Arabic influences that did so much to revitalize European science and commerce. While the people who lived in the Mediterranean basin carried out their trade and warfare on ships and became maritime powers, their dark-skinned counterparts south of the Sahara were mainly concerned with crossing the desert and lacked any motivation for maritime adventures. So when the first Portuguese ships arrived off the Guinea coast in the fifteenth century, they were able to seize control of the ports and seal the fate of Africa for the next 500 years. After exhausting their gold mines, the Africans settled down to hunting slaves to exchange for European cloth and firearms. This led to increased amounts of warfare, rebellion, and the breakup of the indigenous feudal states, cutting short the trajectory of Africa's political development and turning vast portions of the interior into a no-man's-land whose chief product was a human crop bred for export to the sugar, cotton, and tobacco plantations on the other side of the Atlantic.

With the end of the slave trade, the Europeans forced the Africans to farm and mine for them. Meanwhile, colonial authorities made every effort to keep Africa subservient and backward by encouraging tribal wars, by limiting African education to the most rudimentary level possible, and, above all, by preventing colonies from developing an industrial infrastructure that might have made it possible for them to compete on the world market after they achieved political independence. With such a history, Africans will have to be considered not as racial inferiors but as superhumans if they succeed in creating a single advanced industrial society of their own before the middle of the next century.

If you doubt that colonialism could have had such long-lasting consequences, just think of Indonesia and Japan. In the sixteenth century these two island civilizations shared many features of agrarian feudal states. Indonesia became a Dutch colony, while Japan shut its doors to European traders and missionaries, accepting nothing but books as imports from the West, especially technical books that told how to make munitions, build railways, and produce chemicals. After 300 years of close contact with their European masters, Indonesia emerged into the twentieth century an underdeveloped, overpopulated, pauperized basket case, while the Japanese were ready to take their place as the most advanced industrial power in the Far East. Of course, there are other factors to be considered in this story, but race isn't one of them.

DO THE RACES DIFFER IN INTELLIGENCE?

*B*UT WHAT ABOUT the fact that blacks in the United States have lower I.Q. scores than whites? Doesn't this prove that Huxley was right and that blacks have an innate disadvantage in a competition carried on by "thoughts and not by bites"?

No one disputes the fact that, on a national basis, blacks consistently score fifteen points lower than whites on standardized I.Q. tests. But many scientists do dispute the fact that the I.Q. tests measure innate racial differences in intelligence. It seems far more likely that what they measure is the effect of a consistent lack of social preparation for getting high I.Q. scores, including a long history of going to inferior schools, of being brought up in broken families, and of not being exposed to role models who have succeeded in intellectual careers.

Even the proponents of I.Q. tests as measures of intelligence concede that 20 percent of the fifteen-point difference reflects environmental rather than genetic differences between the races. It is important to know how they arrive at this figure. They do it by comparing the I.Q. scores achieved by pairs of identical twins separated by adoption agencies in infancy and raised by different foster parents. Despite the twins' having been reared apart, the I.Q.s of each pair of twins tend to be the same about 80 percent of the time. But the validity of this number depends on being reasonably certain that the separate households in which each pair of twins is raised constitute environments that are no less different than the environments experienced by adopted children who are not identical twins. This condition cannot be satisfied because adoption agencies in general attempt to place children in need of foster care in homes that match their parents' socioeconomic, religious, ethnic, and racial backgrounds. The agencies make a special effort to achieve a close match in the case of identical twins.

The strategy of using twins reared apart to distinguish between environmental and hereditary effects in racial I.Q. scores suffers from an even greater and, to my mind, fatal methodological fault. If one wishes to measure the effects of black children's social environments on their I.Q. scores, it is not admissible to measure the effects of white children's environments on white children's I.Q. scores as a proxy. Since there is no way that the experiences of a white child growing up in a white family and community can be made to duplicate the experiences of a black child growing up in a black family and community, measures of genetic influence derived from studies of white children reared apart in white families never replicate the real intensity and extent of the environmental differences experienced respectively by black and white children in the United States. The only way to get around this impasse would be to rear white children in black homes and black children in white homes and then compare their I.Q. scores. Of course, the oddity of blacks rearing whites would be an additional variable that would have to be controlled. And blacks reared in white homes would still experience the effects of color prejudice outside the family. So it might be necessary to devise some means of changing the children's color in order to identify the effects of their race on their I.Q.s (by painting their faces?). People in their right minds would not propose such an experiment, and if they did, it would be declared unethical and illegal. This says much about the absurdity of claiming that the effects of environment on I.Q. differences between blacks and whites have been scientifically measured. For all practical purposes such measurements cannot be carried out without substantially modifying the whole social universe in which blacks and whites find themselves. As behavior geneticist Jerry Hirsch of Washington University, St. Louis, says, the attempt to measure racial differences in intelligence is "impossible and therefore worthless."

Like the underdevelopment of Africa, the lower I.Q. scores of American blacks are the product of hundreds of years of systematic repression. Those who attribute either the underdevelopment of Africa or the poverty, crime, and addiction from which black America suffers to an innate intellectual deficit are spreading misinformation that can only make the black struggle for parity that much more difficult. There is nothing in the heritage of people of African descent that makes them less capable of being on the cutting edge of technological, scientific, and social change than any other major division of the human species. Their day will come.

A DIFFERENT
KIND OF
SELECTION

WHEN NATURAL SELECTION had brought the body, brain, and behavior of our ancestors to cultural takeoff, culture itself began to evolve, according to its own principles of selection and with its own patterns of order and disorder, chance and necessity. During the ensuing 35,000 years, natural selection continued to shape and adapt the human body to levels of solar radiation, heat, cold, altitude, and nutritional stress encountered in different habitats. But these changes cannot possibly account for the immense differences between the cultural repertories of modern industrial societies and those of prehistoric times. To understand the relationship between Marshack's Paleolithic serpentine punch marks and the key strokes of a personal computer, theories based on natural selection are useless and fundamentally misleading. We who build and use computers are inherently no smarter than the Ice Age observers who possibly watched and recorded the phases of the moon. Nothing in our genes tells our brains to use floppy disks rather than burins and stone plaques. Nor is there anything in our genes that tells us to live in a high-rise apartment rather than in the mouth of a cave or to get our meat from herds of Black Angus cattle rather than from herds of wild horses. We have floppy disks and domesticated animals because there was cultural selection for these items, not because there was natural selection for them.

Let me try to clarify the distinction. Natural selection acts upon changes in the hereditary program contained within the molecules of DNA located inside the nucleus of the body's cells. If the changes in the program and the physical and behavioral traits that they control result in a higher net rate of reproduction for the individuals in whom they appear, then the changes will be favored in succeeding generations and will become part of a population's genetic program.

How does cultural selection take place? As a result of natural selection, our bodies possess a number of specific urges, needs, instincts, limits of tolerance, vulnerabilities, and patterns of growth and decay, which, in sum, roughly define what one means by human nature. Human cultures are organized systems of socially learned behavior and thought that satisfy or attend to the demands and potentialities of human nature. Cultural selection is human nature's servant. It works by preserving and propagating behavior and thoughts that more effectively satisfy the biological and psychological demands and potentials of individuals in a given group or subgroup. During the course of social life, there is a continuous stream of variations in the way individuals think and behave, and these variations are continuously tested for their ability to increase or decrease well-being. This testing or screening may proceed with or without a conscious weighing of costs and benefits by individuals. The important point is that some variations turn out to be more beneficial than others and are preserved and propagated within the group (or subgroup) and across generations, while other variations that turn out to be less beneficial are not preserved or propagated.

Once cultural takeoff has occurred and cultural selection is operating at full force, differential reproductive success ceases to be the means by which variations in behavior and thought are selected for or propagated. In order for calendars, domesticated cattle, or floppy disks to be favored by cultural selection, there does not have to be any increase in the rate of reproductive success of the individuals who invent and propagate these traits. Some great cultural inventions, in fact, increase well-being, satisfy human nature, and are selected for precisely because they reduce rates of reproductive success—contraceptives, for example. Reproductive success does not serve as drive or appetite for cultural selection because such a drive or appetite is not part of human nature (a point that I'll discuss at greater length later on). Of course, if cultural selection results in a continuously falling rate of reproduction, it will eventually lead to the extinction of the population whose well-being it is serving. But this outcome has no bearing on the question of whether cultural selection must, like natural selection, always operate to *increase* rates of reproductive success. As I will emphasize later on, human reproductive behavior during the past 300 years becomes utterly unintelligible if one subscribes to the currently fashionable sociobiological axiom that our kind always strives to maximize the number of children and close relatives in succeeding generations. In a post-takeoff human population, rates of reproductive success may rise or fall depending on whether high or low rates satisfy the urges, needs, instincts, limits of tolerance, vulnerabilities, and other known bio-psychological components of human nature. When people do strive to maximize their reproductive success, it is not because they are driven by irresistible longings for numerous progeny but because under certain circumstances having numerous progeny leads to having more sex, leisure, food, wealth, allies, support in old age, or other benefits that enhance the quality of life.

My next step, then, will be to identify the components of human nature that test and screen for particular patterns of behavior and thought. Despite vaunted powers of speech and consciousness, our kind's great cultural adventures remain tethered to the mundane conditions imposed by our specific humanity. If somewhere in the universe there are intelligent armor-plated asexual social creatures made of silicon who are energized by photovoltaic receptors and reproduce by fission, I am sure that they are given neither to painting reindeer on cave walls nor to pushing carts up and down the aisles of supermarkets.

TO BREATHE

*T*RAINED HUMAN SUBJECTS can hold their breath underwater for thirteen minutes. Most people start to gasp after two. Breathing, then, is a good example of a biopsychological drive that is a component of human nature and that acts as a screen to select cultural alternatives. Grand theories of cultural evolution seldom deign to consider anything so obvious even though the need for oxygen explains why most of the drama of human history has unfolded somewhere between sea level and 14,000 feet. More recently, the need for breathable air, or rather the failure to protect the supply of breathable air, has asserted itself in less obvious ways. Substantial portions of industrial-age life-styles are now actively being selected for or against in conformity with their contribution to satisfying the air quality demanded by human nature.

In former times, air was so ubiquitous and abundant that economists called it a "free good." In so doing, they obscured the fact that automobile, petrochemical, and utility companies were using the atmosphere as a sewer without paying for it and without regard for the effect dirty air would have on the people who had to draw the breath of life from it. Actually, air ceased to be free as soon as our ancestors began to make smoke as a by-product of their heating and cooking fires. They had to pay for getting rid of the smoke by making holes in the roof and building chimneys and windows. With industrialization, the added costs of breathing were small at first, compared to the benefits of new fossil-fuel combustion technologies. But the sky soon proved to have a limited capacity to absorb toxic chemicals, and smog is now a major factor in cultural evolution. We pay to prevent it with catalytic converters, smokestack scrubbers, filters, and air conditioners. And we pay to get away from it by building million-dollar homes precariously perched on the sides of mud-slide-prone hills or by commuting 150 miles a day from and to relatively smog-free suburbs.

Yet it remains true that the need for air has not been as important for cultural evolution as other needs. Industrialization increased the salience of the need for air, but the need for air cannot explain how industrialization itself came to be selected for. Nor can it explain any major part of the evolutionary trajectories that led from the foraging bands of prehistory to the agrarian states and empires that preceded the rise of modern industrial systems. I think it is important to understand the reason for this. Simply put, in the past no one was able to exchange air for goods and services, nor could it be stored, doled out, and made the basis of power over others. Yes, individuals could be deprived of access to air by choking, drowning, or hanging. But the power to do such things was (and still is) based on the control of other kinds of resources and rewards and not on the rationing or sale of air. For the time being, we are safe from tyrants or entrepreneurs who want to corner the market on the breath of life. But given a proven ability to deplete and pollute the skies over small cities like Denver and Salt Lake City as well as over big ones like Mexico City and New York, no one should suppose that access to air is a protected birthright for future generations. Will the day ever come when giant utilities threaten to stop pumping air to homeowners who don't pay their bills on time? Stranger things have happened during the course of cultural evolution.

TO DRINK

*T*HIRST, *LIKE THE NEED* for air, places implacable demands on the human body. With high ambient temperatures, low humidity, and high levels of activity, lack of fluids can lead to fatal dehydration in a few hours. Under humid conditions, one can endure longer. Andress Mihaverz, an Austrian prisoner who was put into a holding cell and left there by mistake, survived after eighteen days without water (or food). Thirst is much more urgent than hunger. Fat individuals who give up everything but liquids can live a surprisingly long time. Angus Barbieri of Tayport, Fife, in Scotland, lived on nothing but tea, coffee, water, soda water, and vitamins for 382 days. When he started his fast, he weighed 472 pounds; when he stopped, 178 pounds. After prolonged deprivation, the craving for food abates; the craving for liquids grows worse.

But thirst, like the need for air, has not played a major role in the evolution of culture, at least not until recent times. Water to quench one's thirst became a problem only after the rise of cities and the movement of people into arid habitats. For most of prehistory and history our kind has lived in regions where water for drinking purposes was almost as abundant as air. Great sheets of it fell from the skies, poured along countless rivers and streams, and collected in numberless ponds and lakes. It was not the kind of stuff for which people would exchange food and services. They could get it themselves. Moreover, most foods consist mainly of water, making it difficult for someone who is well fed to become dehydrated. For this reason, water has played a more crucial role in cultural evolution as a requirement for food production—in irrigation—than as a source of drink.

Water to drink is still abundant enough that it flows into our homes indiscriminately mixed with water to clean dishes and clothes, flush the toilet, and sprinkle the lawn. If we want it pure, clean, and unchlorinated, we can still buy it in bottles at the local supermarket for somewhat less than the cost of a soft drink. The exemplary house guest does not yet arrive bearing a gallon of mountain spring water as a gift to the hostess. But if industrial societies continue to waste and contaminate rivers, lakes, and subterranean aquifers, the value of a bottle of natural, unchlorinated, undistilled, pure water will inevitably come to rival the value of a good bottle of wine. And people will hunt for the best brands at the gourmet shops.

Food is different. Throughout history and prehistory, food has always been exchangeable for other goods and services. Water to drink could become scarce only in a few arid habitats; food could become scarce in any habitat. Food has always required productive effort. No one has ever mistaken food for a free good.

TO EAT

URING WORLD WAR II, the Nazis tried to kill the inhabitants of the Warsaw ghetto by starving them to death. Food smuggled past the guards made it possible for the ghetto residents to consume about 800 calories per day. The ghetto's doctors, who were themselves slowly starving to death, decided to carry out a study of what they called the hunger disease. A portion of their work survived the war and has entered the clinical literature as a unique account of human starvation unto death. The doctors hoped that their observations might someday be useful for understanding the clinical status of other victims of starvation. They reported:

> Constant thirst and persistent increase in urinary output . . . are the first signs of even a short period of hunger. . . . Other early complaints include dryness in the mouth, rapid weight loss, and a constant craving for food.
>
> With prolonged hunger, these symptoms diminish. The patients now experience general weakness and the inability to sustain even the smallest physical effort, and are unwilling to work. They remain in bed all day, covered because they always feel cold, most acutely in the nose and the extremities. They become apathetic and depressed, and lack initiative. They do not remember their hunger, but when shown bread, meat, or sweets, they become very aggressive, grab the food, and devour it at once, even though they may be beaten for it and have no strength to run away. Toward the end of hunger disease the only complaint is complete exhaustion.

As surplus fat disappears, the skin becomes darker, dry, and wrinkled. Pubic and axillary hair fall out. Women miss their menstrual periods and are sterile. Men are impotent. Any children born die within a few weeks.

Vital functions subside simultaneously. Pulse rate and respiratory rate get slower and it becomes more and more difficult to reach the patient's awareness, until life is gone. People fall asleep in bed or on the street and are dead in the morning. They die during physical effort, such as searching for food, and sometimes even with a piece of bread in their hands.

As the Warsaw study shows, although life can be sustained for months on a diet that will end in death, bodily and psychological impairments set in quite rapidly. The hunger we experience when we are well fed is a fail-safe signal of danger ahead, rather than of danger present. As soon as the last meal passes out of the stomach, signals begin arriving in the brain, especially in the part called the hypothalamus, which tell us it is time to eat again. The signals carry information that the stomach is empty, that the level of glucose in the blood has fallen, and that the body reserves of amino acids are becoming unbalanced. We perceive these signals as a mild discomfort that, if not attended, worsens into a relentless, aching obsession. To prevent further punishment, we eat—if we can. But that is not all. Eating need not be just a reflex that diminishes pain like jerking one's hand off a hot stove. Food can also be a rich source of delightful fragrances, textures, and tastes that reward people for eating, even when they are not hungry.

At first, our ancestors scavenged, hunted, and collected their food; later came agriculture and stock-raising; and more recently, mechanized petrochemical factory farms. Whether gathered, planted, scavenged, hunted, or produced in factories, food-production costs run high. Food has always absorbed a considerable portion of our kind's time, energy, and technical know-how. And since people need it and want it several times a day, it is not only expensive, but eminently exchangeable for other goods and services. Later on I shall show how a distinctive organization of hominid social life emerged when food began to be exchanged for sexual service. But I am not ready to tell that part of the story yet.

WHY WE EAT
TOO MUCH

ℑN A *SOCIETY* where obesity is the principal nutritional disease, one easily forgets the horrible things that lack of food and drink can do to the human body. Yet obesity itself is merely a form of hunger in disguise. The specter of overweight stalks some of us the way starvation stalks others, because our need and appetite for food are the products of at least two million years of selection for the ability not only to eat but to overeat. The stomach bears witness. A small muscular sac when empty, it readily expands to take in two or three pounds of food at a time; bulky meals containing 10,000 or more calories pose no mechanical or physiological problems. Worldwide, feasts and banquets attest to our kind's enthusiastic endorsement of overeating, even by well-fed individuals.

Healthy people who have endured considerable weight loss over a number of months as a result of food deprivation can put away astonishing amounts of food. After volunteers in a famous laboratory hunger study carried out by Anselm Keys returned to eating freely, they began to gorge themselves on 10,000 calories a day. Yet, no matter how hungry at the outset, people do not ordinarily continue to stuff themselves so resolutely that they swell to the gargantuan proportions of circus exhibitionists. We have an almost irresistible urge to eat, but we also have at least some built-in controls that reduce our appetite for food and that limit the accumulation of excess fat. In one study, prisoners volunteered to stuff themselves until they had increased their body weight by 20 percent. Upon achieving this goal, they were allowed to eat as much or as little as they wished. Most of them immediately began to consume only a few hundred calories a day until they had gotten back to their original weights. Another indication that our bodies must be equipped with some kind of "foodstat" (like a thermostat) is that the average person gains relatively little weight over a life span. Between ages eighteen and thirty-eight, Americans usually put on no more than ten or twenty pounds while eating their way through twenty tons of food. Nutritionists estimate that to keep the weight gain to such a small percentage of food consumed means that the foodstat operates with a tolerance of less than 1 percent. Impressive as this may sound, the human foodstat cannot be relied on to keep people from eating too much. Putting on ten to twenty extra pounds by age thirty-eight often means being ten to twenty pounds overweight at age thirty-eight. And the same seemingly low tolerance for deviation will allow a lot of us to become twenty to forty pounds overweight by the time we reach age fifty-eight. According to the National Center for Health Statistics, 24.2 percent of adult men and 27.1 percent of adult women weigh 20 percent more than is good for them. What is really remarkable about the modern-day incidence of obesity is that it persists—despite fashions and aesthetic standards that demean fat persons, despite an intense educational effort conducted by public health authorities linking obesity with cardiovascular diseases, and despite billion-dollar industries devoted to fitness, diet foods, and weight control. With half the adult population of Western nations on one diet or another, I think one has to conclude that the foodstat doesn't work very well under the present circumstances. And the reason for this seems clear enough: For most of the time that hominids have been on earth, it wasn't foodstats that kept them from becoming overweight. It was lack of food.

WHY WE
FEAST

OVEREATING BY ITSELF is not the culprit in obesity. No physiological law dictates that overeating must lead to overweight. Excess food could simply be eliminated. The trouble lies in the extraordinary efficiency with which our bodies convert excess food into fat and in the storage of this fat in special "depots" located in the breasts, abdomen, buttocks, hips, and thighs. In converting excess energy to depot fat, the body saves 98 percent of the calories that are not needed for immediate metabolic functions. And to make matters worse, there is a large amount of variation from one individual to the next in the number of calories that are needed for maintaining metabolic equilibrium. At the same weight and height, some people will lose weight with 2,000 calories, while others will gain. An even greater calamity results from the ability of the body to become more efficient in converting food to energy when the amount of calories consumed is reduced. Dieting trains the body to become a more efficient energy machine. As a result, persistent dieters find themselves pushing a stone up a hill that gets steeper every time they push. Of course, none of this is a problem to the two-thirds of the world's population who cannot afford to consume enough food to get fat, no matter how efficient their bodies have become in converting food to energy.

The ability to turn excess food energy into depot fat is a biological heritage shaped by the hominid experience over the entire course of preindustrial time. Hunger lay at the core of that experience. Not only the hunger-to-death of other Warsaw ghettos brought on by the battles, sieges, and routs of wars gone by, or by killing winds, droughts, frosts, and earthquakes, but also by cyclical periods of food deprivation linked to seasonal scarcities of animals to hunt or of plants to collect and harvest. Few were the ancestors who did not have to contend with an annual rhythm of scarcity and plenty.

Hungry seasons afflict modern hunter-gatherers and village farmers as well. They occur at different times of the year, depending on the system of food production. Among the Eskimo, winters of discontent occurred in the summer, when seals could no longer be harpooned as they came to the surface to breathe through holes in the ice. In Amazonia, it was the rainy season that brought hunger, as rivers became too wide and swift to catch fish, and terrestrial prey species dispersed and became difficult to hunt. Agricultural peoples generally experience their hungry times when crops are maturing but not yet ready for harvest. This was shown in a classic study of hungry season in Africa carried out by anthropologist Audrey Richards among the Bemba of Zambia. The Bemba seldom harvested enough of their staple crop, millet, to last them more than nine months. For the remaining three months until the new harvest, they ate one instead of their usual two meals a day, gave up their snacks and millet beer, and subsisted on gourds, mushrooms, and caterpillars. To reduce their calorie deficit, they sat around doing nothing for much of the time and on some days they simply stayed in bed, drinking water and taking snuff. Weight losses of 8 percent or more are common during Africa's hungry seasons.

When a hungry season ends, people do not merely resume their average rate of food consumption. Seasonal harvests, whether of planted or wild foodstuffs, characteristically lead to ritual bouts of overeating. Feast follows fast, exactly as among Keys's volunteers.

Recent advances in the study of prehistoric human bones and teeth provide evidence that our Stone Age ancestors followed a pattern of episodic fasts and feasts mixed with occasional periods of prolonged hunger. Clinical observations show that when children and adolescents suffer serious food deprivation for as little as a week, the long bones of their legs and arms stop growing. Upon resumption of normal growth, the density of the bone where the growth process was interrupted is different from that of the rest of the bone. X rays reveal periods of interrupted growth as thin transverse lines called "Harris lines." Archaeologists use these lines as a source of information about the nutritional status of prehistoric hunter-gatherers. The lines often tell the story of short bouts of hunger followed by bouts of eating during which growth spurted ahead.

Teeth provide other telltale signs of nutritional stress among prehistoric populations. Periods of prolonged malnutrition often lead to dental defects known as hypoplasias—discolored bands and small pits and imperfections in the enamel surface. Researchers believe that hypoplasias represent longer and more severe periods of nutritional deprivation than the Harris lines. An important finding is that Harris lines occur more frequently and dental hypoplasias less frequently in prehistoric hunter-gatherer populations than in later prehistoric populations who lived in villages and depended on agriculture for their food supply. The implication is that hunter-gatherers were more likely to suffer temporary food shortages, but less likely to suffer from prolonged starvation since they were highly mobile and could improve their diet by moving to areas less affected by drought and other natural disasters. Agriculturalists, in contrast, were likely to have only one hungry season per year. But from time to time their crops would fail and they would suffer prolonged famine without being able to abandon their villages and fields.

I doubt that our Ice Age ancestors were able to gain weight consistently enough to get fat. For one thing, their fat reserves were drawn down several times a year by temporary scarcities of some animals and harvestable wild plants. For another, the amount of walking, running, digging, and carrying they had to do would have burned up most of the extra calories they consumed when food was plentiful. But what about the remarkable Ice Age Venus figurines that depict women with enlarged breasts, bellies, thighs, hips, and buttocks? I venture to say that the artists had never really seen a fat woman in the flesh. But they could not help noticing that plump women endured prolonged bouts of hunger better than skinny ones, and accordingly endowed their ideal images of womanhood with superhuman reserves of fat.

For better or worse, industrial-age celebrants have lost touch with the primordial significance of overeating. At Thanksgiving time, for example, Americans do not emerge from months of semi-starvation in urgent need of replenishing their depleted fat depots. Calorically speaking, modern holiday, marriage, birthday, or anniversary banquets are merely occasions for raising prior consumption levels from more than enough to far more than enough. The extra calories will do us no good, but, for our ancestors, to feast was to store fat, and to store fat was to survive the next frost, drought, or hungry season.

WHY WE GET FAT

IF IT IS TRUE that our ancestors found it hard to get enough to eat to get fat, then it becomes clear why our kind now gets fat so easily. Natural selection never had a chance to select against people who ate so much that they became obese and damaged their hearts and arteries. Too long have the victims of obesity been blamed for their affliction. Overeating is not a character defect, a longing to return to the womb, a substitute for sex, or a compensation for poverty. Rather, it is a hereditary defect in the design of the human body, a weakness that natural selection was unable to get rid of, just as it was unable to get rid of the tendency for our S-shaped spinal column to fail under a heavy load; for the arch in our foot to collapse; for too many teeth to crowd into our small jaws; for our appendix to get infected; or for the human baby's head to be too big for its mother's pelvic opening. Do we chastise and ridicule people who get slipped disks, flat feet, impacted wisdom teeth, appendicitis, or babies stuck in the birth canal? Whose fault is it that food tastes just as delicious and hunger aches just as painfully when we are fat as when we are thin? Of course, I don't intend this to be an argument in favor of giving up the effort to fight obesity by restricting caloric consumption and increasing physical activity. My point is that we ought to recognize that for many people weight control is a never-ending lifelong battle against great odds.

This brings me to a paradox: In the past, it was the poor who were most likely to undereat; today, in developed countries it is the poor who are most likely to overeat. From the time that major differences of rank and power among the members of society began to appear, it was the subordinate classes that suffered most from having too little to eat. Archaeological excavations of ancient burials almost always show that the people who were buried with the richest assortment of jewels, pots, weapons, and other symbols of rank were taller than the people who were buried in unadorned graves. At Tikal in

Guatemala, for example, the ancient Maya male elite averaged 5 feet 7 inches, as compared with commoner males, who averaged only 5 feet 1 inch, presumably because commoner diets were deficient in calories and proteins. The same kind of class difference existed in England during the nineteenth century. English schoolboys who were wealthy and attended elite private schools were, on average, five inches taller than those who were poor and attended ordinary government or council schools. Although the elites were not necessarily obese, the poor were undoubtedly not only short but skinny. The situation today is at least partially reversed. The poor continue to be shorter than the wealthy, but now they are also fatter. I am not forgetting that hunger and undereating still occur among many desperately poor, homeless, and psychologically impaired Americans. But overeating is far more common among low-income Americans, especially among low-paid adult service and factory workers. There are several explanations for this paradox. Weight control presumes knowledge about calories and nutrition and about the health-damaging consequences of obesity that the poor do not possess. Jogging, aerobics, and sports are time-consuming and often expensive activities. Foods high in sugar and starch are cheaper than low-calorie and more nutritious meat and fish. Finally, low-paid service and nonunion factory employees and people on welfare or the edge of it lack the motivation to conform to standards of dress and physical appearance that middle-class status-seekers must maintain. Now that food calories are cheaper than clean air, fatness bears the taint of poverty and failure. No longer do our Julius Caesars seek to have people about them who are fat. To gain the confidence of the higher circles, one must have a lean and hungry look.

INNATE
TASTES

A FUNCTIONING HUMAN BODY consists of thousands of different proteins, fats, carbohydrates, and other molecules. The body itself synthesizes most of these substances out of a relatively small number of elements and molecules called "essential nutrients." Were it not for this chemical wizardry, we would be dependent on eating each other for getting a balanced supply of all the molecules necessary for sustaining human life. But the body is a great chemist, so there need be very little resemblance between the chemical profile of the organisms we consume and the chemical profile of our bodies. (A good thing, because a species that could eat only its own kind would promptly cease to exist.) In addition to air and water, we have to ingest forty-one substances: one carbohydrate that can be broken down into the sugar glucose; one fat that contains linoleic acid; ten amino acids, the building blocks of proteins; fifteen minerals; thirteen vitamins; and a source of indigestible roughage to help clean the lower end of the gut.

Nature has left us remarkably free to obtain these essential nutrients from any convenient combination of plants and animals. We are not at all like koalas, which eat only eucalyptus leaves; pandas, which eat only bamboo shoots; seals, which eat only fish; whales, which eat only plankton; or lions, which eat only meat. Our strongest innate preference is probably for variety and against concentrating on any single kind of plant or animal food meal after meal, day after day. We are, to repeat, omnivores.

Yet we do not come into the world entirely without taste preferences. Infants grimace and turn away from substances that taste bitter, sour, sharp, peppery, or salty. This makes sense in terms of natural selection, since most poisonous or indigestible plants, animals, and animal products have telltale bitter, sour, sharp, peppery, or salty tastes. But these innate avoidances are extremely weak relative to our predilection for omnivory. The forces of cultural selection therefore easily override the influence of innate aversions during the evolution of particular cuisines.

Growing up usually leads to marked reversals of some or all of the innate infantile taste aversions. The Chinese love their tea scalding hot and bitter. Gauchos have their equivalent bitter drink, maté, sucked up hot from a communal cup. Americans savor their morning grapefruit chilled and cut into bite-size pieces. Spaniards squeeze lime juice on their fish. The English like their alcohol mixed with quinine water. The Germans take their meat with dollops of bitter horseradish. Sourness also abounds in world cuisines: sour milk, sour cream, sauerkraut, sourdough, sour apple. Not to mention vinegar used to pickle meat, fish, and vegetables and to mingle with oil in Italian salad dressings. Most remarkable, perhaps, is the reversal of the infantile aversion to peppery foods. In much of China, Central America, India, Southeast Asia, and Africa, people expect to experience a tingling, burning, mouth-watering fulsomeness of fiery, hot condiments at every meal. Take away the malabar or chili pepper, and they will rise from the table in disgust. What babies abhor, children and adults learn to crave. Incidentally, I think the widespread yen for salt belongs in the same category. Infants reject salt but adults crave it. Yet I know of at least one culture—the Yanomami—whose adults find it thoroughly unpalatable.

So much for innate taste aversions. But what about taste preferences? Aren't there some tastes that people are born to like and that cultural selection finds difficult to override? Perhaps. At birth, babies show a strong preference for sweetness. That toothless humans should possess a sweet tooth accords well with the sweet taste of mother's milk, the sole item on the infant's obligatory menu. Mother's milk is sweet because it contains the sugar called lactose. In the presence of lactase, an intestinal enzyme, lactose gets broken down into the digestible, calorie-rich sucrose and galactose. An innate taste for sweetness, therefore, guides us away from potentially harmful substances and toward our wholesome first meal.

Until a few hundred years ago, sweetness junkies had to get their fix from honey and ripe fruit, neither of which was readily available or cheap. It took the invention of industrial processes for extracting sucrose from cane and later from beets to introduce the demon sweetness into the bosom of the human family. In its purest crystalline form, we call it sugar; in less pure liquid form, we call it syrup or molasses. Mixed with cacao, we call it chocolate. By what-ever name, no cuisines seem to be able to resist its allure. According to anthropologist Sydney Mintz, "To date, there have been no reports of any group with a nonsugar tradition rejecting the intro-duction of sugar, sweetened condensed milk, sweetened beverages, sweetmeats, pastries, confectionary, or other sweet dietary items." But is it the sweetness of sugar or the cheap calories that sugar can provide that account for the irresistible spread of the sugar demon? Nutritionists condemn sugar because of its "empty" calories, but calories for most of the world are nothing to sneer at. As Mintz shows, the industrial working class could not have carried out its historic mission without the cheap calories that sugar provided, empty or not. Stirred in copious quantities into tea, coffee, and other bitter-tasting effusions, sugar became the preferred pick-me-up for lightening the burden of industrial drudgery. No need to look over your shoulder as you take your morning coffee break (or do you prefer tea?). The boss approves. After all, it could be gin (or worse) and that would put you to sleep (or worse) before the next pause that refreshes.

The fact that no culture with a nonsugar tradition has ever rejected the use of sugar does not convince me that the taste for sweets in adults is largely the result of an innate preference. A point that I shall be returning to later on is that the universality of a cultural trait does not prove that it is part of human nature. It may simply be so useful under a broad variety of conditions that it has been culturally selected for over and over again. (No culture has ever resisted flashlights or matches, either.)

Much of the impetus for the spread of sugar arose from its utility as a source of energy that gave the caffeine in coffee, tea, and cacao an extra kick. Would sugar have spread as fast apart from these stimulants, simply for its taste? Now that we have artificial, nonca-loric sweeteners, one can ask another interesting question. Would the penchant for sweet foods have spread as relentlessly if there had been no calories in sugar?

As the worldwide sugar binge takes its toll in rotted teeth, late-onset diabetes, obesity, and cardiovascular disease, signs of a reaction to sweeteners, natural or artificial, have begun to appear. At the moment, the economic and social forces favoring sugar- and sweetener-consumption are much greater than those arrayed against it. Even so, many people find that they can easily resist the insidious spread of sweeteners into salads, hamburgers, vegetables, and bread, spurn sweet desserts, and enjoy unsweetened coffee and tea. This raises the possibility that the infantile preference for sweetness may someday be converted into an adult loathing for sweets. Tastes are not forever.

ACQUIRED
TASTES

OW DO CULTURES arrive at their particular combinations of preferred foods and flavors? Are food preferences arbitrary or are they selected for in conformity with general principles of cultural evolution? I have given a great deal of thought to this matter and have become convinced that specific cuisines mainly represent practical solutions to the problem of providing the essential nutrients to populations under definite natural and cultural conditions. Seemingly arbitrary variations in the basic components of food traditions usually have nutritional, ecological, or economic causes. The passion for hot, peppery foods, for example, correlates with three conditions: warm climates; mainly vegetarian diets with legumes instead of meat; and marginal caloric intake with little variation in menu from day to day. Since malabar or chili peppers require frost-free, warm, moist climates, the centers of the taste for hot foods can be expected to occur in the tropics. Also, people who obtain their essential nutrients primarily from legumes such as beans, soybeans, or lentils combined with rice, maize, or starchy roots generate a great deal of intestinal flatus. Some scientific evidence supports the folk belief that peppery sauces relieve this problem. Finally, for people whose menu changes little from meal to meal and who must often go to sleep hungry, peppery condiments stimulate the salivary glands and produce a sensation of fullness that makes a meal seem bigger and more variegated than it is. The absence or diminished presence of these conditions plausibly explains the relative blandness of northern European and Anglo–North American cuisines.

A basic point that should not be missed in trying to explain why some groups relish foods that others spurn is that it would be extremely wasteful for people to acquire an equal appetite for every possible edible substance. Depending on the natural and cultural context, there will always be some food sources that are better bargains than others. Western cuisines, for example, display a marked prejudice against the consumption of animal tidbits such as insects, earthworms, and spiders, all of which find favor in many non-Western food traditions. I think that the key to this disparity may lie in the availability of such tidbits compared with the availability of alternative sources of animal flesh. While insects, worms, and spiders are nutritious, their small size and dispersed distribution make it quite costly to find and collect them compared to the cost per pound of hunting or raising large animals like deer or cattle.

A simple formula predicts the extent to which different cultures will reject or accept animal tidbits. The variables that need to be taken into account are the abundance, concentration, and size of the available insects and other small edible creatures; and the abundance, concentration, and size of available larger animals. The bigger, more abundant, and more concentrated the small creatures, the more likely that they will be regarded as good to eat, provided that at the same time larger animals are scarce and difficult to obtain. This explains the extreme popularity of insect-eating among the native peoples of Amazonia and among other tropical forest societies; insects are big and available in dense swarms, while there are few genuinely large animals to be hunted and no domesticated species other than dogs available as animal flesh alternatives. The reverse situation occurs in Europe, where there are few large swarming tidbit species but an abundance of domesticated animals such as cattle, pigs, sheep, and chickens. This explanation seems to me preferable to the popular notion that Europeans and Americans don't eat insects because such things carry disease and are too disgusting to look at. If insects spread disease, well, so do pigs, cattle, and chickens. Besides, insects can be made perfectly safe to eat the way we make other foods safe to eat: by cooking them. As for not eating things because they look disgusting, the only people who find them disgusting are the ones who don't eat them.

Over the years I have spent a great deal of effort showing that the same kind of principle applies to such seemingly wasteful taboos as the ban on pork in the Old Testament and in the Koran. Pigs, which need shade and have to have their skin wetted down to prevent heat stroke and which don't give milk, can't pull plows or carts, and can't thrive on grass, are a poor investment in the hot, dry Biblical heartlands compared with alternative domestic species, especially the ruminants: cattle, sheep, and goats. In famous passages in the Book of Leviticus, the ancient Israelite priests banned the flesh of not only the pig, but essentially all other land animals that were non-cud-chewers, which is to say, nonruminants. Camels were the only ruminant (actually, pseudoruminant) in the prohibited category. I offer the following balance sheet as evidence that these ancient culturally selected prohibitions contain a core of ecologically sound, economically efficient, and nutritionally safe collective wisdom.

CATTLE

Costs	*Benefits*
feed (cheap grass)	traction for carts
herding (little labor)	traction for plows
disease (brucelosis, anthrax)	meat
	milk
	dung
	hides

PIGS

Costs	*Benefits*
feed (cheap waste)	meat
herding (much labor)	dung
wallows	hides
shade	
disease (trichinosis, anthrax)	

Some of the most puzzling and seemingly arbitrary cultural determinations of food preferences and avoidances involve trade-offs between animals as a source of flesh and animals as a source of important products or services. In some contexts, certain animals are simply worth more alive than dead. This holds true, for example, of cattle in India. Used alive for plowing and as a source of dung for fertilizers and cooking fuel, as well as a source of milk, cattle in India provide more benefits kept in service to a ripe old age than if they were to be butchered and sold for meat. Moreover, when they finally do keel over after a lifetime of essential services, their flesh rarely goes to waste since their masters promptly notify members of castes that specialize in the consumption of dead cattle to dispose of the carcass.

Perhaps this is an appropriate point to say something once

again about the weighting of natural and cultural selection in post-takeoff cultural evolution. The distribution of enormously diverse socially acquired preferences for flavors and foods cannot conceivably result from closely controlling genetic tendencies. Surely no one would seriously wish to invoke red-pepper genes to explain the Mexican passion for peppers; antipork genes to explain why Jews and Moslems abhor pork; cow-protection genes to explain the Hindu rejection of beef; or insect-loathing genes to explain why Euro-Americans abhor insects. I also would find little merit in the claim that food traditions are generally adopted because they increase reproductive success. If, as I think I have shown, food preferences and avoidances generally result in efficaciously satisfying the need for food, why should anyone insist that they would not be culturally selected unless they also increased reproductive success? The recent history of the Western world shows that the best-nourished people are not necessarily the ones who have the most babies. My point is not that natural selection and reproductive success never influenced the evolution of food traditions after cultural takeoff, but that they have been influential only in rare instances. One such instance is the aversion to milk. I present it next as an example of how natural selection and cultural selection sometimes do interact even after cultural takeoff.

ONE FOR
THE GENES

$\mathcal{E}$AST ASIANS, AFRICANS, AND AMERICAN INDIANS do not like to drink milk when they grow up, while northern Europeans and their American descendants, young or old, like to drink it by the glassful. To understand why, genetic differences must be recognized.

Like other mammals, as they grow older, most humans lose the ability to produce lactase, which, as I mentioned earlier, is the enzyme that breaks down lactose—milk sugar—into digestible sucrose and galactose. Lactase deficiency in adults makes biological sense because human milk is normally the only source of lactose and mother's milk is crucial for the survival of infants but not for the survival of adults.

Before proceeding, let me explain why milk does not contain a less complex and more easily digestible sugar. The answer is that lactose not only provides energy but it also helps infants digest the calcium that is present in milk. As you already know, the body needs this essential mineral to build and harden bones. Adults can get their supply of calcium from plant foods, especially from green leafy vegetables. But infants must depend on mother's milk for their calcium supply. Another factor important for digesting calcium is vitamin D, which, as I explained earlier, can be either obtained from oceanic fish and fish-eating mammals, or synthesized in the body by exposing the skin to sunlight. Infants, unlike adults, can get their vitamin D only from sunlight because there is no vitamin D in milk. The contribution that lactose makes to calcium absorption in infants, therefore, outweighs the problem of its being a complex rather than simple sugar.

About 12,000 years ago, milkable animals were domesticated in the Middle East. For the first time it became possible for humans to obtain copious amounts of milk from nonhuman mammary glands. The earliest dairying people soon found that they could not digest this new food resource if they drank it in raw form. They were able to digest it only if they let it sour or turned it into yogurt or cheese, since fermentation changes the lactose into sucrose, thereby avoiding the need for adults to produce lactase in order to add animal milk to their diet.

The loss of the effect of lactase on calcium absorption for Middle Eastern dairying populations had no impact on their reproductive success, since they could get all the vitamin D they needed from sunshine and all the calcium they needed from leafy green vegetables. This explains why the descendants of ancient dairying people such as Jews, Arabs, Greeks, Sudanese, and South Asians often suffer severe intestinal discomfort after drinking a glass or two of unfermented milk. It was only after dairying began to spread into northern Europe that the ability to produce lactase at all ages became associated with marked differences in rates of reproductive success. As I explained earlier, the northern dairying people lived in a mist-shrouded environment and had to bundle up against the cold most of the year. They were without access to vitamin D in fish and sea mammals, and lacked green leafy vegetables as an alternative source of calcium. Under these conditions, individuals who were genetically capable of digesting large quantities of *unfermented* milk were better able to maintain normal bone growth and avoid crippling bone diseases such as rickets and osteomalacia, and therefore enjoyed higher rates of reproductive success than individuals who obtained their calcium through fermented milk, yogurt, or cheese. Within 4,000 or 5,000 years, the gene that controls for lactase production in adulthood spread to over 90 percent of the individuals in northern European dairying populations.

An interesting link in this explanation concerns the different biological, cultural, and gastronomic trajectories followed by India and China. The peoples of India long ago accepted dairying and made milk products basic to their cuisine, but not being stressed for calcium, they consumed milk primarily in fermented form. The incidence of low levels of lactase in adulthood is therefore much more common in India than in northern Europe, despite the love of milk and milk products in both traditions. China, on the other hand, never accepted dairying and the Chinese people view a glass of milk as a loathsome secretion, akin to a glass of saliva. Over 90 percent of the Chinese and nondairying East Asians have insufficient lactase to digest unfermented milk when they are adults. But note that the answer to the question of why the Chinese loathe milk cannot be simply that milk makes them sick. If they had accepted dairying as a mode of food production, the Chinese, like the South Asians, could easily have overcome their insufficiency of lactase by consuming fermented milk products. The crux of the problem, therefore, is why the Chinese never adopted dairying. The answer to this question has to do with the difference between the ecological restraints and opportunities of the Chinese and Indian habitats and has to be given in terms of cultural rather than natural selection.

To pursue this inquiry here would take me too far afield. So I shall have to confine myself to pointing out that China relied on trade with inner Asia pastoralists for a supply of plow animals. Hence China's farmers had no reason to keep cows in their villages. No cows, no milk, no milk-based cuisines. But India was sealed off from pastoralist societies by the Himalaya and Hindu Kush mountains. To supply the need for plow oxen, India had to raise and keep cows in the villages. This led to the prominence of milk products in India's cuisine, and to an intermediate frequency of the gene for adult lactase sufficiency. A final interesting point is that in India, cows get their food by scavenging garbage and other village wastes. In China, where there were no cows in the villages, pigs filled the principal scavenger niche. Except for Christian castes, no one raises pigs in India. Pork and lard, therefore, are to Chinese cuisine what milk and butter are to Indian cuisine.

But enough of food for the moment. Culture does not evolve by hunger alone. It is time to move on to another great drive and appetite that culture must serve.

SEXUAL
PLEASURE

SEX RANKS CLOSE to hunger as a motivation of human action and as a selective force in cultural evolution. Like hunger, sex is both a drive and an appetite. In an acute state of sexual deprivation, humans feel a powerful need to alleviate an inner tension. But the relief of that tension provides pleasures that make us crave additional sexual acts, even if we are not acutely deprived. Nonetheless, the balance of drive and appetite in food hunger is quite different from the balance of drive and appetite in sex hunger. The aversive effects of prolonged sexual deprivation are not as severe as the aversive effects of prolonged starvation. Abstention from food (or air or water) leads to profound physical torture as well as to obsessive desires that can be ignored only at the risk of death. Abstention from sex leads to relatively mild discomfort and to obsessive desire ignored only at the risk of additional obsessive desire. Sex is less powerful than hunger as a selective force in cultural evolution because when hunger reaches starvation levels, humans lose their drive and appetite for sex. The reverse does not hold. Sexually deprived humans do not lose their drive or appetite for food. In fact, they may try to eat more as a means of alleviating their sexual distress. But when the two drives and appetites are placed on a level playing field, sexual desire can easily preempt the desire for food. Well-nourished humans experience no difficulty in postponing the pleasures of a gourmet table for the pleasures of a lover's bed.

Worried parents, irate spouses, snooping police, and ecclesiastical commandments may depress or divert human copulatory behavior, but they can never completely extinguish the drive and appetite for sexual release and pleasure. People fight, kill, rape, and risk their fortunes, health, and their very lives on behalf of achieving sexual goals. Sexual desire can persist even at the risk of disfiguring gonorrhea, maddening syphilis, itching herpes, and cancerous AIDS. Many have struggled against it to achieve a higher spiritual existence, but I doubt if there ever was a healthy young human being who could completely suppress his or her genital feelings. As Saint Paul confessed, "I see another law in my members, warring against the law of my mind, and bringing me into captivity to the law of sin which is in my members" (Romans 7:23).

The lack of adverse physiological consequences from abstention, the extraordinary lengths to which people will go to experience orgasms, the repetitive, compulsive search for additional orgasms, and the futility of trying to prevent oneself from doing it, all suggest a close resemblance between the pursuit of sexual pleasure and addiction to psychotropic drugs. Among heroin addicts, for example, the need for a "fix" often overrides the need for food, rest, and shelter. The fact that nothing is ingested to produce a sexual high does not invalidate the analogy. We know that the body can dose itself with internally manufactured euphoria-producing substances when it is stimulated to do so.

Experimentation on rats and dogs has shown that there are parts of the brain that serve as pleasure centers and that animals will go to extraordinary lengths to have a mildly stimulating electric current delivered to these centers. When electrodes implanted in their brain are connected to switches that the animals themselves can operate, they compulsively stimulate themselves for hours on end. Given a choice between pressing the button for a pleasure center or a button for food and water, the animals continue to stimulate themselves until they die of thirst and starvation. Researchers have also performed similar experiments on humans in the course of preparing patients for brain surgery. The human brain, too, has centers, which, when activated electrically or by infusions of chemicals called neurotransmitters, produce intensely pleasurable sensations. Some patients describe these sensations as like having an orgasm. But researchers have yet to find a center that keeps people pressing buttons as compulsively as rats.

In 1975, a team of scientists working in the United States, Scotland, and Sweden simultaneously discovered a substance called enkephalin, which binds to the very same neurone receptors in the brain to which heroin binds and which deadens pain and produces a feeling of euphoria. Shortly afterward, other scientists discovered a second class of endogenous opiumlike substance called endorphins. A logical inference that one might draw from these discoveries is that the concentrated pleasure of orgasm results from a cascade of the body's own opiates across the gaps that separate neurons from each other in the brain's pleasure centers. This inference was tested in 1977 by administering naloxone to a human subject prior to his attempt to achieve orgasm by masturbation. Naloxone is the chemical that is the antidote to heroin and that acts by blocking the transmission of opiates across the gaps between neurons. The researchers found no diminution in the subject's ability to reach orgasm, and the subject reported no reduction in pleasurable sensation.

Electrical stimulation of the portion of the brainstem known as the septum produces sensations of pleasure in humans. In one male subject, the electrical activity of the septum was recorded during orgasm and showed a pattern of brainwaves similar to those found during epileptic seizures—indicative of the synchronous discharge of a very large number of neurons. Injection of a female subject's septum with the neurotransmitter acetylcholine produced intense sensations of sexual pleasure, culminating in repeated orgasm. These experiments leave too many variables uncontrolled, and the exact pharmacology and neurophysiology of the human addiction to sexual ecstasy remains one of nature's best-kept secrets. But can the day be far off when one of the major pharmaceutical houses announces that it is ready to market substances that induce the mental sensation if not the physiological reactions of orgasm?

If it were not for the intermittent nature of orgasmic highs, sexual appetites might easily override essential life-supporting drives and appetites and turn us into veritable sex junkies. Natural selection has made sobriety the norm and euphoria the exception. We need to feel pain and anxiety in order to cope effectively with the world outside our heads. And so natural selection has seen to it that we get our biggest high only as a reward for stimulating the organs that initiate the process of reproduction and not for stimulating our fingers and toes. Through cultural evolution we have learned how to defeat nature's connection between sexual pleasure and reproduction. Are we now on the threshold of learning how to defeat nature's connection between sexual pleasure and sex?

CARNAL
IGNORANCE

VER SINCE ADAM AND EVE'S expulsion from the Garden of Eden, Western cultures have associated human sexuality with sin, dirt, and animals. "Man" may have been made in God's image, but, as Saint Augustine warned, it is only "that part of him by which he rises above those lower parts he has in common with the beasts, which brings him nearer to the Supreme." Even Sigmund Freud, that great champion of libido, relegated sex to "id," the animal basement of the human psyche. But do we really resemble the beasts more from the waist down than from the waist up? I say no. Among the 200 or so species of living primates, not a single one can be said to have lower members or to delve and spawn quite as humans do.

Genesis states that Adam and Eve lost their innocence about sex after eating fruit from the tree of knowledge. But the serpent didn't tell them one important thing: As Adam delved, he didn't know when Eve spawned. And so it has been to this day, with consequences that reach to the deepest levels of our social existence. Wise as we came to be, our carnal knowledge remains incomplete. Outside of a laboratory, we still can't tell when a woman's egg is ready to be fertilized.

The significance of this best-kept secret of nature will become clear after I recount some familiar and perhaps some not so familiar facts of life.

Approximately every twenty-eight days, one or another of the two ovaries in a woman's body releases a tiny egg into the corresponding left or right fallopian tube. If a sperm fertilizes the egg before it has descended the length of the tube, it will embed itself in the specially prepared, spongy, blood-filled lining on the wall of the uterus. Otherwise, this lining sloughs off, creating the familiar monthly phenomenon of menstruation. The most remarkable thing about this cycle is that sperm and unfertilized egg have very short lifetimes. If the egg is not penetrated by a sperm in twenty-four hours, it loses its capacity to be fertilized. And if the sperm does not penetrate the egg within forty-eight hours after having been ejaculated into the vagina, its little tail stops beating and it dies. Therefore, on the average, only if intercourse takes place coincident with or no more than forty-eight hours before or twenty-four hours after ovulation can fertilization occur. Altogether this provides a window of opportunity of approximately three days out of twenty-eight when copulation can lead to pregnancy. On average, the crucial seventy-two hours occur about midway in the menstrual cycle, that is on the twelfth, thirteenth, and fourteenth days after the beginning of the menstrual flow. (But don't count on these numbers for having sex without running the risk of pregnancy. The interval between menstruation and ovulation can be off as much as five to ten days in any particular cycle.) In most mammalian species whose sperm and ova have a similar narrow window of opportunity (unlike bats, for example, whose females store sperm for months), the female emits an array of signals and engages in behavioral routines that assure her and her mate that a viable egg awaits his ejaculate. Or it may be the other way around: The egg doesn't get released until viable sperm are present, as in mice. Female "heat," familiar to owners of unaltered cats or dogs, is one of the most common strategies for synchronizing copulation and ovulation. The female becomes edgy and whimpers and releases a powerful scent that attracts the neighborhood males.

Like cats and dogs, monkeys and apes do not let ovulation come and go without some kind of assurance that sperm will be there to fertilize the egg. A capuchin brown monkey, for example, markedly changes her behavior as she approaches ovulation. She wears a grimace on her face, produces a distinctive continuous soft whistle that turns into a pulsing, hoarse whine, and follows a dominant male around for hours at a time, approaching him very closely and touching or pushing him on the rump or shaking a branch near him and then running away.

Odors also play an important role in several primate species. Among rhesus monkeys, secretions of vaginal fatty acids attract the male and increase his responsiveness to female solicitations as ovulation approaches. Other species reveal when they are close to ovulation by means of visual signals exhibited in the perineal (anal-genital) skin. Common chimpanzees develop pink perineal swellings that reach the size of grapefruits as ovulation approaches and then subside. Other parts of the female may also "light up." Female gelada baboons, who spend most of their time sitting on their rumps pulling up clumps of grass, develop bright necklaces of swellings on their chest, in addition to swellings on their often difficult-to-see posteriors.

The most prominent swellings seem to occur in primate species like chimpanzees and baboons that mate promiscuously. Promiscuous females rely on vivid signals to attract as many mates as possible during each ovulation. These matings establish friendly bonds between males and females and discourage males from molesting infants (which they might be inclined to do, according to the sociobiological theory of inclusive fitness, if they could be certain that the infants were sired not by themselves but by another male). Chimpanzee males seldom fight over access to females in heat. As many as twenty males may patiently wait their turn with a single female. This does not mean that males do not compete for reproductive success. On the contrary, they compete fiercely with each other to fertilize the most females. But this competition is carried out in a manner that does not lead to threatening, maiming, or killing their competitors. Common chimpanzees have extremely large and heavy testicles compared with other apes; and their average ejaculate contains about ten times more sperm than a gorilla's or an orangutan's ejaculate. During their numerous promiscuous matings, reproductive victories go to the male chimps with the highest sperm count and the most vigorous sperm. The average size of their penis is also commensurate with their commitment to sperm competition. Proportionate to body size, it is more than three times as long as the gorilla's.

A different mating pattern and form of competition exist among gorillas and orangutans, neither of which signal ovulation with prominent sexual swellings. Gorilla males, who are twice as big as females, keep exclusive harems and prevent other males from copulating with their females when they are in heat. Females nearing ovulation, therefore, would derive no advantage from sending up flares and rockets to attract a lot of males. Their one mate can be alerted to their ovulatory condition by means of less conspicuous and elaborate signals. Orangutan males do not keep harems, but the same logic applies. They are monogamous, which means that the females again have to attract only one mate and can therefore dispense with raucous advertisements for additional suitors. Since both orang and gorilla males maintain exclusive control over females by fighting or scaring off competitors, they need not compete for access to ova by having large testicles, a high sperm count, and a big penis.

The evolution of female promiscuity, combined with male sperm competition and mutual toleration among males who mate with the same female, has gone furthest among the pygmy chimpanzees (*Pan paniscus*). What I am about to recount of the sex life of these remarkable animals was unknown until a few years ago. Living in the densest and most remote parts of the Congo rain forest, they were the last of the great apes to be studied in their natural habitat by primatologists using modern field methods. Because they are genetically at least as closely related to the hominids as the better known common chimp (*Pan troglodytes*), their unique sexual and social behavior provides new insights into the role of sexuality in the origin of human societies. Unlike the common chimpanzee, which exhibits a peak in copulations at the maxima of its perineal swellings, the pygmy chimp copulates all year round throughout the entire ovulatory cycle. During the thirty-six to forty-two days that the cycle lasts, there is a phase of maximal swelling for fifteen to eighteen days. But on a daily basis, the rate of copulation does not vary much throughout the whole cycle, except for a few days when there is minimal swelling. I should add that adult female pygmy chimpanzee swellings never subside as far as they do in the common chimpanzee, so that females are, in effect, continuously sending out signals to attract males. As a result, both males and females copulate several times a day, during most of the month, throughout the year.

In comparison with other ape species, the pygmy chimpanzees can be described only as hypersexual. The male's penis is larger and more conspicuous than that of any other ape and, relative to body size, larger than that possessed by our kind. Not to be outdone, the pygmy chimp female possesses the largest clitoris of any primate species. It stays plainly in view throughout the ovulatory cycle. During periods of sexual excitement, the clitoris doubles in length and both shaft and tip become engorged as they do in the male's penile erection. The enlargement of the clitoris seems to be associated with a unique form of female homosexuality that has been termed "genito-genital rubbing": Two females embrace face to face, stare into each other's eyes, and rub their genitals together in rapid, lateral movements. In general, one of the partners wraps her legs around the other's waist as they rub. On occasion, female partners use the erect clitoris for the thrusting behavior that is typical of male-female copulations. Males also engage in homosexual pseudocopulatory bouts, although less frequently than females. Adult male homosexual mountings in other primate species can usually be interpreted as attempts on the part of a subordinate to placate a dominant male or as an attempt on the part of a dominant male to intimidate a subordinate. Relatively little of this behavior occurs among pygmy chimps because males are unusually tolerant of each other in conformity with their investment in sperm competition as a reproductive strategy.

Copulation does not take place until both sexes have indicated their readiness by facial and vocal signals. They stare into each other's eyes fifteen minutes prior to copulation and maintain eye contact while copulating. And more than other nonhuman primates, pygmy chimps use the ventral-ventral (face-to-face) position. Evidently, the pygmy chimps have been able to do away with linking copulation to ovulation by substituting continuous intense sexuality for ovulatory signals that other apes use to ensure the meeting of ovum and sperm. To what extent can we use the pygmy chimps as a model for human origins?

AND NOW
FOR
SOMETHING
COMPLETELY
DIFFERENT

ATURAL SELECTION has designed a simple but extravagant method for getting human sperm and egg together on the three days that count. It has endowed us with sexual needs and appetites so strong that people are predisposed to tolerate, if not to crave, sex every day of the month, every day of the year over a span of many years. This takes the guesswork out of the reproductive shell game: To find out where the prize is hidden, we turn over all the shells. Need I add that this doesn't mean that men automatically have erections as soon as they encounter women nor that women will be receptive to any man who solicits sexual intercourse. As we all know, both men and women possess a considerable degree of latitude in regard to whom they solicit and whom they reject or accept as well as when, where, and how often. But the essential point is that for both men and women, sex is an intensely pleasurable experience and there are no physiological or hormonal barriers to having it one or more times a day every day of the year, at least from adolescence to middle age. And it is this astonishing shotgun approach to hitting a three-day target that humans, even more than pygmy chimpanzees, use as a substitute for the precisely aimed rifle fire of species that copulate primarily only when the ovum is there to be hit.

Despite a voluminous ejaculate, human sperm counts are smaller than those of many other primate species, and the percentage of motile sperm is also unusually low. But this is a murky and somewhat alarming subject because studies show that human sperm and motility counts have sharply declined since 1950, possibly as a result of chemical pollution of air, food, and water. In all other respects, humans are one of the sexiest species in the animal kingdom. The human penis is longer and thicker than that of any other primate, and the testes are heavier than in a gorilla or orang. Our kind spends more time in precopulatory courtship, and copulatory sessions last longer than among other primates. The capacity for female orgasm, while not unique to humans as once thought, is highly developed. Copulatory frequency is not as high as among chimpanzees, but then again humans confront the greatest amount of socially imposed restrictions on sexuality. These restrictions lead to peculiarly human nocturnal emissions among males—wet dreams—and to rates of masturbation among both human males and females that are matched only in primates kept in zoos or laboratories. The human male's psychological preoccupation with sex has no parallel in other species. American adolescents aged twelve to nineteen report thinking about sex on average every five minutes during their waking hours, and even at age fifty, American males think about sex several times a day. How did this peculiar pattern of sexuality originate?

Since we have no direct knowledge of the reproductive cycles and mating patterns of afarensis or habilis, this question has to be approached by looking for possible antecedents or "models" in the behavior of pygmy chimps. The relentless economizing of natural selection makes it unlikely that the pygmy chimp's sexual extravagances are merely there to add zest to life. There must be some reproductive payoff that compensates them for their wasteful approach to hitting the ovulatory target. Could it be that this payoff consists of a more intense form of social cooperation between males and females? And could this in turn lead to a more intensely cooperative social group, a more secure milieu for rearing infants, and hence a higher degree of reproductive success for sexier males and females?

Certain contrasts between the social organization of the common chimpanzees and the pygmy chimps support this interpretation. As I said a while back, chimpanzee sexual swellings are associated with promiscuous mating and heightened male tolerance of females and infants. Among common chimpanzees, these mating patterns are further associated with loose, shifting coalitions of adult males who receive visits from sexually receptive females and their infants. About a third of the time, common chimps can be found in these multimale groups temporarily accompanied by females and infants. Another third of the time they live in smaller groups consisting only of adults of both sexes. And during the rest of the time they either live in groups that contain only females and infants or only males. In contrast, the pygmy chimpanzees have a far more integrated form of social organization. They spend three-quarters of the time in groups containing adults of both sexes, juveniles, and infants and can seldom be found in all-male groups or in female-and-infant groups without adult males. In sum, several adult males and several adult females and their progeny remain close to each other most of the time, traveling, eating, grooming, copulating, and resting together.

I believe that it is plausible to conclude that the intense sexuality of pygmy chimps was selected for because it intensified the solidary bonds among males and females and their progeny. Common chimps have also moved in this direction by their promiscuous matings and their substitution of sperm competition for direct aggression. But since their copulatory behavior is regulated by the tumescence and detumescence of their sexual swellings, mothers (and young) were frequently separated from fathers and from the help that fathers might render in feeding and in protecting mothers and infants. Pygmy chimp females, with their virtually permanent sexual swellings and their continuous sexual receptivity, are in a much better position to receive male support for themselves and their infants.

My theoretical expectation is borne out by another remarkable feature of pygmy chimp social life. Males do in fact regularly share food with females and with young. This applies both to the small animals that they occasionally capture and to certain large fruits that are handed back and forth. Sueshi Karoda of the Laboratory of Physical Anthropology of Kyoto University reports that there is a clear tendency for dominant pygmy males to share food more frequently than dominant common chimpanzee males. Females often approach dominant males to take or beg food. Juveniles also frequently take or beg food from dominant males. Subordinate males tend to be less generous. If they come into possession of a prized fruit such as a pineapple, they try to climb up to a secluded spot. But dominant males are often surrounded by beggars and compelled to share food. Among common chimpanzees, females seldom share food with anyone except their infants; in contrast, among pygmy chimps, females frequently share food with adult members of their group as well as with infants. While both common and pygmy chimp females obtain prized food by begging with their outstretched arm, pygmy females do something seldom observed among any other species, except humans. They precede their begging, or dispense with it entirely, by copulating with the individual who possesses the desired food. Karoda gives these examples: "A young female approached a male, who was eating sugar cane. They copulated in short order, whereupon she took one of the two canes held by him and left. In another case a young female persistently presented to a male possessor, who ignored her at first, but then copulated with her and shared his sugar cane." And females do not restrict themselves to exchanging sex for food with males. Females precede nearly half of all food-sharing incidents with other females with a bout of genitogenital rubbing initiated by the supplicant.

All this new information about pygmy chimpanzees has revolutionary implications for our understanding of the probable forms of social life adopted by the earliest hominids. But before I tell that part of the story, let me pause to admire a peculiar anatomical feature that appears in human females and no other primate.

WHY WOMEN
HAVE
PERENNIALLY
ENLARGED
BREASTS

ONHUMAN PRIMATE FEMALES, including the great apes, develop enlarged breasts only while they are lactating. Human females develop enlarged, often pendulous breasts at puberty, and the breasts remain that way regardless of whether lactation takes place or not. Their size is determined primarily by the presence of fatty tissues that have nothing to do with the glands that secrete milk and that are not related to how much milk a woman can produce during lactation.

As I mentioned a moment ago, perineal sexual swellings in pygmy chimps undergo only partial detumescence after ovulation and menstruation. These swellings no longer function to arouse and excite males only if the female is close to ovulation, as in common chimpanzees. Rather, in keeping with the near-permanent state of sexual readiness maintained by female pygmy chimpanzees, they function as a permanent stimulus for male sexual arousal.

The development of quasi-permanent perineal swellings in pygmy chimps may shed light on the question of why human females are the only primates whose breasts remain permanently enlarged. Perineal signals are more readily detected by species that walk and run on all fours than by species that walk upright or maintain a vertical orientation while feeding. I have already mentioned gelada baboons as an example of vertically oriented feeders whose sexual swellings occur on their chests as well as their rumps. In humans, pendulous breasts, therefore, seem to combine the permanence of a pygmy chimp's perineal swellings with the visibility of a gelada's "necklace."

The theory that swollen breasts represented a translocation of sexual signals from rump to front was first proposed by Desmond Morris in his book *The Naked Ape*. As Morris pointed out, pubic hair and the orientation of the external male and female genitalia conform to the use of the vertically oriented front-facing torso for sexual displays.

Morris also had the idea that female hominid breasts actually mimicked an ape ancestor's genital-anal swellings and that the breasts gained their effectiveness as sexual signals because they built on visual susceptibilities possessed by these ancestral apes. As a final touch, Morris claimed that a woman's lips and breasts formed a unit in which the red-rimmed opening of the mouth became a proxy for a red-rimmed opening of an ape vagina.

But one does not have to go to such fanciful lengths to understand why breast signals would have been selected as substitutes for perineal signals in humans. The reason why full bosoms acquired the power to excite human males is that there is a link between full bosoms and reproductive success. Males who were attracted by large breasts had more progeny than males who were not attracted by them. And females who possessed them had more progeny than those who did not possess them. These reproductively favorable consequences resulted from the fact that female breasts consist mainly of stored fat. Women use about 250 extra calories a day while they are pregnant and about 750 extra calories a day when they are lactating. Large-breasted women are likely to have ample stores of fat not only in their bosoms but in the rest of their bodies—fat that can be converted into calories if dietary intake fails to meet the extra demands of pregnancy or lactation. Stored fat would have been especially advantageous during the movement to savanna habitats, where our earliest hominid ancestors had to contend with a less certain and more variable food supply than forest-dwelling apes. Large breasts would have signalled to potential mates the fact that females were in good condition and physiologically prepared to withstand the extra burdens that pregnancy and lactation impose. So natural selection would have favored females whose breasts were perennially large and pendulous at the same time that it favored males who found large-breasted women sexually attractive.

This theory has been criticized on the grounds that large breasts should have turned males off rather than on because, among apes, the female's breasts enlarge, as I have said, only during lactation, and lactation in turn suppresses the ovulatory cycle, rendering females temporarily sterile. Large breasts would have served as a signal that a female was not ready to become pregnant and therefore would have repelled rather than attracted male suitors. But this objection would not hold in the case of a protohominid whose copulatory behavior resembled that of the pygmy chimpanzees. In keeping with their generally hypersexual life-style, pregnant pygmy chimpanzees and mothers with nursing infants continue to copulate. If the reproductive payoff for continuous sexual receptivity was mediated by its social bonding effects, wouldn't one expect there to be a gradual extension of sexual activity through later and later phases of pregnancy and earlier and earlier phases of lactation?

Perhaps a word of caution about the erotic appeal of large breasts is needed at this point. From the European and African perspective, American males seem pathologically obsessed with this aspect of the female anatomy. Writing of the Ulithi islanders of Micronesia, William Lessa notes that Ulithi men claim not to find women's bare breasts exciting and wonder why foreigners make such a fuss over them. Obviously there is a strong cultural component in the allure of the female bosom. Scarification, body paint, and brassieres may enhance male excitement at the sight of breasts far beyond their natural allure. The same may hold for the practice of wearing clothing to conceal the sight of a woman's bosom from every male except her husband or lover. Keeping any part of the female anatomy from public view may lead to its becoming an erotic fetish. Chinese males, for example, were aroused by the sight of the naked feet of aristocratic women, who normally kept them tightly bound and hidden from view. Fashions may also decree that female breasts be inconspicuous. During the 1920s, for example, a small-bosomed "boyish" look dominated the design of Western female attire. Males seem to have courted these boyish-looking women as ardently as males courted the big-breasted, padded-brassiere-clad women of the 1950s. I consider it likely, therefore, that the innate signal power of large female breasts is not as strong as it was in an earlier phase of hominid evolution prior to cultural takeoff. But let me get back to the relationship between human sexuality and the evolution of human social life.

GIVING
AND
TAKING

*G*IVING AND TAKING, or exchange, is the glue that holds human societies together. The primordial form of exchange is the giving and taking of services as embodied in copulation: sex for sex. Primates also take turns carefully picking parasites and dirt from each other's hair and skin, another example of the exchange of a service for a service. But beyond the transfer of milk from mother to infants, or of ejaculate to vagina, the exchange of service for *goods* seldom occurs. The pygmy chimps are the big exception, for, as I emphasized a while back, female pygmy chimps exchange sex for food. And this has momentous implications, for it suggests how afarensis and habilis could have achieved unprecedented levels of social cooperation that prepared them for group life on the perilous savannas. With more regular exchanges of sex for food, females would have been able to obtain a significant part of their food supply from male consorts. Moreover, as females competed for the attention of productive and generous males, they would inevitably discover the well-known path that lies through a male's stomach, and fed him with a choice morsel of their own—ants and termites or a big tuber, perhaps (regrettably, I can't say that it was an apple).

The bonding effects of the exchange of goods for goods increase if each party gives the other something the other wants but doesn't have. Since we already have seen that, among common chimps, males obtain meat more often than females, but females obtain insects more often than males, there is every likelihood that afarensis and habilis males and females engaged in similar kinds of exchanges—probably insects and plant foods obtained by females for morsels of scavenged or hunted meats obtained by males. An inevitable effect of increasing the volume and types of exchange would be the establishment of partnerships among subsets of male and female givers and takers. Individuals could afford to give sexual services indiscriminately to everyone in the troop—they had more than enough of that to give—but they could not afford to give food indis-

190

criminately, since food was far more limited than sex. Partnerships that concentrated food exchanges in two or three groups smaller than the troop as a whole, would have constituted the protocultural beginnings of families. Yet to prevent the permanent dissolution of the troop, some degree of exchange between these protofamilies had to be maintained. Within and between protofamilies, givers had to have confidence that the flow would be reversed, not necessarily with an equal return, nor immediately, but to some degree, from time to time. Otherwise they would stop giving.

Let me point out that none of the steps in the process of building social complexity through exchange relationships presupposes close genetic control over give-and-take response. Our ancestors were no more born to "truck and barter," as Adam Smith and other classical economists believed, than they were born to make hand axes and digging sticks. The expansion of the sphere of exchange beyond the prototypical give-and-take of copulation and mutual grooming required that a simple behavioral relationship be generalized: Afarensis and habilis had merely to learn that if they gave to those from whom they took, they could take again. But generalizing this rule to satisfy more needs and drives to encompass more individuals and longer delays between taking and giving, all the while keeping track of the balance in each "account," does presuppose major advances in memory, attention, and general intelligence. Truly complex exchanges and institutions would have had to await the evolution of language, with its capacity to formalize long-term rights and obligations implicit in each individual's history of giving and taking goods and services.

But once cultural takeoff had been passed, exchange relationships could evolve rapidly into different kinds of economic transactions: gift exchange, barter, trade, redistribution, taxation, and eventually buying and selling, salaries, and wages. And to this day it is exchange that binds people into friendships and marriages, creates families, communities, and higher order political and corporate bodies. By iterations and recursions, by permutating and combining different rewards appropriate to different drives and needs, by spinning fantastically complex webs connecting individuals to individuals, institutions to institutions, and groups to groups, exchange was destined to make our kind not merely the most intensely sexual creatures on earth, but the most intensely social as well.

HOW
MANY
MATES?

I WOULD LIKE to be able to say more about what kind of mating system and family organization prevailed during the formative phases of hominid social life.

Over the entire span of four or five million years that separate us from the first afarensis, there is not a simple piece of hard evidence bearing on this question. And the record is equally blank when it comes to post-takeoff Stone Age sapiens hunter-gatherers. This lack of evidence has not deterred various scholars from attempting to identify the form of mating to which all hominids are supposedly innately predisposed. Much popular support can always be found for those who insist the first humans were monogamous and that they lived in troops or bands composed of several nuclear families, each in turn consisting of a mated pair and their children. The logic behind this view is that human sexuality with its personalized, eye-to-eye, frontal orientation naturally leads to strong bonds between one man and one woman. Such pair-bonds supposedly provide the best assurance that human infants will be fed and nurtured during their long period of dependency. Some anthropologists like to round out this scenario by postulating a connection between monogamy and the existence of a home base. Wife and child supposedly stay near the home base while husband/father goes off to hunt at a greater distance, returning at night to share the catch.

While I agree that exchanges of food and sex would lead to the development of stronger bonds between some males and some females, I do not know why these would have to be exclusive pair-bonds. What about contemporary mating patterns? Do they not show that alternative modes of mating and family organization are perfectly well suited to the task of satisfying human sexual needs and rearing human children? Polygyny is an ideal in more societies than is monogamy. And it occurs among foraging societies as well as among state-level societies. Moreover, as a result of the high frequency of divorce, of keeping mistresses and concubines, and having "affairs," most ideologically monogamous societies are behaviorally polygamous. Let's be realistic. One of the fastest growing forms of family in the world today is the single parent family headed by a woman. Sexual practices that go along with this family often correspond to a form of polyandry (one female, several males). In U.S. central cities and throughout much of South America, the Caribbean islands, and urbanizing parts of Africa and India, women have temporary or visiting mates who father the woman's children and contribute marginally to their support.

In view of the frequent occurrence of modern domestic groups that do not consist of, or contain, an exclusive pair-bonded father and mother, I cannot see why anyone should insist that our ancestors were reared in monogamous nuclear families and that pair-bonding is more natural than other arrangements.

I am equally skeptical about the part of the pair-bond theory that postulates a primordial home base tended by homebody females whose males roamed widely in search of meat. It seems to me much more likely that afarensis and habilis males, females, and infants moved together across the land as a troop and that females who were not nursing took an active part in dispersing scavengers, combating predators, and in pursuing prey animals. My evidence? Women marathon runners. Competing against men in grueling twenty-six-mile races, they are steadily closing the gap between male and female winners. In the Boston Marathon, the women's record of 2:22:43 is only 9 percent off the men's record. This is scarcely the kind of performance of a sex whose ancestors stayed home minding the babies for two million years.

What I have just been saying should not be taken to mean that our presapiens forebears never formed monogamous pair-bonds. The point is simply that they were no more likely than modern-day humans to have mated and reared children according to a single plan. Given an ability to mediate potentially disruptive social arrangements by exchanging services for goods, goods for goods, and goods for services, our presapiens ancestors could have adopted mating and childrearing systems as diverse as the systems that exist today or that existed in the recent past.

We know that modern-day mating and childrearing systems are constantly adjusting to levels of technological competence, population density, deployment of males and females in production, and local environmental conditions. Polygyny prevails, for example, where there is an abundance of land and a shortage of labor so that men can become prosperous by adding additional wives and children to their households. These conditions often occur in newly occupied lands, as among the Mormons of Utah, for whom polygyny was a means of establishing control over a vast and sparsely settled region in the American West. At the opposite extreme, polyandry represents an adjustment to extreme scarcity of resources. It occurs in Tibet, where agricultural land is so scarce that two or three brothers are willing to share one wife in order to limit the number of heirs to their jointly owned farmland. Monogamy seems to prevail at intermediate levels of population pressure and land scarcity. Many other factors may be relevant in particular cases. Ecclesiastical and political policies, themselves rooted in particular conditions, may enjoin one or another mating system. I'll have more to say later on about some of the processes that give rise to different mating systems. Until then, one need merely consider the changes taking place in marriage and childrearing in industrial societies to realize that it is cultural selection and not closely controlling genetic predispositions that accounts for today's high rates of divorce, declining fertility rates, and an increase in people living alone. Nor does it account for the strange new high-tech forms of making babies by uniting ovum and sperm in a laboratory dish and planting the conspectus in a biological or surrogate mother's uterus.

In sum, each of these variations is as "natural" as the other, since each represents a socially constructed pattern of mating dictated by prevailing social and natural conditions, rather than by specific genetic instructions. It is certainly human nature to have a powerful sex drive and appetite, and it is certainly human nature to be able to find diverse ways of satisfying these species-given needs and appetites. But it is not human nature to be exclusively promiscuous or polyandrous or monogamous or polygynous.

GENES
AGAINST
INCEST?

HY IS IT THAT around the globe people feel queasy, disgusted, horrified, enraged to find out that a father and daughter, or a mother and son, or a brother and sister have slept together? Can it be that something so widespread and powerful as the taboo against incest is also a product of cultural rather than natural selection? Yes, I am rather convinced of it. To be more specific, I think that the incest taboos are, at bottom, another manifestation of the principle of exchange. I'll explain what I mean in a moment.

The theory that incest-avoidance is under tight genetic control holds that since mother-son, father-daughter, brother-sister prohibitions are well-nigh universal, they cannot be accounted for by cultural selection. This is a very shaky inference. A universal practice can result from cultural selection as readily as from natural selection. Every society today without exception makes fire, boils water, cooks food. Does this mean that these practices are under close genetic control? Of course not. Some cultural traits are just so useful that they get passed on from one culture to another or get invented and reinvented over and over again. Therefore, the wide occurrence of incest taboos may merely show that they are extremely useful, not that they are innate.

Besides, the taboo on incest is not all that universal. Rulers of several ancient kingdoms and empires were allowed to marry full sisters. Although the evidence about how often such marriages actually took place remains scanty, the fact is that they did occur. In ancient Peru, Tupa Inca married his full sister; his son, Huayna Capac, married a full sister; and Huascar, one of Huayna Capac's sons by another wife, also married a full sister. During Egypt's Ptolemaic dynasty, eight out of thirteen pharaohs took a full sister or half-sister as one of their wives. Similar patterns of permissible or actual brother-sister marriages prevailed among Hawaiian royalty, the emperors of ancient China, and in several East African kingdoms.

Brother-sister marriage was not confined to royalty. During the first 300 years A.D., Egyptian commoners widely practiced brother-sister marriage. Keith Hopkins, a historian who has made a careful study of this period, reports that brother-sister marriages were regarded as perfectly normal relationships, openly mentioned in documents concerning family matters and in business negotiations when selling crops, engaging in law suits, and petitioning officials.

Moreover, we have no way of knowing the actual rate of incest in societies where those who break the taboos face severe punishment if they are discovered. Today, in the United States, psychiatrists, social workers, and law enforcement agencies report that the sexual abuse of children is on the rise. Father-daughter incest, one of the most common forms of sexual abuse, is punishable by up to thirty or forty years in prison. If people innately feel so disinclined to commit incest, why do they persist in doing it, even at the risk of such severe punishment? Given the hypersexual history of our species, our continuous sexual receptivity and preparedness, the high incidence of sexual "affairs," and of other sexual liaisons prohibited by law and public opinion, is it not likely that incest is a temptation that many people experience but avoid out of fear of detection, punishment, and public disgrace?

Advocates of genetic theories of incest-avoidance long ago recognized that it was unlikely that genes contained definite instructions for shutting down sex drives in the presence of siblings, children, and parents. Following the lead of Edward Westermark, they propose, instead, that there is an innate tendency for members of the opposite sex to find each other sexually uninspiring if they have been brought up in close physical proximity to each other during infancy and childhood. Westermark's principle is much in favor among sociobiologists because it provides a way out of the dilemma posed by the relatively high rates at which brother-sister incest may sometimes take place, as in Roman Egypt. If the brother and sister were brought up apart from each other in different houses or by different nurses and caretakers, then, according to the Westermark principle, they might very well find each other sexually attractive enough to mate.

Behind the Westermark theory and other genetic explanations of incest-avoidance is the assumption that close inbreeding results in an increased likelihood that individuals who carry defective genes will mate with each other and give birth to children who suffer from pathological conditions that lower their rate of reproduction. Also, simply by lowering the amount of genetic diversity in a population, inbreeding might have an adverse effect on its ability to adapt to new diseases or other novel environmental hazards. So, those individuals who find themselves "turned off" through the Westermark effect would have avoided inbreeding, reproduced at a higher rate, and gradually replaced those who were "turned on" by their close kin.

There are several soft spots in this part of the argument. It is true that in large modern populations incest leads to a high rate of stillbirths and congenitally diseased and impaired children. But the same results need not occur from close inbreeding practiced in small preagricultural societies. Inbreeding in small preagricultural societies leads to the gradual elimination of harmful recessive genes because such societies have little tolerance for infants and children who are congenitally handicapped and impaired. Lack of support for such children eliminates the harmful genetic variations from future generations, and results in populations that carry a much smaller "load" of harmful gene variants than modern populations.

To test the Westermark theory, one cannot point to the mere occurrence of incest-avoidance. One has to show that sexual ardor cools when people grow up together, independent of any existing norms that call for incest-avoidance. Since this cannot be done experimentally without controlling the lives of human subjects, advocates of the theory lean heavily on two famous case studies that allegedly demonstrate the predicted loss of sexual ardor. The first of these concerns a Taiwanese form of marriage called adopt-a-daughter-marry-a-sister. A senior couple adopts a young girl from another family. They raise her along with their son with the intention of making her his bride. Since the son and his bride will remain with his parents after the marriage, the seniors train their adopted daughter to be obedient to them so that later there will be harmony in the household. Studies have shown that these marriages, in which husband and wife grow up together at close quarters, lead to fewer children, greater adultery, and higher divorce rates than normal marriages, in which future wives and husbands grow up in separate households. But these observations scarcely confirm Westermark's theory. The Taiwanese explicitly recognize that adopt-a-daughter-marry-a-sister is an inferior, even humiliating, form of marriage. Normally to seal a marriage bond, the families of bride and groom exchange considerable wealth as a sign of their support for the new-lyweds. But these exchanges are smaller or absent altogether in adopt-a-daughter-marry-a-sister. This makes it impossible to prove that sexual disinterest rather than chagrin and disappointment over being treated like second-class citizens is the source of the couple's infertility.

The second case used to confirm Westermark's theory concerns an alleged lack of sexual interest displayed by boys and girls who attended the same classes from nursery school to age six in the Israeli cooperative community known as a kibbutz. Allegedly these boys and girls were so thoroughly "turned off" that among marriages contracted by people who were reared in a kibbutz, not one involved men or women who had been reared together from birth to age six. This seems impressive, but there is a fatal flaw. Out of a total of 2,516 marriages, there were 200 in which both partners were reared in the same kibbutz, although they were not in the same class for six years. Given the fact that all kibbutz youth were inducted into the army and commingled with tens of thousands of potential mates from outside their kibbutz before they got married, the rate of 200 marriages from within the same kibbutz is far more than could be expected by chance. One must now ask, of the 200 marriages from within the same kibbutz, what was the chance that not a single one would be between a boy and a girl who had attended the same class? Since girls were generally three years younger than the boys they married, only a very few marriages between people who were reared for six years in the same class could be expected. Actually, it turns out that five marriages did occur between boys and girls who had been reared together for part of the first six years of their life. Since Westermark's theory does not predict how long it takes for reared-together boys and girls to lose their interest in each other, these five marriages actually disconfirm the theory.

THE MYTH OF
THE GREAT TABOO

CULTURAL SELECTION THEORIES of incest fit the evidence better than natural selection theories. They go back to E. B. Tylor, one of the nineteenth-century founders of British anthropology. Tylor proposed that the basic set of incest taboos originated during the foraging phase of cultural evolution when people were compelled by the limited availability of plants and animals to live in small bands (the equivalent of protohominid troops) of about twenty to thirty members. Studies of modern-day foraging bands show that in such groups the prevention of matings within the band is essential, not because of the danger of having physically impaired offspring, but because groups of that size are too small to satisfy their biopsychological needs and appetites on their own and risk extinction if they do not establish peaceful and cooperative relationships with their neighbors.

An endogamous band—one that mated within the group—would be confronted by perpetually hostile neighbors and confined to a territory that might prove too small in years of droughts, floods, and other climatic perturbations. With only twenty to thirty people, it would also run the risk of an unlucky string of births that would leave too few women to breed a new generation. Bands that form alliances with each other exploit larger territories, participate in larger breeding populations, assist each other in defense against intractable warlike neighbors, and help each other in times of food scarcity. How could such alliances have originated?

Since exchanges of goods and services lay at the foundation of the harmony within afarensis or habilis troops, it was no great innovation to create alliances between neighbors through the exchange of valued goods and services. What was the most effective form of exchange open to them? Through trial and error they inevitably discovered that it was the exchange of their most valuable possessions, their sons and daughters, brothers and sisters, to live, work, and reproduce in each other's midst. But precisely because human beings are so valuable, each group is tempted to keep sons and daughters and brothers and sisters at home, to enjoy their economic, sentimental, and sexual services. As long as the exchange of persons proceeds smoothly, the loss of one is compensated by the acquisition of another, and both sides gain from the resulting alliance. But any prolonged delay in reciprocating, especially if caused by the refusal of one group to live up to the bargain, would have devastating effects on all concerned. The dread and horror and anger surrounding incest reflect the dangers to which a breakdown in the exchange of persons exposes all members of the group, and at the same time function as an antidote to the temptation felt by people who have been brought up together to have sex together.

The economic and social value of incest-avoidance remained high throughout the evolution of more complex societies after the beginnings of agriculture. Among agricultural groups, marital exchange between extended family households is still essential for economic and social well-being. Intermarrying households have an advantage in land clearance, harvests, and ditching and mounding operations that require temporary concentrations of labor. Furthermore, where warfare poses a threat to group survival, the ability to mobilize large numbers of warriors is decisive. Militaristic, male-dominated village societies frequently use women as pawns in the establishment of alliances. These alliances do not necessarily eliminate warfare between intermarrying groups, but they make it less common, as might be expected from the presence of sisters and daughters in the enemy's ranks.

Alliances based on exogamic exchanges also formed a vital part of the political and military strategy of ruling elites in ancient kingdoms and empires. Royal brother-sister marriage proclaimed that the incestuous pair were so powerful and exalted that they did not have to abide by the principles of marital exchange. Yet, the pharaohs, Incas, and Chinese emperors always had multiple marriages that included women from royal lineages who were cousins or even nonrelatives as a means of forming and reinforcing alliances with potential rivals for the throne.

With the evolution of money, of buying and selling, and of other price-market forms of exchange, the importance of incest-avoidance as a means of establishing intergroup alliances is no longer as great as it was in previous epochs. Today, money buys everything (well, almost everything), including friends and allies. True, the right kind of marriage may still be the key to worldly success, but families nowadays need a good job or a fat annuity more than they need incest taboos in order to enjoy peace, security, and the good things in life.

I should point out that one of the consequences of incest that keeps the emotions boiling may have little to do with incest per se. Mother-son and father-daughter incest not only threatens the maintenance of external relationships, but it threatens the basic bonds of family organization. After all, these two forms of incest are also two forms of adultery. Mother-son incest is a special threat to the institution of marriage. Not only is the wife "double-dealing" against her husband, but the son is "double-dealing" against his father. This may explain why the least common and most feared and abhorred form of incest is that between mother and son (as in the Ancient Greek myth of Oedipus). It follows that father-daughter incest will be somewhat more common since husbands enjoy double standards of sexual conduct more often than wives and are less vulnerable to punishment for adultery. Finally, the same consideration suggests an explanation for the relatively high frequency of brother-sister matings and an additional reason for their legitimization in elite classes— they do not conflict with father-mother adultery rules.

The Great Taboo, in other words, is greatly overrated. It is not just one thing but a set of sexual and mating preferences and avoidances that are selectively subject to change during the evolution of culture. In this age of sexual liberation and experiment, for example, brother-sister mating is probably on the verge of becoming just another "kinky" sexual preference of little interest to society, provided that incestuous siblings use contraceptive safeguards and seek genetic counseling. It has already been decriminalized in Sweden. Father-daughter, mother-son incest is another story, not only because of its overlap with adultery but because the age differences involved imply lack of informed consent if not outright rape and child abuse.

For many pages now, I have been casting an eye over some of the diverse ways in which humans seek to satisfy their powerful sexual drive and appetite. I hope I have shown that the origins and continuing evolution of the choice of heterosexual partners can better be understood by invoking cultural selection rather than by invoking close control by genetic propensities related to reproductive success. Permit me now to change the focus to an even more fundamental question: Do humans instinctively attempt to maximize their reproductive success?

THE MYTH
OF THE
PROCREATIVE
IMPERATIVE

AMONG NONHUMAN PRIMATES, sexual stimulation usually leads to coitus and coitus virtually guarantees conception. And once sperm and ovum unite, pregnancy usually proceeds relentlessly to the stage of labor and birth. Thereafter, powerful hormones compel the mother to suckle her infant, carry it about, and protect it from danger.

In human beings, this system of genetically controlled guarantees for linking sex with the birth and the rearing of progeny no longer exists. Sex does not guarantee conception; conception does not lead relentlessly to birth; and birth does not compel the mother to nurse and protect the newborn. Cultures have evolved learned techniques and practices that can prevent each step in this process from occurring. For better or worse, we have been decisively liberated from the reproductive imperative that reigns throughout the rest of the animal kingdom. Unlike every other creature on earth, therefore, our behavior no longer gets selected exclusively for its ability to increase reproductive success; rather, it gets selected for its ability to increase the satisfaction of our drives and needs, even if this does not increase or even if it actually lowers the rate of reproductive success for ourselves and our closest relatives.

What made this momentous change possible is that natural selection never endowed modern sapiens with a procreative drive or appetite. It merely endowed us with a powerful sexual drive and appetite and an internal hiding place where the fetus could grow. In the absence of a strong procreative drive or appetite, cultural selection was able to co-opt all of the psychological and physiological mechanisms that formerly linked sex to reproduction.

The decoupling of sex from its reproductive consequences long preceded the age of technologically advanced contraceptives and abortions. For starters, preindustrial couples made use of the contraceptive effects of prolonged and intensive nursing to lengthen the interval between births. They avoided untold additional numbers of births by practicing nonreproductive forms of sex such as masturbation, homosexuality, and coitus interruptus. Then, if unwanted pregnancies developed, they tried to abort the fetus by drinking toxic concoctions, twisting tight bands and ropes around the pregnant woman's abdomen, jumping on a board laid across her stomach until blood spurted out, or jabbing pointed sticks into her uterus. Because these techniques were as likely to destroy the mother as the fetus, abortion was far less common in the past than it is today. Nonetheless, in a survey of world cultures, George Devereux found that 464 societies practiced one or another form of abortion.

It seems to me that the high frequency of noncoital sex, contraception, and abortion conclusively shows that women have no closely controlled genetic predisposition to become pregnant or to protect the fetus. But what about the next step? Surely humans have an innate predisposition to nurse, protect, and rear their infant progeny? The evidence against this notion may be less well known, but I regret to say that it is equally convincing. In fact, because of the dangers mothers confront in practicing abortions in preindustrial societies, women often prefer to destroy the infant rather than the fetus. I want to stress the fact that infanticides are not merely committed by direct means such as strangulation, drowning, exposure, and head bashing, but more commonly by indirect means such as slow starvation, physical and psychological neglect, and "accidents."

Anthropologists have only recently awakened to the likelihood that a large portion of infant and child deaths formerly attributed to unavoidable starvation and disease may actually represent subtle forms of de facto infanticide. Indirect, surreptitious, and unconscious denials of nurturance to infants and children are extremely common, especially in Third World countries that combine the condemnation of infanticide with the condemnation of contraception and abortion. Under these circumstances, mothers may be motivated to unburden themselves of unwanted children, but may find it necessary to hide their intentions not only to others but to themselves as well. Research carried out by Nancy Scheper-Hughes in northeast Brazil, where 200 out of 1,000 babies die within the first year of life, provides insights into the complex psychological nuances that affect a mother's decision to rear or not to rear a particular baby. Scheper-Hughes found that women depicted the deaths of certain children as a "blessing." They habitually judged each child on a rough scale of readiness or fitness for life. Children whose mothers perceived them as being quick, sharp, active, and physically well developed received more food and medical attention than their sisters and brothers. Others, whose mothers perceived them to be lethargic, passive, and as having a "ghostlike" or "animallike" appearance, received less food and medical attention and were in fact likely to become ill and die within the first year of life. Mothers spoke of them as children who wanted to die, whose will to live was not sufficiently strong or developed.

When children with the fatal stigmata expire, their mothers do not display grief. They told Scheper-Hughes that there was no remedy and that even if anyone had tried to treat the disease, the child would "never be right." Some say that the death was "God's will," and others that their baby had been called to heaven to become a "little angel."

I myself had many occasions to witness funeral processions for babies during the course of fieldwork in northeast Brazil. Down the street came an older child of the family holding the tiny open wooden casket with the deceased in view; then a group of skipping and laughing children, followed at the rear by father and mother, holding hands and grinning sheepishly.

I cannot provide precise numbers on how often human parents have used direct and indirect infanticide to rid themselves of unwanted progeny. Joseph Birdsell estimated that the Australian Aborigines destroyed as many as 50 percent of all infants. Various samples drawn from preindustrial societies indicate that between 53 percent and 76 percent practiced direct forms of infanticide. Whatever the precise figures, enough is known to warrant the statement that human fathers and mothers are not "hard-wired" to do everything they can to enhance the life prospects of their progeny.

The first European explorers to reach China were shocked at the wastage of infant lives. They were even more shocked when the first census figures became available in the nineteenth century indicating that in some regions boys outnumbered girls four to one. The greatest imbalance coincided with regions of rural poverty and landlessness, such as the lower Yangtze Valley and Amoy, in the province of Fukien. In these areas, parents would not raise more than two daughters. Out of 175 female babies to whom 40 women in Swatow had given birth, 28 were destroyed. Combined samples from various regions show that 62 percent of girls born alive, as compared with 40 percent of boys, did not survive to the age of ten. In Fukien province as a whole, between 30 percent and 40 percent of female infants were not permitted to live, while in particular villages, rates of direct or indirect infanticide could range from 10 percent to 80 percent of live female births.

Northern India was another region where people systematically killed unwanted infants, especially females. Early nineteenth-century censuses indicated that boys outnumbered girls four to one among certain castes in Gujurat; and three to one in the northern provinces. British administrators were astounded by recurrent reports of castes and villages that prevented even one female baby from surviving past infancy.

Europeans expressed horror when they found out how common infanticide was in Asia. They seemed oblivious to the fact that it was almost as common in Europe itself. Christianity notwithstanding, European parents destroyed large numbers of unwanted babies. To accommodate laws against homicide, they favored indirect rather than direct methods. One peculiarly European form of indirect infanticide was called overlaying. Mothers took their nursing infants to bed and "accidentally" rolled over on them, suffocating them. Europeans also made much use of "wet nursing" to rid themselves of unwanted babies. Parents contracted for the services of surrogate mothers who had the reputation of being "she-butchers" to nurse children. The low fee and the poor condition of these wet nurses guaranteed that life would be brief for the unwanted. Europeans also rid themselves of large numbers of infants by abandoning them in front of government foundling hospitals whose main function appears to have been to keep small corpses from accumulating in the streets and waterways. To facilitate the collection of unwanted infants, the French installed revolving night depositories at the entrances of their foundling facilities. Admissions rose from 40,000 in 1784 to 138,000 in 1822. By 1830, there were 270 revolving boxes in use throughout France, with 336,297 infants legally abandoned during the decade 1824–1833. "Mothers who left their babies in the box knew that they were consigning them to death almost as surely as if they dropped them in the river." Between 80 percent and 90 percent of the children in these institutions died during their first year of life.

Just as pro-choice activists define the fetus as a nonperson, societies that tolerate or encourage infanticide usually define newborn infants as nonpersons. Almost every society has rituals that confer upon an infant and a child the status of being a member of the human race. They baptize it, give it a name, put a garment on it, or show the face to the sun or moon. In all cultures that practice systematic direct infanticide, the unwanted child is destroyed before these ceremonies take place. On the basis of his intensive study of birth records in two nineteenth-century Japanese villages, G. William Skinner of Stanford University estimates that one-third of all couples destroyed their firstborn child. Another researcher, Susan Hanley, states that infanticide was so prevalent in premodern Japan that it became the custom not to congratulate a family on the birth of a child until it was learned whether or not the child was to be raised. If the answer was negative, nothing was said; if positive, the usual congratulations and gifts were offered.

All of this would not be possible if the bond between parents and child were a natural outcome of pregnancy and delivery. Whatever the hormonal basis for mother love and father love, there evidently is not a sufficient force in human affairs to protect infants from culturally imposed rules and goals that define the conditions under which parents should or should not strive to keep them alive.

I once supposed that the regular systematic worldwide decoupling of sex from reproduction would be sufficient to prove that reproductive success is not the governing principle of cultural as well as natural selection. But sociologists do not regard this evidence as conclusive or even relevant. They argue that by preventing a certain number of conceptions and births and by destroying a certain number of infants, parents merely make it possible for the maximum number of children to survive and reproduce where resources are insufficient for all to survive and reproduce. I will respond to this argument in a moment. But first let me indicate how I think cultural selection sets the number of children parents decide to have and to bring up.

HOW MANY CHILDREN?

*M*ODERN-DAY INDUSTRIAL-AGE parents have forgotten just how useful children can be around the house. But in other times and cultures, adults knew that if they didn't manage to rear a certain number of children, life would be extremely harsh. Despite the situation that prevails in industrial societies, children have almost always been expected to "earn their keep" in a material sense. In the Brazilian Amazon, Thomas Gregor recorded these poignant words of advice addressed by the village headman to his son: "My son, Kupate, make more children. Like a copulating frog, thrust your semen deep inside. Look at yourself all alone with no kinsmen. Make children and they will help you later. They will get fish for you when they grow up and you are old."

In preindustrial farm families, children start to do household chores when they are still toddlers. By age six, they help gather firewood and carry water for cooking and washing; take care of younger siblings; plant, weed, and harvest crops; grind and pound grains; peel and scrape tubers; take food to adults in the fields; sweep floors; and run errands. By puberty, they are ready to cook meals, work full-time in the fields, make pots, containers, mats, and nets, and hunt, herd, fish, or do almost anything that adults do, although somewhat less efficiently. Studies carried out among Javanese peasant families by anthropologist Benjamin White show that boys of twelve to fourteen years of age contribute thirty-three hours of economically valuable work per week and that girls nine to eleven contribute about thirty-eight hours. Altogether, children perform about half of all work done by household members. White also found that Javanese children themselves do most of the work needed to rear and maintain their siblings, freeing adult women to engage in income-producing tasks. Meade Cain, a researcher for the Population Council, came to similar conclusions about the benefits of child labor in rural Bangladesh. Male children begin to produce more than they consume by age twelve. By age fifteen they have already made up for all the years during which they were not self-supporting.

In past eras, children became more valuable as parents grew older and lost the physical strength to support themselves by hunting, foraging, or farming. Aging parents in Third World countries cannot rely on company pension funds, social security payments, welfare allotments, food stamps, or bank accounts; they can rely only on their children.

The faster children pass from consuming more than they produce to producing more than they consume, the greater the number of children parents will strive to bring up. But in seeking to take full advantage of their offspring's potential contribution to parental well-being, couples must allow for the fact that even if they make a total commitment to rearing each child born, some will unavoidably fall victim to injuries and diseases at an early age. Consequently, couples commonly "overshoot" the targeted ideal and increase the number of births in proportion to the rates of infant and child mortality. In rural India, for example, studies have shown that many couples consider three children to be optimal, but knowing that more than one out of three children born will die before reaching adulthood, they will not use contraceptives or other means of separating sex from reproduction until after they have had four or five children. This is why one need not fear that efforts to reduce infant and child mortality will lead to a worsening of the population problem. Healthier babies generally mean fewer babies per couple. But one cannot expect that lowering infant and child mortality rates will actually lower the rate of population growth since, if nothing else changes, couples will still aim at having the same number of living children.

Third World parents also take into account the different kinds of costs and benefits that can be expected from rearing male children versus female children. Where men make a more critical contribution to agricultural production than women, Third World couples prefer to rear boy babies rather than girl babies. As I'll show later in more detail, brute strength frequently accounts for the preference. Although men are only marginally stronger than women, marginal differences in productivity can mean life or death. The preference for boys is especially strong where hard-packed soils must be prepared with a hand-held plow and a pair of reluctant yoked animals. This is true of wheat-growing north India, where peasant couples set their sights on rearing at least two boys to maturity and are quite happy not to have any daughters at all. But to ensure survival of at least two males, they must "overshoot" for three. And since in all probability some births will be female, they can easily go through five or six births before they achieve their target of three survivable sons. In southern India and most of Southeast Asia and Indonesia, the principal crop is not wheat but rice. Plowing rice paddies takes second place to "puddling"—walking animals around in the mud— while the most critical operations are transplanting and weeding, both of which tasks women can perform as well as men. In these regions parents are not biased against female children and rear as many girls as boys.

Japan's country folk were at one time the world's most efficient managers of human reproduction. During the nineteenth century, Japanese farm couples precisely fitted the size and sexual composition of their broods to the size and fertility of their land holdings. The small-holder's ideal was two children; one boy and one girl; people with larger holdings aimed for two boys and one or two girls. But the Japanese did not stop there! As expressed in a still-popular saying, "first a girl, then a boy," they tried to rear a daughter first and a son second. According to G. William Skinner, this ideal reflected the practice of assigning much of the task of rearing firstborn sons to an older sister. It also reflected the expectation that the firstborn son would replace his father as the farm's manager at an age when the father was ready to retire, and the son was not yet so old as to have grown surly while waiting to take over. A further complexity was the age at which couples got married. An older man would not dare to delay having a son; and so, if the firstborn was a male, he would count himself fortunate. Since the parents had no way of telling the sex of a child before birth, they were able to achieve these precise reproductive goals only by practicing systematic infanticide.

Any reduction of the value of child labor in agriculture can be expected to depress the rate of childrearing. If, at the same time, the expected economic returns from parental investment in children can be increased by sending them to school and training them to get white-collar jobs, birth rates may fall very rapidly. Parents, in effect, substitute a strategy of rearing only a few well-educated but potentially well-paid and influential children for a strategy of raising a lot of poorly educated farm hands. Numerous case studies support this conclusion, but I'll just give one key example. In the 1960s, Harvard University researchers selected a village called Manupur, located in the state of Punjab in northwest India, as the site of a project that aimed at reducing reproduction rates by providing contraceptives and vasectomies. In a follow-up study, Mahmood Mamdani reported that the villagers had no trouble accepting the idea of family planning, but they accepted sterilization and contraceptives only after they had reached their target of two survivable males. "Why pay 2,500 rupees to an extra [hired] hand?" they wanted to know. "Why not have a son?" Fifteen years later, researchers returning to Manupur were astonished to find that women were using contraceptives to achieve substantial reductions in birth rates and that the number of sons desired per couple had fallen considerably. The underlying reason for this shift was that after the first study had been completed, the villagers became involved in a number of technological and economic changes that made the Punjab one of India's most developed states. The increased use of tractors, irrigation wells, chemical weed-killers, and kerosene cooking stoves had greatly reduced the value of children as farm hands. Children were no longer needed to take the cattle to pasture, weed the crops, or collect cattle dung to provide cooking fuel. At the same time, Manupur villagers were becoming aware of opportunities for employment in commercial and governmental firms and offices. They needed to acquire new literacy and mathematical skills just to run their mechanized and bank-financed farm operations. Many parents now want to keep their children in school rather than have them contribute manual labor. As a result, high school enrollment rose from 63 percent to 81 percent for boys and from 29 percent to 63 percent for girls. And Manupur's parents now want at least one son to have a white-collar job so that the family will not be entirely in agriculture; many even plan to send sons and daughters to college.

There is an interesting resemblance between rates of reproduction among disadvantaged ethnic and racial minorities and those of Third World countries. In both cases, it appears as if people are being driven to have more children than they can afford to rear, and at the expense of parental well-being. But I doubt if this is what is really going on. In the United States, for example, it seems as if inner-city women get pregnant over and over again in reckless disregard of their own futures. Yet I think that the key to this situation is not that they cannot control their sexuality but that by getting pregnant they become entitled to welfare subventions that substantially raise the net benefits of rearing children over the net benefits that nonwelfare women of their class can expect from their pregnancies. In New York City, having a child entitles a welfare mother to monthly support payment, housing subsidies, free medical care, and educational benefits. Ghetto mothers also receive support from a wide network of kin and temporary husbands. And ghetto children, unlike middle-class children, begin to pay for their keep in their teens with incomes derived from part-time jobs, petty theft, and drug sales. Furthermore, inner-city welfare women want sons almost as badly as Indian families want them. Studies conducted by Jagna Sharff in the Lower East Side of Manhattan show that mothers need sons for protection against thieves, muggers, and hostile neighbors. And with homicide the principal cause of death among young ghetto males, ghetto mothers, like Indian farmers, must "overshoot" their target if they want this protection. Given the generally dismal prospects that ill-educated ghetto women confront when they try to compete with educated middle-class women for jobs and status, they are probably no worse off having three or four children than having one or two. Certainly they are better off, on the average, having one or two children than having none, in the circumstances in which they find themselves.

Of course, the life to which these children are condemned guarantees the perpetuation of an underclass at great expense and moral shame to the rest of society. But the irrationality of the system does not lie at the level of the individual ghetto mother. It is not she who created the ineffectual educational system, the lack of good jobs, or the cancer of racial discrimination. It is not her fault that she is paid more to have children than not to have them. The examples I have been discussing show that parents adjust their investment in childrearing to bring about improvements in the net contribution that children make to their well-being. Therefore, one can predict whether reproductive rates will go up or down without taking into consideration the effect that a particular adjustment will have on the overall rate of reproductive success. All one has to know is whether the parents' biopsychological needs, drives, and appetites under the particular circumstances are better served by having more or fewer children. Yet the possibility remains that natural selection has some-how been able to ensure that any adjustments up or down in rearing children that humans may make in conformity with principles of cultural selection will also always maximize overall reproductive success in conformity with principles of natural selection. What is needed to break this impasse is evidence that downward changes in numbers of children reared per woman often unambiguously lower rather than raise the overall rates of reproductive success. This evidence lies close at hand.

REPRODUCTIVE
FAILURE

RECENT DEMOGRAPHIC EVENTS in modernizing parts of the Third World such as the Punjab strongly resemble the great changes in reproduction rates that marked transitions from agrarian to industrial societies in the nineteenth and twentieth centuries. As in Manupur, shifting costs and benefits associated with childrearing account for the lowered reproduction rates that have come to prevail in advanced industrial societies east and west. Why? Because industrialization raised the cost of rearing children. Skills essential for earning a living took longer to acquire. So parents had to wait longer before they could receive any economic benefits from their offspring. At the same time, the whole pattern of how people earned their living changed. No longer did family members work on the family farm or in the family shop. Instead, they earned wages as individuals in factories and offices. The return flow of benefits from rearing children came to depend on their willingness to help out in the medical and financial crises that beset parents in old age. But longer life spans and spiraling medical costs now make it increasingly unrealistic for parents to expect such help from their children. Industrial nations have no choice but to substitute old-age and medical insurance and retirement homes for the preindustrial system in which children took care of their aged parents. No wonder that in many industrial nations the fertility rate has fallen below the 2.1 children per woman needed to prevent a population from shrinking. Further transformation of industrial economies from the production of goods to service-and-information production is exacerbating this trend. Since modern middle-class couples will not rear children unless both husband and wife have incomes, marriages are being postponed. Late-marrying couples are aiming at only one child, and more and more young people are refusing to invest in the traditional forms of familial and sexual togetherness.

Over the entire course of this transition from large to small families, high rates to low rates of rearing children, and high rates to low rates of population growth, the standard of living of the working and middle classes has steadily improved. With the exception of certain ethnic and racial minorities, more people today enjoy access to more of the basic necessities of life, such as food and shelter, and to a wider variety of luxuries, such as entertainment and travel, than people did 200 years ago. It is therefore surely incorrect to insist that the postponement of marriage, the delay in having children, and the decline in birthing from over four per mother or more early in the last century to two per mother or less today is nature's way of assuring that reproduction is maximized. When young people in the full flush of fecundity invest in college and graduate school rather than in nurseries, buy stereo televisions, gourmet meals, and $20,000 sports cars rather than bassinets, baby food, and $20 strollers, and don't have children until they reach their thirties, one can safely conclude that they are responding to something other than a naturally selected tendency to rear as many children as they possibly can.

It looks as if those who can have the most children are having the fewest. To test for this inverse relationship, the demographer Daniel Vining compared the number of children fathered by white men listed in *Who's Who* with the average number of children of same-age white women in the population as a whole. Starting with the cohort born from 1875 to 1879, Vining found that the average number of children born to the nation's most educated and successful males has generally been substantially lower than the average per woman. When white women born in 1875 were having 3.50 children, the *Who's Who* male was having only 2.23 children. For the cohort born from 1935 to 1939, the ratio was 2.92 to 2.30. Vining obtained a similar result for men listed in the Japanese *Who's Who*. Over a span of almost one century, Japan's most educated and esteemed men had only about 70 percent of the number of children that the average woman in the same cohort had.

Today's service-and-information middle classes are scarcely the first humans to exhibit a preference for children that is inversely related to the resources available for rearing them. In nineteenth-century India, for example, the most lopsided ratios of young males to young females occurred among the Rajputs and other high-ranking military and land-owning castes. As reported by British officials, the rajahs of Mynpoorie, the crème de la crème of Rajput aristocracy, systematically killed off every one of their female heirs: "Here when a son, a nephew, a grandson was born to the reigning chief, the event was announced to the neighboring city by the large discharge of wall-pieces and matchlocks; but centuries had passed away and no infant daughter had been known to smile within those walls."

Sociobiologists have attempted to deal with the puzzle of female infanticide among elite castes by arguing that wealthy and powerful parents actually have more offspring even if they rear only males. The logic is that each elite male can have sex with scores of women and father scores of children, while daughters are limited to no more than a dozen or so pregnancies no matter how many men they have sex with. So by rearing sons instead of daughters, elite parents are maximizing their reproductive success. But if the reproductive behavior of the rajahs of Mynpoorie had really been selected for its contribution to reproductive success, children born to daughters would have been a welcome addition to those born to sons, because being the crème de la crème, the rajahs could easily afford to provide the necessities of life for daughters as well as sons.

Cultural selection, not natural selection, accounts best for the practice of elite female infanticide. The root of it is the struggle on the part of elite men to keep their lands and other sources of wealth and power from being divided among too many heirs. It was not reproductive success that governed their behavior, but a refusal to give up the luxurious style of life to which they had grown accustomed. Having lots of children with concubines, mistresses, and courtiers did not pose a threat to the Rajputs because these children could not back up a claim to a share of the estate with a threat of force. But sisters and their male children did pose such a threat because their husbands would have been high-caste Rajputs themselves, capable of demanding a portion of the estate. By destroying their daughters and sisters, the Rajput elites were employing one extreme of a continuum of strategies all of which aimed at preventing the dispersal of wealth and power among females and their descendants. The most common solution was to preempt a woman's claim to landed wealth by having her husband accept a payment in jewels, gold, silk, or cash, known as a dowry, in lieu of any future claims on the estate. To this day in northern India, reluctance to pay dowry for daughters or sisters results in high rates of indirect female infanticide and lopsided ratios of boys to girls. The Rajputs simply took the next step, eliminating the need to pay any dowry by refusing to rear any female infants. (More about dowry later.)

I do not see how we can avoid concluding that our kind is by nature just as likely to act in ways that reduce rates of reproductive success as to act in ways that increase it. When having more children increases their biopsychological well-being, people will have more children; when having fewer children increases their biopsychological well-being, people will have fewer children. Let us not be confused by the fact that throughout most of history and prehistory, modes of production were such as to be more likely to reward those who could rear large numbers of children. With industrialization, this likelihood was reversed. Large numbers of children became an obstacle to maximizing parental biopsychological well-being. And so people generally chose to have fewer children. To insist that having few or even no children is actually a strategy that leads to greater reproductive success at some future date is to render inexplicable one of the most fundamental features of modern life. There are a billion people in the world today who crave a second income, a second car, and a second house more than they crave a second child. Cultural selection, not natural selection, has brought us to this point, and cultural and natural selection will get us to another, whatever it may be.

THE NEED
TO BE
LOVED

F RATES OF MAKING BABIES depended exclusively on their contribution to satisfying parental needs for air, water, food, sex, bodily comfort, and security, fertility rates in Japan and the industrialized West would have dropped to zero by now. On a strictly dollars-and-cents basis, modern-day parents have virtually no hope of recouping their expenditures for day schools and kindergartens, baby sitters and pediatricians, stereos and designer jeans, summer camps and orthodontists, music lessons and encyclopedias, tricycles, bicycles, and cars, and college tuition. Not to mention room and board for eighteen years. Add it all up and you have a bill that's over $200,000. And that does not include the cash value of the services parents render while nursing, bathing, diapering, and burping their little one or the bills for sleepless nights and jangled nerves the next day. Here again, one might be tempted to see the selfish gene at work, compelling people to reproduce like salmon leaping upstream, no matter what the cost to themselves. But biological parents are not the only ones who are prone to rearing children at great expense. How are we to explain the heavy demands placed on adoption agencies and the thriving black market where desperate couples pay cash for babies? Why should adopted children, who have no genetic relationship to their foster parents, be raised with the same extravagant care that parents lavish on "their own flesh and blood"?

I see no way to answer these questions other than to postulate the existence of another biopsychological component of human nature. Children fulfill exceptionally well not a parental need to reproduce, but a need for close, affectionate, emotional relationships with supportive, concerned, trustworthy, and approving beings. In short, we need children because we need to be loved. A long series of studies initiated by Harry Harlow and associates in the 1950s provided experimental evidence that primates brought up in isolation, but otherwise well cared for, quickly turn into the equivalent of

230

human nervous wrecks. Fortunately, no one has tried raising human babies in solitary confinement to see how they react to a lack of companionship and emotional support, but plenty of evidence from clinical psychology shows that people who have been deprived of parental affection during their early years have difficulty functioning as adults. Up until the late 1980s, the standard policy with regard to premature infants placed in incubators was to touch them as little as possible. Through the work of psychologist Tiffany Field, it was found that premature infants who received a gentle massage for fifteen minutes three times a day gained weight 47 percent faster and were ready to leave the hospital six days earlier than infants who were not massaged. After eight months massaged infants were still heavier than the others and outperformed their unmassaged agemates on tests of mental and motor ability. But love is not selfless; it requires an exchange just like every other human bond. And in the support parents lavish on children there is a culturally instructed expectation that a balance will be struck with the love and affection that children can be so good at giving in return.

I disagree here with an esteemed colleague, Melvin Konner, of Emory University, who has conducted his own inquiry into the mysteries of modern parenthood. In an eloquent passage in *The Tangled Wing,* Konner likens his own first few months with a colicky baby daughter to an unrequited adolescent love affair:

> You suffered every known variety of emotional abuse, neglect, rejection, anguish, and humiliation. If you managed somehow to steel yourself for an hour, to become convinced that you could stay on an even keel, you were thrown a scrap —here an appropriately timed belch, there a split second of eye contact—and you tumbled back down into the well with the glazed walls, stewing in your damned affectional juices. This set you up nicely for the next diaper change when, almost literally, you would have more offal dumped on your pitiful head.

Konner could understand why his wife, who was "rocked with hormonal changes, filled breasts urging from within," found herself doting on their baby, but he was completely baffled by his own positive parental emotions. Konner simply could not believe

231

that the "crazy emotions" he felt were the product of "cultural nudging"—that he felt these things "because someone told him he should be a good father."

I cannot see how the crazy emotions and hormonal juices that flow after a child is born can explain why reproductive rates have not dropped closer to zero. It is the decision taken nine or more months before the child is born, to remove carefully maintained barriers against conception, that needs to be explained. Faced with twenty years of economic hara-kiri and not so much as a zygote to stir the hormonal brew, the aspiring parents could only be committing themselves to parenthood because they have been nudged culturally to believe that children will help them to solve their need for love.

And let me not forget to point out that in a society whose interpersonal relations are dominated by laissez-faire individualism and ruthless competition for wealth and status, whose hostile streets are filled with crime and neighbors who are afraid to say hello, and where next of kin and best friends are scattered over the face of the earth, the hunger for affection runs very strong. Since couples also suffer from the isolation and alienating effects of consumerism and an impersonal bureaucratic workplace, let me add as an additional inducement for becoming a parent the anticipation that a baby will help us give each other the love we crave.

Why the bleary-eyed and besotted couple submit to their baby's insatiable demands seems evident. Committed to building a temple of love in an indifferent and unloving world, it does not take more than a crumb or two for us to renew our faith in the love to come. Even in their least giving mood, babies respond with warm, wet sucking and mouthing; they grasp your fingers and try to put their arms around you. Already you can anticipate the ardent hugs and kisses of early childhood, the tot who clings to your neck, the four-year-old tucked in bed, whispering "I love you," the six-year-old breathless at the door or running down the path as you come home from work. And with a little more imagination you can see all the way to a grateful son or daughter, dressed in cap and gown, saying, "Thanks, Mom and Dad. I owe it all to you."

The fact that many rewards of parenthood are delayed does not mean that dreams rule the economy of love. As in every other kind of exchange, mere expectation of a return flow will not sustain the bonds indefinitely. The family sanctuary is a fragile temple. People will not forever marry and have children no matter how far the actual experience departs from expectation. Contemporary society has much to fear from growing numbers of couples who argue over rather than delight in their progeny, and from children, themselves corrupted by the social conditions that make the need for love so strong, who metamorphose into monsters with a single mission, to take all and give nothing, not even a belch or a fleeting instant of eye contact. Rising divorce rates suggest that these cruel disappointments are spreading. If so, prepare for the state to intervene. Society needs children even if sexually active adults do not. I wonder how far away we are from corporations chartered to rent the wombs of surrogate mothers to fill targets set by a Bureau of Procreation. Will there also be a choice of surrogate children for those who cannot or will not get a license to raise real human babies? Already any number of pet owners will be glad to tell you that they get as much love from their cats or dogs as others get from people and at less monetary and emotional expense as well.

WHY
HOMOSEXUALITY?

*L*ATEST ESTIMATES place the percentage of adult American men who have had sexual contact to orgasm with another man at 20.3 percent. Given the many ways in which humans separate sexual pleasure from unwanted reproduction, the widespread occurrence of homosexual behavior should come as no surprise. More surprising are the many people who masturbate themselves or their partners, who take birth control pills, use condoms and spermicidal jellies, have abortions, and practice various gymnastic forms of noncoital heterosexuality, but who condemn and ridicule homosexual behavior on the grounds that it is "unnatural." Nor does the linkage between homosexual behavior and AIDS render the fierce prejudices against those who find pleasure in homophile or lesbian relationships any less irrational. Were it not for medical advances, good clean natural heterosexual men and women would still be dying in vast numbers from syphilis, a venereal scourge that once was of far greater magnitude than AIDS.

To say that homosexuality is as natural as heterosexuality is not to say that the majority of men and women find same-sex individuals to be as arousing and erotically satisfying as members of the opposite sex. On the contrary, I'll soon tell about societies in which most males behave as homosexuals for a considerable portion of their lives without losing their preference for women. Much evidence exists also that a small percentage of men and women in every human population is genetically or hormonally predisposed to prefer same-sex relationships. (But in anthropological perspective most homosexual behavior cannot be traced to genetic or hormonal factors.) I do not claim, therefore, that people come into the world with a sexual tabula rasa. What I am saying is that preferences do not necessarily entail avoidances. One can prefer steak without avoiding potatoes. I see no evidence that people endowed with opposite-sex preferences are also endowed with a predisposition to loathe and avoid same-sex relationships. And this holds the other way as well. That is, I strongly doubt that the small numbers of humans who are predisposed to prefer same-sex relationships are born with phobic tendencies toward the opposite sex. I doubt, in other words, that there are any obligatory modes of human sexuality at all outside of those imposed by cultural prescription.

Why should there be? Humans have sex to spare. Are we not unfettered by breeding seasons or estrus cycles? Do our males not possess a penis that is the largest and testicles that are next to the largest among the primates? Do our females not possess a clitoris whose prominence surpasses all others except that of the raunchiest chimpanzees? Are our skins not uniquely glabrous and more erotically sensitive than that of any furry ape? If pygmy chimps engage in daily heterosexual encounters plus frequent bouts of genitogenital rubbing and homosexual pseudocopulatory thrusting, why should one expect *H. sapiens,* the sexiest and most imaginative of the primates, to be any less versatile? In truth, it takes a great deal of training and conditioning, parental disapproval, social ridicule, threats of fiery hell, repressive legislation, and, now, the threat of AIDS to convert our kind's bountiful sexual endowment into an aversion against even the mere thought of homosexual congress. Most societies—about 64 percent, according to one survey—don't make the effort to create this aversion and either tolerate or actually encourage some degree of same-sex along with opposite-sex erotic behavior. If one includes clandestine and noninstitutionalized practices, then it is safe to say that homosexual behavior occurs to some extent in every human population. But as I'll show in a moment, homosexual behavior in different cultural contexts is as variegated as heterosexual behavior. I think this astonishing variety testifies not only to the protean potential of human sexual needs and drives, but to the even more protean ability of human cultures to sever the connection between sexual pleasure and reproduction.

MALE
WITH
MALE

ESTERN HETEROSEXUALS have a penchant for stereotyping male homosexuals as effeminate. But historically and ethnographically, the most common institutionalized form of male homosexual relationships occurs among men being trained not as hairdressers or interior decorators, but as warriors. In ancient times, for example, Greek soldiers were regularly accompanied into battle by young boys who served as their sexual partners and sleeping companions in return for being taught the martial arts. Thebes, an early city-state north of Athens, possessed an elite battalion known as the Sacred Band, whose reputation for invincible courage rested on the unity and devotion of its male warrior couples.

Anthropologists have encountered similar forms of military homosexuality in many parts of the world. The Azande, a people of the southern Sudan, maintained a standing military force of young bachelors. These young warriors "married" boys and satisfied their sexual needs with them until they could accumulate the cattle wealth required to marry a woman. Azande homosexual boy-marriage mirrored aspects of the heterosexual woman-marriage to come. The bachelor gave to the boy-bride's family a token bride-price consisting of a few spears. The boy addressed his senior partner as "my husband," ate apart from him just as women ate apart from their husbands, gathered leaves for his daily toilet and for his bed at night, and brought him water, firewood, and food. During the day, the boy-wife carried the warrior's shield and at night the two slept together. The preferred form of sexual congress was for the senior to insert his penis between the boy's thighs while the "boys got what pleasure they could by friction of their organs on their partners' belly or groin." When the bachelor warriors grew older, they left the military encampments, gave up their boy-wives, paid bride-price for a female wife, and had children. Meanwhile the former boy-wives

240

graduated into the bachelor corps, and it became their turn to marry a new set of boy-bride warrior apprentices.

In highland Papua New Guinea, homosexual relations between boy warrior apprentices and junior warriors are part of an elaborate and prolonged male initiation cycle aimed at making macho warriors out of effeminate youths. Gilbert Herdt reports that among the warlike Sambia, prepubescent boys are separated from their mothers and taken to live in all-male clubhouses along with young men in their teens and early twenties. For seven years or so, the younger boys fellate the seniors. Only if he swallows semen ejaculated into his mouth by his older companions, from as many of them and as often as possible every day, can a boy grow up to be a successful adult and manly warrior. For the Sambia, like many other Papua New Guinea people, believe that men are men only because they have semen and that semen can best be obtained by fellating someone who has a supply of it. When the young men who serve as semen donors reach about twenty-five years of age, they end their homosexual relations, get married, and use their semen to make babies. Sambia husbands are careful not to have sex too often with their wives lest they fall victim to women's powers of pollution and weaken themselves by "wasting" so much precious male substance. But in spite of their universal involvement in homosexual activities, when they achieve adulthood, Sambia men say that they prefer genital sex with women to oral sex with other men, a point to which I alluded a bit earlier as indicating the greater innate appeal of the heterosexual option for most human males.

Semen not only makes boys into men, it also makes babies and mother's milk. Sambia males form solidary lineages consisting of men who believe they have created and nourished each other virtually without female assistance. Permit me to warn against regarding these androcentric beliefs and their homosexual enactments as arbitrary products of bizarre primitive musings. Among the Sambia and similar Papua New Guinea societies, the solidarity forged in the men's house, the training for hardness and masculinity, the sharing of life-giving semen, have their payoff on the battlefield. More about this later on, but first let me continue with other varieties of male-male homosexuality.

It was the peculiar genius of classical Greek civilization to

appropriate the form of junior-senior homosexual warrior apprenticeships for the transfer of philosophical rather than military knowledge. Almost all of the famous Greek philosophers engaged in
homosexual relationships with young apprentices. Their attitude, as
revealed in Plato's *Symposium,* was that sleeping with women merely
leads to the procreation of the body, whereas sleeping with men leads
to the procreation of the life of the mind. As Jeremy Bentham
pointed out, to the dismay of Victorian scholars who recoiled at the
idea that Socrates, Plato, Xenophon, and Aristotle were all "per-
verts," "everybody practiced it; nobody was ashamed of it."

Actually, most of the male homosexuality in classical Greece
took place in a context that was only remotely reminiscent of junior-
senior apprenticeships whether for war or for philosophy. As in
China, Byzantium, and medieval Persia, homosexuality in Greece
was mainly devoted to the expropriation of the bodies of people of
inferior rank, which meant slaves and commoners of both sexes, by
the powerful androcentric ruling classes of the ancient empires. Aristocratic men could indulge themselves with any form of hedonistic
amusement that struck their passing fancy. So when they were jaded
by their wives and concubines and female slaves, they tried boys as a
temporary expedient, and if any people thought that such indul-
gences were worthy of comment, they kept it to themselves.

The Azande, Papua New Guinea, and Greek varieties of
homosexuality all have one thing in common: No one believed that
the men who engaged in homosexual and heterosexual intercourse
had succumbed to abnormal impulses that placed them in a special
gender status. In all of these societies, ordinary men can be, indeed
should be, bisexual. Many forms of institutionalized homosexuality,
however, place the "insertee"—but not the "insertor"—(terms that
are more accurate than "active" and "passive") in a special gender
category that heterosexuals regarded as abnormal or deviant. This
distinction between insertees and insertors apparently exists to some
degree among American males and is implicated in the infamous
persecution of gay men by Senator Joseph McCarthy and his legal
advisor, Roy M. Cohn, both of whom were undoubtedly accustomed
to having sexual relations with males. From their point of view, they
were not the monumental hypocrites that others saw, but simply
men who were so virile that they would do it even to "queers" as a
means of showing their contempt for such people.

In other cultures, the fact that a man is an insertee for other men does not demean either insertee or insertor. On the contrary, he may simply be regarded as an in-between, third sex, or not-man-not-woman. Males who acquire this status, far from being demeaned as "queers," often enjoy considerable prestige and are especially valued for their ability to act as intermediaries between the natural and supernatural worlds. Siberian male shamans, for example, enhance their air of mystery and otherworldliness by wearing women's dress, performing female chores, and acting as insertees for their male clients. In Afro-Brazilian spirit-possession cults known as macumba and condomble, successful, charismatic cult leaders are also generally homosexuals. Clients come to them for help in finding lost valuables, missing persons, the causes of misfortune, and cures for illnesses. Why should they expect a person who has the gift to do these things to dress and behave like everybody else?

The North American Indian homosexuals known as *berdache* are another variant of respected not-man-not-woman gender endowed with supernatural gifts and shamanic powers. Berdache dressed like women and rendered sexual services to a successful warrior as a de facto "wife" along with the warrior's other wife or wives. Because berdache were devoted to domestic chores and were skilled at beadwork and quillwork, their female co-wives accepted or even welcomed their presence. For the warrior, having a berdache was a considerable honor and in no way impugned his masculinity. Many berdache used their supernatural gifts to become shamans. Among the Oglala and Tetons, for example, they bestowed new names on young men and women at puberty, marriage, and other life crises. The Crow berdache chopped down the first tree for the Sun Dance; Cheyenne berdache organized and conducted the Scalp Dance; and Navajo, Creek, and Yokut berdache performed special functions at funerals. Berdache could serve several warriors at a time, and a warrior could have more than one berdache at a time. But berdache had no sexual interest in each other. As for the warriors, they professed no interest in homosexual relations with anyone other than a berdache.

India, an inexhaustible treasure house of ethnographic examples, does not lack for its male homosexual holy persons, known as *hijras*. The anatomically male not-men-not-women undergo castration to gain admission to one of the seven "houses" of the hijra community. They dress like women, wear their hair long, pluck rather than shave their facial hair, take women's names, sit in places reserved for "ladies only" on public conveyances, and have been agitating for the right to be counted as women in the national census. Hijras often acquire male "husbands" who are married and have children, but who provide steady financial support in return for the opportunity to indulge in sexual maneuvers that their wives know nothing about. Less fortunate or less enterprising hijras earn their living by acting as male prostitutes. Hijras also earn part of their income by begging, an activity they excel at when they threaten to lift their saris and expose their mutilated genitals unless alms are forthcoming. But traditionally the hijras derive most of their sustenance by performing certain rituals, especially at male birth ceremonies. Summoned to the house of the newborn male, the hijra picks the infant up, holds it in his/her arms, and goes into a dance during which he/she inspects its genitals and thereby confers fertility, prosperity, and health on the infant and the family.

Finally, there is the case of the modern gay male, a form of institutionalized homosexuality that has probably never existed anywhere except in recent Western culture. What makes the gays unique is that the American heterosexual majority condemns all manifestations of homosexual behavior and up until a few years ago used the criminal justice system to punish anyone found guilty of even a single homosexual encounter. Because of the unremitting hostility and ridicule to which they have been subjected, gay men form a community apart, very much like a caste or an ethnic minority. In this respect they resemble the hijras, except that when hijras have intercourse with nonhijras, the nonhijras do not become homosexuals, whereas any American male, married or not, who has intercourse with a gay becomes, by social convention, a person of indeterminate status whom the gay community seeks to recruit and the heterosexual majority seeks to expel.

How did all this come to pass? As I said in "The Need to Be Loved," society needs children even if sexually active adults do not. In reaction to the prospect of widespread reproductive failure brought on by the shift from agrarian to industrial economies, employers of labor pushed legislation that condemned and severely punished every form of nonreproductive sex. The objective of this movement was to make sex a privilege granted by society only to people who would use the privilege to make babies. As a glaring example of nonreproductive sex, homosexuality became a major target of the pronatalist forces, along with masturbation, premarital sex, contraception, and abortion.

But my tour of the homosexual universe is only half over.

FEMALE
WITH
FEMALE

ECAUSE OF THE PREDOMINANCE of androcentric observers among anthropologists, details about lesbian practices are scarce. But I think it is correct to say that institutionalized forms of female homosexuality are not as well developed as the male forms. I'll explain why in a moment.

Anthropologists have reported on only a handful of female initiation rituals that entail lesbian behavior. Among the Dahomey of West Africa, for example, adolescent girls prepared for marriage by attending all-female initiation schools where they learned how to "thicken their genitalia" and engage in sexual intercourse.

Since women seldom bear the brunt of military combat, they have little opportunity to use same-sex erotic apprenticeships to form solidary teams of warriors. Similarly, enforced absence from the classical Greek academies precluded women's participation in homosexual philosophical apprenticeships, and since men regarded women as their sexual "object," the incidence of overt lesbian dalliance between women of rank and slave girls or other social inferiors could never be very high. More commonly, women do adopt socially sanctioned not-man-not-woman gender roles, dressing like men, performing manly duties such as hunting, trapping, and going to war and using their in-between gender status to establish their credibility as shamans. Among several western Native American tribes, female not-men-not-women entered into enduring lesbian relationships with women, whom they formally "married." But little concrete evidence supports the surmise that lesbian relationships were entailed in the majority of cultures that allowed for not-man-not-woman gender roles.

Several reported cases of institutionalized lesbianism are related to the migration of males in search of work. On the Caribbean island of Carriacou, where migrant husbands stay away from home for most of the year, older married women bring younger single women into their households and share the absent husband's remittances in exchange for sexual favors and emotional support. A similar pattern exists in South Africa, where it is known as the "mummy-baby game."

One of the most interesting forms of institutionalized lesbianism occurred in mid-nineteenth-century–early twentieth-century China in several of the silk-growing districts of the Pearl River Delta region in southern Kwangtung. Single women provided virtually all of the labor for the silkworm factories. Although poorly paid, they were better off than their prospective husbands. Rather than accept the subordinate status that marriage imposed on Chinese women, the silk workers formed antimarriage sisterhoods that provided economic and emotional support. While not all of the 100,000 sisters formed lesbian relationships, enduring lesbian marriages involving two and sometimes three women were common.

It seems clear that even when allowance is made for blind spots in the ethnographic reports of male observers, there are fewer forms of institutionalized female than of male homosexuality. Does this mean that females engage in homosexual behavior less often than males? Probably not. More likely most female homosexuality has simply been driven underground or has been expressed in noninstitutionalized contexts that escape observation. Although seldom reported, adolescence is probably an occasion for a considerable amount of female homosexual experimentation the world over. Only recently, for example, has it come to light that among the Kalahari !Kung, young girls engage in sexual play with other girls before they do so with boys.

Polygynous marriage is another context in which lesbian relationships probably flourish. The practice seems to have been common in West Africa among the Nupe, Haussa, and Dahomey, and among the Azande and Nyakusa in East Africa. In Middle Eastern harems, where co-wives seldom saw their husbands, many women entered into lesbian relationships despite the dire punishment such male-defying behavior could bring.

The female gay movement provides further evidence that institutionalized female homosexuality is not a mirror image of its male counterpart. As a social movement, lesbianism has been overshadowed both by male homosexual politics and by the political agenda of women's liberation. Both male and female gays belong to socially segregated communities that provide their members with essential everyday services as well as with emotional and physical security. But the male gay community networks have more members, a greater span of occupations, and more political clout. This follows, ironically enough, from the fact that males in general benefit from childhood training in the art of self-assertion and have greater access to high-paying jobs and professions. "Coming out," therefore, may have been more difficult for gay women than for gay men because female gays have had to contend with their subordination as women as well as with their ostracism as sexual deviants, while male gays have had to contend only with their ostracism as sexual deviants. As Evelyn Blackwood has remarked, "Enforced heterosexuality is tied to women's lack of economic power and the restriction of female activity to the domestic sphere." Being gay, whether male or female, challenges the foundations of the modern family. In addition, being a lesbian challenges the heterosexual male's definition of woman as a sex object for males only. Therefore, women of different sexual orientation have found a common cause in the struggle to overturn the male construction of female gender.

SPERM

VERSUS

EGG?

WE KNOW THAT HUMAN males and females belong to the same species, but one might think otherwise from the way they look, speak, and behave. Are men and women fundamentally different kinds of beings? Are the female sex organs and the female body and the male sex organs and the male body parts of a larger genetic package that includes hard-wired programs for fundamentally different kinds of sex-specific thought and behavior?

The central focus of modern-day biological theories about supposedly innate sexually mandated patterns of thought and behavior is the notion that men and women by nature have distinct and competitive reproductive strategies: a female egg strategy and a male sperm strategy. The egg strategy supposedly mandates that women be more picky in choosing a mate, have fewer mates, and expend more care and effort than men on nurturing infants and children. Sperm strategy obliges men to seek to mate indiscriminately with a lot of different females and to spend less care and effort than women on nurturing infants and children. These two opposed strategies in turn allegedly reflect the differences between the size and quantity of eggs and sperm. In their lifetime, women can have only a small number of opportunities to pass on their genes to their offspring. They have a fixed supply of eggs, which they can use at the rate of only one a month. Once pregnant, they cannot have another baby until at least eighteen months go by. Males, in contrast, produce sperm by the tens of millions. Since it is the female whose body devotes itself to the task of nurturing the fetus, it is to the reproductive advantage of the males to go about impregnating one female after another in rapid succession with their cheap little sperm. During the time it takes for a woman with her one expensive egg per month to produce one baby, a male who listens to the call of his genes can father a dozen or more. What a woman allegedly wants from her mate, therefore, is the opposite of what a man wants from his. She wants him to stay nearby and provide support for her and her child. He wants to wander about seducing as many women as possible. Writes E. O. Wilson, "It pays males to be aggressive, hasty, fickle, and indiscriminating. In theory it is more profitable for females to be coy and to identify the male with the best genes—who are more likely to stay with them after insemination. Human beings obey this biological principle faithfully." The egg and sperm strategies also supply an explanation for why men rape women—to escape entirely from the costs of parenting; and why polygyny is so much more common than polyandry—men recoil from investing their sperm in a single pregnancy, especially when one cannot be certain if he is the father.

This set of theories rests on the sociobiological generalization that I have already rejected, namely that investments in reproductive success always receive priority in the allocation of resources among post-takeoff human populations. But I have more specific reasons for rejecting the view that males and females possess contradictory natures dictated by different reproductive strategies. First of all, there is nothing in the behavior of our closest primate relatives that supports the idea of innate female sexual coyness. Female chimpanzees, especially female pygmy chimpanzees, are as bold as males in seeking sexual satisfaction. They copulate with one male after another for variety's sake, and then do it again with females. This behavior gains in relevance to the human condition, when one considers the anatomical basis for female pygmy chimp hypersexuality— the prominence of the clitoris and its capacity for inducing multiple orgasms in quick succession. If women are coy by nature, why are they equipped with a capacity to have more orgasms than any single male can provide? Furthermore, as I pointed out earlier, millions of women live in female-centered households and have multiple lovers as well as a series of temporary husbands. Similar quasi-polyandrous female-centered households are especially common among the urban poor in many parts of the world. These households develop when men cannot earn enough to pay for anything beyond their own subsistence needs. One might argue that because of their poverty, women in female-centered households have no choice but to be more promiscuous than women in monogamous households, and that if they could find one man wealthy enough to support them and their children, they would heed the call of reproductive success and become monogamous. I have to agree that if the choice is between impoverished polyandry and relatively affluent monogamy, women will submit to the discipline of monogamy. But let us level the playing field. Suppose women were free to choose between affluent monogamy and affluent polyandry, what then? According to the sociobiological view, they would choose monogamy. But I believe that if they were really free to choose, women would choose as many partners as men choose when they are free to do so. Women by nature are at least as capable of enjoying sex with a variety of men as men are interested in experiencing sex with a variety of women.

What has kept us from recognizing this truth is that women have never been as free to choose the option of multiple sexual partnerships as men have been. And this lack of freedom has nothing to do with sexual strategies for reproductive success but is rather a product of the sexual politics of the double standard, whereby men have sought to dominate women and to combat their sexuality as part of their attempt to control women's productive and reproductive powers. With few exceptions, women have been able to have numerous sexual partners only when it was advantageous for numerous males to let them do it. As a consequence, female promiscuity occurs primarily among prostitutes, who are obliged by adversity to submit to males indiscriminately, not for gratification of female sexual drive or appetite—the busier prostitutes uniformly report that they feel nothing when servicing their customers—but to eke out a meager living. While ordinary honorable males in most state-level societies could be unfaithful in marriage, keep mistresses, and visit prostitutes, ordinary honorable women were almost universally subject to severe punishment if they displayed any promiscuous or polyandrous tendencies.

It is the female's body and not the male's body that endures the risks and costs of pregnancy, birth, and lactation. This surely also has something to do with the tendency of women to be sexually more conservative than men. In the absence of effective contraception, or medical abortion, sexual promiscuity leads to very different consequences for females. Men have never had to balance sexual pleasures against the painful ordeal that terminates a pregnancy nor have they had to worry about dying in childbirth. As family planning agencies discover when they attempt to introduce contraceptive practices to Third World countries, wives are far more eager than husbands to avoid having more children. Not because they are following a female egg-oriented reproductive strategy, but because they are sick and tired of being pregnant and giving birth so often. To the higher costs that women naturally confront in traditional societies as a potential consequence of being sexually adventurous, add the culturally elaborated male-imposed penalties aimed at punishing women whose pregnancies can be shown to result from premarital or extramarital affairs. When women are subject to everything from being gang-raped, whipped, stoned, or divorced for sexual adventures leading to pregnancy out of wedlock, shall we say that women are merely following their genetic instructions when they have fewer sexual adventures than men? In other words, if we want to identify the natural limits of female sexuality, we cannot merely observe women in situations where they are culturally constrained to be virginal, chaste, or monogamous or where a woman's indulgence in sex with different men leads to being branded as a prostitute, a whore, a fallen woman, or a nymphomaniac; or where children born out of wedlock become a moral and economic burden to the mother but not to the father. Otherwise, the inferences about female nature will be totally confounded with the effects of male dominance.

Because of the pervasiveness of male supremacist institutions and values, there are very few, if any, societies in which women's sexual freedom is not curtailed more than men's. But I need not present societies in which politics allows exactly equal degrees of sexual freedom to males and females to prove the point. The issue is, do women choose more mates when they are free to do so?

STOLEN
PLEASURES

*B*RONISLAW MALINOWSKI was the first anthropologist to describe female sexuality in a society where some familiar components of male supremacy were absent or greatly attenuated. His classic study, *The Sexual Life of Savages,* depicts young unmarried girls in the Trobriand Islands of Melanesia as having the same number of sexual escapades with different partners as young men. The principal limitation on female premarital sex was that girls had to refrain from being too forward and openly solicitous of male consorts. To the extent that their charm and beauty aroused suitors to ask for liaisons, they could have premarital sex, provided they did it discreetly. The censure of young women who were too sexually aggressive was founded, according to Malinowski, not on the sense that there was anything wrong in having many partners, but on the sense that young girls who were brazenly solicitous were erotic failures. And young men who were too aggressively lecherous were censured on the same basis. Discretion seems to have been the watchword. Yet Malinowski notes that there were clear cases of girls who were not satisfied with "moderate sexual intercourse and required a number of men every night." These Malinowski regarded as "nymphomanics." But I wonder if this judgment corresponded to the Trobriander women's view of it.

Young women in Samoa, according to Margaret Mead, also enjoyed a high rate of sexual activity with different male partners. Clandestine assignations, arranged by go-betweens, were consummated "under the palm trees" or by daring midnight "night-crawling" intrusions into the girl's hut. Mead wrote that "these affairs are usually of short duration and both girl and boy may be carrying on several at once." I should point out that before the Samoans came under the influence of Christian missionaries, premarital sexual freedom for girls was probably much greater than when Mead did her fieldwork.

For a better picture of traditional female sexuality in the

South Seas, one can turn to the island of Mangaia. Here both sexes experimented freely before puberty and enjoy an intense premarital sex life. Girls received nightly suitors in their parents' house and boys competed with their rivals to see how many orgasms they could achieve. Mangaian girls were not interested in romantic protestations, extensive petting, or foreplay. Sex was not a reward for masculine affection; rather, affection was the reward for sexual fulfillment:

> Sexual intimacy is not achieved by first demonstrating personal affection: the reverse is true. The Mangaian . . . girl takes an immediate demonstration of sexual virility and masculinity as the first test of her partner's desire for her and as the reflection of her own desirability. . . . Personal affection may or may not result from acts of sexual intimacy, but the latter are requisite to the former—exactly the reverse of the ideals of western society.

The Trobrianders, Samoans, and Mangaians expect adult men and women to give up their sexual adventures after they get married. But ideals of marital fidelity are flouted the world over despite the threat of punishment. Again, because of the asymmetrical distribution of power, the adulterous woman is usually at greater risk than her accomplice if she is discovered. And so studies of women's extramarital sex life are extremely difficult to carry out. There is only one anthropological study that I know of that actually provides a tally of the number of "affairs" married men and women engage in. It was carried out by Thomas Gregor in a small village inhabited by the Mehinacu Indians of central Brazil. The village contained thirty-seven adults—twenty men and seventeen women. All of the men were having at least one affair while Gregor was living with them, and fourteen of the seventeen women were similarly engaged.

The women actually averaged more affairs than the men, 5.1 to 4.4 per person, and if we count only those women who were playing the game, their batting average was 6.3 affairs per woman. (The women who were not having affairs were presumably "the old, the sick, and the extremely unattractive" who, according to Gregor, did not excite sexual interest among the men.)

Gregor, like Malinowski, denies that his data show that women have as much of a hedonistic interest in sex as men do. "The

Number of affairs per person	Number of persons having the affairs	
	Men	Women
0	0	3
1	2	0
2	3	0
3	4	3
4	3	1
5	0	4
6	4	1
7	2	1
8	1	1
9	0	1
10	1	0
11	0	1
14	0	1
	20	17

men's principal motivation for initiating affairs is sexual desire," he writes. "The women, on the other hand, seem to value the social contact and the gifts they receive in the course of the affair as well as the physical side of the relationship." But males, even when they are anthropologists, are not to be trusted when it comes to explaining what motivates women to have sexual intercourse. I place more trust, therefore, in Marjorie Shostak's woman-to-woman account of extra-marital affairs among the San. According to Nisa, the subject of Shostak's deeply personal and moving study, "Having affairs is one of the things God gave us." Nisa had over twenty of them. She made it clear that her motivations were not exclusively sexual.

> One man can give you very little. One man gives you only one kind of food to eat. But when you have lovers, one brings you something and another brings you something else. One

comes at night with meat, another with money, another with beads.

As hunters and gatherers, the !Kung do a great deal of visiting from one camp to another. "A woman," says Nisa, "should have lovers wherever she goes. Then she will be well provided for with beads, meat, or other food."

At first it seems as if Nisa is more interested in getting gifts than in having sex. But she soon exhibits a sophisticated knowledge of the erotic satisfactions that various kinds of lovers can provide and it becomes clear that if a man does not satisfy her—"Let her finish her work"—gifts will not induce her to continue the affair. Nisa says that "a woman's sexual desire is always with her and even if she doesn't want a certain man she still feels her desire inside." Moreover, having a lover does not mean that one cannot still enjoy one's husband: "A woman has to want her husband and her lover equally; that is when it is good."

Like all dominant groups, men seek to promote an image of their subordinate's nature that contributes to the preservation of the status quo. For thousands of years, males have seen women not as women could be, but only as males want them to be.

ARE MEN
MORE
AGGRESSIVE
THAN
WOMEN?

FEMINISTS AND MALE SEXISTS tend to agree on one thing: Men are innately more aggressive than women. To male sexists, this explains why women are and should be politically subordinate. To feminists, it explains why women, rather than men, should be in charge of government and the armed forces. Both sides think the basic premise is unassailable. Men have a greater amount of the male hormone testosterone circulating in their blood than women. Therefore, men are more aggressive. Don't the testes secrete testosterone, and isn't that why we say in the vernacular that a man has "balls," referring to his courage and combativeness? (Women, however, also have testosterone secreted in small amounts by the outer portion of the adrenal glands.) Doesn't castration transform bulls brave enough for the bull ring into oxen meek enough for plowing? Yes, that is true. But the effects of castration are not so clear among primates, including humans. Castrated rhesus monkeys are not significantly less aggressive than normal males. And as far as humans are concerned, castration lowers or eliminates sexual drive and potency, but it has very little if any deterrent effect on aggression. Both men and women can become very aggressive with low levels of testosterone.

Attempts to use physical or chemical castration as a means of controlling aggressive male prisoners have not had the desired results. The officials who sanctioned these experiments could have saved everyone a lot of trouble had they acquainted themselves with the history of eunuchism. In China, Ancient Rome, Persia, and Byzantium, castrated male youths entered the service of their emperors at an early age and rose to positions of great trust and responsibility. Because of their reputation for fierceness in battle, they were placed in command of the palace guards and given the rank of general or admiral in the armed forces. Bagoas, one of the most famous eunuchs of history, became commander-in-chief of the Persian army. Conqueror of Egypt in 343 B.C., Bagoas murdered the emperor Artaxerxes III and all his sons, placed Darius III on the throne, and when Darius III was not cooperative enough, tried to murder him, too.

In China, the most famous eunuch was Cheng Ho, a veteran of the Mongol wars who became commander of the largest navy ever launched in Chinese history, even to this day. According to family records, Cheng Ho was seven feet tall, had a waist about five feet in circumference, glaring eyes, and a voice as loud as a bell. Under his direct command, an armada consisting of 300 ships and carrying 28,000 men voyaged to ports as far away as India, fighting pirates, subduing hostile armies, and collecting tribute.

But surely in normal males the amount of testosterone increases at the outset of an aggressive episode? Not so! Typically, the amount of testosterone is highest at the end of an aggressive encounter, rather than at the beginning or middle. Monkeys that fight to form dominance hierarchies have higher testosterone levels after they become successful, not before. When attacked and defeated by a group of strangers, male monkeys show a sharp drop in testosterone levels. Although this leads to a correlation between high rank and high levels of testosterone, it scarcely proves that high testosterone levels cause high rank in monkeys any more than fire engines cause fires.

Turning to humans, studies of college wrestlers show that testosterone levels are lower just before the start of the match than at its end. Similarly, just after winning their prize money at tennis matches or receiving their M.D. degrees, young men show an increase in testosterone. But men have a sharp drop in testosterone levels just before surgery, just as Americans who were about to go on patrol during the Vietnam War had less, not more, testosterone in their blood. If the level of testosterone determines the level of aggression, why isn't the amount circulating in the blood at least as high at the beginning of an aggressive encounter as at the end?

I am not saying that testosterone has no influence on aggressive behavior. There is a positive feedback between the two, but it is weak and there are many factors that can override, distort, or suppress that relationship. In the words of Irwin S. Bernstein and his associates at the Yerkes Primate Research Center, "With the elaboration of the cerebral cortex in the primate, hormonal influences on behavior are not lost, but may be superseded." If this is true of monkeys, it must be even more true of humans. I am willing to grant that the possession of higher levels of testosterone may predispose men to learn aggressive roles somewhat more readily than women, but the primate evidence does not indicate the existence of a hormonal barrier that would prevent women from learning to be more aggressive than men if the exigencies of social life were to call for women to assume aggressive gender roles and for men to be more passive. These exigencies are already present to a significant extent in industrial societies where men in two-wage-earner families are learning to perform nurturant childrearing tasks that were formerly the exclusive responsibility of stay-at-home housewives. At the same time, women are learning to compete aggressively against men for preferred positions as professionals and managers. An interesting finding in this connection is that independent of age, women in professional, managerial, and technical occupations have higher levels of testosterone than woman clerical workers and housewives. Does this mean that some women become professionals, managers, and technicians because they have a higher testosterone level, or does it mean that they have higher testosterone levels because they became professionals, managers, and technicians? I do not believe that a proper answer consists of saying that both relationships are equally probable. There has been a vast increase in the number of women in the wage labor force and a corresponding vast increase in the number who have attained preferred positions. Can this increase be accounted for by postulating a general rise in the female testosterone level at birth? Did the vast social and economic changes that brought about the demise of smokestack industrialism and its male-breadwinner families result from a surge of testosterone that masculinized the female sex? Of course not. Then why should one believe that hormonal differences would prevent the further "masculinization" of female gender roles if post-smokestack societies continue to select for such roles?

OF TOMBOY
GIRLS AND
PENIS-AT-
TWELVE BOYS

*S*OME SCIENTISTS CONTEND that the intrauterine exposure to testosterone permanently modifies a portion of the male's brain, making him prone to violence throughout the rest of his life. They believe that John Money and Anke Ehrhardt's study of twenty-five girls who were exposed to abnormally high levels of male hormones during their fetal growth supports this theory. All these girls were born with an enlarged clitoris and according to their own and their mothers' estimation, were far more boylike as children than other girls. They engaged in "a high level of physical energy expenditure, especially in vigorous outdoor play, games, and sports commonly considered the prerogative of boys." This the researchers attributed to the "masculinizing effect on the fetal brain" of the high levels of male hormones to which they had been subject during embryonic growth. But there were social effects that were at least as important as the hormonal effects: The girls' mothers probably did not treat them as normal females. Not only would the masculinized clitoris have induced mothers to treat them more like boys, but the ability of both mothers and daughters to recall and estimate the amount of tomboyism would have been biased by their expectations of the kinds of behavior masculinized girls could be predicted to exhibit. An additional confounding factor is that all of the girls underwent an operation—clitoridectomy—to reduce the size of the clitoris. This procedure would have constituted an additional source of atypical behavior. Studies show that male infants who undergo circumcision are more active, wakeful, and irritable than those who do not, and clitoridectomy entails a more drastic form of surgery than circumcision.

Other researchers claim that the masculinizing of behavioral tendencies, including heightened levels of aggressivity, occurs primarily at puberty rather than when the male embryo is in the womb.

This view rests to a large extent on studies carried out by the endo-crinologist Julianne Imperato-McGinley and her associates among nineteen genetic males from three neighboring villages in the Dominican Republic. As a result of hereditary testosterone deficien-cies, these individuals were born with female genitals and were reared as girls. At puberty, under the influence of a normal male surge of testosterone, they failed to develop breasts, their voices deepened, their testicles descended, and the clitoris changed to a normal male penis. According to Imperato-McGinley and her associ-ates, seventeen of these men, despite having worn dresses and having been reared as females for twelve years, became typical, aggressive Latin machos who married and fathered children, proving that "the effects of testosterone predominated, overriding the effect of rearing as girls." Or transposed to a larger screen: *Men will act like men no matter how much you teach them to act like women.*

But how much of an effort did anyone really make to bring up the penis-at-twelve children as girls? In view of the fact that the Dominican Republic is a typical, Latin male-sexist society, parents would continue to hope that their "girls" would eventually become "boys" as other children with the same affliction had done. Wouldn't parents of anatomically normal male adolescents do everything they possibly could to make men rather than women out of them? Even so, the retraining was not easy. It took years of confusion and psy-chological anguish for some to make the transition. As far as I can see, what we learn from the much celebrated penis-at-twelve males is not that the effects of testosterone override the effects of rearing as girls, as Imperato-McGinley maintains, but simply that adolescents can change their behavior to accord with what their culture defines as appropriate for their sexual anatomy. Certainly there is nothing in this study that would support the view that men are naturally more aggressive than women primarily as a result of the big dose of testos-terone that males get at puberty.

If I am right about the extent to which cultural selection can override the relationship between testosterone levels and aggressive behavior, what accounts for the near universal occurrence of higher levels of aggressivity in males? Why haven't any cultures turned the tables, so to speak, and obliged women to be more aggressive than men?

269

I promise to supply an explanation. But first, permit me one more delay in order to bring certain additional claims about innate differences between human males and females into the orbit of the discussion. Do men and women naturally think differently? Is one sex more innately mathematical or more intelligent than the other?

MIND, MATH,
AND THE SENSES

*A*RE MEN SMARTER than women? Back in the nineteenth century, scientists answered without hesitation: Women have smaller brains than men so men must be smarter. Today we know better: Human brain size varies with body weight. Corrected for average disparity in body weight, women's brains are slightly bigger than men's.

What about I.Q. tests? On the most widely used test, the Stanford-Binet, men and women have the same average scores. But this doesn't prove much one way or the other because the Stanford-Binet test was engineered to produce just that result. Early on, psychologists realized that men answered some kinds of questions better than women and that women answered some kinds of questions better than men. Rather than conclude that no single test could measure general intelligence (the most plausible conclusion), test designers added and subtracted various types of questions until the average scores reached by males and females came out even.

Psychologists interested in the comparison of male and female aptitudes have concentrated on differences in specific aspects of intelligence. For example, on the basis of the differential performance of boys and girls on aptitude tests, many psychologists conclude that men are by nature better mathematicians than women. Research by Camilla Benbow and Julian Stanley seems to confirm this view. Benbow and Stanley examined the scores of 10,000 seventh- and eighth-grade children who scored in the top 3 percent of the mathematics part of the Scholastic Aptitude Test and found that the boys' average scores were consistently higher than the girls' average scores even when boys and girls had taken equal numbers of math courses. In a follow-up based on the test scores of 40,000 participants in a Johns Hopkins University talent search, Benbow and Stanley found that males averaged 416, females 386 out of a possible score of 800. The higher the scores, the greater the disproportion between the number of boys versus girls achieving that score. (Four times as many boys as girls scored over 600.)

As many feminists, social scientists, and mathematicians quickly pointed out, Benbow and Stanley had made virtually no attempt to control for differences in the socialization of boy and girl mathematicians other than the number of math classes children in their sample had taken. The researchers seem oblivious of the larger context of family and community life in which young people acquire their incentive to excel, form images of themselves, and develop career goals. Traditionally, fathers, not mothers, helped children with mathematics homework, effectively conveying the message that mathematics was a male sphere of endeavor. Counselors and teachers have traditionally joined parents in defining mathematical ability as a sex-linked characteristic that is essential for male careers—but not for female careers. In one study of this problem, 42 percent of girls interested in careers in mathematics reported being discouraged by counselors from taking advanced courses in mathematics. As two female professors of mathematics wrote in response to Benbow and Stanley, "Anyone who thinks that seventh graders are free from environmental influences can hardly be living in the real world." And as feminist-scientist Ruth Bleier pointed out, "At an age when pressures are high to conform to expected gender roles and behaviors, many girls do not want to be seen as 'unfeminine' in a culture that equates math and science skills with 'masculinity'."

But aren't the brains of men and women "wired" differently? The left and right hemispheres of the human brain are specialized for somewhat different functions. In most humans, the left hemisphere is more active during verbal tasks, while the right hemisphere is more active when a person thinks about or visualizes objects and their spatial relationships. Could it be that women are "wired" to use the left hemisphere more than the right and that this accounts for their higher verbal aptitude? And since ability to visualize objects and spatial relationships is correlated with mathematical skills, could it be that men have greater mathematical aptitude because they are "wired" to make more use of their right hemisphere? No, I have not been able to find any evidence to support these hypotheses. No one has yet demonstrated that female brains have more highly developed left hemispheres than do male brains or that male brains have more highly developed right hemispheres than do female brains. Moreover, there is a logical flaw in the hypothesis, because the left and right hemispheres each have additional functional specializations that are contrary to what the sex-linked aptitudes are supposed to be. The right hemisphere not only predominates in the "masculine" visualization of objects, it also predominates in holistic and intuitive modes of thought that are popularly supposed to be feminine specialties. The same kind of mix-up occurs in the left hemisphere. It is more active in tasks that involve logical analysis, a supposedly masculine ability, as well as in supposedly "feminine" verbal tasks.

In reviewing the minutiae of sex-linked physiological differences, one can easily lose sight of the major issue. The question is not whether there are measurable sex-linked differences in capacities, tolerances, and drives, but whether these differences are large enough to produce recurrent patterns of sexually specialized social behavior. Even if one grants that observed differences in I.Q. and aptitude scores are primarily a result of differences in brain structure, the overlap in male and female test scores does not match up with the overlap in male and female representation in the fields of mathematics, science, and engineering. Suppose that four times as many men as women score over 600 and that half of that results from sex-linked genetic factors, then the proportion of men to women in math-related fields should be 2 to 1, when in fact the actual ratio is closer to 9 to 1. Clearly, cultural selection has intervened between biology and behavior and has amplified the influence of any innate differences that actually exist.

It seems to me that if you admit that cultural selection has the power to amplify genetic differences on such a scale, you must also grant that cultural selection possesses the power to create sharp differences in performance when no genetic differences exist at all— as I think will ultimately be shown to be true of mathematical aptitudes.

In fact, I can think of no reason why cultural selection could not result in the genetically impaired sex outperforming the gentically favored one. Take the sense of hearing. Women appear to have a keener sense of hearing, as measured by their ability to detect pure tones at various wavelengths. The disparity between the sexes appears to increase with age. Men begin to lose their hearing when they reach thirty-two years of age; women, when they reach thirty-seven. (Of course, some of this may reflect men's greater exposure to noisy occupations that put their hearing at risk.) Despite greater hearing impairment among males, a glance at the sex ratio of any major symphony orchestra will show that male musicians greatly outnumber female musicians. I admit that auditory acuity is not the only prerequisite for playing a musical instrument, but this kind of caveat applies as well when the supposed genetically favored sex is also the socially favored sex, as in the case of mathematicians. No single genetic predisposition can explain anything about real human behavior.

Women also appear to have a more acute sense of taste. They can detect the presence of small amounts of sweet, sour, salty, and bitter substances more readily than men. If only genes counted, one might predict that women make the best chefs. Why, then, are more men than women chefs in five-star restaurants?

There are two other senses for which slight genetically controlled discrepancies between the sexes may exist. Men perform better on tests of visual acuity, while women exhibit greater sensitivity to pressure on the skin. But I am not aware that anyone has ever invoked these differences to explain universal aspects of male and female roles, so we need not tarry to sort out how much of the discrepancy results from cultural and how much from natural selection. As for the sense of smell, despite popular stereotypes that give women an edge over men, the sexes appear to be equal in their ability to detect the majority of odors.

I fear that I may be creating the impression that biological differences between the sexes are irrelevant, when it is merely the hypothetical and speculative status of some of the alleged differences to which I object. Rather than lend credence to such unobservable entities as genes for male and female reproductive strategies, genes for right- and left-hemisphere brain functions, or genes for specific verbal or mathematical abilities, I recommend that we pay more attention to the anatomical and physical facts about male and female bodies, whose sex-linked hereditary character cannot be impugned, and that we use these known biological differences to construct parsimonious explanations of culturally selected gender roles.

SEX, HUNTING, AND DEADLY FORCE

EN ARE 11.6 CENTIMETERS (4.6 inches) taller than women on average. Women have lighter bones and more fat than men, and therefore weigh less for their height (fat weighs less than muscle). Women are about two-thirds to three-quarters as strong as men, depending on the group of muscles tested. The biggest strength differences are concentrated in the arms, chest, and shoulders. There is no mystery, therefore, about why men outperform women in track-and-field athletic contests. In archery, for example, the woman's hand bow record for distance is 15 percent less than the male record. In compound bow competition, the gap is 30 percent. In javelin hurling, it is 20 percent. Add to these differences a 10 percent gap in various kinds of sprints and intermediate- and long-distance races. As I mentioned earlier, there is a 9 percent gap in the marathon. The same for 100-meter dashes, but larger, about 12 percent, for intermediate distances. While athletic training programs and psychological incentives improve women's track-and-field performance, there is little prospect that the gap that now exists in sports based on muscular strength and body build will ever be significantly narrowed (except, perhaps someday, through genetic engineering).

On the basis of what anthropologists know about simple band-and-village societies, I think we can be fairly confident that these differences were responsible during early post-takeoff times for the recurrent cultural selection of males as the sex responsible for hunting large animals. There are a few exceptions—the Agta of the Philippines, for example, among whom some women hunt for wild pigs—but in 95 percent of known cases, men specialize in bringing down big game. As to whether earlier presapiens and protocultural hominid species had the same division of labor, I shall say nothing because we cannot extrapolate from modern foragers to such remote times. Men were culturally selected to prey on large animals because their height, weight, and brawn advantages made them, on the average, more efficient at this task than women. Moreover, the male height, weight, and brawn advantages in the use of hand-held hunting weapons increase considerably for the many months during which women are less mobile because they are pregnant or lactating.

Sex-linked anatomical and physiological differences do not preclude women from participating in hunting to some degree. But the systemically rational alternative is to train men rather than women to be responsible for big-game hunting, especially since women are never at a disadvantage in hunting smaller game or collecting wild fruits, berries, or tubers, which are just as important in many foragers' diets as meat from big game.

The selection of males to do the hunting of large game means that at least since Paleolithic times men have been the specialists in the manufacture and use of weapons such as spears, bow and arrows, harpoons, clubs, and boomerangs—weapons that have the capacity to wound and kill human beings as well as animals. I am not saying that male control over these weapons automatically leads to male dominance and the sexual double standard. On the contrary, many foraging societies with a sexual division of labor between male hunters and female gatherers have nearly egalitarian relations between the sexes. For example, writing of her fieldwork among the Montagnais-Naskapi foragers of Labrador, anthropologist Eleanor Leacock notes that "they gave me insight into a level of respect and consideration for the individuality of others, regardless of sex, that I had never before experienced." And in his study of the forest-dwelling Mbuti of Zaire, Colin Turnbull found a high level of cooperation and mutual understanding between the sexes and considerable authority and power vested in women. Despite his skills with bow and arrow, the Mbuti male does not see himself as superior to his wife. He "sees himself as the hunter, but then he could not hunt without a wife, and although hunting is more exciting than being a beater or a gatherer, he knows that the bulk of his diet comes from the foods gathered by the women."

Marjorie Shostak's biography of Nisa shows the !Kung to be another foraging society in which nearly egalitarian relationships between the sexes prevail. Shostak states that the !Kung do not show any preference for male children over female children. In matters relating to childrearing, both parents guide their offspring, and a mother's word carries about the same weight as the father's. Mothers play a major role in deciding whom their children will marry, and after marriage, !Kung couples live near the wife's family as often as they live near the husband's. Women dispose of whatever food they find and bring back to camp as they see fit. "All in all, !Kung women have a striking degree of autonomy over their own and their children's lives. Brought up to respect their own importance in community life, !Kung women become multifaceted adults and are likely to be competent and assertive as well as nurturant and cooperative."

Nonetheless, I cannot agree with Eleanor Leacock and other feminist anthropologists who claim that gender roles in foraging societies are completely egalitarian. My reading of the ethnographic evidence indicates that in the realm of public decision making and conflict resolution, men generally have a slight but nonetheless significant edge over women in virtually all foraging societies. As Shostak points out for the !Kung, "Men more often hold positions of influence—as spokespeople for the group or as healers—and their somewhat greater authority over many areas of !Kung life is acknowledged by men and women alike." Men's initiation rites are held in secret; women's are held in public. If a menstruating woman touches a hunter's arrows, his quarry will escape; but men never pollute what they touch. The !Kung, therefore, are somewhat short of having a perfectly balanced set of separate-but-equal gender roles.

The same is true of the Mbuti. Turnbull writes "that the hunters (i.e., the men) may be considered the political leaders of the camp and that in this the women are almost, if not fully, the equals of the men." But "a certain amount of wife beating is considered good," even if "the wife is expected to fight back," and for children, "mother is associated with love," while "father is associated with authority."

Richard Lee recorded thirty-four cases of nonlethal bare-handed fighting among the !Kung. Fourteen of these involved a man attacking a woman; only one involved a woman attacking a man. Lee remarks that despite the higher frequency of male-initiated attacks, "women fought fiercely and often gave as good as or better than they got." But the men in these encounters may have been restrained by the presence of a newly installed government constable and therefore did not use their weapons. Delving deeper into the past, Lee learned about twenty-two killings that had taken place prior to his fieldwork. None of the killers, but two of the victims, were women. Lee interpreted this to mean that men were unable to victimize women as freely as they do in really oppressive male sexist societies. Another interpretation seems more apt. !Kung women may have been more timid in the past when there were no constables nearby and refrained from getting into brawls with men, knowing that they would be in mortal danger if the men began to use their spears and poisoned arrows.

Why are women almost, but not fully, the equals of men in public authority and conflict resolution among foragers? I think it is because of the monopoly men maintain over the manufacture and use of hunting weapons, combined with their advantages in weight, height, and brawn. Trained to kill large animals with deadly weapons from boyhood on, men can be more dangerous and hence more coercive than women when conflicts between them break out. "I'm a man. I've got my arrows. I'm not afraid to die," say the !Kung hunters when disputes start to get out of hand. If these are the reactions of men trained to kill animals, what will men who have been trained to kill people do? How will women fare when the hunters hunt each other?

FEMALE
WARRIORS?

*W*HEREVER CONDITIONS FAVORED the intensification of warfare among bands and villages,
the political and domestic subordination of
women also became more intense. This theory
has been tested by anthropologist Brian Hayden of Simon Frazer
University and his associates on a sample of thirty-three hunter-
gatherer societies. The correlation between low status for females and
more deaths due to armed combat was "unexpectedly high." As Hayden and his coauthors note, "The reasons for overwhelming male
dominance in societies where warfare is pronounced seem relatively
straightforward. The lives of group members depend to a greater
degree on males and male assessment of social and political conditions. Male tasks during times of warfare are simply more critical to
the survival of everyone than is female work. Moreover, male aggres-
siveness and the use of force engendered by warfare and fighting
renders female opposition to male decisions not only futile but dangerous."

Men rather than women were trained to be warriors and
therefore to be more aggressive, fearless, and more capable of hunting and killing other human beings without pity or remorse. Males
were selected for the role of warriors because the anatomical and
physiological sex-linked differences that favored the selection of men
as hunters of animals favored the selection of men as hunters of people. In combat with hand-held weapons dependent on muscle power,
the slight 10 or 15 percent edge that men hold over women in track-
and-field performances becomes a life-and-death issue, while the
restrictions imposed on women by pregnancy loom as an even greater
handicap in war than in hunting, especially among preindustrial
societies that lack effective contraceptive technology.

No, I have not forgotten that women in more evolved societies have formed combat brigades and fought alongside men as
guerrillas and terrorists and that they are now finding a measure of

acceptance as police officers, prison guards, and graduates of military academies. It is true that thousands of women served as combat troops in the Russian Revolution and in World War II on the Russian front, as well as in the Viet Cong and in many other guerrilla movements. But this does not alter the importance of warfare in shaping gender hierarchies among band-and-village peoples. The weapons used in all of these instances are firearms, not muscle-powered weapons. The same holds true for the famous corps of female warriors who fought for the West African kingdom of Dahomey during the nineteenth century. Of a force of about 20,000 in the Dahomey army, 15,000 were men and 5,000 were women. But many of the women were unarmed and performed duties as scouts, porters, drummers, and litter-bearers rather than as direct combatants. The elite of the female fighting force—numbering between 1,000 and 2,000—lived inside the royal compound and acted as the king's personal bodyguard. During several recorded battles, the female corps seems to have fought as fiercely and as effectively as the men. But their principal arms were muskets and blunderbusses, not spears or bows and arrows, thereby minimizing the physical differences between them and their adversaries. In addition, the Dahomey king viewed pregnancy among his female soldiers as a serious threat to his security. Although they were technically married to him, he did not have sex with them. And those who became pregnant were accused of adultery and were executed. Clearly the circumstances that made it possible for the Dahomey to rely on female warriors, even to a limited extent, did not exist in war-making bands and villages. The populations of bands and villages were too small to maintain a professional standing army; they lacked centralized leadership and the economic resources needed to train, feed, house, and discipline a standing army, male or female; and above all they were militarily dependent on bows and arrows, spears, and clubs rather than on firearms. As a consequence, among band-and-village societies, the more warfare there was, the more women suffered from male oppression. Let me give a few examples.

WAR AND
SEXISM

*T*O HAVE WAR, one must have teams of armed combatants. None of the killings reported by Richard Lee were carried out during raids by combat teams and therefore were not acts of war. Two of Lee's informants indicated that raiding by armed teams did take place long ago before the Bechuanaland Protectorate Police appeared in the area. If so, it could not have been very common or intense, or more people would have remembered. The virtual absence of raiding or any other warlike manifestation among the !Kung therefore goes hand in hand with their primarily egalitarian gender roles.

Although the !Kung seldom resort to organized armed conflict, they fall short of being the peaceful paragons depicted in Elizabeth Thomas's book, *The Harmless People*. Richard Lee's estimate of twenty-two homicides over a period of fifty years mentioned a moment ago works out to a homicide rate of 29.3 per 100,000 persons per year, considerably less than Detroit's 58.2 but considerably more than the F.B.I.'s overall U.S. average of 10.7. I admit the Kalahari Desert is no Eden, but as Lee points out, the rate of homicide in modern industrial nations is much higher than official criminal-justice figures show because of a peculiar semantic deception: Killings carried out during wartime by modern states against the "enemy" are not counted as murders. Deaths caused by military action against combatants and civilians boost the homicide rate of modern state societies far above that of the !Kung, with their virtual absence of warfare.

Unlike the !Kung, many band-level societies do engage in moderate amounts of warfare and have correspondingly more pronounced forms of male sexism. This was true of the native peoples of Australia when they were first encountered and studied by European scientists. The Aborigines of Queensland in northeast Australia, for example, who were organized into bands of forty to fifty people and made their living exclusively from foraging for plants and animal life, regularly dispatched teams of warriors to avenge the wrongdoings of enemy bands. Eyewitness accounts testify to a moderately high level of organized intergroup killing, which culminated in cooking and eating captives, a reward reserved exclusively for male warriors, but a fate that mainly befell women and children.

Along with these warlike interests, the Aborigines possessed a well-developed but far from extreme form of male supremacy. Among older males, polygyny was common, some men acquiring as many as four wives. Men discriminated against women in the distribution of food. Carl Lumholtz reported that a man "often keeps the animal food for himself, while the woman has to depend principally upon vegetables for herself and her child." The sexual double standard prevailed. Men beat or killed their wives for adultery, but wives did not have similar recourse. And the division of labor between the sexes was anything but equal. Lumholtz has this to say about it:

> [The woman] must do all the hard work, go out with her basket and her stick to gather fruits, dig roots, or chop larvae out of the tree-stems. . . . [She] is often obliged to carry her little child on her shoulders during the whole day, only setting it down when she has to dig in the ground or climb trees. . . . When she comes home again, she usually has to make great preparations for beating, roasting, and soaking the fruits, which are very often poisonous. It is also the woman's duty to make a hut and gather the materials for the purpose. . . . She also provides water and fuel. . . . When they travel from place to place the woman has to carry all the baggage. The husband is therefore always seen in advance with no burden save a few light weapons, such as spears, clubs, or boomerangs, while his wives follow laden like packhorses with even as many as five baskets containing provisions. There is frequently a little child in one of the baskets, and a larger child may also be carried on the shoulders.

None of this adds up to a pattern of ruthless subordination of women. What Lloyd Warner had to say about gender roles among the Murngin, another group of bellicose foragers who lived in northern Australia, probably applied to the Aborigines of Queensland as well:

A wife has considerable independence. She is not the badly treated woman of the older Australian ethnologists' theories. She usually asserts her rights. Women are more vocal than men in Murngin society. Frequently they discipline their husbands by refusing to give them food when the men have been away too long and the wives fear they have had a secret affair.

Village-organized societies that derive their subsistence in part from rudimentary forms of agriculture often carry warfare and male dominance to greater extremes than band-organized foraging societies. Let me illustrate this contrast with the case of the Yanomami, a much-studied people who inhabit the border region between Brazil and Venezuela. Yanomami boys start to train for warfare at an early age. As reported by anthropologist Jacques Lizot, when little boys strike each other, their mothers urge them to return blow for blow. Even if a child gets knocked down by accident, the mother shouts from afar, "Avenge yourself, go on, avenge yourself!" Lizot saw one boy bite another. The victim's mother came running, told him to stop crying, grabbed the other boy's hand, and put in into her son's mouth and said, "You bite him now!" Should another child hit her son with a stick, the mother "places the stick into her son's hand and, if necessary, she herself will move his arm." Yanomami boys learn cruelty by practicing on animals. Lizot watched as several male juveniles gathered around a wounded monkey. They poked their fingers into the wounds and pushed sharp sticks into its eyes. As the monkey dies, little by little, "its every contortion stimulates them and makes them laugh." Later in life, men on the warpath treat their enemies the same way. In one engagement, a raiding party wounded a man who had tried to escape by jumping into the water. Lizot says that the pursuers dove into the water after him, dragged him onto the bank, lacerated him with the tips of their arrows, shoved sticks through his cheeks, and gouged his eyes by pushing the end of a bow into them.

The Yanomami's favorite form of armed engagement is the surprise raid at dawn. Under cover of darkness, the members of the raiding party pick a trail outside the enemy village and wait for the first man or woman to come along at daybreak. They kill as many men as they can, take the women as captives, and try to leave the scene before the whole village can be roused. On other occasions, they get close enough to the village to shower it with arrows before retreating. A deadly form of attack occurs when one village visits another, ostensibly for a peaceful purpose. Once the guests settle down and put aside their arms, their hosts attack them. Or it can be the other way around; unsuspecting hosts can find themselves the victims of their supposedly friendly guests. These raids, counterraids, and ambushes take a heavy toll on Yanomami life—about 33 percent of adult male deaths result from armed combat, leading to an overall homicide rate of 166 per 100,000 people per year.

In keeping with this intense pattern of warfare, relations between Yanomami men and women are markedly hierarchical and androcentric. To begin with, the Yanomami are polygynous. Successful men usually have more than one wife; some have as many as six at a time. Occasionally, a second husband may be forced on a wife as a favor to the husband's brother. Husbands beat their wives for disobedience, but especially for adultery. During domestic squabbles, husbands yank on the sticks of cane that women wear through their pierced earlobes. Anthropologist Napoleon Chagnon reported one case of a husband who chopped off his wife's ears and another of a husband who chopped a big piece out of his wife's arm. In other reported cases, husbands battered wives with sticks of firewood, swung at them with machetes and axes or burned them with firebrands. One shot a barbed arrow into his wife's leg; another aimed wrong and shot his wife in the stomach.

The Yanomami father chooses a husband for his daughter while she is still a child. But betrothals may be altered and contested by rival suitors. Jacques Lizot and Judith Shapiro independently describe scenes in which rival husbands-to-be grabbed a girl's arms and pulled in opposite directions while she shrieked in pain.

But the Yanomami are far from being the world's worst warmongers and most ardent male chauvinists. That dubious distinction belongs to certain village societies found throughout highland Papua New Guinea, whose central institution is the Nama, a male initiation cult that trains men simultaneously to be fierce warriors and to dominate women. Inside the cult house, which no woman may ever enter, the Nama men store their sacred flutes whose sounds terrorize the women and children. Only male initiates learn that it is their fathers and brothers who make the sounds and not carnivorous supernatural birds. They swear to kill any woman or child who learns the secret even by accident. Periodically, the initiates make their noses bleed and induce vomiting to rid themselves of the polluting effects of contact with women. After being secluded in the cult house, the initiates emerge into adulthood. They are given a bride, whom they promptly shoot in the thigh with an arrow "to demonstrate . . . unyielding power over her"; women work in the gardens, raise pigs, and do all the dirty work while men stand around gossiping, making speeches, and decorating themselves with paint, feathers, and shells.

According to Daryl Feil of the University of Sydney:

> Women were severely punished for adultery by having burning sticks thrust into their vaginas, or they were killed by their husbands; they were whipped with cane if they spoke out of turn or presumed to offer their opinions at public gatherings; and were physically abused in marital arguments. Men could never be seen to be weak or soft in dealings with women. Men do not require specific incidents or reasons to abuse or mistreat women; it is part of the normal course of events; indeed, in ritual and myth, it is portrayed as the essential order of things.

Extreme among extremists are the Sambia, the eastern highland Papua New Guinea group whose obsession with semen and homosexuality I described some pages ago. Here not only do men exclude women from their sacred clubhouse, but they so fear women's breath and vaginal odors that they partition the whole village into men's and women's areas, complete with separate paths for each sex. Sambia men assault their wives both verbally and physically, equate them with enemies and treachery, and treat them as worthless inferiors. For many women, suicide was the only way out. As in the eastern highlands in general, Sambia men faced a multiplicity of physical dangers. A man could be ambushed, cut down in battle, or axed to death in his gardens; his only defense was lifelong training for physical strength, stamina, and phallic mastery. Women were his primary victims.

As for warfare, it was "general, pervasive and perpetual." People lived in villages protected by palisades, yet so endemic was the raiding and counterraiding that a man could not eat without looking over his shoulder or leave his house in the morning to urinate without fear of being shot. Among the Bena Bena, raiding was so common that the men, armed to the teeth, would cautiously escort the women out of the stockade in the morning and stand guard over them while they worked in the fields until it was time to go back in. I cannot cite reliable statistics on deaths due to homicide for these groups. The carnage probably surpassed that of the Yanomami since whole villages consisting of 200 people were from time to time wiped out entirely. If figures from other parts of highland New Guinea are applicable, the Sambia's homicide rate could have been over 500 per 100,000 people per year, or seventeen times greater than the !Kung's.

Here I rest my case for believing that warfare is the key variable for predicting and understanding variations in gender hierarchies —at least among band-and-village societies. But this conclusion leaves me with a dissatisfied feeling since it answers one very important question only at the expense of raising another very important one: If war explains band-and-village sexism, what explains band-and-village war?

WHY WAR?

OR EXPLAINING WARFARE, theories of innate aggression seem to me to have as little merit as they do for explaining sexism. Innate, aggressive potentials must surely be part of human nature in order for there to be any degree of sexism or warfare, but cultural selection wields the power that activates or inactivates these raw potentials and channels them into specific cultural expressions. (Or shall we believe that the !Kung San have genes for peace and equality, while the Sambia have genes for war and inequality?)

I propose, in brief, that bands and villages make war because they find themselves in competition for resources such as soils, forests, and game upon which their food supply depends. These resources become scarce as a result of being depleted or as a result of rising population densities, or a combination of the two. Local groups then recurrently face the prospect of having to reduce their rate of population growth or their level of resource consumption. To reduce their population is in itself costly, given the lack of industrial-age means of contraception and abortion. And reductions in the quality and quantity of resource consumption inevitably subvert a people's health and vigor, causing extra deaths through malnutrition, hunger, and disease.

For band-and-village societies that confront these alternatives, warfare offers a tempting solution. If one group can succeed in driving away its neighbors or thinning their ranks, there will be more land, trees, soil, fish, meat, and other resources for the victors. Since warfare as practiced by bands and villages does not guarantee mutual destruction, groups can rationally accept the risk of battlefield fatalities in return for the chance of improving their living conditions by forcibly lowering their neighbor's population density.

In his study of warfare among the Mae Enga of the western highlands of Papua New Guinea, Mervyn Meggitt estimates that aggressor groups succeeded in gaining significant amounts of enemy land in 75 percent of their wars. "Given that the initiation of warfare usually pays off for the aggressors, it is not surprising that by and large the Mae count warfare as well worth the cost in human casualties," comments Meggitt. On the basis of their study of a carefully drawn representative sample of 186 societies, anthropologists Carol and Melvin Ember found that preindustrial peoples mostly go to war to moderate or cushion the impact of unpredictable (rather than chronic) food shortages and that the victorious side almost always takes some resources from the losers. Human societies find it difficult to prevision recurrent but unpredictable drops in food production caused by droughts, floods, storms, killing frosts, and insect swarms and to adjust population levels accordingly. Incidentally, the Embers have this to say about the prevalence of warfare: "Most societies known to anthropology have had warfare, i.e., fighting between territorial units (bands, villages, and aggregates thereof). And the warfare probably occurred a lot more often than even we are used to in the modern world: in the societies we have looked at that were described before pacification, nearly 75 percent had warfare at least once every two years."

But the problem of balancing population against resources can't be solved simply by thinning out the neighbors and taking over their resources. The fecundity of the human female is so great that even if raiding reduces the density of a territory by half, all it takes is twenty-five years of unrestrained breeding for the population to reach its former level. Warfare, therefore, does not dispense with the need to control population by other costly means such as abstinence, prolonged lactation, abortion, and infanticide. On the contrary, it may actually achieve its most important demographic effects not by eliminating but by increasing one particular costly practice—female infanticide.

In the absence of warfare and its androcentric bias, there would be no marked preference for rearing more children of one sex than the other, and rates of infanticide for male and female infants would tend to be equal. But warfare places a premium on maximizing the number of future warriors, which leads to the preferential treatment of male infants and higher rates of direct and indirect female infanticide. So in many band-and-village societies the greatest population-regulating consequences of warfare may result not from short-term effects of raiding but from the long-term effects of female infanticide and the ill-treatment of women in general. For what counts most in the regulation of population growth is not the number of males—one or two will suffice if there is polygyny—but the number of females.

A study that William Divale and I carried out on a sample of 112 societies lends circumstantial support to the proposal that warfare leads to high rates of direct and indirect female infanticide. We found that in the age group from birth to fourteen, boys outnumbered girls 127 to 100 before warfare was repressed by colonial powers. After warfare was repressed, the sex ratio for the same age group fell to 104 to 100, which is about normal for modern populations.

Warfare among band-and-village peoples, in other words, is no mere venting of fears and frustrations generated by population pressure. By thinning out the density of people to resources, and by slowing rates of reproduction, warfare in its own right acts to slow or reverse the rise of regional population pressure. And it is because of these systemic ecological and demographic advantages, and not because of a genetic imperative, that warfare has been recurrently selected for during the evolution of band-and-village peoples.

My intention here is not to praise warfare but simply to damn it less than some of its alternatives when certain conditions prevail. As practiced by band-and-village peoples, warfare was a wasteful and brutal way to cope with population pressure. But given the absence of effective contraception or medical abortion, the alternative was also wasteful and brutal: malnutrition, hunger, disease, and short, mean, and nasty lives for everyone. Of course, the favorable accounting of the balance of effects applies far more to winners than to losers. And perhaps it does not apply at all, when, on occasion, conflicts became so endemic, remorseless, and unrelenting that there were no winners and more people died from the effects of war than would have died from the effects of malnutrition. But then, again, no system is fail-safe.

Let me pause a moment to attend to a few additional conceptual problems. First, I need to point out that population pressure is not a static condition but a process in which increasingly unfavorable balances develop between the effort people put into obtaining their food and other necessities and the output from that effort. The process begins as soon as people encounter diminishing returns, as, for

298

example, when hunters find that they must search longer and harder to kill as many animals as they used to. If people do nothing to slow or reverse it, the process will eventually reach the point where it permanently degrades their habitat through extinctions of flora and fauna or depletions of other nonrenewable resources, and they will be obliged to find other means of subsistence.

Another issue is how signs of hunger and malnutrition relate to population pressure. One should not expect a one-to-one correlation between them. By working harder and by rearing fewer children, the adult members of band-and-village societies may avoid presenting any clinical signs of hunger or malnutrition. In such cases, the only indicators of population pressure may be the means employed to restrict numbers of children reared, on the assumption that costly practices such as infanticide, abortion, and abstinence would not be employed unless a group was pressing against its resource limits, at least to a moderate extent. Naturally, if people engage in infanticide, abortion, and prolonged abstinence and at the same time display symptoms of acute malnutrition and hunger, one would regard them as experiencing a more intense level of population pressure.

The final point concerns the relationship between population pressure and a society's overall population density. Sociologist Gregory Leavitt found a high correlation between settlement size and warfare in a sample of 133 societies of all types. But one must be careful not to assume that bigger settlements and more people per square mile always indicate greater pressure on essential resources. This relationship only holds true when comparing societies that have similar modes of subsistence. The Netherlands, with a population density of over 900 people per square mile, has less population pressure, measured by indices of malnutrition and hunger, than Zaire, with 40 people per square mile, or even some foraging societies with population densities of less than one person per square mile. Groups possessing domesticated plants and animals generally have higher population densities than hunter-gatherers. But hunter-gatherers and those who possess domesticated plants and animals are equally vulnerable to population pressure, albeit usually at different densities.

Because of these caveats and complications, I cannot provide precise measurements of the relative degrees of population pressure found in different societies. Rough approximations must suffice. But the cumulative indications of stresses and strains strongly suggest that band-and-village societies must pay a heavy price for keeping population and food supply in balance, and warfare is part of that price. How well does this explanation of warfare fit the cases under discussion?

MEAT, NUTS,
AND CANNIBALS

*T*HE *!KUNG SAN* appear to be the least subject to population pressure as I have defined it. They derive the bulk of their subsistence from the protein- and fat-rich nuts of mongongo trees, groves of which grow wild throughout their arid habitat. Mongongos are so plentiful some nuts even remain on the ground unused at the end of the year. But harvests of wild varieties of nuts are notorious for their unreliability, due to insect invasions, plant diseases, and aberrant weather patterns, so that their bounteousness in the short run may prove deceptive. Lacking permanent settlements, the !Kung are free to move about from grove to grove and from water hole to water hole in search of big game animals as a supplement to their plant food staples— warthogs, gemsbok, kudu, and wildebeest being the most common of the big game species that live in their habitat. During the two least productive months of the year, the !Kung may have to tighten their belts and eat less, but most of the time their diet is well balanced, if somewhat skimpy in calories. Moreover, they regulate the size of their families by primarily relying on prolonged lactation, eschewing the more costly alternatives of abstinence, abortion, or infanticide (except for twins). Virtual absence of warfare, separate-but-equal gender roles, and relative freedom from food scarcity and other symptoms of population pressure all go together in this case.

Yet as I have already admitted, the Kalahari Desert is no Garden of Eden, even if the discontents generated by population pressure are insufficient to lead to warfare. A dark cloud does in fact hang over the !Kung's apparent well-being. Although the !Kung do not practice infanticide, demographic records show that about half of their children die before reaching maturity. Nutritional factors must account for part of this toll of young lives. Perhaps the fault lies with the prolongation of nursing which, as I mentioned earlier, can last up to four years. Too great a reliance on mother's milk can lead to iron deficiency anemia in young children and perhaps to calorie deficits as well. If so, !Kung lactation is more costly than it seems at first sight. But how hard-pressed are the !Kung compared with more warlike foragers, like the Queensland Aborigines?

The Queensland Aborigines, like the !Kung, nursed their children for several years. But in addition, women abstained from sex during the lactation period. Consequently, except for males who had several wives, both sexes were obliged to be sexually abstemious for many months at a time. In contrast to the !Kung, they also practiced direct infanticide, especially female infanticide. Coupled with the practice of polygyny, female infanticide led to late marriage or no marriage at all for junior males. In addition, the Queensland Aborigines seem to have had more of a problem maintaining an adequate diet than the !Kung. During part of the year they lived in permanent thatched huts in settlements of forty to fifty people that were like small villages. They too derived most of their calories from nuts—not mongongos but wild walnuts and almonds—and what I said about the unreliability of nuts as staples applies here as well. But their rain forest habitat was much more poorly endowed with animal resources than the open country inhabited by the !Kung, possibly as a result of too much hunting. They consumed snakes, beetle larvae, rats, opposum, an occasional tree kangaroo, and fish in season, but they never seemed to get enough meat, especially fatty meat. This problem affected the women more than the men for, as I mentioned earlier, when men distributed meat from the hunt, they often excluded women and children.

Perhaps the most telling symptom of population pressure among the Queensland Aborigines was their penchant for capturing enemy women and children and eating them. Humans are the most expensive and dangerous source of animal fats and proteins. For this reason societies that have abundant alternative sources of protein in the form of big game or of domesticated animals tend to shy away from eating their enemies, even when bodies are available as a by-product of warfare. But cannibalism can become well-nigh irresistible if no other big game is available. Humans are not only big animals, but like most domesticated species, we are a lot fatter than wild game. Indeed, the Queensland Aborigines most prized the fat around the kidney, and their expressed preference for consuming women and children may also have reflected an interest in portions that had more fat than they could obtain by eating adult males. I shall leave further discussion on the finer points of people-eating to a later segment. But the time has come for us to take a closer look at why a low intake of animal foods in general is usually a symptom of population pressure and a provocation for attacking one's neighbors.

A DISSERTATION
ON FATTY MEAT

*H*UMANS ARE OMNIVORES —consumers of both plants and animals. Yet virtually all human groups as well as most of our primate cousins (remember Worzle's tantrum) make a fuss about the production, exchange, and consumption of meat and other animal foods. (Even vegetarians like India's Brahmans or Jains prize the consumption of milk and butter over plant foods.) This does not mean that humans are compelled by genetic programming to seek out and consume flesh foods, the way lions or eagles and other true carnivores are driven to eat meat. A more plausible view is that our species-given physiology and digestive processes predispose us to learn to prefer animal foods. We and our primate cousins pay special attention to such foods because they are exceptionally nutritious.

Meat is a more concentrated source of essential amino acids, the building blocks of proteins, than any plant food. Proteins in turn are crucial for all body-building and body-regulating functions. In addition, meat is also an excellent source of vitamins A and E and of the entire B complex, including B-12, which cannot be obtained from plant foods at all. Significant amounts of all the other vitamins and all of the essential minerals are also present in meat. Perhaps even more important, meat is a source of fats that are hard to obtain from plants and essential for the absorption and transport of vitamins A, D, E, and K.

Much of the craving for meat and the excitement it generates reflects the unique nutritional benefits that preindustrial populations derive from consuming a food that often contains both high-quality protein and lots of fat in one concentrated package. The first priority of a hungry person's body is to convert whatever food it consumes into energy. Supplied with nothing but lean meat, the body uses the protein in it for energy rather than for body-building and body-regulating functions. One way to "spare" the protein in meat is to eat it along with calorie-rich starchy foods, a practice followed around the world, as in steak and potatoes, chicken and rice, spaghetti and meat balls, and pork and dumplings. Among the Yanomami the protein-sparing combination is meat and plantains. Kenneth Good has told me that the Yanomami absolutely refuse to eat meat if it is not accompanied by plantains, although they will eat plantains without meat. The best protein-saving combination of all, however, is fatty meat, since fat contains twice as many calories per gram as starch. For this reason alone, one might expect that fatty meat (or high-fat-content milk, among dairying peoples) would be a food held in high esteem among preindustrial societies.

But there is another benefit of meat as a source of fat that is unrelated to the problem of conserving proteins for body-building and body-regulating functions. As I pointed out in an earlier context, among people who experience hungry seasons and other marked fluctuations in food supply, the conversion of calories into body fat during good times is essential for survival during bad times. In order to build up fat reserves, the body has to expend calories. If the food to be converted to fat is a starch, almost a quarter of its caloric value is wasted as a cost of the conversion and storage process. But if the source of the stored fat is fat itself, only 3 percent of the ingested calories are lost.

In a world full of people struggling to lose weight and to cut back on cholesterol and saturated fats, meat does not seem like a resource worth fighting over. But preindustrial people are in no danger of consuming too much cholesterol or saturated fats and their lives are not cut short by clogged arteries. The animals they hunt are in general much leaner than modern feed-lot finished beef, and meatless meals are the rule rather than the exception. If modern states threaten to go to war to put gasoline in their cars, should one be surprised that band-and-village peoples go to war to put meat in their larders?

And now on to population pressure among the Yanomami.

GAME WARS?

*T*HE PROBLEM OF GETTING ENOUGH animal fats and proteins seems to be the underlying cause of the Yanomami's intense warfare and male supremacist complex. Unlike the !Kung and the Queenslanders, the Yanomami practice a rudimentary form of agriculture. They clear and burn a few acres of forest at a time, raising plantains and bananas in the nitrogen-rich ashes. While proteinaceous and oily wild plant products such as palm fruits grow wild in the forest, these are available only on an intermittent or seasonal basis and do not provide an effective substitute for meat.

Despite the notion that the Amazon teems with big game, large huntable species are scarce, much scarcer than in open grasslands. What jungles teem with by way of animal life are insects and earthworms, duly consumed by native peoples, but seasonally or under duress, when they cannot find other sources of animal flesh. As I indicated in discussing acquired tastes, the preference for larger animals that occurs universally among band-and-village peoples reflects the prohibitive costs involved in capturing and processing thousands of small, dispersed creatures in order to get the equivalent food value of one big one. Although they are not malnourished, the Yanomami do engage in high levels of female infanticide, resulting in sex ratios from birth to fourteen years of age of about 130 boys to 100 girls. It seems likely that this practice is part of their attempt to slow or reverse diminishing returns in hunting and reflects a considerable degree of population pressure, despite the great expanse of jungle available to them.

As Yanomami villages grow in size, game must be sought in more and more distant areas, and per capita meat consumption falls. Raiding between villages helps to slow or temporarily reverse this decline by dispersing and thinning the regional population.

Kenneth Good, who has studied the Yanomami for over a decade, sees them as virtually obsessed with the problem of obtaining a regular supply of meat. Despite their "meat-hunger," they consume meat only once or twice a week on the average. Moreover, Good found that hunting efficiency rapidly declines in areas close to villages, necessitating frequent long-distance hunts, some of which take the whole village on protracted treks. Were it not for these long sojourns away from the village, game near the village would soon be completely wiped out.

Several Amazonists have argued against the theory that game depletions are responsible for Yanomami warfare. They point to the fact that there are no clinical signs of malnutrition among the Yanomami. Also, they have shown that in at least one village, whose population is thirty-five, daily per capita overall protein intake is seventy-five grams per day per adult, far more than recommended by the Food and Agricultural Organization. They have also shown that Yanomami villages with low levels of protein intake (thirty-six grams) seem to engage in warfare just as frequently as those that have high protein intake (seventy-five grams) per adult.

But as Good's studies show, the average daily amount of meat produced can be misleading. Because of fluctuations in the number and size of animals captured, there is little or no meat available most of the time, and, as I have already forewarned, the absence of clinical signs of malnutrition cannot be taken as evidence for no population pressure. The fact that villages with both high and low per capita meat consumption engage equally in warfare also does not assure an absence of such pressure. Warfare necessarily pits villages at different stages of growth and resource depletion against each other, and groups with lower levels of consumption and larger populations will seek out smaller groups with higher levels of consumption as their targets.

As an alternative to game-war explanations, Napoleon Chagnon proposes that the Yanomami males go to war in order to maximize their reproductive success. Not only do warriors capture women and bring them home to be wives, but, by being fierce in combat, a warrior can intimidate the people of his village, get married earlier, have more wives and affairs, and consequently have more children. The flaw in this argument, aside from my previously expressed reservations about reproductive success as the arbiter of cultural selection, is the Yanomami's high rate of female infanticide, an extremely effective method of minimizing, not maximizing, reproductive success. The best way for Yanomami males to satisfy their desire for women would be to rear more girls than boys. Why do precisely the opposite? Because they have passed the point of diminishing returns in their effort to extract a nutritionally sound diet from their jungle habitat and therefore are under pressure to limit their population growth. It is this pressure that makes them so warlike, and it is because they are so warlike that they are such consummate male chauvinists.

Let us see if this logic applies to the even more warlike and sexist Papuans.

HUNGRY
PAPUANS

INITIALLY, IT MIGHT SEEM as if the bellicose Papuans should be less stressed by diminishing returns than the Yanomami because they get plant food from domesticated sweet potatoes and animal proteins and fats from domesticated pigs. But the population density of the highland groups is far greater than anything found among Amazonian villages (thirty persons per square mile compared to less than one person per square mile), making the relationship between food-related resources and the demand for animal fats and proteins even more precarious than among the Yanomami. Moreover, not only were the Papuans confronted with diminishing returns, but they had to contend with severe depletions of their basic resources. Like the Yanomami, the Papuans plant their gardens in the midst of trees that have been felled and burned and whose ashes provide fertilizer for their crops. Without trees to burn, they cannot grow their crops and feed themselves or their pigs (at least not unless they change over to a much more intensive and complex form of agriculture). Their population density is too great for them to allow sufficient time between harvests for the trees to regenerate after being felled and burned. As a result, grasslands have replaced forests over wide areas, and there can be no doubt that the fierce wars that these people wage have as their principal objective the forceful expropriation of land suitable for cultivation. Here signs of protein-calorie deficits abound, attesting to a higher level of population pressure than in the previous cases. Children, women, and old men are especially malnourished, subsisting mainly on fibrous, low-protein-content sweet potatoes, with very occasional and irregular consumption of pork.

Moreover, these groups employed costly means of limiting reproduction. Among the Gahuka-Gama, for example, where families averaged only one child, men firmly believed that their women would either try to abort the fetus or kill the infant every time they got pregnant. The neighboring Bena Bena practiced female infanticide, and even said in explanation that they did it because girls can't become warriors. Recall also that many of the eastern highland groups prohibited heterosexual intercourse for extensive periods of the year, substituting the obligatory practice of homosexual intercourse during the men's cult rituals.

What the Papuans gained in sweet potato and pig husbandry they lost in the wild animals and plants that once lived in the forests. So, despite their possession of domesticated pigs, they were, if anything, even more obsessed than the Yanomami with obtaining a steady supply of animal flesh. Men fared better than women and children because they monopolized the eating of pork. To satisfy their meat hunger, women and children had to be content with insects, frogs, and mice. Nothing that crawled or crept was wasted. Midwives ate even the placentas of newborn infants, and so great was their craving for animal fats and proteins that women of the Fore peoples took to digging up the partly decomposed bodies of deceased relatives and eating the flesh. They also ate the maggots, which they regarded as a great delicacy. And perhaps this explains why they let the corpses begin to decompose before eating them. Is it any wonder these people wanted to kill off their neighbors and take over their lands?

Since I have been misunderstood in my previous writings about the relationship between warfare and sexism, let me emphasize that the formula the-more-warfare-the-more-sexism holds for band-and-village societies but not for chiefdoms and states. Chiefdoms, unlike bands and villages, engage in warfare with distant enemies. This improves, rather than worsens, the status of women. And in state-level societies, most males no longer receive the training or possess the weapons that make men such formidable adversaries among the Yanomami and the Sambia. But first let me attend to the effect that long-distance warfare had on gender hierarchies.

WHERE
WOMEN
RULE THE
ROOST

ONE OF THE CIRCUMSTANCES that makes life so difficult for women in Papua New Guinea and among the Yanomami is that the societies they live in practice patrilocality. That is, when women get married they leave the village or neighborhood in which their mother, father, and brothers are living and move in with their husband's paternal relatives. This isolates women from their closest kin who might otherwise intervene if they were being mistreated. Women in patrilocal village societies are doubly disadvantaged since they usually come from different villages and are comparative strangers to each other as well as to their husband's relatives, while all the men have lived together since infancy and know each other intimately The practice of patrilocality in these villages clearly reflects the influence of warfare, since success in war depends on the formation of combat teams, teams of men who have trained together, trust each other, and have reason to hate and kill the same enemy. What better way to form combat teams that meet these criteria than to have them consist of coresident fathers, sons, brothers, uncles, and paternal nephews?

But to remain together after they get married, these paternally related males must bring their wives to live with them rather than go off to live with their wives' families. There is one drawback. Success in raiding depends not only on well-coordinated teamwork but on the size of the combat force. For groups living in small villages, the only possibility of enlarging the combat force lies through forming alliances with neighboring villages.

In evolutionary perspective, military alliances can be seen as part cause and part effect of the process by which single-village political units become transformed into bigger and more complex multivillage chiefdoms. As this transformation progresses, unallied villages recede into the distance, to be encountered only after several days on the trail. Multivillage combat forces consisting of several hundred men now take to the field for months at a time, motivated by the opportunity to hunt in distant no-man's-lands, to trade with faraway villages, or to raid their enemy's granaries and storehouses.

But these long sojourns away from a man's fields, crops, and storehouses create a dilemma. Who can care for them in his absence? His wife is not to be trusted since, as I said, she comes from another village and is loyal to her own father and brother and other paternal kin rather than to her husband and his kin. The woman a man can trust most is his sister, for she alone shares with him a common interest in their paternal lands and property. Men who must be away from the village for weeks and months therefore recurrently refuse to let their sister follow the patrilocal rule, denying her in marriage unless the husband agrees to live with her rather than she with him. As increasing numbers of brothers and sisters adopt this strategy, the rule of patrilocal residence gradually gives way to its opposite: the rule of matrilocal residence. Followed consistently across several generations, a matrilocal rule of marriage results in the coresidence of a continuous line of mothers, sisters, and daughters. Husbands become the outsiders; it is they who feel isolated and who must cope with a united front of members of the opposite sex who have been living together all their lives. Where matrilocality prevails, therefore, women tend to take control of the entire domestic sphere of life. Husbands become more like visitors than permanent residents and divorce is frequent and as easy for women as for men. If a man mistreats his wife, or if she grows tired of him, she and her sister, mother, and maternal aunts send him packing to his own maternal family. And the fact that he is frequently away makes divorce that much easier to carry out.

The effects of matrilocality on women's status extend beyond the domestic sphere. As men transfer responsibility for managing the cultivation of their lands to female kin, women come to possess the means for influencing political, military, and religious policies.

Let me illustrate these general points with a specific example. From their palisaded villages in upstate New York, the matrilocal Iroquois dispatched armies composed of as many as 500 men to raid targets as far away as Quebec and Illinois. Upon returning to his native land, the Iroquois warrior joined his wife and children at their hearth in a village longhouse. The affairs of this communal dwelling were directed by a senior woman who was a close maternal relative of his wife. It was this matron who organized the work that the women of the longhouse performed at home and in the fields. She took charge of storing harvested crops and drawing on them as needed. When husbands were not off on some sort of expedition—absences of a year were common—they slept and ate in the female-headed longhouses but had virtually no control over how their wives lived and worked. If a husband was bossy or uncooperative, the matron might at any time order him to pick up his blanket and get out, leaving his children behind to be taken care of by his wife and the other women of the longhouse.

Turning to public life, the formal apex of political power among the Iroquois was the Council of Elders, consisting of elected male chiefs from different villages. The longhouse matrons nominated the members of this council and could prevent the seating of the men they opposed. But they did not serve on the council itself. Instead, they influenced the council's decisions by exercising control over the domestic economy. The longhouse matrons could withhold the stored foods, wampum belts, feather work, moccasins, skins, and furs under their control if a proposed action was not to their liking. Warriors could not embark on foreign adventures unless the women filled their bearskin pouches with the mixture of dried corn and honey men ate while on the trail. Religious festivals could not take place, either, unless the women agreed to release the necessary stores. Even the Council of Elders did not convene if the women decided to withhold food for the occasion. But in the final reckoning, matrilocal societies such as the Iroquois fall far short of subordinating men in the way that the fiercely male chauvinist villages of highland Papua New Guinea subordinate women. Despite their control over the longhouses and the agricultural and craft components of production, Iroquois women did not humiliate, degrade, and exploit their men. And when it comes to the public domain, the most that I can say is that women possessed almost as much influence as men but only by indirect means. Why is this the case?

Why doesn't matrilocality result in the full reversal of the patrilocal complex? Why this asymmetry? Why are there patriarchies but no matriarchies?

One answer that I cannot accept is that it is women's feminine nature that prevents them from doing unto men what men have done unto them. This idea (which serves, incidentally, as a common bed for sociobiologists and some radical feminists) is refuted by the role that women in matrilocal societies play in the treatment of enemy captives. The Tupinamba of Brazil, for example, tortured, dismembered, and ate their prisoners of war. This practice served several functions: It was a form of psychological warfare intended to demoralize the enemy; it hardened future warriors to the process of inflicting pain and suffering on human beings; and it discouraged thoughts of surrender, since the enemy could be expected to be equally brutal. Women participated enthusiastically in these torture deaths, taunting the bound prisoners, shoving burning sticks against their genitals, howling for pieces of their flesh when they finally expired and were cut up to be eaten. So I strongly doubt that the absence of matriarchy has anything to do with "feminine" restraints on being cruel and ruthless. As long as men monopolized the weapons and skills of armed combat, women lacked the means to boss, degrade, and exploit them in a mirror image of patriarchy. It was lack of power and not lack of masculinity that prevented women from turning the tables. For just as warfare created the conditions that led to matrilocality, so did warfare set the limits on how far matrilocal matrons could subordinate men without supplanting them on the battlefield.

WOMEN UP,
WOMEN DOWN

N EVOLUTIONARY PERSPECTIVE, band-and-village societies and egalitarian chiefdoms (like the Iroquois) recurrently evolved into stratified chiefdoms and states characterized by ruling classes and centralized governments. Later on I'll examine these transformations and try to explain why they occurred. But I should say something right now about the accompanying ups and downs of women's status. Stratified societies have bigger armies and wage war on a much grander scale than classless societies, but the effect of warfare on women is less direct and generally less invidious than in patrilocal band-and-village societies. What makes the difference is that soldiering becomes a specialty reserved for professionals. Most males no longer train from infancy to be killers of men, nor even to be killers of animals (since there are few animals left to hunt, except in royal preserves). Instead, they find themselves reduced to being unarmed peasants who are no less terrified of professional warriors than are their wives and children. Under these conditions, other determinants of sex and gender roles come to the fore. I don't mean to say that warfare ceased to create a demand for suitably macho men to be trained as warriors. But most women no longer had to deal with husbands whose capacity for violence was honed in battle. Female status, therefore, rose or fell, depending on other circumstances.

Favorable female gender relationships among preindustrial chiefdoms and states occurred in the forested areas of West Africa. Among the Yoruba, Ibo, Igbo, and Dahomey, women had their own fields and grew their own crops. They dominated the local markets and could acquire considerable wealth from trade. To get married, West African men had to pay bride-price—iron hoes, goats, cloth, and, in more recent times, cash—a transaction that in itself indicated that the groom and his family and the bride and her family agreed that the bride was a very valuable person and that her parents and relatives would not give her away without being compensated for her economic and reproductive capabilities. In fact, West Africans believed that to have many daughters was to be rich.

There was no double standard. Although men practiced polygyny, they could do so only if they consulted their senior wife and obtained her permission. Women, for their part, had considerable freedom of movement to travel to market towns, where they often had extramarital affairs. Furthermore, in many West African chiefdoms and states, women themselves could pay bride-price and "marry" other women. Among the Dahomey (whose female warriors I discussed a while back), a female husband built a house for her "wife" and arranged for a male consort to get her pregnant. By paying bride-price for several such "wives," an ambitious woman could establish control over a busy compound and become rich and powerful.

West African women also achieved high status outside the domestic sphere. They belonged to female clubs and secret societies, participated in village councils, and mobilized en masse to seek redress against mistreatment by men.

Among the Igbo of Nigeria, women met in council to discuss matters that affected their interests as traders, farmers, or wives. A man who violated the woman's market rules, let his goats eat a woman's crops, or persistently mistreated his wife ran the risk of mass retaliation. The miscreant would be awakened in the middle of the night by a crowd of women banging on his hut. They danced lewd dances, sang songs mocking his manhood, and used his backyard as a latrine until he promised to mend his ways. They called it "sitting-on-a-man."

The supreme rulers of these West African chiefdoms and states were almost always males. But their mothers and sisters and other female relatives occupied offices that gave women considerable power over both men and women. In certain Yoruba kingdoms, the king's female relatives directed the principal religious cults and managed the royal compounds. Anyone wanting to arrange rituals, hold festivals, or call up communal labor brigades had to deal with these powerful women first before they could gain access to the king. Among the Yoruba, women occupied an office known as "mother of all women," a kind of queen over females, who coordinated the voice of women in government, held court, settled quarrels, and decided what position women should take on the opening and maintenance of markets, levying of taxes and tolls, declarations of war, and other important public issues. And in at least two Yoruba kingdoms, Ijesa and Ondo, the office of queen-over-women may have been as powerful as the office of king-over-men. For every grade of male chief under the king-of-men there was a corresponding grade of female chief under the queen-of-women. Each met separately with his or her council of chiefs to discuss matters of state, reported what their respective followers had advised, relayed this information to the councils, and awaited further approval or disapproval before taking action. Unfortunately, my source does not state what happened when the two sides disagreed. I suspect that since the male half controlled the army, it probably got its way in any final showdown. But the degree of gender equality in West Africa as compared with other agricultural chiefdoms and states remains impressive.

Take northern India for example. Neither the high rate of female infanticide nor the preference for sons that I discussed in "Reproductive Failure" exists in West Africa. Another striking contrast is that a north Indian man who had many daughters regarded them as an economic calamity rather than an economic bonanza. Instead of receiving bride-price, the north Indian father paid each daughter's husband a dowry consisting of jewelry, cloth, or cash. In recent years, disgruntled or merely avaricious husbands have taken to demanding supplementary dowries. This has led to a spate of "bride-burnings" in which wives who fail to supply additional compensation are doused with kerosene and set on fire by husbands who pretend that the women killed themselves in cooking accidents. And speaking of burnings, north Indian culture has always been extremely unfriendly to widows. In the past, a widow was given the opportunity of joining her dead husband on his funeral pyre. Facing a life of seclusion with no hope of remarrying, subject to food taboos that brought them close to starvation, and urged on by the family priest and their husband's relatives, many women chose fiery death rather than widowhood. The contrast with how widows were treated in West Africa is striking. West African widows often married their deceased husband's brother—an institution called the levirate—and their prospects were seldom as ominous as in northern India.

What accounts for these differences?

HOES, PLOWS,
AND COMPUTERS

*T*HE UPS AND DOWNS of women's status in chiefdoms and states mirror the extent to which men were able to use their muscle and height advantages to gain control over technological processes vital for both warfare and production. When men and women are equally competent to perform vital military and production tasks, then women's status rises to parity. But if there are vital aspects of production or warfare that men carry out more effectively than women, then women's status will be lower.

The contrast between women's status in West Africa and northern India exemplifies this principle. These regions had two very different kinds of agriculture and divisions of labor—one in which both sexes were equally competent and the other in which men had a crucial physical advantage. In West Africa, the main agricultural implement was not an ox-drawn plow, as in northern India, but a short-handled hoe. The West Africans did not use plows because in their humid shady habitat the tsetse fly made it difficult to rear plow animals. Besides, West African soils do not dry out and become hard-packed as in arid northern India so that women using nothing but hoes were able to be as competent as men in preparing fields and had no need for men to grow, harvest, or market their crops. In northern India, the contribution of the sexes to agriculture was less favorable to women. Men maintained a monopoly over the use of ox-drawn plows, and these implements were indispensable for breaking the hard-packed soils. Men achieved this monopoly for essentially the same reasons that they achieved a monopoly over the weapons of hunting and warfare: Their greater bodily strength enabled them to be 15 percent to 20 percent more efficient than women. This advantage often meant the difference between survival and starvation, especially during prolonged dry spells when every inch to which a plowshare penetrates beneath the surface and every minute less it takes a pair of oxen to complete a furrow was critical for retaining moisture. As Morgan D. Maclachlan of the University of South Carolina found in his study of the sexual division of labor in a village in the state of Karnataka, the question is not whether Indian peasant women could be trained to manage a plow and a pair of oxen but whether in most families training men to do it leads to larger and more secure harvests. Maclachlan found that a plow typically weighs about 40 pounds and that a pair of small oxen exerts a pull of about 180 pounds. To get to the end of the day, the plowman has to guide his bulky ensemble back and forth for a distance of almost twenty miles, keeping the furrows straight and at a maximum uniform depth. According to Maclachlan, youths who lack the strength of full-grown men do all right for a short period, but after a few hours the plow begins to wobble and bucks up out of the soil and the furrows begin to wander.

The influence of alternative forms of agriculture on gender hierarchy stands out clearly within India itself. The states in the extreme south lack most of the harsh features that define male dominance in the north. In these states, especially in Kerala, which is famous for its strong female-centered family life and complementary gender roles, rainfall is more abundant, dry seasons are much shorter than in the north, and the principal crop is not wheat but rice grown in postage-stamp-sized paddy fields. The principal farm animals are water buffalo, not cattle, and their principal function is not to pull plows but to mix and "puddle" the mud by walking round and round in it up to their knees. Women and children can be as efficient as men in guiding these animals. The same is true of transplanting, which requires much stooping over and manual dexterity to uproot the clumps of rice seedlings in order to thin them out and stick them back into the mud.

The connection between rice paddy subsistence tasks and the development of complementary gender statuses holds true for vast regions to the south and east of Kerala as well. The agrarian states of Sri Lanka, Southeast Asia, and Indonesia are all based on "wet" rice production, in which women are at least as important as men for accomplishing crucial tasks, and it is precisely in these lands that women traditionally enjoyed an exceptionally high level of freedom and power in public as well as domestic relations.

Is a factor as simple as male control over plowing sufficient to explain female infanticide, dowry, and widows throwing themselves onto their husband's funeral pyre? Perhaps not, if one thinks only of the direct effects of plowing on agriculture itself. But in evolutionary perspective this male specialty set in motion a whole train of additional specializations that cumulatively do point to a plausible explanation of almost every feature of the depressed status of women in northern India and in other preindustrial societies with similar forms of agriculture. As a result of learning how to plow, men learned how to yoke and drive oxen. Therefore, with the invention of the wheel, men yoked oxen to carts and acquired the specialty of driving animal-drawn wheeled vehicles. This put them in charge of transporting crops to market and from there it was a short step to their domination of both local and long-distance trade and commerce. As trade and commerce increased in importance, records had to be kept, and it was to men active in trade and commerce that the task of keeping these records fell. Therefore, with the invention of writing and arithmetic, men came to the fore as the first scribes and accountants. By extension, men became the literate sex; they read and wrote, and did arithmetic. And this explains why men, not women, came to the fore as the first historically known philosophers, theologians, and mathematicians.

Moreover, all of these indirect effects of plowing acted in concert with the continuing androcentric effects of warfare. By dominating the armed forces, men gained control over the highest administrative branches of government, including state religions. And the continuing need to recruit male warriors made the social construction of aggressive manhood a focus of national policy in every known state and empire. And that is why at the dawn of modern times men dominated politics, religion, art, science, law, industry, commerce, and the armed forces wherever people depended on animal-drawn plows for their basic food supply.

If this line of reasoning explains the evolution of so-called patriarchical institutions, it also should explain the current deflation of such institutions in advanced industrial societies. I think it does. Is not consciousness of women's rights rising as the strategic value of masculine brawn declines? Who needs 10 percent or 15 percent more muscle power when the decisive processes of production take place in automated factories or while people sit at desks in computerized offices? Men continue to fight for the retention of their old androcentric privileges, but they have been routed from one bastion after another as women fill the need for service and information workers by offering competent performance at lower wages than males. Even more than the market women of West Africa, women in today's advanced industrial societies have moved toward gender parity based on an ability to earn a living without being dependent on husbands or other males. But there is one last barrier to equality between the sexes. Despite the waning importance of brute strength in warfare, women continue to be excluded from combat roles in the world's military forces. Can women be trained to be as competent as men in armed combat with intercontinental ballistic missiles, smart bombs, and computerized firing systems? I see no reason to doubt it. But women must decide whether to push for equality of opportunity in the killing fields or to push for something else—the end of war and an end to the social need to raise macho warriors, whether they be males or females.

In the meantime, males would do well not to regret the passing of their sexist privileges. As I'll explain next, men are paying more than they know for their glittering Rambo image.

WHY DO
WOMEN LIVE
LONGER THAN
MEN?

HY DO WOMEN throughout the industrial world outlive men by four to ten years? Although life expectancy for both sexes rose during this century, women made much larger gains than men. As recently as 1920, life expectancy at birth for white women in the United States was only eight months more than for white men. Now it is 6.9 years more. White females gained 23 years of additional life, while their male counterparts gained fewer than 17 years. In 1920, among blacks, males outlived females. Today, black women in the United States live 8.4 years longer than black men.

Four to ten years is no laughing matter for the men who won't live them; nor is it good news for most of the women who will. The male's shorter life ruins the marriage prospects of younger divorced and widowed women and forces healthy older women to spend a good part of their existence taking care of sickly husbands. As its demographic effects accumulate, the longevity gap is creating a subculture of spinsters, widows, and divorcees whose life-styles are adjusted to sharing men or doing without them entirely.

My mailbox is stuffed every day with appeals to help needy, sick, homeless, and hungry people who suffer from all kinds of gaps —a generation gap, a poverty gap, a racial gap, and, yes, a gender gap, if you're talking wages and job opportunities. But I have never gotten an urgent "mailogram" to make men's life spans equal to women's. People seem to think there is nothing to be done about this problem because that is how nature made us. Being the biologically stronger sex, women naturally live longer.

The human male already displays what appears to be a built-in inability to grasp life as firmly as females even when he is just an embryo. At conception, male fetuses outnumber female fetuses 115 to 100, but at birth, as a result of more male intrauterine deaths, this ratio drops to 105 to 100. Male babies seem to show the same weakness, for they have higher rates of infant mortality than do female babies. Irrefutable evidence that males are congenitally weaker than females? No, not as long as alternative explanations are available. One would expect male fetuses and male neonates to present a greater challenge to their mother's body during pregnancy and at childbirth since male embryos and neonates are bigger than female embryos and neonates. While the precise cause of the attrition suffered by male embryos remains obscure, difficult births leading to injuries play a major role in higher rates of stillborn males and early male infant mortality. Studies show that sex differences in late fetal and early infant mortality rates became less pronounced in Europe, the United States, and New Zealand during this century, presumably in response to improved gynecological and obstetrical procedures.

Then there is the matter of the X and Y chromosomes. All of the twenty-three different chromosomes in the nucleus of human cells occur in matching pairs except for the chromosomes called X and Y. Women have a pair of X chromosomes but no Y; men have an X and a Y. Because their X chromosome is paired with another X chromosome, women have less of a risk of suffering deleterious consequences if an X chromosome has a defective gene, since the other X with a normal gene can serve as a "backup" and override the defect. Males with a defective gene on their unpaired Xs and Ys do not have this backup potential. That is why males more often suffer from X-linked hereditary diseases. Muscular dystrophy, for example, is caused by a defective gene on the X chromosome. Men get the disease more often than women because if they inherit the defective variant, they have no paired X chromosome with a normal gene to take over. Much remains to be learned about the function of the genes on the X and Y chromosomes, but given the present state of knowledge, there is no evidence that they could account for anything more than a week or two of the longevity gap.

I should also mention the possibility that estrogen, the female sex hormone, offers protection against heart disease by decreasing the level of low-density fats and cholesterol in the bloodstream, while androgens such as testosterone have the opposite effect. Unfortunately, estrogens are a mixed blessing, since they promote cancer of the breast, the most common form of fatal cancer among women in the United States and other industrial societies. In addition, as numerous studies show, high-cholesterol food, not androgens, are the primary cause of too much cholesterol and low-density fats in the bloodstream.

Male and female hormones probably also have different effects on the immune response system. Dosing female mice with androgens reduces antibody production; and castration of male mice leads to higher antibody production. But if human females do in fact have a more powerful immune system than males, it is, again, not an unmixed blessing. Rheumatoid arthritis, lupus (a disfiguring skin disease), and myasthenia gravis (a muscular disorder) are diseases produced by hyperimmune reactions that occur in women three to ten times more often than in men. In sum, while males and females do have distinctive sex-linked genetic predispositions that could influence mortality rates, the advantages are not all on the female side.

The balance of intrinsic factors for and against the greater life expectancy of one sex or the other remains obscure. But even if this balance favors females, it will not help us understand the longevity gap as it exists today. For the changes in the longevity of females, without which there would be no longevity gap, were entirely caused by cultural changes. These changes consist of general improvements in public health, with a higher valuation of the female gender role, fewer pregnancies, and improved care during pregnancy, delivery, and the postpartum period. We know that in the absence of these culturally selected changes, women's longevity would have remained much shorter than it is today and perhaps even shorter than men's.

At least a dozen Third World countries, including India, Bangladesh, Pakistan, Indonesia, and Iran, either have equal life expectancies at birth for males and females or a longevity gap that slightly favors males. And there may be many similar cases that remain unknown because census figures for Third World countries overestimate the life expectancy of females at birth. Given the widespread neglect of daughters in South Asia, for example, parents tend not to register or enumerate female infants who die in the first few months of life. Females with extremely short lives, therefore, are less likely to appear in the vital statistics than females who survive into early childhood. So the real life expectancy of females in many countries may be considerably shorter than the official data indicate. In contrast, Third World parents are more likely to remember early male deaths and to report them to the census taker.

In South Asia, where the longevity gap favors males rather

than females, mortality associated with pregnancy and childbirth is alone responsible for 25 percent of the deaths of women under age forty-five and between 33 percent and 100 percent of the excess rate of the mortality of women over the mortality of men.

Returning to the years of life gained by women in developed countries, are there any genetic changes experienced by women that can account for these gains? None whatsoever. Therefore *all* of the differences in female life expectancy between developed and underdeveloped countries as well as *all* of the female life expectancy changes since the beginning of the century in developed countries result from cultural selection. If so, the question that should be uppermost in our minds is not whether men naturally live shorter lives than women but why cultural changes and interventions failed to raise male life expectancy by at least the same number of years that female life expectancy was raised. This failure, as I'll show next, is not a consequence of having reached a biologically decreed upper limit of male longevity, but a culturally decreed consequence of male sexism.

THE HIDDEN
COST OF
MACHISMO

CAN THE FAILURE of males to gain life expectancy as fast as females also be accounted for entirely in terms of modifiable social and medical practices? I see no reason to doubt it. Males smoke more cigarettes than women, eat more fatty red meat, drink more alcohol, take more hard drugs, expose themselves to more industrial poisons and on-the-job hazards, drive faster and more recklessly, possess more firearms and other deadly weapons, and more often acquire tension-building competitive personalities. As a result, they die more often from heart attacks, strokes, and other cardiovascular diseases, from cancer of the lungs and cirrhosis of the liver, from automobile and industrial accidents, and from being murdered and committing suicide. Studies show that cigarette smoking alone could account for most of today's longevity gap.

The grim irony of this saga of woes is that it faithfully expresses the traditional macho gender role. Have our young men not been brought up to believe that it is manly to eat lots of meat, smoke two packs a day, drink their buddies under the table, ignore discomforts, take risks, drive fast, be quick on the draw, and show no fear? This sets me to wondering whether the strange silence that surrounds the longevity gap is itself an unintended by-product of the macho syndrome and the antagonisms that machismo has spawned between men and women. Have men simply done the "manly" thing and decided not to whine and complain? Men have only themselves to blame. Women could not be expected to take the lead in exposing the cultural secret of their longer lives. With feminists arguing that women are victims of sexism, the fact that they outlive men is a political inconvenience. Whoever heard of downtrodden serfs, peasants, slaves, colonials, outcastes, or proletariats who outlived their oppressors? And, of course, not all women dread the early demise of their spouses, especially heavily insured male chauvinist ones.

No matter how one chooses to explain the downplaying of

the longevity gap as a social issue, it seems to me to be important that both men and women understand it for what it really is: not the price that men have had to pay for being born with XY chromosomes; but the price they have to pay for living up to a culturally constructed macho image of what it takes to be a man.

I think it should be clear by now why the various degrees and kinds of subordination associated with human sexual differences are primarily the consequence of cultural rather than natural selection. Can one say the same about distinctions of rank in general? Are we compelled by our genes to live always in groups divided into the high and mighty and the weak and lowly? And if not, why does hierarchy pervade our lives?

WAS THERE LIFE BEFORE CHIEFS?

CAN HUMANS EXIST without some people ruling and others being ruled? The founders of political science did not think so. "I put for a general inclination of all mankind, a perpetual and restless desire for power after power, that ceaseth only in death," declared Thomas Hobbes. Because of this innate lust for power, Hobbes thought that life before (or after) the state was a "war of every man against every man"— "solitary, poor, nasty, brutish, and short." Was Hobbes right? Do humans have an unquenchable desire for power that, in the absence of a strong ruler, inevitably leads to a war of all against all? To judge from surviving examples of bands and villages, for the greater part of prehistory our kind got along quite well without so much as a paramount chief, let alone the all-powerful English leviathan King and Mortal God, whom Hobbes believed was needed for maintaining law and order among his fractious countrymen.

Modern states with democratic forms of government dispense with hereditary leviathans, but they have not found a way to dispense with inequalities in wealth and power backed up by an enormously complex system of criminal justice. Yet for 30,000 years after take-off, life went on without kings, queens, prime ministers, presidents, parliaments, congresses, cabinets, governors, mayors, police officers, sheriffs, marshals, generals, lawyers, bailiffs, judges, district attorneys, court clerks, patrol cars, paddy wagons, jails, and penitentiaries. How did our ancestors manage to leave home without them?

Small populations provide part of the answer. With 50 people per band or 150 per village, everybody knew everybody else intimately, so that the bonding of reciprocal exchange could hold people together. People gave with the expectation of taking and took with the expectation of giving. Since chance played a great role in the capture of animals, collection of wild foodstuffs, and the success of rudimentary forms of agriculture, the individuals who had the luck of the catch on one day needed a handout on the next. So the best way for them to provide for their inevitable rainy day was to be generous. As expressed by anthropologist Richard Gould, "The greater the amount of risk, the greater the extent of sharing." Reciprocity is a small society's bank.

In reciprocal exchange, people do not specify how much or exactly what they expect to get back or when they expect to get it. That would besmirch the quality of the transaction and make it similar to mere barter or to buying and selling. The distinction lingers on in societies dominated by other forms of exchange, even capitalist ones. For we do carry out a give-and-take among close kin and friends that is informal, uncalculating, and imbued with a spirit of generosity. Teenagers do not pay cash for their meals at home or for the use of the family car, wives do not bill their husbands for cooking a meal, and friends give each other birthday gifts and Christmas presents. But much of this is marred by the expectation that our generosity will be acknowledged with expressions of thanks. Where reciprocity really prevails in daily life, etiquette requires that generosity be taken for granted. As Robert Dentan discovered while doing fieldwork among the Semai of central Malaysia, no one ever says "thank you" for the meat received from another hunter. Having struggled all day to lug the carcass of a pig home through the jungle heat, the hunter allows his prize to be cut up into equal portions, which he then gives away to the entire group. Dentan explains that to express gratitude for the portion received indicates that you are the kind of ungenerous person who calculates how much you give and take. "In this context saying thank you is very rude, for it suggests first that one has calculated the amount of a gift and second, that one did not expect the donor to be so generous." To call attention to one's generosity is to indicate that others are in debt to you and that you expect them to repay you. It is repugnant to egalitarian peoples even to suggest that they have been treated generously.

Richard Lee tells how he learned about this aspect of reciprocity through a revealing incident. To please the !Kung, he decided to buy a large ox and have it slaughtered as a present. After several days searching Bantu agricultural villages looking for the largest and fattest ox in the region, he acquired what appeared to be a perfect specimen. But his friends took him aside and assured him that he had been duped into buying an absolutely worthless animal. "Of course, we will eat it," they said, "but it won't fill us up—we will eat and go home to bed with stomachs rumbling." But when Lee's ox was slaughtered, it turned out to be covered with a thick layer of fat. Later, his friends explained why they had said his gift was valueless, even though they knew better than he what lay under the animal's skin:

> Yes, when a young man kills much meat he comes to think of himself as a chief or a big man, and he thinks of the rest of us as his servants or inferiors. We can't accept this, we refuse one who boasts, for someday his pride will make him kill somebody. So we always speak of his meat as worthless. This way we cool his heart and make him gentle.

Lee watched small groups of men and women returning home every evening with the animals and wild fruits and plants that they had killed or collected. They shared everything equally, even with campmates who had stayed behind and spent the day sleeping or taking care of their tools and weapons.

> Not only do families pool that day's production, but the entire camp—residents and visitors alike—shares equally in the total quantity of food available. The evening meal of any one family is made up of portions of food from each of the other families resident. Foodstuffs are distributed raw or are prepared by the collectors and then distributed. There is a constant flow of nuts, berries, roots and melons from one family fireplace to another until each person resident has received an equitable portion. The following morning a different combination of foragers moves out of camp and when they return late in the day, the distribution of foodstuffs is repeated.

What Hobbes did not realize is that it was in everybody's best interest in small, prestate societies to maintain each other's freedom of access to the natural habitat. Suppose a !Kung with a Hobbesian lust for power were to get up and tell his campmates, "From now on, all this land and everything on it belongs to me. I'll let you use it but only with my permission and on the condition that I get first choice of anything you capture, collect, or grow." His campmates, thinking that he had certainly gone crazy, would pack up their few belongings, take a twenty- or thirty-mile walk, make a new camp, and resume their usual life of egalitarian reciprocity, leaving the man who would be king alone to exercise a useless sovereignty.

To the extent that political leadership exists at all among simple band-and-village societies, it is exercised by individuals called headmen, who lack the power to compel others to obey their orders. But can a leader be powerless and still lead?

HOW TO BE
A HEADMAN

HEN A HEADMAN gives a command, he has no certain physical means of punishing those who disobey. So if he wants to stay in "office," he gives few commands. In contrast, the political power of genuine rulers depends on their ability to expel or exterminate any readily foreseeable combination of disobedient individuals and groups. Among the Eskimo, a group will follow an outstanding hunter and defer to his opinion with respect to choice of hunting spots. But in all other matters, the "leader's" opinion carries no more weight than any other man's. Similarly, among the !Kung, each band has its recognized "leaders," most of whom are males. These men may speak out more than others and are listened to with a bit more deference, but they have no formal authority and can only persuade, never command. When Lee asked the !Kung whether they had "headmen" in the sense of powerful chiefs, they told him, "Of course we have headmen! In fact we are all headmen . . . each one of us is headman over himself."

Headmanship can be a frustrating and irksome job. Among Brazilian Indian groups such as the Mehinacu of Brazil's Xingu National Park, headmen remind one of zealous scoutmasters on overnight cookouts. The first one up in the morning, the headman tries to rouse his companions by standing in the middle of the village plaza and shouting at them. If something needs to be done, it is the headman who starts doing it, and it is the headman who works at it harder than anyone else. He sets an example not only for hard work but for generosity. After a fishing or hunting expedition, he gives away more of the catch than anyone else; and in trading with other groups, he is careful not to keep the best items for himself.

In the evening, he stands in the center of the plaza and exhorts his people to be good. He calls upon them to control their sexual appetites, work hard in their gardens, and take frequent baths in the river. He tells them not to sleep during the day or bear

350

grudges against each other. All the while he carefully avoids making accusations of wrongdoing against a specific individual.

Robert Dentan refers to a similar pattern of leadership among the Semai of Malaysia. Despite attempts by outsiders to bolster up the power of Semai leaders, the headman was merely the most prestigious figure among a group of peers. In Dentan's words, the headman

> keeps the peace by conciliation rather than coercion. He must be personally respected. . . . Otherwise people will drift away from him or gradually stop paying attention to him. . . . Furthermore, most of the time a good headman gauges his general feeling about an issue and bases his decision on that, so that he is more a spokesman for public opinion than a molder of it.

Then let me hear no more of our kind's natural necessity to form hierarchical groups. An observer viewing human life shortly after cultural takeoff would easily have concluded that our species was destined to be irredeemably egalitarian except for distinctions of sex and age. That someday the world would be divided into aristocrats and commoners, masters and slaves, billionaires and homeless beggars would have seemed wholly contrary to human nature as evidenced in the affairs of every human society then on earth.

COPING WITH
FREELOADERS

*D*URING THE REIGN of reciprocal exchange and egalitarian headmen, no individual, family, or other group smaller than the band or village itself could control access to rivers, lakes, beaches, oceans, plants and animals, or the soil and subsoil. Reports to the contrary have not survived close scrutiny. Anthropologists once thought that families and even individuals among Canadian hunter-collectors owned private hunting territories, but these ownership patterns turned out to be associated with the colonial fur trade and did not exist aboriginally.

Among the !Kung, a core of people born in a particular territory say that they own the water holes and hunting rights, but this has no effect on the people who happen to be visiting and living with them at any given time. Since !Kung from neighboring bands are related through marriage, they often visit each other for months at a time, do not have to ask permission to do so, and have free use of whatever resources they need. While people from distant bands must make a request to use another band's territory, the "owners" seldom refuse them.

The absence of private possession in land and other vital resources means that a form of communism probably existed among prehistoric hunting and collecting bands and small villages. Perhaps I should emphasize that this did not rule out the existence of private property. People in simple band-and-village societies own personal effects such as weapons, clothing, containers, ornaments, and tools. But why should anyone want to steal such objects? People who live in bush camps and move about a lot have no use for extra possessions. And since there are only a few-score people and everybody knows everybody else, stolen items cannot be used anonymously. If you want something, better to ask for it openly, since by the rules of reciprocity, such requests cannot be denied.

I don't want to create the impression that life within egalitarian band-and-village societies unfolded entirely without disputes over possessions. As in every social group, nonconformists and malcontents tried to use the system for their own advantage at the expense of their fellows. Inevitably there were freeloaders, individuals who consistently took more than they gave and who lay back in their hammocks while others did the work. Despite the absence of a criminal justice system, such behavior was eventually punished. A widespread belief among band-and-village peoples attributes death and misfortune to the malevolent conspiracy of sorcerers. The task of identifying these evildoers falls to a group's shamans, who remain responsive to public opinion during their divinatory trances. Individuals who are well liked and who enjoy strong support from their families need not fear that the shaman will accuse them. But quarrelsome, stingy people who do not give as well as take or who are aggressive and outspoken had better watch out.

FROM HEADMAN
TO BIG MAN

ECIPROCITY WAS NOT the only form of exchange practiced by egalitarian band-and-village peoples. Our kind long ago found other ways to give and take. Among them the form of exchange known as redistribution played a crucial role in creating distinctions of rank during the evolution of chiefdoms and states.

Redistribution occurs when people turn over food and other valuables to a prestigious figure such as a headman, to be pooled, divided into separate portions, and given out again. The primordial form was probably keyed to seasonal hunts and harvests, when more food than usual became available. As illustrated by Australian Aboriginal practice, when wild seeds ripened and game was abundant, neighboring bands gathered together to hold their corroborees. These were occasions for singing, dancing, and the ritual renewal of group identity. With more people and more meat and other delicacies being brought into camp, ordinary channels of reciprocal exchange may not have sufficed for making sure that everyone was treated fairly. Perhaps senior males took charge of making up and distributing the portions that people consumed. A small step separates these rudimentary redistributors from eager "scoutmaster" headmen who exhort their companions and kinfolk to hunt and harvest more intensely so that all may enjoy bigger and better feasts. True to their calling, headmen-redistributors not only work harder than their followers, but they give more generously and reserve smaller and less desirable portions for themselves than for anyone else. Initially, therefore, redistribution strictly reinforced the political and economic equality associated with reciprocal exchange. The redistributors were compensated purely with admiration and in proportion to their success in giving bigger feasts, in personally contributing more than anybody else, and in asking little or nothing for their effort—all of which initially seemed an innocent extension of the basic principle of

358

reciprocity. But how little our ancestors understood what they were getting themselves into!

If it is a good thing to have a headman give feasts, why not have several headmen give feasts? Or better yet, why not let their success in organizing and giving feasts be the measure of their legitimacy as headmen? Soon, where conditions permit or encourage—I'll explain what this means later on—there are several would-be headmen vying with each other to hold the most lavish feasts and to redistribute the most food and other valuables. In this fashion there evolved the nemesis that Richard Lee's informants had warned about: the youth who wants to be a "big man."

A classic anthropological study of big men was carried out by Douglas Oliver among the Siuai, a village people who live on the island of Bougainville in the Solomon Islands in the South Pacific. In the Siuai language, the big man was known as a *mumi*. Every Siuai boy's highest ambition was to become a mumi. He began by getting married, working hard, and restricting his own consumption of meat and coconuts. His wife and parents, impressed with the seriousness of his intentions, vowed to help him prepare for his first feast. Soon his circle of supporters widened and he began to construct a clubhouse in which his male followers could lounge about and in which guests could be entertained and fed. He gave a feast at the consecration of the clubhouse, and, if this was a success, the circle of people willing to work for him grew still larger and he began to hear himself spoken of as a mumi. Larger and larger feasts meant that the mumi's demands on his supporters became more irksome. Although they grumbled about how hard they had to work, they remained loyal as long as their mumi continued to maintain or increase his renown as a "great provider."

Finally the time came for the new mumi to challenge the older ones. He did this at a *muminai* feast, where both sides kept a tally of all the pigs, coconut pies, and sago-almond puddings given away by the host mumi and his followers to the guest mumi and his followers. If the guests could not reciprocate in a year or so with a feast as lavish as that of his challengers, their mumi suffered a great social humiliation and his fall from mumihood was immediate.

At the end of a successful feast, the greatest of mumis still faced a lifetime of personal toil and dependence on the moods and inclinations of his followers. Mumihood did not confer the power to coerce others into doing one's bidding nor did it elevate one's standard of living above anyone else's. In fact, since giving things away was the essence of mumihood, great mumis consumed less meat and other delicacies than ordinary men. Among the Kaoka, another Solomon Islands group, reported on by H. Ian Hogbin, there is the saying, "The giver of the feast takes the bones and the stale cakes; the meat and the fat go to the others." At one great feast attended by 1,100 people, the host mumi, whose name was Soni, gave away thirty-two pigs plus a large quantity of sago-almond puddings. Soni and some of his closest followers went hungry. "We shall eat Soni's renown," they said.

THE BIRTH
OF THE
GREAT
PROVIDERS

NOTHING IS MORE SYMPTOMATIC of the difference between reciprocity and redistribution than the acceptance of boastfulness as an attribute of leadership. In flagrant violation of prescriptions for modesty in reciprocal exchanges, redistributive exchange involves public proclamations that the redistributor is a generous person and a great provider.

Boasting was carried to extremes by the Kwakiutl of Vancouver Island during the competitive feasts called potlatches. Seemingly obsessed with their own importance, Kwakiutl redistributor chiefs said things like this:

> I am the great chief who makes people ashamed. . . . I bring jealousy to the faces. I make people cover their faces by what I am continually doing in this world. Giving again and again [fish] oil feasts to all the tribes . . . I am the only great tree. . . . You are my subordinates, tribes . . . I am the first to give you property, tribes. I am your Eagle, tribes! Bring your counter of property, tribes, that he may try in vain to count the property that is to be given away by the great copper maker, the chief.

Redistribution is not an arbitrary economic style that people pick and choose according to whim, since the career of a redistributor is predicated on his ability to increase production. Selection for redistribution occurs only when conditions are such that the extra effort really does pay off. But getting people to work harder can affect production negatively. In simple foraging societies like the !Kung, individuals who try to intensify the capture of animals and collection of wild plants increase the risk of overkill and the depletion of plant resources. To encourage a !Kung hunter to act like a mumi is to place him and his followers in imminent danger of starvation. In contrast, depletions are less of an immediate menace for agricultural-ists such as the Siuai and the Kaoka. Crops can often be planted over a wider area, cultivated and weeded more meticulously, and helped along with extra water and fertilizer without imminent danger of depletions.

But I need to avoid placing too much emphasis on the formal distinction between foraging and agricultural modes of production. The Kwakiutl were not agriculturalists, yet their mode of production was highly intensifiable. They got most of their food from prodigious annual upriver runs of salmon and candlefish, and as long as they used only aboriginal dip nets, they could not readily deplete these species. In their aboriginal form, potlatches therefore were an effec-tive means of stimulating production. Like the Kwakiutl, many soci-eties that lacked agriculture nonetheless lived in permanent communities that had marked inequalities in rank. Some, like the Kwakiutl, even possessed lowly commoners whose status resembled that of slaves. The majority of these nonegalitarian foraging societies seem to have developed along seacoasts and rivers, where localized beds of shellfish, concentrated fish runs, or sea mammal colonies encouraged the building of permanent settlements and where extra labor could be used to increase the productivity of the habitat.

Yet in general, it is among agricultural societies that the greatest leeway for intensification existed. And in general, the more intensifiable the agricultural base of a redistributive system, the greater its potential for giving rise to sharp divisions of rank, wealth, and power. But before I tell the story of how those whom the mumi served became the servants of the mumi, let me pause to consider another issue. Granted that mumihood was good for production, why was it good for the mumi? Why would people go to such lengths to be able to boast about how much they gave away?

WHY WE
CRAVE
PRESTIGE

ARLIER, I PROPOSED that we have a genetically determined need for love, approval, and emotional support. To gain rewards in the currency of love, our kind limits satisfactions expressed in the currencies of other needs and drives. Now I propose that the same need accounts for the strenuous efforts of headmen and mumis to improve the general well-being of their fellows. Society pays them not with food, sex, or increased bodily comforts, but with approval, admiration and respect—with prestige, in short.

Personality differences decree that some humans crave affection more than others (a truism that applies to all our needs and drives). It seems likely, therefore, that headmen and mumis are individuals who have an especially strong desire for approval (presumably as a result of a mix of childhood experience and heredity). In addition to possessing outstanding organizational, oratorical, and rhetorical skills, egalitarian leaders come to the fore as individuals who have a large appetite for praise, a reward that others happily supply in return for basketfuls of delicacies and a safer, healthier, and more exciting existence.

Initially, the rewarding of prestige for socially useful services seemed, like redistribution, to weigh against the development of distinctions of rank based on wealth and power. If Soni tried to keep the meat and fat for himself or if he tried to get things done by command rather than request, people would give their admiration and support to a more authentic big man. But the generosity of the big man is intrinsic to the structure of egalitarian societies, not to the nature of prestige. With the evolution of distinctions of rank in advanced chiefdoms and states, retention of wealth and concentration of power mingle with continued expectations of approval and support. Being rich and powerful is compatible with being loved and admired, as long as you don't comport yourself in a selfish and tyrannical manner. Paramount chiefs and kings expect to be loved by their subjects and often are, but, unlike mumis, they take their reward in all the currencies to which human nature subscribes.

Current thinking about the role of prestige in human affairs follows the lead of Thorstein Veblen, whose classic, *Theory of the Leisure Class*, has lost none of its appeal as a mordant commentary on the foibles of consumerism. Noting the frequency with which ordinary consumers attempt to emulate the exchange, display, and destruction of luxury goods and services by members of the higher classes, Veblen coined the phrase "conspicuous consumption." Ad agencies and their clients have been grateful ever since as they map their strategies for selling fashionable locations for office buildings and residences, limited-edition Maseratis, Oscar de la Renta dresses, and upscale wines and foods.

But I must demur when it comes to Veblen's attempt to answer the question of *why* people value clothing, jewelry, houses, furnishings, food and drink, skin complexion, and even body odors that emulate the standards of persons of superior rank. His answer was that we crave prestige because we have an innate need to feel superior. By emulating the leisure class we hope to satisfy that craving. In Veblen's words: "With the exception of the instinct of self-preservation, the propensity for emulation is probably the strongest and most alert and persistent of the economic motives." This propensity is so powerful, he argued, that it regularly leads us to engage in foolish, wasteful, and painful behavior. As examples, Veblen cited foot-binding among the Chinese and corseting among Americans—practices that rendered women conspicuously unfit for work and therefore candidates for membership in the superior class. He also recounted the story (obviously apocryphal) of a "certain king of France" who, in order to avoid "menial contamination" in the absence of the functionary whose office it was to shift his master's seat, "sat uncomplaining before the fire and suffered his royal person to be toasted beyond recovery."

Veblen's universal drive to emulate the leisure class presupposes that a leisure class exists universally, which is factually untrue. The !Kung, Semai, and Mehinacu get along quite well without manifesting any marked propensity to show themselves superior. Instead of boasting about how great they are, they belittle themselves and their accomplishments precisely in order to reassure each other that they are all equal. As for an emulative instinct leading people into

foolish patterns of consumption, what appears to be silly in one perspective makes good economic and political sense in another. No
doubt conspicuous consumption does cater to our desire to feel superior, even if we must pay dearly for it. But our susceptibility to such
desires is socially constructed and has motives and consequences that
go beyond the mere pretense or illusion of high rank. In evolutionary
perspective it was an integral and practical part of the process of the
formation of ruling classes and higher circles and of achieving or
maintaining membership in them.

WHY WE CONSUME CONSPICUOUSLY

CONSPICUOUS EXCHANGE, conspicuous display, and conspicuous destruction of valuables—all implicit in Veblen's notion of conspicuous consumption—are culturally constructed strategies for achieving and protecting power and wealth. They evolved because they provided evidence in symbolic form that paramount chiefs and kings *were* superior and therefore rightfully richer and more powerful than ordinary mortals. Generous redistributors like Soni have no need to impress their followers with a sumptuous life-style; lacking power, they have no need to justify it and would lose their followers' admiration if they did. But redistributors who reward themselves first and in greater measure have always needed ideologies and rituals that legitimize their appropriation of social wealth.

Among advanced chiefdoms and early states, the most influential ideological justification of royal prerogatives was the claim of divine descent. The paramount chiefs of Hawaii, the emperors of ancient Peru, China, and Japan, and the pharaohs of Egypt all independently maintained that they were the direct descendants of the sun, the god who created the universe. In conformity with rules of descent and inheritance appropriately designed for maximizing the benefits of this relationship, reigning monarchs became divine beings and rightful owners of the world their incandescent ancestor had created and bequeathed to them. Now, gods and their close relatives cannot be expected to look and behave like ordinary mortals (unless they side with ordinary mortals against the rich and powerful). Their consumption standards in particular must be appropriate to their celestial orgins and on a level so far above the capabilities of their subjects as to demonstrate an unbridgeable gap between them. By wearing embroidered garments made from the finest cloths, bejeweled turbans, hats, and crowns, by sitting on intricately carved thrones, by eating only elaborately prepared foods served on dishes made from precious metals, by residing in sumptuous palaces in life, and equally sumptuous tombs and pyramids in death, the high and mighty fashioned a life-style intended to awe and intimidate their subjects and any potential rivals.

Much conspicuous consumption focuses on a class of portable artifacts that archaeologists call preciosities—gold cups, jade figurines, bejeweled scepters, swords, and crowns, silk robes and dresses, ivory bracelets, diamond necklaces, ruby and sapphire rings, pearl earrings, and other examples of fine jewelry. Why did these items have such great value? Is it because of their intrinsic qualities such as color, hardness, brightness, and durability? I don't think so. As poets tell us, one can find as much beauty in a blade of grass, a leaf of a tree, or a pebble on a beach. Yet no one has ever conspicuously consumed leaves, blades of grass, or pebbles. Preciosities acquired their value because they were tokens of concentrated wealth and power, actual material embodiments and manifestations of the ability of godlike humans to do godlike things. For an item to be a preciosity, it had to be scarce or extremely difficult for ordinary people to find, hidden underground or underwater, available only in distant lands, or reachable only after long and hazardous journeys, or it had to embody the concentrated labor, cunning, and genius of great craftsmen and artists.

During the Shang and Chou dynasties in ancient China, for example, emperors were great patrons of metallurgical craftsmen whose supreme achievements were intricately designed bronze vessels. Writing in the year 552 B.C. the scholar Tso Ch'iu-ming applauded the functions of these bronze masterpieces: "When the powerful have conquered the weak, they use their bounty to make ritual vessels and to cast inscriptions to record the deed, to show to their descendants, to publicize the bright and the virtuous, and to penalize those without rituals."

In conspicuous consumption our kind culturally reinvented the brightly colored feathers, loud roars, gyrating dances, flashing teeth, and ponderous antlers that individuals of noncultural species use to intimidate their rivals. I have read that among crickets, the dominant males chirp the loudest. Silence them by waxing their legs, and they still continue to mate more than their rivals, but the amount of time they spend in combat greatly increases. "In other words," notes Adrian Forsyth, "it pays to advertise your strength to your rivals, otherwise you will waste much in the process of affirming it."

In preindustrial times preciosities were notices, attention-grabbing advertisements, warnings, whose meaning was, "As you can see, we are extraordinary beings. The greatest artists and artisans labor at our command. We send miners into the bowels of the earth, divers to the bottom of the ocean, caravans across the desert and ships across the sea. Obey our commands because anyone who can possess such things has the power to destroy you."

To this day preciosities have continued to play a critical role in the construction and maintenance of social rank. But their message has changed, as we shall see next.

WHY
YUPPIES?

CONSPICUOUS CONSUMPTION in modern consumer economies differs from conspicuous consumption in early states and empires. Lacking closed hereditary classes, modern market societies encourage anyone who can afford preciosities to acquire them. Since the source of wealth and power for modern upper classes lies in stepping up consumption, everyone is encouraged to indulge their emulative inclinations to the highest degree. The more Maseratis and Oscar de la Rentas the better, providing, of course, that when they become too commonplace, new brands of even greater exclusivity are ready to take their place. But in early states and empires, any attempt on the part of commoners to emulate the ruling class without that class's consent was viewed as a subversive threat. To make sure this did not happen, the elites passed sumptuary laws, making it a crime for commoners to emulate their superiors. Some of the most exquisitely detailed sumptuary restrictions arose in conjunction with India's caste system. The dominant Rajputs of northern India, for example, forbade low-caste Chamar men to wear sandals or any garment that extended above their hips or below their knees. Chamar men were also forbidden to have their hair cut or to carry umbrellas. As for Chamar women, they had to go bare-breasted, could not use saffron paste as a cosmetic or wear flowers, and were not allowed to use anything but earthenware vessels in their home. (Anyone who still doubts the power of culture to make and remake the world we live in might wish to ponder the following observation: While feminist women in the West have been struggling to liberate themselves by going bare-breasted in public, the women of India have been liberating themselves by refusing to go bare-breasted in public.)

Let me give another example of sumptuary laws from a less familiar political context. According to Diego Duran, a great early source of information about pre-Columbian Mexico, commoners could not wear cotton garments, feathers, or flowers; nor could they

374

drink chocolate or eat fine foods. One of the main thrusts of ancient forms of conspicuous consumption, in other words, was to thwart any attempt on the part of the rabble to emulate their superiors.

Emulation, which Veblen placed next to survival as an economic motive, became a major economic force only when ruling classes ceased to be composed of inbreeding, hereditary elites. But Veblen's ideas about emulation apply with considerable accuracy to the transition in Europe from feudal monarchies to capitalist parliamentary democracies with their mercantile and industrial upper classes, who did indeed lavish their new wealth on mansions, tombs, and preciosities to demonstrate that they were the equals of their erstwhile superiors. But I cannot accept Veblen's caricature of bourgeois status-seekers as people whose craving for prestige leads them into silly nonutilitarian patterns of consumption. The emergent capitalist elites were not interested in destroying aristocrats but in joining them, and to do this they had no choice but to ape aristocratic standards of consumption.

Is this a case of things remaining the same the more they changed? On the contrary, the new elites of capitalism overturned the traditional relationships of preciosities to the maintenance of wealth and power. In capitalist societies, rooms at the top are not reserved for people who insist that they alone are entitled to rare and exotic possessions. As I mentioned a moment ago, power and wealth flow from buying and selling in open markets and, with a few exceptions (like the crown jewels of England?), everything is up for sale. Not only are there no laws today against ordinary people acquiring Rolls-Royces, country estates, race horses, yachts, every kind of gem and precious metal and rare perfume, the works of great artists and artisans, and the latest in haute couture and haute cuisine, but the wealth and power of the people on top improve in proportion to the volume of such purchases.

And this brings me to the plight of the much-maligned Yuppies, perhaps the most voracious and predatory consumers of preciosities the world has ever seen. Yuppies are much maligned because their purchasing of symbols of wealth and power is not another example of a weird propensity to emulate at any cost. Rather, it is an unrelenting condition of success imposed from above in a society where wealth and power depend on mass consumption. Only people who can prove themselves loyal to the ethos of consumerism are

375

admitted to the higher circles of consumer society. For upwardly mobile youth (or even for youth who merely wish not to fall to lower social ranks), conspicuous consumption is less a benefit than a cost of success. Designer clothes, Italian sports cars, laser disks, hi-fi systems, frequent shopping trips to the glass-and-chrome souks at Bloomingdale's, weekends in the Hamptons, lunches at Maxim's—you'll never meet the right people or get the right job without them. If this means going heavily into debt on charge accounts instead of putting money in the bank, and postponing marriage and living in child-free condominiums instead of tract housing in the suburbs, what better proof could there be of loyalty to one's superiors? But let us return to the world as it was before there were ruling classes or Bloomingdale's to shop in.

FROM BIG MAN
TO CHIEF

THE SLIDE (OR ASCENT?) toward social stratification gained momentum wherever extra food produced by the inspired diligence of redistributors could be stored while awaiting *muminai* feasts, potlatches, and other occasions of redistribution. The more concentrated and abundant the harvest and the less perishable the crop, the greater its potential for endowing big men with power over people. While others would possess some stored-up foods of their own, the redistributors' stores would be the largest. In times of scarcity, people would come to him, expecting to be fed, and, in return, he would call upon those who had special skills to make cloth, pots, canoes, or a fine house for his own use. Eventually, the redistributor no longer needed to work in the fields to gain and surpass big-man status. Management of the harvest surpluses, a portion of which continued to be given to him for use in communal feasts and other communal projects such as trading expeditions and warfare, was sufficient to validate his status. And increasingly, people viewed this status as an office, a sacred trust, passed on from one generation to the next according to rules of hereditary succession. The big man had become a chief; his dominion was no longer a single small, autonomous village, but a large political community, a chiefdom.

Returning to the South Pacific and the Trobriand Islands, one can catch a glimpse of how these pieces of encroaching stratification fell into place. The Trobrianders had hereditary chiefs who held sway over more than a dozen villages containing several thousand people. Only chiefs could wear certain shell ornaments as the insignia of high rank, and it was forbidden for commoners to stand or sit in a position that put a chief's head at a lower elevation. Malinowski tells of seeing all the people present in the village of Bwoytalu drop from their verandas "as if blown down by a hurricane" at the sound of a drawn-out cry warning that an important chief was approaching.

Yams were the Trobrianders' staff of life; the chiefs validated their status by storing and redistributing copious quantities of them acquired through donations from their brothers-in-law at harvest time. Similar "gifts" were received by husbands who were commoners, but chiefs were polygynous, and having as many as a dozen wives, they received many more yams than anyone else. Chiefs placed their yam supply on display on racks specifically built for this purpose next to their houses. Commoners did the same, but a chief's yam racks towered over all others. They used their yams when entertaining guests, to hold lavish feasts, and to feed canoe-building specialists, artisans, magicians, and family servants. In former times, the yam stores also furnished the base for launching long-distance trading expeditions among friendly groups and raids against enemies.

This pattern of giving food as a gift to hereditary chiefs who store, display, and redistribute it was not an isolated oddity of the South Seas. The pattern recurs over and over again, with minor variations, on several continents. Striking parallels were seen, for example, 12,000 miles away from the Trobrianders, among chiefdoms that flourished throughout the southeastern region of the United States. I am thinking especially of the Cherokee, former inhabitants of Tennessee as described by the eighteenth-century naturalist William Bartram.

At the center of the principal Cherokee settlements stood a large circular house where a council of chiefs discussed issues involving their villages and where redistributive feasts were held. The council of chiefs had a paramount who was the principal figure in the Cherokee redistributive network. At harvest time a large crib, identified as the "chief's granary," was erected in each field. "To this each family carries and deposits a certain quantity according to his [sic] ability or inclination, or none at all if he so chooses." The chief's granaries functioned as "a public treasury . . . to fly to for succor" in the case of crop failure, as a source of food "to accommodate strangers, or travellers," and as a military store "when they go forth on hostile expeditions." Although every citizen enjoyed "the right of free and public access," commoners had to acknowledge that the store really belonged to the supreme chief who had "an exclusive right and ability . . . to distribute comfort and blessings to the necessitous."

Supported by voluntary prestations, chiefs and their families could now enjoy life-styles that set them increasingly apart from their followers. They could build bigger and finer houses for themselves, eat and dress more sumptuously, and enjoy the sexual favors and personal services of several wives. Despite these harbingers, people in chiefdoms voluntarily invested unprecedented amounts of labor on behalf of communal projects. They dug moats, threw up defensive earthen embankments, and erected great log palisades around their villages. They heaped up small mountains of rubble and soil to form platforms and mounds on top of which they built temples and big houses for their chief. Working in teams and using nothing but levers and rollers, they moved rocks weighing fifty tons or more and set them in precise lines and perfect circles forming sacred precincts for communal rituals marking the change of seasons. Donated labor created the megalithic alignments of Stonehenge and Carnac, put up the great statues on Easter Island, shaped the huge stone heads of the Olmec in Vera Cruz, dotted Polynesia with ritual precincts set on great stone platforms, and filled the Ohio, Tennessee, and Mississippi valleys with hundreds of mounds, the largest of which, at Cahokia near East St. Louis, covered fourteen acres and was 100 feet high. Not until it was too late did people realize that their boastful chiefs were about to keep the meat and fat for themselves while giving nothing but bones and stale cakes to their followers.

POWER:
WAS IT SEIZED
OR GIVEN?

HE POWER, so alien to the Mehinacu or Semai headmen, to give orders and have them obeyed, was incubated, like the power of men over women, in the wars that were waged by big men and chiefs. Without warfare, the potential for control inherent in the egg of redistribution would never have hatched.

Big men were violent men and chiefs were even more so. The mumis were as famous for their ability to get men to fight as they were for their ability to get men to work. Warfare had been suppressed by the colonial authorities long before Douglas Oliver carried out his study, but the memory of mumis as war leaders was still vivid. As one old man put it: "In the olden times there were greater mumi than there are today. Then they were fierce and relentless war leaders. They laid waste to the countryside and their clubhouses were lined with the skulls of people they had slain." In singing praises of their mumis, the generation of pacified Siuai call them "warriors" and "killers of men and pigs." Oliver's informants told him that mumis had more authority in the days when warfare was still being practiced. Mumi war leaders even kept one or two prisoners whom they forced to work in their gardens. And people could not talk "loud and slanderously against their mumis without fear of punishment."

But the mumis' power remained rudimentary, as shown by the fact that they had to provide their followers with lavish gifts, including meat and women, in order to keep them loyal. "If the mumi didn't furnish us with women, we were angry. . . . All night long we would copulate and still want more. It was the same with eating. The clubhouse used to be filled with food, and we ate and ate and never had enough. Those were wonderful times." Furthermore, the mumi who wanted to lead a war party had to be prepared personally to pay an indemnity for any of his men who were killed in battle and to furnish a pig for each man's funeral feast.

Kwakiutl chiefs were also war leaders and their boasting and potlatches recruited men from neighboring villages to fight alongside them on trading and raiding expeditions. The Trobriand chiefs were equally keen on fighting. Malinowski states that they conducted systematic and relentless wars, venturing across the open ocean in their canoes to trade, or, if need be, to fight, with islands over a hundred miles away. The Cherokee also undertook annual long-distance raiding and trading expeditions organized under the auspices of the council of chiefs. As the quotation from Bartram indicated, Cherokee chiefs used food from their granaries to feed the members of these expeditions.

I am not saying that warfare led directly to the qualitatively new form of hierarchy embodied in the state. Initially, when chiefdoms were small, chiefs could not use force of arms to compel people to do their bidding. As in band-and-village societies, virtually every male knew the arts of combat and possessed the requisite arms and skills in roughly equal measure. Furthermore, internecine strife might expose a chiefdom to defeat at the hands of its foreign enemies. Yet the opportunity to break away from the traditional restraints on power would increase as chiefdoms expanded their territories and grew more populous, and as stores of food and other valuables available for redistribution increased proportionately. By allocating different shares to those who were most cooperative, loyal, and effective on the battlefield, chiefs could begin to build the nucleus of a noble class backed up by a police force and a standing army. Commoners who shirked their gift-giving duties to their chiefs, failed to meet production quotas, or refused to donate labor to building monuments and other public works found themselves threatened with bodily harm.

One school of thought concerned with the origin of the state rejects the idea that ruling classes gained control over commoners as a result of a violent conspiracy carried out by the chiefs and their militia. In contrast, they see commoners submitting peacefully out of gratitude for the services that ruling classes provided. These services included emergency rations in times of famine, protection against enemy attacks, and construction and management of agricultural infrastructures such as dams and irrigation and drainage canals. Also, people believed that the rituals carried out by chiefs and priests were essential for everyone's survival. Furthermore, no reign of terror was needed to get people to obey orders from above because the priests avowed that their rulers were gods on earth.

My position on this issue is that both voluntaristic submission and violent repression were present. Ethnographically and archaeologically known advanced chiefdoms and incipient states must be reckoned as among the most violent societies that have ever existed. Incessant warfare often involving wholesale massacres of rebellious villages and the torture and sacrifice of prisoners of war accompanied the rise of advanced chiefdoms in pre-Roman Celtic Europe, Homeric Greece, Vedic India, Shang China, and precontact Polynesia. The Walls of Jericho testify to the practice of warfare as early as 6000 B.C. in the Middle East. Fortified towns appear in Egypt during predynastic and postdynastic times and the earliest Egyptian monuments from the late Gerzean and First Dynasty (3330–2900 B.C.) glorify the military exploits of "unifiers" who bore bellicose names such as "Scorpion," "Cobra," "Spearer," and "Fighter." Numerous war clubs and a knife depicting battle scenes have been found at the predynastic site of Hierkanpolis. Men are shown engaged in combat employing knives, maces, and clubs; boats carry fighting men while people struggle in the water.

Evidence for warfare appears to be absent from only one major case in the transition from advanced chiefdoms to the state, the Susiana Plain in southwestern Iran. But this evidence is based on an absence of fortifications, artifacts, and pictorial elements. Similar negative evidence had long been used to deny that warfare was a factor in the evolution of the Maya states, a position that recent discoveries and the interpretation of glyphs have shown to be completely untenable. Given the central role played by warfare in the formation of advanced chiefdoms and early states, I think it highly improbable that violence against commoners or the threat of violence would not be used to establish and consolidate the hegemony of the earliest ruling classes. This does not mean that stratified societies resulted from nothing but the constant threat of force.

Archaeologist Antonio Gillman contends that in Bronze Age Europe "the rise of an elite has nothing to do with the 'common good' and that whatever benefits accrued to the commoners from the managerial and redistributive activities of their rulers could have been secured at lesser cost." These remarks inspired one commentator to propose what might be called the Mafia theory of state formation, involving ". . . an industrious but downtrodden peasantry unable to refuse protection money to a mob of flashily dressed racketeers for fear of having their plough oxen kneecapped, pirogues pirated and olive trees set in cement overshoes." I see no reason why both commoners and elites could not have benefitted from the managerial and redistributive activities of the state, although I feel certain that the elite's share of benefits was greater than the commoner's share.

Whether by the sword, rewards, or religion, many chiefdoms were called but few made it through the transition to the state. Rather than obey commands to work and pay taxes, commoners tried to flee to no-man's-lands or unpopulated frontiers. Others stood their ground and tried to fight off the militia, thereby providing an opportunity for other chiefs to invade and take over. Whatever the precise course of rebellion, the great majority of chiefdoms that attempted to impose crop quotas, taxation, labor conscription, and other coercive and asymmetrical forms of redistribution on a commoner class either fell back to more egalitarian forms of redistribution or were destroyed entirely. Why did some succeed while others failed?

THE THRESHOLD
OF THE STATE

*T*HE *FIRST STATES* evolved from chiefdoms but not all chiefdoms could evolve into states. For the transition to take place, two conditions were necessary. The population not only had to be large (about 10,000 to 30,000 people), but it had to be "circumscribed," that is, it had to be confronted with a lack of unused lands to which people who were unwilling to be taxed, conscripted, and ordered about could flee. Circumscription was more than a question of how much land was available; it was also a matter of the quality of soils and natural resources and whether groups of refugees could support themselves at a standard of living that was not substantially lower than what they could expect under their oppressive chiefs. If the only places a dissident faction could flee to were high mountains, deserts, tropical forests, or other undesirable habitats, there was little incentive for them to hive off.

The second condition had to do with the nature of the food contributed to the central store for redistribution. When the chief's storehouse was filled with perishable root crops like yams and sweet potatoes, the potential for coercion was much less than when it was filled with rice, wheat, maize, or other domesticated grains that could be stored safely from one harvest to the next. Chiefdoms that were not circumscribed or that lacked storageable crops often reached the threshold of kingdoms only to break apart as a result of the mass exodus or rebellion of disaffected commoners.

Hawaii in the days before Europeans appeared is an example of a society that rose to, but never quite got across, the threshold of becoming a kingdom. All the islands of the Hawaiian archipelago were uninhabited until Polynesian voyagers in ocean-going canoes came ashore sometime early in the first millennium A.D. The homeland of these first settlers probably was the Marquesas Islands, some 2,000 miles to the southeast. If so, they were probably already familiar with big-manship or simple egalitarian chiefdoms. A thousand years later, when observed by the first Europeans to contact them, the Hawaiians were living in highly stratified societies that possessed all of the characteristics of states except for the fact that rebellion and usurpation occurred as frequently as war against external enemies. The population of these states or protostates varied from 10,000 to 100,000 persons. Each was divided into several districts and each district in turn was composed of several village communities. At the apex of the political hierarchy was a king or a would-be king called *ali'i nui*. Paramount chiefs called *ali'i* ruled over districts, and their agents, lesser chiefs called *konohiki,* were in charge of the local communities. The greatest percentage of the population—the people who did the fishing, farming, and craft products—were commoners.

Sometime before the first Europeans arrived, the Hawaiian redistributive system had crossed the Rubicon that divides unequal gift giving from outright taxation. Food and craft products were siphoned off from the commoners to the district chiefs and on to the ali'i nui. The konohiki were in charge of seeing to it that each village produced enough to satisfy the district chief who, in turn, had to satisfy the ali'i nui. The ali'i nui and the district chiefs used the food and crafts flowing through the redistributive network to feed and support retinues of priests and warriors. Very little trickled back down to the commoners except during times of drought and famine when the most industrious and loyal villages could expect to be favored with emergency rations furnished by the ali'i nui and the district chiefs. As David Malo, a nineteenth-century Hawaiian chief, noted, the storehouses of the ali'i nui were designed as a means of keeping people contented, so that they would remain loyal to him: "As the rat will not desert the pantry, so the people will not desert the king while they think there is food in his storehouse."

How had this system developed? Archaeological evidence shows that as the population grew, settlements slowly spread from one island to another. For almost a thousand years the principal populated areas remained close to the coast, where marine resources could supplement yams, sweet potatoes, and taro, planted in the most fertile patches of soil. Finally, in the fifteenth century, settlements began to spread inland into the higher ecozones, where poor soils and inadequate rainfall prevailed. As the population increased further, the interior forests were cut or burned down and large areas were lost to erosion or turned into grasslands. With the ocean on one side and barren slopes on the other, the population now had no place to go to escape from chiefs who wanted to be kings. Circumscription had set in. Oral tradition and legends tell the rest of the story. After 1600, various districts waged incessant warfare with each other, resulting in temporary control by certain chiefs over whole islands. While these ali'i nui held great power over commoners, their relationship with the paramount chiefs, priests, and warriors, as I indicated, was extremely unstable. Dissident factions fomented rebellions or waged wars, destroying the fragile political unity until a new coalition of would-be kings set up another configuration of equally unstable alliances. That was more or less the situation when Captain James Cook sailed into the harbor of Waimea in 1778, opening the way for the sale of firearms to the Hawaiian chiefs. The ali'i nui, Kamehameha I, obtained a monopoly over the purchase of these new weapons and promptly turned them against his spear-wielding rivals. After defeating them once and for all, he set himself up in 1810 as the first king of the entire Hawaiian archipelago.

We are left to wonder whether the Hawaiians would have gone on to develop a stable state-level society if they had remained isolated. I doubt it. They had intensive agriculture, large harvest surpluses, elaborate hierarchical redistributive networks, taxation, work quotas, dense circumscribed populations, and external warfare. But there was one thing that was missing: a food crop that could be stored from one year to the next. Yams, sweet potatoes, and taro are calorie-rich but perishable foods. They could be stored for only a few months. So the Hawaiian chiefs' storehouses could not be counted on to feed large numbers of followers during shortages brought on by drought or by the ravages of sustained wars. In David Malo's terms, the pantry was empty too often for chiefs to be kings.

And now it is time to tell what happened elsewhere when the pantry was full.

THE FIRST
STATES

THE FIRST TIME a chiefdom became a state was in the Middle East, specifically in Sumer in southern Iran and Iraq, between 3500 and 3200 B.C. Why the Middle East? Probably because this region was better endowed than other early centers of state formation with wild grasses and animal species suitable for domestication. The progenitors of wheat, barley, sheep, goats, cattle, and pigs all thrived in the upland sections of the Levant and the foothills of the Zagros Mountains, facilitating an early abandonment of foraging modes of subsistence in favor of sedentary village life.

What motivated people at the end of the Ice Age to give up their hunter-gatherer existence remains a matter of dispute among archaeologists. But it seems likely that with the warming of the earth after 12,000 B.C., a combination of environmental changes and hunting overkill brought about the extinction of many species of big game, which reduced the attractiveness of the old means of subsistence. In several regions of the Old and New Worlds, people compensated for the extinction of large game species by foraging for a broader variety of plants and animals, including the wild progenitors of today's familiar grains and barnyard animals.

In the Middle East, which had never been as richly endowed with large game as other regions during the Ice Age, hunter-gatherers turned to exploiting wild stands of wheat and barley over thirteen millennia ago. As their dependence on these plants increased, they were obliged to become less nomadic because the seeds all ripened at the same time and had to be stored for the rest of the year. Since the wild seed harvest could not be moved about from camp to camp, people like the Natufians, who flourished in the Levant about 10,000 B.C., stayed put, built storage houses, and established permanent villages. It was a relatively short step from settling down near wild stands of wheat and barley to propagating the plants whose seeds were bigger and did not fall off at the slightest touch. And as the wild stands gave way to cultivated fields, they attracted animals like sheep and goats into closer association with humans, who soon found it was more practical to put these animals in pens, feed them, and breed the ones with the most desirable characteristics rather than simply hunt them all to extinction. And that is how the period that archaeologists call the Neolithic began.

The first settlements quickly evolved beyond headman or big-man village stages to simple chiefdoms. Jericho, situated in an oasis in what is modern-day Jordan, for example, already covered ten acres and had 2,000 inhabitants as long ago as 8000 B.C., and by 6000 B.C., Çatal Hüyük in southern Turkey covered thirty-two acres and had 6,000 people. Its ruins contain a dazzling array of art objects, woven cloth, murals, and wall sculpture. Wall paintings—the earliest known inside houses—depict a large bull, hunting scenes, dancing men, and vultures attacking human bodies done in red, pink, mauve, black, and yellow. The people of Çatal Hüyük grew barley and three varieties of wheat. They kept sheep, cattle, goats, and dogs and lived in attached houses opening on courtyards. There were no doors; the only way in was through holes in the flat roofs.

Like chiefdoms everywhere, early Neolithic villages seem preoccupied with the threat of attack by marauders from afar. Jericho was surrounded by moats and walls (long before Biblical times) and had a circular watch tower on top of one of the walls. Other early Neolithic settlements such as Tell-es-Sawwan and Maghzaliyah in Iraq were also surrounded by walls. I should note that at least one archaeologist claims that the first walls built at Jericho were for protection against mudslides rather than against armed attacks. But the tower with its narrow lookout slits clearly was designed to serve defensive functions. Nor can one doubt that the walls around Tell-es-Sawwan and Maghzaliyah were the equivalent of the wooden palisades characteristic of chiefdoms in lands where trees were abundant. These were no peaceful, harmonious, and harmless farmers concerned only with cultivating their fields and tending their flocks. At Çayönü in southern Turkey, not far from Çatal Hüyük, James Mellaart excavated a large stone slab that had once been covered with human blood. Nearby he found several hundred human skulls without the rest of their skeletons. And why else, if not for protection against marauding strangers, would the people of Çatal Hüyük have built their houses without openings at ground level?

Like chiefdoms everywhere, Neolithic societies engaged in long-distance trade. Their favorite items for exchange with other far-away settlements were obsidian, a volcanic glass used for making knives and other cutting tools, and pottery. Çatal Hüyük seems to have been a center for the domestication, breeding, and export of cattle in exchange for a variety of imported artifacts and raw materials, including fifty-five different kinds of minerals.

The degree of specialization within and between Neolithic settlements also bespeaks of much trade and other forms of exchange. At Beidha in Jordan, one house concentrated on making beads, while others concentrated on flint making, and still others on butchering animals. At Çayönü, a group of houses specialized in making beads. At Umm Dabajioua in northern Iraq, the whole settlement seems to have been devoted to tanning animal skins, while the inhabitants of Yarim Tepe and Tell-es-Sawwan specialized in the mass production of pottery.

There is also evidence for redistribution and distinctions of rank. For example, at Bougras in Syria, a storage structure adjoins the largest house in the village, and at Çatal Hüyük and Tell-es-Sawwan, burial chambers differ in size and in the amount of grave goods interred with different individuals.

In the earliest centers of agriculture and stockraising, people depended on rainfall to water their crops. As the population increased, they experimented with irrigation and began to fission off and colonize the drier parts of the region. Sumer, situated in the rainless but swampy and flood-prone deltaic zones of the Tigris-Euphrates, was settled in this manner. Confined at first to the margins of a natural watercourse, the Sumerians soon became totally dependent on irrigation to water their fields of wheat and barley, unknowingly trapping themselves into the final condition for the transition to statedom. As their would-be kings pressed for more taxes and more public labor, Sumer's commoners found that they had lost the option to move out. How could they take the artificial waterways and their irrigated fields, gardens, and orchards, representing the investment of generations of labor, with them? To live away from the rivers, they would have to adopt a pastoral nomadic way of life for which they lacked the prerequisite skills and technology.

Archaeologists are not able to say exactly where and when in

Sumer the transition took place. But by 4350 B.C., mud-brick structures with ramps and terraces called ziggurats, combining the function of fortress and temple, began to loom over the larger settlements. Like the mounds, tombs, megaliths, and pyramids found throughout the world, ziggurats attest to the presence of advanced chiefdoms capable of organizing large amounts of donated labor and were the forerunner of the great tower of Babylon, which was over 300 feet high, and of the Biblical tower at Babel. By 3500 B.C., there were streets, houses, temples, palaces, and fortifications covering several hundred acres at Uruk in Iraq. Perhaps the transition occurred there. If not, it took place at Lagash, Eridu, Ur, or Nippur, all flourishing as independent kingdoms by 3200 B.C.

Driven by the same internal pressures that sent chiefdoms to war, the Sumerian kingdom had one important advantage. Chiefdoms were likely to try to exterminate their enemies and to kill and eat their prisoners of war. Only states possessed the managerial know-how and the military might for extracting labor and resources from conquered people. By aggregating defeated populations into a peasant class, states rode an amplifying wave of territorial expansion. The more populous and productive they became, the greater their power to defeat and exploit additional peoples and territories. At various times after 3000 B.C., one or the other of the Sumerian kingdoms held sway over Sumeria. But other states soon formed farther upstream on the Euphrates. Under Sargon I, in 2350 B.C., one of them conquered all of Mesopotamia including Sumeria and lands extending from the Euphrates to the Mediterranean Sea. For the next 4,300 years it was one empire after another: Babylonian, Assyrian, Hyskos, Egyptian, Persian, Greek, Roman, Arabian, Ottoman, British. Our kind had created and mounted a wild beast that ate continents. Will we ever be able to tame this, our own creation, the way we tamed nature's sheep and goats?

WHY WE
BECAME
RELIGIOUS

*H*UMAN SOCIAL LIFE cannot be understood apart from the deeply held beliefs and values that in the short run, at least, motivate and mobilize our transactions with each other and the world of nature. So let me interrupt the story of political and economic evolution in order to confront certain questions concerning our kind's religious beliefs and behavior.

First, are there any precedents for religion in nonhuman species? The answer is yes, only if one accepts a definition of religion broad enough to include "superstitious" responses. Behavioral psychologists have long been familiar with the fact that animals can acquire responses that are falsely associated with rewards. For example, a pigeon is placed in a cage into which food pellets are dropped by a mechanical feeder at irregular intervals. If the reward is delivered by chance while the bird is scratching, it begins to scratch faster. If the reward is delivered while a bird happens to be flapping its wings, it keeps flapping them as if wing-flapping controls the feeder. Among humans, one can find analogous superstitions in the little rituals that baseball players engage in as they come up to bat, such as touching their caps, spitting, or rubbing their hands. None of this has any real connection with getting a hit, although constant repetition assures that every time batters get hits, they have performed the ritual. Some minor phobic behavior among humans also might be attributed to associations based on coincidental rather than contingent circumstances. I know a heart surgeon who tolerates only popular music piped into his operating room ever since he lost a patient while classical compositions were being played.

Superstition raises the issue of causality. Just how do the activities and objects that are connected in superstitious beliefs influence one another? A reasonable, if evasive, answer is to say that the causal activity or object has an inherent force or power to achieve the observed effects. Abstracted and generalized, this inherent force or power can provide the explanation for many extraordinary events and for success or failure in life's endeavors. In Melanesia, people call it *mana*. Fishhooks that catch big fish, tools that make intricate carvings, canoes that sail safely through storms, or warriors who kill many enemies, all have mana in concentrated quantities. In Western cultures, the concepts of luck and charisma closely resemble the idea of mana. A horseshoe possesses a concentrated power that brings good luck. A charismatic leader is one who is suffused with great powers of persuasion.

But are superstitions, mana, luck, and charisma religious concepts? I think not. Because, if we define religion as a belief in any indwelling forces and powers, we shall soon find it difficult to separate religion from physics. After all, gravity and electricity are also unseen forces that are associated with observable effects. While it is true that physicists know much more about gravity than about mana, they cannot claim to have a complete understanding of how gravity achieves its results. At the same time, couldn't one argue that superstitions, mana, luck, and charisma are also merely theories of causality involving physical forces and powers about which we happen to have incomplete understanding as yet?

True, more scientific testing has gone into the study of gravity than into the study of mana, but the degree of scientific testing to which a theory has been subjected cannot make the difference between whether it is a religious or a scientific belief. If it did, then every untested or inadequately tested theory in science would be a religious belief (as well as every scientific theory that has been shown to be false during the time when scientists believed it to be true!). Some astronomers theorize that at the center of each galaxy there is a black hole. Shall we say that this is a religious belief because other astronomers reject such a theory or regard it as inadequately tested?

It is not the quality of belief that distinguishes religion from science. Rather, as Sir Edward Tylor was the first to propose, the basis of all that is distinctly religious in human thought is animism, the belief that humans share the world with a population of extraordinary, extracorporeal, and mostly invisible beings, ranging from souls and ghosts to saints and fairies, angels, and cherubim, demons, jinni, devils, and gods.

Wherever people believe in the existence of one or more of these beings, that is where religion exists. Tylor claimed that animistic beliefs were to be found in every society, and a century of ethnological research has yet to turn up a single exception. The most problematic case is that of Buddhism, which Tylor's critics portrayed as a world religion that lacked belief in gods or souls. But ordinary believers outside of Buddhist monasteries never accepted the atheistic implications of Gautama's teachings. Mainstream Buddhism, even in the monasteries, quickly envisioned the Buddha as a supreme deity who had been successively reincarnated and who held sway over a pantheon of lower gods and demons. And it was as fully animistic creeds that the several varieties of Buddhism spread from India to Tibet, Southeast Asia, China, and Japan.

Why is animism universal? Tylor pondered the question at length. He reasoned that if a belief recurred again and again in virtually all times and places, it could not be a product of mere fantasy. Rather, it must have grounding in evidence and in experiences that were equally recurrent and universal. What were these experiences? Tylor pointed to dreams, trances, visions, shadows, reflections, and death. During dreams, the body stays in bed; yet another part of us gets up, talks to people, and travels to distant lands. Trances and drug-induced visions also bring vivid evidence of another self, distinct and separate from one's body. Shadows and mirror images reflected in still water point to the same conclusion, even in the full light of normal wakefulness. The concept of an inner being—a soul —makes sense of all this. It is the soul that wanders off when we sleep, that lies in the shadows, and that peers back at us from the surface of the pond. Most of all, the soul explains the mystery of death: a lifeless body is a body permanently deprived of its soul.

Incidentally, there is nothing in the concept of soul per se that constrains us to believe each person has only one. The ancient Egyptians had two, and so do many West African societies in which both patrilineal and matrilineal ancestors determine an individual's identity. The Jívaro of Ecuador have three souls. The first soul—the *mekas*—gives life to the body. The second soul—the *arutam*—has to be captured through a drug-induced visionary experience at a sacred waterfall. It confers bravery and immunity in battle to the possessor. The third soul—the *musiak*—forms inside the head of a dying warrior and attempts to avenge his death. The Dahomey say that women have three souls, men have four. Both sexes have an ancestor soul, a personal soul, and a mawn soul. The ancestor soul gives protection during life, the personal soul is accountable for what people do with their lives, the mawn soul is a bit of the creator god, Mawn, that supplies divine guidance. The exclusively male fourth soul guides men to positions of leadership in their households and lineages. But the record for plural souls seems to belong to the Fang of Gabon. They have seven: a soul inside the brain, a heart soul, a name soul, a life force soul, a body soul, a shadow soul, and a ghost soul.

Why do Westerners have only one soul? I cannot answer that. Perhaps the question is unanswerable. I accept the possibility that many details of religious beliefs and practices may arise from historically specific events and individual choices made only once and only in one culture and that have no discernible cost-benefit advantages or disadvantages. While a belief in souls does conform to the general principles of cultural selection, belief in one rather than two or more souls may not be comprehensible in terms of such principles. But let us not be too eager to declare any puzzling feature of human life forever beyond the pale of practical reason. For has it not been our experience that more research often leads to answers that were once thought unattainable?

THE EVOLUTION
OF THE
SPIRIT WORLD

*A*LL VARIETIES OF SPIRIT BEINGS found in modern religions have their analogues or exact prototypes in the religions of prestate societies. Changes in animistic beliefs since Neolithic times involve matters of emphasis and elaboration. For example, band-and-village people widely believed in gods who lived on top of mountains or in the sky itself and who served as the models for later notions of supreme beings as well as other powerful sky gods. In Aboriginal Australia, the sky god created the earth and its natural features, showed humans how to hunt and make fire, gave people their social laws, and showed them how to make adults out of children by performing rites of initiation. The names of their quasi-supreme beings—Baiame, Daramulum, Nurunderi—could not be uttered by the uninitiated. Similarly, the Selk'nam of Tierra del Fuego believed in "the one who is up there." The Yaruro of Venezuela spoke of a "great mother" who created the world. The Maidu of California believed in a great "slayer in the sky." Among the Semang of Malaysia, Kedah created everything, including the god who created the earth and humankind. The Andaman Islanders had Puluga whose house is the sky, and the Winnebago had "earthmaker."

Although prestate peoples occasionally prayed to these great spirits or even visited them during trances, the focus of animistic beliefs generally lay elsewhere. In fact, most of the early creator gods abstained from contact with human beings. Having created the universe, they withdrew from worldly affairs and let other lesser deities, animistic beings, and humans work out their own destinies. Ritually, the most important category of animistic beings was the ancestors of the band, village, and clan or other kinship groups whose members believed they were bonded by common descent.

I've already mentioned that people in band-and-village societies tend to have short memories concerning specific individuals who have died. Rather than honor the recent dead, or seek favors from them, egalitarian cultures often place a ban on the use of a dead person's name and try to banish or evade his or her ghost. Among the Washo, a native American foraging people who lived along the border of California and Nevada, souls of the dead were angry about being deprived of their bodies. They were dangerous and had to be avoided. So the Washo burned the dead person's hut, clothing, and other personal property and stealthily moved their camp to a place where they hoped the dead person's soul could not find them. The Dusun of North Borneo curse a dead person's soul and warn it to stay away from the village. Reluctantly, the soul gathers up belongings left at its grave site and sets off for the land of the dead.

But this distrust of the recent dead does not extend to the most ancient dead, nor to the generality of ancestor spirits. In keeping with the ideology of descent, band-and-village people often memorialize and propitiate their communal ancestral spirits. Much of what is known as totemism is a form of diffuse ancestor worship. Taking the name of an animal such as kangaroo or beaver or a natural phenomenon such as clouds or rain in conformity with prevailing rules of descent, people express a communal obligation to the founders of their kinship group. Often this obligation includes rituals intended to nourish, protect, or assure the increase of the animal and natural totems and with it the health and well-being of their human counterparts. Aboriginal Australians, for example, believed that they were descended from animal ancestors who traveled around the country during the dream-time at the beginning of the world, leaving mementos of their journey strewn about before turning into people. Annually, the descendants of a particular totemic ancestor retraced the dream-time journey. As they walked from spot to spot, they sang, danced, and examined sacred stones, stored in secret hiding places along the path taken by the first kangaroo or the first witchetty grub. Returning to camp, they decorated themselves in the likeness of their totem and imitated its behavior. The Arunta witchetty-grub men, for instance, decorated themselves with strings, nose bones, rattails, and feathers, painted their bodies with the sacred design of the witchetty grub, and constructed a brush hut in the shape of the witchetty-grub chrysalis. They entered the hut and sang of the journey they had made. Then the head men came shuffling and gliding out, followed by all the rest, in imitation of adult witchetty grubs emerging from a chrysalis.

In most village societies an undifferentiated community of ancestral spirits keep a close watch on their descendants, ready to punish them if they commit incest or if they break the taboos against eating certain foods. Important endeavors—hunting, gardening, pregnancy, warfare—need the blessings of a group's ancestors to be successful, and such blessings are usually obtained by holding feasts in the ancestors' honor according to the principle that a well-fed ancestor is a well-intentioned ancestor. Throughout highland New Guinea, for example, people believe that the ancestral spirits enjoy eating pork as much as living persons enjoy eating it. To please the ancestors, people slaughter whole herds of pigs before going to war or when celebrating important events in an individual's life such as marriage and death. But in keeping with a big-man redistributive level of political organization, no one claims that his or her ancestors merit special treatment.

Under conditions of increasing population, greater wealth to be inherited, and intrasocietal competition between different kin groups, people tend to pay more attention to specific and recently deceased relatives in order to validate claims to the inheritance of land and other resources. The Dobuans, South Pacific yam gardeners and fishermen of the Admiralty Islands, have what seems to be an incipient phase of a particularized ancestor religion. When the leader of a Dobuan household died, his children cleaned his skull, hung it from the rafters of their house, and provided it with food and drink. Addressing it as "Sir Ghost," they solicited protection against disease and misfortune, and, through oracles, asked him for advice. If Sir Ghost did not cooperate, his heirs threatened to get rid of him. Actually, Sir Ghost could never win. The death of his children finally proved that he was no longer of any use. So when the grandchildren took charge, they threw Sir Ghost into the lagoon, substituting their own father's skull as the symbol of the household's new spiritual patron.

With the development of chiefdoms, ruling elites employed specialists whose job it was to memorize the names of the chief's ancestors. To make sure that the remains of these dignitaries did not get thrown away like Sir Ghost's skull, paramount chiefs built elaborate tombs that preserved links between generations in a tangible form. Finally, with the emergence of states and empires, as the rulers' souls rose to take their places in the firmament alongside the high gods, their mummified mortal remains, surrounded by exquisite furniture, rare jewels, gold-encrusted chariots and other preciosities, were interred in gigantic crypts and pyramids that only a true god could have built. But I have already told that part of the story.

THE BASIC ANIMISTIC RITUALS

$\supset$N EARLIEST TIMES, belief in the existence of a spirit world recurrently gave rise to the hope that spirit beings could be induced or compelled to help humans lead longer, healthier, and more satisfactory lives. Every known culture has a repertory of techniques for obtaining such help. But among simple band-and-village societies, most adults possess a working knowledge of these techniques in keeping with an open and egalitarian use of natural resources.

Among the Eskimo, a man had to have a hunting song, a combination of chant, prayer, and magic formula that he inherited from his father or his father's brothers, or purchased from some famous person. This he would sing under his breath as he prepared himself for the day's activities. Around his neck he wore a little bag filled with tiny animal carvings, bits of claws and fur, pebbles, insects, and other items, each corresponding to a personal "spirit helper," who protected him against hostile spirits and helped him in the hunt. A similar individualistic relationship with guardian spirits once prevailed throughout much of North America. Among the Crow Indians of the Great Plains, a man had to have a "guardian spirit" if he wanted to be successful as warrior, hunter, or lover. To obtain such a spirit was not easy: One had to have a vision in which the guardian would appear and make its identity known. Lacking hallucinatory drugs and in keeping with a code of personal bravery and indifference to pain, the young Crow sought his vision through self-inflicted torture. He went alone into the mountains, stripped off his clothes, and abstained from food and drink. If this was not sufficient, he chopped off part of the fourth finger of his left hand. Coached from childhood to expect that a vision would come, most of the Crow vision-seekers were successful. A buffalo, snake, chicken hawk, thunderbird, dwarf, or mysterious stranger would adopt him, teach him a secret song, and promise him success in battle, horse-raiding, or some other life goal.

410

Despite the emphasis on do-it-yourself religion among band-and-village peoples, every known society acknowledges that some individuals, known as shamans, have a special aptitude for obtaining help from the spirit world. (Shaman is a word borrowed from the Tungus-speaking people of Siberia.) Shamans are adept at communicating with and visiting the spirit world during dreams and trances. To go into a trance, they take hallucinogenic substances, dance to a monotonous drumbeat, or simply close their eyes and concentrate. Their bodies become rigid, and they start to sweat, moan, and tremble as they enter the spirit world and call upon their guardians to help cure the sick, predict the future, find lost persons, or ward off malevolent forces.

We know that shamans everywhere have a bag of Wizard-of-Oz tricks that they use to impress their clients. Siberian shamans held seances inside a darkened tent whose corners were attached by long thongs hidden under the rugs to the shamans' feet. With the arrival of a guardian spirit, the shamans had only to wiggle their toes to make the tent shake violently. The spirits would then speak in a high-pitched voice, which appeared to float about near the top of the tent, for Siberian shamans were accomplished ventriloquists. Other acts of deception were practiced in relation to the belief, widely held in preindustrial societies, that disease is caused by malevolent objects that sorcerers insert into people's bodies. Shamans, with the assistance of their spirit helpers, tried to remove these objects, usually by sucking them out with their mouths pressed against the patient's skin. In North and South America, shamans prepare for the removal of the offending objects by getting intoxicated on huge whiffs of tobacco smoke that they exhale over their patient. Huffing, puffing, and sucking with all their might, the practitioner finally falls back and triumphantly spits or vomits forth a sliver of bone, a thorn, or a dead spider, which he or she knows was never in the patient's body.

Michael Harner, a modern exponent of shamanic practice, insists that there is nothing fraudulent about the sucking cure. Shamans put the offending object in their mouths because its presence helps to withdraw the *spiritual* counterpart of such objects that are, in fact, inside the patient's body and causing the illness. And so by spitting or vomiting up the intrusive object, the shamans are merely displaying a material symbol of the spirit-world reality. Perhaps. But I prefer a slightly different interpretation. Modern medical theory holds that ill persons who intensely believe that they are going to get better have stronger immunological reactions and a greater chance of recovering than those who think their condition is hopeless. Both shamans and patients undoubtedly believe that intrusive objects cause illness. But to obtain the therapeutic benefit of such beliefs, the patient has to be convinced that the shaman has successfully removed the objects. Cultural selection, therefore, favored the use of deception and sleight of hand in producing the evidence needed for achieving a therapeutic effect, although from the shaman's point of view the real business of curing involved the removal of intangible spirit-world objects.

Even after the rise of chiefdoms and states, shamanism continued to be an important component of religious life. In fact, it has never lost its popular appeal and many people continue to practice it in modern times as a means of establishing contact between the living and the dead. Shirley MacLaine's "channeling"—tuning in on our past incarnations with the aid of "spirit guides"—is just one among hundreds of modern variants.

So am I saying that religious rituals today are more or less what they were in the beginning? Not at all. The rise of chiefdoms and states resulted in new layers of religious belief and practice appropriate to evolved and centralized societies. Along with advanced chiefdoms and states came ecclesiastical institutions staffed by professionally trained, full-time specialists—the first churches and the first priests. Unlike shamans, priests lived apart from ordinary people, studied astronomy, cosmology, and mathematics, kept track of the seasons and other calendrical events, and interpreted the will of the governing class's exalted ancestors and high gods. Yet there was continuity. For a long time, the rituals of ecclesiastical specialists remained what they had been for the lineage heads of simple ancestor cults. Like Sir Ghost and the pork-hungry ancestors of New Guinea, the gods of early ecclesiastical religions wanted to eat. It was the responsibility of the first priests to make certain they ate well.

DIVINE
EXCHANGES

*H*UMANS HAVE ALWAYS related to the gods with an enormous variety of emotions, motives, and expectations. Yet it would be hypocritical to deny that, underlying all other sentiments, one impulse has been salient since the beginning of animistic thought. Our kind has always wanted gods and other spirit beings to provide us with certain kinds of benefits. In Ruth Benedict's words, "Religion was first and foremost a technique for success." Most frequently, the sought-after benefits have been quite tangible and mundane: recovery from illness, success in trading ventures, rains to water parched crops, victory on the battlefield. Requests for immortality, resurrection, and eternal bliss in heaven may seem less crass, but they nonetheless also involve the gods in the delivery of goods and services. Even when sought-after benefits consist of nothing more than help in acting and thinking in conformity with the wishes of the deity or in achieving inner peace, however lofty our motives, it is a service that we seek. Has there ever been a religion that did not ask what the gods could do for humans as well as what humans could do for the gods? I don't think so.

Certainly ecclesiastical religions in ancient chiefdoms and states did not equivocate about the practical objectives of their interactions with deities. People expected to receive goods and services from the spirit world and it was the primary task of ecclesiastical specialists—the consummate objective of all their lore and learning —to satisfy such expectations.

Ecclesiastical experts dispose of a limited set of options in their attempt to obtain benefits from the gods. In fact, they are largely constrained to use stratagems that humans use in trying to obtain goods and services from each other. One can try an aggressive approach and threaten harm to gods who do not cooperate. Alternatively, one can engage in some form of exchange of goods and services that are valuable to the gods in order to get benefits in return.

414

Or one can appeal to the mercy and generosity of the superior trading partner, promising to even the score with the gifts of love and devotion. Finally, in extremis, there is sacrifice, which I define as an expression of love and gratitude backed up by harmful actions such as self-mutilation, slaying of a loved one, or the destruction of property that the supplicant regards as precious.

Few ecclesiastical religions approach their deities in the belligerent and vindictive style that Dobuans adopt toward Sir Ghost. If the gods of ecclesiastical religions are maltreated, it is at the hands of disgruntled commoners. In rural Mexico, for example, villagers have been known to whip the images of patron saints who have mismanaged the rains or failed to ward off sickness. But the ecclesiastical authorities take a dim view of such actions. The reason ecclesiastical religions refrain from taking tough measures against recalcitrant gods is that tough measures could only work against minor and relatively weak deities. How could gods that, like Sir Ghost, yield to puny threats and punishments deliver the great things that ecclesiastical religions expect of them?

Exchange has always seemed a more fitting approach for those who wish to enlist the help of the high gods of ecclesiastical religions. But exchange presumes that people have something that the gods want. What can it be? A common answer is that the gods value most what humans value most. That is why food and drink, without which humans cannot survive, were once at the top of the list of godly needs in virtually all ecclesiastical religions. In fact, many early divine exchanges seem implicitly to assume that the reason the gods bothered to create humans in the first place was that they needed humans to feed them. As recounted in the Babylonian myth of Gilgamesh, the gods grew famished along with humans when a great flood swept over the earth. Traces of mutual dependence remain in the Biblical version of the flood story. When the water subsides, Noah offers burnt parts of every clean beast and every clean fowl to the Lord, who smells the "sweet savor" and promises never to produce another flood.

To put it bluntly, early ecclesiastical religions saw humans and gods as if they were enmeshed in a food cycle. Without help from gods, humans would never be able to feed themselves. But humans must feed gods to obtain that help. By assuming the burden of feeding ever-hungry gods, doesn't it seem as if humans would only trap themselves ever deeper into shortages of food? No. There was an easy way out of this dilemma. Food set out for spirit beings to eat did not suddenly disappear: It rotted just like ordinary food left uneaten. Clearly, gods, being of spirit, eat only the spiritual essence of the food that is offered to them. The corporeal substance can then be redistributed under the auspices of ecclesiastical and political authority and consumed as food that gods have given permission for humans to enjoy. Does this sound familiar? It should, for what I am describing is the spiritual side of redistributive exchange systems whose role in the evolution of political hierarchies I have already discussed.

As relations between ruling elites and commoners became more hierarchical, redistributive exchanges became more materially lopsided and what began as gifts from people to their ancestors ended as compulsory donations—taxes in kind—collected by church and state. But can one say that commoners whose donations supported the ecclesiastical elites had struck a bad bargain? Not if the ecclesiastical experts were correct, for humans would have starved and the earth and everything on it would have come to grief if the priests hadn't fed the gods on time.

MEAT
OFFERINGS

LTHOUGH MOST GODS are omnivores and enjoy plant foods and beverages (especially alcoholic beverages), wherever one catches a glimpse of early religions, meat is the central focus of the food exchange cycle linking humans and the spirit world. This follows as an extension of the principle that gods and humans value the same things. Since meat is the most prestigious and universally desired food among humans, it is also the most prestigious and universally desired food among the gods. As a consequence, animal slaughter and religious ritual became closely entwined during the development of ecclesiastical institutions. Over wide areas of Europe, Asia, Africa, and Oceania, to be a priest was to possess the knowledge, skill, and authority necessary for killing animals in a fashion that was pleasing to divine tastes. The Massai, Nuer, Dinka, and other East African people could not eat domesticated animals, especially cattle, unless the beasts had been ritually slaughtered by experts. Furthermore, slaughter and meat-eating did not occur at the whim of anyone who wished to eat meat, but only on special occasions such as births, marriages, funerals, and graduation from puberty schools, when meat could be redistributed and shared by members of the community. Sacred texts that allude to beliefs and practices in ancient Iran and India indicate that remarkably similar rituals of redistribution lay at the center of the earliest known ecclesiastical religions. In the Yasna, a sacred text from Iran, there is a passage that reads: "The cow calls to the priest who should sacrifice but does not. 'May you become childless and dogged by ill-fame, you who do not distribute me when I am cooked, but fatten me for your wife or your son or for your own belly!' "

As this passage indicates, cattle could not be consumed in ancient Iran without being ritually slaughtered, and ritual slaughter was integrally involved with the redistribution of meat. Vedic tombs from India point to the same restrictions. Brahmans, members of the priestly caste, were in charge of ritually slaughtering domesticated animals and of serving portions according to a fixed formula. People ate meat only from animals that Brahmans ritually killed, offered to gods and ancestors, and redistributed to invited guests. As the Indo-Iranian scholar Bruce Lincoln affirms, Indo-Iranian ritual slaughter took place in the presence of deities summoned for the occasion, not merely as approving onlookers but as active consumers of spiritualized flesh. And through hymns and prayers, the presiding priests declared what they expected in return. "With overwhelming consistency, these requests have a temporal focus—wealth, success, and well-being."

Celtic pre-Roman Europe also had its caste of ecclesiastical experts, known as Druids. Julius Caesar states that Druids were in charge of sacred matters, the interpretation of all holy things, and "public and private sacrifices." Other sources make it clear that Druidic rituals centered on the slaughter and redistribution of domestic animals, especially cattle and horses, undoubtedly in connection with ideas about feeding the gods in exchange for material benefits. Finally, as every reader of the Old Testament knows, there are the Levites, descendants of Aaron and designated hereditary priests of ancient Israel, who were in charge of the ritual slaughter of domestic animals for offerings and redistribution. As among modern-day East Africans, the Israelites "could never eat beef or mutton except as a religious act." The Book of Leviticus sets forth the where, when, and how of ritual slaughter in great detail, often prescribing the animal's sex, age, color, and physical condition. Leviticus mentions at least seven kinds of offerings: "burnt," "peace," "sin," "trespass," "heave," "wave," and "free will."

With the exception, perhaps, of "burnt offerings," ritual slaughter did not render the carcass inedible, although the animal's blood was invariably drained and sprinkled over the altar. The Levites apparently retained a significant share of animal offerings for their own consumption. In Numbers 8, the Lord explicitly states that Levites may eat the holy things that are offered to Him, provided they do so in a hallowed place. Also according to the Book of Numbers (7:1–89), 36 oxen, 144 sheep and lambs, and 72 goats and kids were ritually slaughtered over a twelve-day period at the dedication of the first tabernacle. As the Israelites advanced from the level of semipastoral chiefdoms to sedentary states, the scale of animal offerings increased. At the dedication of the first temple in Jerusalem, King Solomon sacrificed 22,000 oxen and 120,000 sheep as a "peace offering." Since all that meat was obviously not left to rot, the description of the festivities as a sacrifice obscures its eminently practical outcome in consonance with ancient redistributive feasting the world over. Actually, Solomon's redistributive feast was a pale shadow of what a really great provider could do for his loyal followers. When the Assyrian king Assurnasirpal completed his palace at Nimrod, he threw a party for 16,000 inhabitants of the city, 1,500 members of royalty, 47,074 men and women from the rest of the country, and 5,000 foreign envoys. The total of more than 69,000 guests stayed for ten days, during which they consumed 14,000 sheep and drank 10,000 skins of wine. But the era of great providers was drawing to a close.

HUMAN
SACRIFICE

ARLY ECCLESIASTICAL RELIGIONS made frequent use of human beings as offerings to the gods. But they seldom viewed human flesh as a food that gods liked to eat, nor did they redistribute human remains like animal flesh at festivals sponsored by generous kings. (I'll come to the one great documented exception in a moment.) To the extent that ecclesiastical experts used humans as offerings, they often did so as genuine sacrifices—offerings that were intended to win the sympathy of the gods through extravagant self-inflicted deprivation rather than through balanced reciprocity and food cycles. Offerings of children epitomize the genre. In the Old Testament, Jaweh demands that Abraham demonstrate obedience by putting his only son, Isaac, to death. God relents at the last minute and Isaac is spared. Not so with the child sacrifice carried out during the reign of three apostate kings (Agaz in II Kings 16:3, Manassa in II Kings 21:6, and Ahab in I Kings 16:34). Neighboring kingdoms also used children as sacrificial victims. Archaeological excavations at Gezer, for example, indicate that the Biblical Canaanites killed children and placed them beneath the foundations of temples and palaces. And early Assyrian documents refer to the burning of children as sacrificial offerings.

Other evidence suggests that at one time child sacrifice was not uncommon among the Israelites themselves. In Jeremiah 7:31 we learn that "they have built the high places of Tophet which is in the Valley of Ben-Hinnon to burn their sons and daughters in the fire; which I commanded not, neither came it into my heart." The tophet was a sacred precinct just south of Jerusalem where parents gave their infants and children to priests to be burnt alive in honor of Baal, as we learn from II Kings 17:16–17: "And . . . they served Baal . . . and they caused their sons and daughters to pass through the fire." Additional mention of tophets occurs in II Kings 23:10 and Jeremiah 32:35, where they appear to be associated with the worship of Moloch.

The Jerusalem tophet was dismantled by the king Josiah, who reigned in the seventh century B.C. But the building of tophets by other Mediterranean and Middle Eastern peoples continued long after the ancient Hebrews desisted. Phoenicians, who shared many cultural features with their Canaanite ancestors, constructed tophets in their colonies in Sicily, Sardinia, and Tunisia. At Carthage, near modern-day Tunis, they built the largest tophet of all, interring the charred remains in special urns placed under stone markers. Carthaginians sacrificed their children for at least 600 years, until the Romans destroyed the city in 146 B.C. Archaeologists Lawrence Stager and Samuel Wolff estimate that 20,000 urns were interred in the Carthage tophet between 400 B.C. and 200 B.C. alone, making it the largest cemetery of sacrificed humans ever discovered. That doesn't make the Carthaginians the most zealous sacrificers of human beings. Others excelled them but didn't bother to inter the remains in cemeteries, as we shall see.

Prisoners of war were another common source of sacrificial victims. Since enemy warriors could be taken prisoner only as a result of costly and dangerous battles, they were eminently suited to convey an impression of their captors' sacrificial zeal. Inscriptions from early Mesopotamia record the frequent sacrifice of prisoners of war by temple priests. Similar practices probably existed among early Greeks and Romans. According to Homer's account of the battle of Troy, the Greek hero Achilles put twelve captured Trojans on the funeral pyre of his comrade-in-arms, Patroclus. And as late as the great naval battle of Salamis in 480 B.C. between the Greeks and Persians, Themistocles, the Greek commander-in-chief, ordered the sacrifice of three Persian captives to assure victory. But by classical times, the Romans and Greeks generally condemned human sacrifice as suitable only for the religion of "barbarians." They had in mind such people as the Scythians, who lived on the lower Danube and shores of the Black Sea and who, according to Herodotus, actually slit the throat of one out of every one hundred prisoners taken on the battlefield. The Celts of northern and western Europe frequently practiced prisoner sacrifice, although they preferred to weave a wickerwork basket around the victim and set fire to it. On other occasions, they disemboweled or stabbed prisoners so that Druids could foretell the future from the condition of the entrails or from the position of the limbs when the writhing stopped.

A great deal is known about prisoner-of-war sacrifice as practiced in Shang China (second century B.C.). Shang priests used fire-induced cracks on cattle shoulder blades and turtle carapaces to predict the future. They incised the bone or shell with written questions they wanted answered, put them in the fire, and then interpreted the answers as indicated by the pattern of cracks made by the heat. One of the oft-repeated questions inscribed on these "oracle bones" was whether or not and how many cattle, sheep, goats, and prisoners of war needed to be sacrificed to satisfy the king's ancestors: "Should the king's ritual be performed with the sacrifice of ten prisoners of war from Chiang? Or twenty? Or thirty?" was the way the matter was put. One bone asked if 400 prisoners might not be the appropriate number. When summed, all questions concerning the number of Chiang to be sacrificed suggested that over an extended period, Shang priests used their oracle bones to decide the fate of at least 7,000 such prisoners, and Chiang was not the only place from which prisoners were obtained. Archaeological evidence confirms the tale told by the oracle bones. More than 600 prisoners were put to death at Hsiao-t'un for the consecration of a single royal residence.

The most widespread form of human sacrifice occurred at the death and burial of kings and other royal personages. When monarchs died, during the earliest dynasties of Egypt and Sumer, as well as in ancient China and Peru and in such African kingdoms as Uganda and Dahomey, wives, concubines, cooks, grooms, and other retainers could expect to be ritually killed as part of the great one's funeral. The prevalence of this custom has been confirmed archaeologically for China's eastern Chou period (770–221 B.C.). At Leigudum in Suixian, Hubei, twenty-one women ranging in age from thirteen to twenty-five were interred in a single tomb, along with one male who was forty-five years old. Retainer burial was still being practiced in China as late as the third century B.C. during the Ch'in Dynasty. The second emperor, for example, ordered that all of his father's childless concubines should accompany their master to the grave.

The sacrificial logic of these rites focuses on the new ruler's renunciation of the departed ruler's prized human possessions. Rather than keep them for their own use, the new rulers sent them off to serve the late great one in heaven as on earth, thereby hoping to win favor with exalted ancestor gods upon whose cooperation a new ruler's success depended. At the same time, of course, the burial of a king's retainers and wives was one more proof of the fact that kings were no ordinary mortals. Not only could they enjoy the services of an immense staff of servants, wives, and concubines during their reign, but they could take the whole operation with them into the tomb along with the world's most expensive and beautiful clothing, jewelry, furniture, and other craft projects. Let me note a still more mundane function of retainer burial. Could anything more encourage wives and servants to be protective of the life of their king than the knowledge that if he died they died with him?

As I said a moment ago, the gods of early ecclesiastical religions were not fond of human flesh. Hence human sacrifice was seldom accompanied by redistributive feasting. The gods accepted human sacrifices, but not as part of a food exchange. Why was this the case? If early ecclesiastical gods almost universally relished animal flesh, why didn't they dine on human flesh as well? Since the gods liked to eat what people liked to eat, their rejection of human flesh simply reflected the prevalent human distaste for eating our kind. That leaves us with the question of why advanced chiefdoms and early states were averse to eating their enemies.

THE GODS
WHO WOULD
NOT EAT
PEOPLE

WISH I COULD SAY that the widespread taboo on cannibalism expressed an ethical impulse to protect human life. But the warlike nature of advanced chiefdoms and early states tells a different story. Much of the slaughter of animals at the altar was nothing but a prelude to the slaughter of humans on the battlefield. Nowhere is there the slightest bit of evidence suggesting that warriors who were forbidden to eat each other were less inclined to kill each other. So we must look for a more down-to-earth explanation of why the gods of early ecclesiastical religions were disinclined to accept human flesh as a food offering.

Before I go on with my explanation, let me make it clear that our kind does not have any natural aversion to the consumption of human flesh. I assure you that it is no great challenge to find cases other than those provoked by extreme hunger, in a besieged Leningrad or among victims of shipwrecks and airplane crashes. Karen Gordon-Grube of the Free University of West Berlin points out that anthropologists have been so preoccupied with seeking evidence of institutionalized cannibalism among "primitives" that they have overlooked a well-documented cannibal tradition that flourished in their own backyard. From the sixteenth to the eighteenth century, medical textbooks in England and on the Continent recommended the use of "mummy"—"a medicinal preparation of the remains of an embalmed, dried, or other 'prepared' human body that had ideally met with a sudden, preferably violent death." London pharmacies kept this cure-all in stock, but for high-quality products, physicians recommended that it be purchased at a mummy shop.

Many unimpeachable reports, including eyewitness accounts such as Lumholtz's about the Queensland Aborigines, testify to the widespread practice of cannibalism among chiefdoms as well as among band-and-village societies. Of the several forms that cannibalism can take, the one of greatest interest with regard to the evolution

428

of ecclesiastical religions is warfare cannibalism: the consumption of the bodies of prisoners of war, frequently at the conclusion of a public spectacle in which the victim has been tortured. As I mentioned earlier, Jesuit missionaries provide detailed eyewitness descriptions of this custom among native inhabitants of both North and South America, and anthropologists and other scientists have confirmed that it was practiced in New Guinea. Since the band-and-village societies and chiefdoms of Europe and Asia were wiped out by state-level societies thousands of years ago, there are no eyewitness accounts of the existence of prestate warfare cannibalism in Europe and Asia. It is to archaeological evidence, therefore, that one must turn to decide whether prestate peoples in Eurasia did in fact eat each other.

Archaeologists have found many decapitated skulls and broken human bones at early sites in Europe and Asia. But the problem has been to determine whether the bones tell the story of warfare cannibalism or of effects produced by carnivores and rodents plus the ritual treatment of bodies of deceased relatives. These uncertainties have been resolved at one site, Fontebregona Cave in southeastern France, which was inhabited by village-level peoples during the fifth and fourth millennia B.C. Fontebregona's excavators encountered several distinct clusters of disarticulated and fractured groups of human bones, each of which contained the remains of six or seven individuals. Microscopic analysis demonstrates that the bones had been broken to extract marrow, and defleshed with exactly the same implements and in exactly the same manner as the animal bones found nearby in the same cave. Furthermore, the vertical and horizontal distribution of the human bones indicates that the individuals must have been killed and butchered as part of a single event. Finally, the possibility that the remains were produced by funerary rituals performed for deceased relatives seems remote since the bone clusters were not buried but were scattered about the cave and interspersed with similar clusters of animal bones. A likely explanation for those clusters is that the filleting and the marrow fracturing of both human and animal bones were done on an animal skin spread on the floor of the cave, after which the inedible debris was dumped over and formed a single heap.

Now that I have set forth some of the reasons for believing that cannibalism occurred widely among warring band-and-village

and chiefdom societies, let me return to the question of why ecclesiastical religions found in early state societies generally placed
restraints on cannibalism but not on warfare. I think the crux of the
matter is the ability of politically evolved societies to integrate van-
quished populations into their labor force. This ability, in turn,
relates to the greater productivity of farmers and other workers in
these societies. Each farmer and worker in a state society can produce
a surplus of goods and services. Therefore, the larger a state's population grows, the greater the amount of surplus production, and the
bigger the tax and tribute base, the more powerful the governing
class becomes. Large-scale killing and eating of captives would
thwart the governing class's interest in expanding its tax and tribute
base. Since captives can produce a surplus, far better to consume the
products of their labor than the flesh of their bodies, especially if the
meat and milk of domesticated animals (not available to most band-
and-village people) are part of the surplus. In contrast, band-and-
village societies are incapable of producing large surpluses, lack a
military and political organization that is capable of uniting defeated
enemies under a central government, and have no governing class
that stands to benefit from taxation. For band-and-village societies,
the military strategy that most benefits the victors, therefore, is to
kill or disperse the population of neighboring groups in order to
lower the pressure of population on resources. Because of their low
productivity, band-and-village societies cannot derive long-term benefits from capturing enemy personnel. Since captives cannot usually
produce a surplus, bringing one home to serve as a slave simply
means one more mouth to feed. Killing and eating captives is the
predictable outcome; if captive labor cannot yield a surplus, captives
are worth more as food than as producers of food.

I hasten to add that no human group would ever find cannibalism cost-efficient outside of the context of warfare. Humans are
the most costly and troublesome creatures to capture and domesticate. But if band-and-village people were at war (for reasons I've
discussed earlier), why wouldn't they eat each other when the opportunity arose?

THE GODS
WHO ATE
PEOPLE

*T*HE PRE-COLUMBIAN religion of the Aztecs was the great exception to which I referred a moment ago. Unlike other ecclesiastic deities, the gods of the Aztec state craved human flesh, especially fresh human hearts. According to Aztec belief, unless this craving was satisfied, the gods would destroy the world. Human sacrifice, therefore, became the most important function of the Aztec priesthood. Most of the people sacrificed were captives brought back to Tenochtitlán, the Aztec capital, by military commanders. Forced to ascend the flat-topped pyramids that dominated the city's ceremonial precincts, the victim was seized by four priests, one for each limb, and bent backward face up, over a stone altar. A fifth priest then opened the victim's chest with an obsidian knife, wrenched out the heart, and while it was still beating, smeared it over the nearby statue of the presiding deity. Attendants then rolled the body down the steps. Other attendants cut off the head, pushed a wooden shaft through it from side to side, and placed it on a tall latticework structure or skull rack alongside the heads of previous victims.

To remove any doubts about what happened next, permit me to quote from Bernadino de Sahagún's *General History of the Things of New Spain,* the most fundamental and scrupulously honest source on Aztec religion:

> After having torn their hearts from them and poured the blood into a gourd vessel, which the master of the slain man himself received, they started the body rolling down the pyramid steps. It came to rest upon a small square below. There some old men, whom they called Quaquacuitlin, laid hold of it and carried it to their tribal temple, where they dismembered it and divided it up in order to eat it.

Again and again Sahagún asserts that the common fate of the victim's corpse was to be eaten:

After they had slain them and torn out their hearts, they took them away gently, rolling them down the steps. When they had reached the bottom, they cut off their heads and inserted a rod through them, and they carried the bodies to the houses which they called *calpulli,* where they divided them up in order to eat them. . . . and they took out their hearts and struck off their heads. And later they divided up all the body among themselves and ate it. . . .

Diego Duran, another major chronicler, clarifies the nature of the occasion on which the "masters"—warriors who had captured the victims and marched them to Tenochtitlán—devoured the corpses.

Once the heart had been wrenched out it was offered to the sun and blood sprinkled toward the solar deity. Initiating the descent of the sun in the west the corpse was toppled down the steps of the pyramid. After the sacrifice the warriors celebrated a great feast with much dancing, ceremonial and cannibalism.

Can there be any doubt that Aztec human sacrifice was the precise counterpart of the redistributive feasting that so many other early ecclesiastical religions carried out with animal rather than human offerings?

Aztec redistributive cannibal feasting provided warriors with substantial amounts of meat as a reward for success in combat. Members of Cortez's expedition found that the principal skull rack in Tenochtitlán's main square contained the heads of 136,000 sacrificial victims. But they were unable to count another group of victims whose heads had been heaped into two tall towers made entirely of crania and jawbones, nor did they count the skulls displayed on five smaller racks that were located in the same central area. According to one of my critics, the principal rack could not have held more than 60,000 skulls. Even if this lower figure is more accurate, the amount of human sacrifice and cannibalism practiced in Tenochtitlán remains unique in human history.

Why did Aztecs and their gods eat prisoners of war instead of putting them to work as peasants and slaves, as did other state-level societies? My answer is that unlike virtually all other states, the

Aztecs had never succeeded in domesticating the kinds of animals whose flesh other ecclesiastical societies relied on for redistributive feasting. That is, they lacked ruminants like sheep, goats, cattle, llamas, or alpacas, which eat grasses and leaves that humans cannot eat. Nor did they possess swine, which were so important as domestic scavengers in East Asia. Instead, their principal domesticated sources of meat were turkeys and dogs, both of which are ill-suited for the mass production of meat under preindustrial conditions. Neither turkeys nor dogs can thrive on grass or other high-cellulose plants and hence must be fed on plant foods that humans themselves consume. As carnivores, dogs are especially ill-suited for the mass production of animal flesh. Why feed meat to dogs in order to get meat for people? The Aztecs did try to develop breeds of dogs that could be fattened on *cooked* plant food, but the fact that they did this is a measure of their unsatisfied craving for meat.

There is similar significance to the astonishing variety of small, inefficient wild sources of animal fats and proteins that the Aztecs eagerly devoured at every opportunity, including snakes, frogs, beetles, dragonfly larvae, grasshoppers, ants, worms, tadpoles, waterflies, and waterfly eggs. Of course, they also ate larger animals such as deer, fish, and waterfowl whenever they could get their hands on them, but shared among the million and a half people who lived within a twenty-mile radius of Tenochtitlán, the combined intake from all wild sources of meat could not have amounted to more than a few grams per day. As a consequence, the balance of costs and benefits in forgoing the consumption of the flesh of prisoners of war was different in the Aztec case than in other state societies. Prisoners continued to be "produced" as a by-product of warfare, but their utility as slaves and peasants was greatly diminished. Preserving their lives could not solve the pressing problem of scarce animal resources since there was no way additional labor power could be harnessed to the task of improving the supply of animal food. In contrast to the rulers of other early state societies, Aztec elites had no motivation to save the lives of prisoners of war. By using war captives as a source of meat for redistributive feasting, the Aztec elites were able to play the role of being great providers worthy of the loyal support of their followers far more effectively than by using captives to increase the production of plant food.

I maintain that the hunger for human bodies of the Aztec

gods faithfully mirrored the hunger for meat of the Aztec people. Some of my critics have found it hard to accept the idea that a whole system of religious beliefs could be shaped by something they consider as crude and vulgar as a desire to provide meat for redistributive feasting. Perhaps one of the reasons for this reaction is that in an age of industrial agriculture, meat is no longer a luxury food. In most developed countries, people confront more of a threat from too much animal fat and protein than from too little. But this was not true of societies like the Yanomami, for whom meat hunger denoted a distinct form of physiological deprivation. Most so-called vegetarian diets include milk, cheese, and yogurt, which were conspicuously absent from the Aztecs' cuisine since they possessed no milkable animals. Real vegetarianism, by which I mean no eggs, dairy products, fish, fowl, as well as no red meat, is a life-threatening diet. True, a healthy adult can obtain all essential amino acids by eating large quantities of cereals alone. But such diets remain deficient in minerals (e.g., iron) and vitamins (e.g., vitamin A). Moreover, the protein levels that are adequate for normal adults and that can be obtained from cereals alone or from combinations such as corn and beans are hazardous for children, pregnant and lactating women, and anybody suffering from parasitical or viral infections or other diseases and body trauma caused by accidents or wounds. Hence, the high value that the Aztecs placed on the consumption of human flesh was not an arbitrary consequence of their religious beliefs. Rather, their religious beliefs (i.e., the cravings of their gods for human meat) reflected the importance of animal foods in relation to human dietary needs and the scant supply of every animal in their habitat except the human one.

I encourage critics who scoff at the idea that meat hunger was the selective force responsible for the evolution of the Aztecs' cannibal kingdom to reflect on the seriousness with which per capita consumption of animal food, especially meat, is regarded by the leaders of Soviet bloc countries. When the Polish government announced a 20 percent reduction in subsidized meat rations in 1981, martial law had to be declared to restore order. The reason why the Soviet Union is incapable of fulfilling its grain requirements without help from abroad is that it uses 186 million tons for animal feed as compared with 126 million tons for cereals and bread. Soviet leaders are not likely to tell their people that they ought to eat less meat because less is good for their health. As Mikhail Gorbachev told the Soviet Central Committee in November 1988: "If we could put 80 kilograms [176 pounds] of meat a year on the consumer's table, all other problems we have would not be as acute as they are now. It is no exaggeration to say that the shortage of meat products is a problem that is worrying the whole nation."

Similar thoughts must surely have crossed the minds of the Aztec kings as they watched people skimming the greenish scum of waterfly eggs from Lake Texcoco and pondered the problem of maintaining the loyalty of their followers. The Soviet Union already consumes enough animal fat and protein per capita to satisfy World Health Organization standards almost twice over, while the Aztecs were probably getting less than half, even with all their cannibalistic feasting. Clearly, they were more in need of a good dose of dietary perestroika than the average Muscovite.

THE
NONKILLING
RELIGIONS

N THE THOUSAND YEARS before the birth of Christ, from the Mediterranean to the Ganges, charismatic leaders arose to challenge ancient ecclesiastical assumptions and practices and to found new religions and philosophies that condemned the role of priests as ritual killers of people or animals and denied the efficacy of food offerings as a means of winning favors from the gods. Instructed by one or another form of transcendental experience or deep meditation, the new leaders insisted that gods could not be swayed by material bribes. Instead, what the gods or their prophets demanded was a lifetime devoted to good deeds defined as love and kindness to people and all living things. In exchange for defending the poor and the weak and for restraining appetites and other egotistical tendencies, one could expect great rewards. But delivery would occur after death in the form of heavenly immortality or eternal peace rather than rewards delivered in life in the form of food and other material benefits.

Zoroastrianism, the religion of ancient Iran, is the oldest nonkilling faith of which any historical record exists. It was founded in either the eleventh or the seventh century B.C. by the prophet Zoroaster, after he received a vision about Ahura Mazda, "Lord of Enlightenment." Ahura Mazda stood for good thoughts, truth, good government, meekness, health, and immortality. But Ahura Mazda was not supreme. He was opposed by Ahriman, who stood for evil thoughts, lies, misgovernment, rebelliousness, sickness, and death. Ahura Mazda and Ahriman were locked in a great struggle. Humans are free to choose to join one side or the other. Those who chose Ahura Mazda must cease the consumption of intoxicants, give up the ritual slaughter of animals, and refrain from the shedding of blood in general. After death, the virtuous will be admitted to Ahura Mazda's heaven; the rest will fall into Ahriman's hell. Mazdaism, a modified form of the religion Zoroaster founded, became the dominant faith of the people of Iran during the reign of the Persian emperors Darius

(522–486 B.C.) and Xerxes (486–465 B.C.). But with the decline of the Persian Empire, Zoroaster's teachings lost their potential for becoming a world religion.

The next historically known religious iconoclast was born a nobleman in Bihar, in northeastern India, during the early part of the sixth century B.C. Prince Vardhamana was his original name but he became known as Mahavira, "the great hero," after he emerged victorious from a prolonged struggle to achieve spiritual fulfillment apart from and in opposition to the Vedic traditions that prevailed among his people. In further recognition of spiritual victories over self-inflicted physical tortures, Mahavira earned the title Jina, "conqueror," from which Jainism, the name of the religion he founded, derives.

Mahavira accepted the idea of rebirth as set forth in Vedic religion, but he opposed the rituals carried out by Brahman priests and challenged the caste distinctions imposed by Vedic beliefs. The objective of Mahavira's teachings was the cleansing and liberation of the human soul from the corrupting influences of passions and desires so that individuals could be reborn at the highest level of bodily purity. The path of liberation begins with five vows: Do not kill, tell lies, steal, fornicate, or acquire excessive riches. Jainism pushed the injunction against killing further than its rivals. Because the lives of all animate beings need to be protected, Jain monks wore gauze masks to prevent the accidental inhalation of flies or gnats and employed sweepers to remove ants and insects from the path ahead of them. For those adepts who had been prepared by previous incarnations, more difficult standards had to be met: complete chastity, and self-mortification, including exposure to hunger, thirst, cold, insect bites, and intense heat. In modified form, Jainism continues to be practiced by about two million people in India, attracting much attention for its sponsorship of charitable institutions such as old-age homes for cows and sealed rooms that serve as sanctuaries for insects.

Like Mahavira, Gautama Siddhartha, the founder of Buddhism, was a nobleman born in Bihar in the Ganges Valley, during the sixth century B.C. He, too, as a young man, fasted and tortured himself in order to free his soul from the cycle of reincarnations. Enlightenment (*bodhi*) came to him only after he had given up this self-inflicted punishment and sat meditating under a tree. Gautama, again like Mahavira, declared his opposition to the old caste-ridden, animal-killing religion of the Veda and set forth a plan—"the eight-fold way"—by which individuals could achieve nirvana, or deliverance from the cycle of reincarnation and its pain and frustration. Calling for both mental and physical discipline, the eightfold way includes such ethical precepts as abstention from lying, lusting, tale-bearing, killing of animals or people, stealing, or engaging in an occupation that brings harm to others. Good deeds combined with deep meditation advance one toward nirvana in this or the next life, bad deeds plus bad thoughts put one further away.

Both Jainism and Buddhism were originally propagated by the cloning of monastic communities, but Buddhist monasteries were more appealing than the Jains' because they did not require the self-inflicted hardships and physical suffering that Mahavira demanded. What Buddha advocated for his disciples was the "middle way" between a life devoted to the futile pleasure of the Vedas and the equally futile self-mortification of the Jains.

Meanwhile, partly as a consequence of the competitive thrust of Jainism and Buddhism, and partly as a response to certain underlying conditions, that I'll get to in a moment, Vedic religion slowly evolved in the direction of modern Hinduism. Instead of continuing to sponsor the ritual slaughter of animals and redistribution of meat, the Brahmans gradually became the most zealous guardians of animal life. Preventing the slaughter of cattle and the consumption of beef became a major preoccupation of all Hindu castes, and ahimsa, reverence for all living beings, emerged as the central ethical component of Hinduism, no less than for Jainism and Buddhism.

By my count, Christianity was at least the fifth historically known ethical, soul-saving, otherworldly religion to appear on the world stage. But this is a very conservative figure. There must have been many similar religious movements during the 600 or more years that separated Zoroaster from Jesus. Northern India alone could have had a dozen embryonic rivals to Jainism and Buddhism about which we know nothing because their founders lived and died outside of the feeble light history shines on these remote times. Not only did Christianity resemble the other four known earlier nonkilling religions of love and mercy, but its relationship to Judaism closely resembled the relationship of these earlier religions to their Indo-Iranian animal-sacrificing, this-worldly redistributive-feasting predecessors. Judaism may have foreshadowed Christian ethic to a larger degree than the religions that foreshadowed the soul-saving Indian and Iranian religions—even the Golden Rule can be found in the Old Testament in the form of "love thy neighbor as thyself" (Leviticus 19:18). But by no stretch of the imagination was Judaism an otherworldly, soul-saving, nonkilling religion in its own right. The Israelites believed that if they faithfully followed Jaweh's commandments, they would be blessed with numerous progeny, freedom from disease, victory over enemies, and an abundance of corn, wine, oil, cattle, and sheep. If they failed to be faithful to Jaweh's commandments, they would suffer the scourges that had once been visited upon the Egyptians (Deuteronomy 7:13–23). The Old Testament has nothing to say about salvation of the soul or even the existence of an afterlife. Moreover, despite the injunction "thou shalt not kill," Biblical Judaism with its imperial ambitions and obsession with bloody rituals, was scarcely a nonkilling religion. Nor is the contrast with early Christianity lessened by the fact that the Israelite priests had begun to abandon large-scale animal offerings before the beginning of the Christian era. Paul, not the Levites, admonished fellow Jews to give up animal sacrifice: "It is not possible that the blood of bulls and of goats should take away sin" (Hebrews 10:4). Since God had sacrificed His only son, there was no need for any more bloody offerings. Henceforth, those who lived without sin would be granted eternal life. "We are sanctified through the offering of the body of Jesus Christ once and for all."

Paul failed to point out that an end to animal offerings also effectively terminated consumption of meat in the redistributive feast that had provided the material substratum of the ancient Hebrew food cycle. Not that redistributive feasting disappeared without a trace. Early Christian communities held feasts during which the wine and bread they consumed were considered to be the symbolic equivalent of Christ's blood and body. Christianity's most important ritual, the Mass or Eucharist, had its origin in the further dematerialization of these early Christian communal meals. Feasting became purely symbolic, as the priest alone drank the wine while passing out nutritionally insignificant portions of bread. And this brings me to some very important questions: Can I account for the demise of the old redistributive food-cycle religions? Why were they recurrently replaced over so vast an area by religions of love and mercy that were destined to become world religions?

THE ORIGIN OF
NONKILLING
RELIGIONS

NONKILLING RELIGIONS arose in response to the failure of early states to deliver the worldly benefits promised by their kings and priests. They arose when these states were being ravaged by brutal and costly wars; when environmental depletions, population growth, and the rise of cities created food shortages and made it difficult to maintain a steady supply of meat for redistributive feasting; and when distinctions of social rank had rigidified and there was widespread poverty among the common people. Let us see if these conditions were actually present in each case.

I must admit the social conditions underlying the origin of Zoroastrianism are quite vague. Scholars set the probable date of Zoroaster's birth by the fact that the oldest surviving Zoroastrian hymns were recorded in an Iranian language that ceased to be used much after 1100 B.C. This corresponds to a period in Iranian history when the Assyrian Empire was losing its grip on Iran and new kingdoms such as Media were vying to fill the political vacuum. The name Zoroaster meant "old camel man," while that of his father meant "gray horse man." This tells us that Zoroaster's family had a pastoral background somewhere on the fringes of the states that were struggling for hegemony over Iran. After receiving his vision, Zoroaster traveled from one kingdom to another until he found a royal patron to support his new religion. So all that one can say is that Zoroaster lived at a time of great political instability and cultural change associated with a struggle against imperial rule and the transition from a pastoral to a more sedentary farming mode of existence.

I can say much more about the social conditions surrounding the births of Buddhism, Jainism, and nonkilling Hinduism. During Vedic times (1500–500 B.C.), the predominant form of political organization in the Ganges Valley was the advanced chiefdom, population was scanty and spread out in small villages, the Gangetic plain was covered with dense forests, fodder for domestic animals was abundant, and there was no conflict between raising cattle for plowing the fields and using them for redistributive feasting. By 600 B.C., the predominant political form was the state, the population had risen into the millions, towns and cities had sprung up, the entire Gangetic plain had become deforested, there was a shortage of pasture and fodder, oxen had become too scarce and costly to be consumed in lavish redistributive feasts, a dozen new states were struggling for regional hegemony, and warfare was incessant. Denuded of its forest cover, the Gangetic plain turned into a dust bowl whenever the monsoon faltered. As recounted in the *Mahabarata,* Hindu India's equivalent of Greece's *Iliad,* droughts brought famines and disorder on an unprecedented scale:

> Lakes, wells and springs were dried up. . . . Sacrifices were in abeyance. Agriculture and cattle-rearing were given up. Markets and shops were abandoned. . . . Festivals died out. Everywhere heaps of bones were seen and cries of creatures heard. The cities were depopulated, hamlets burnt down. People fled from fear of one another or of robbers, weapons, and kings. Places of worship were deserted. The aged were turned out of their houses. Kine, goats, sheep and buffaloes fought and died in large numbers. The Brahmanas died without protection. Herds and plants withered. The earth looked like trees in a crematorium. In that dreadful age when righteousness was at an end, men . . . began to eat one another.

A clear picture also exists of the social and political conditions underlying the birth of Christianity. As a Roman colony, first-century Israel exhibited the classic symptoms of colonial misrule. Jesus lived during a time of guerrilla wars aimed at overthrowing Roman power and purging the Jews who occupied high civil and religious offices as Roman puppets. These uprisings expressed class as well as nationalist discontent, since the high priests, big landowners, and wealthy merchants lived in oriental splendor amidst widespread unemployment, landlessness, and mistreatment of peasants and slaves. The whole colony groaned under the weight of confiscatory taxes, administrative corruption, labor conscription, and runaway inflation. And as in India, shortages of domestic animals made it difficult to continue the practice of ritual slaughter and redistributive feasting.

Many convergent lines of evidence suggest the Romans and their upper-class Jewish clients regarded Jesus as a dangerous revolutionary who was plotting to topple the Roman Empire. In any event, when Paul and the other early missionaries preached the Christian gospel, the kingdom that they promised was not on earth but in heaven. Neither worldly riches nor worldly pain were important because those who loved humankind, lived in peace, and believed in Jesus would be rewarded with the gift of eternal life. The stressful social conditions that existed in Jesus' homeland prevailed throughout other parts of the Roman Empire, including the city of Rome itself. One did not have to be a slave or peasant to be appalled and to feel threatened by the corruption, brutality, class antagonisms, and ceaseless wars that characterized Roman society in the second and third centuries. Under these circumstances, Christianity's promise of otherworldly salvation exerted a strong appeal to people from many different countries and social strata.

But my story of how religions of love and mercy came to be world religions cannot end at this point. However much these religions attracted individuals who yearned for a way to escape from earthly strife and suffering, none of these movements could have achieved their eminence as world religions were it not for their capacity to sponsor and encourage military conquest and to aid and abet harsh forms of political repression and control.

HOW THE
NONKILLING
RELIGIONS
SPREAD

ONCE AGAIN I WISH I could say that the emergence of world religions testified to our kind's innate tendency to adopt higher, more humane principles of spiritual and ethical beliefs and practices. But the historical achievements of the principal religions of love and mercy constitute a decisive refutation of any such view. None of the nonkilling religions has had a detectable influence on the incidence or ferocity of war and each is implicated in devastating inversions of the principle of nonkilling and reverence for life. Indeed, were it not for their ability to sponsor and encourage militarism and harsh measures of state control, there would be no world religions in the world today.

What was it about the religions of love and mercy that appealed to the warlike founders of empires and dynasties? No doubt, kings and emperors were genuinely concerned with the soul's prospects in the next life. But as heads of state, they were also necessarily concerned with maintaining law and order throughout their territories and with crushing their enemies abroad. Nonkilling religions had many advantages with respect to these twin objectives. I've already pointed out that state expansion was predicated on the preservation and incorporation of defeated populations as a source of labor and wealth. Nonkilling religions provided reassurances to the enemy that they could survive capture and thereby hastened their acquiescence to foreign rule. At the same time, the ideological strategy of promising rewards to the soul in lieu of rewards to the body was a great convenience to governing classes. If life on earth was inevitably painful and if poverty and suffering did not stand in the way of salvation, but, on the contrary, actually improved one's chances of finding eternal bliss, then the governing class no longer had to provide wealth and happiness in order to validate its right to govern. This was doubly convenient in the light of the ecological and economic crises that accompanied population growth and the overintensification of production in the homelands of the new religions.

Meanwhile, no longer capable of fulfilling the role of great provider except in their own narrow circle, governing classes willingly abandoned the task of trying to feed both the gods and commoners through animal sacrifice and redistributive feasting. As for reliance on instruments of death and bloody combat in flagrant violation of the most sacred commandments of the nonkilling religions, there was always the excuse of self-defense or of just, good, and holy wars. Interestingly enough, once it was discovered that killing humans on behalf of the state could be reconciled with doctrines of the sacredness of all life, even of butterflies and cows, the followers of the new faiths turned out to be a cut above the average soldiers, for they went into battle convinced that their souls would be rewarded if they died in combat.

Take Buddhism. After an initial phase of peaceful missionization and the cloning of monastic communities, Buddhism became involved in the process of state formation in South and Southeast Asia. In Sri Lanka, militant Buddhist kings appear as early as the second century B.C., driving out the hated Hindu forces from Tamil Nadu. A thousand years of petty wars ensued, culminating with the reign of the Buddhist king Parakrama Bahu, who promptly but unsuccessfully tried to conquer southern India and Burma. When the light of history first falls on the rest of Southeast Asia, it reveals a series of Buddhist states led by divine kings locked in a struggle to conquer each other. Khmers attacked Cambodia and Vietnam in the tenth century, and in the fourteenth century, the Thais attempted to subdue the Malay Peninsula, to mention only a few of the wars that were promulgated under Buddhist religious auspices in Southeast Asia.

North of India, Buddhism played an important role in the formation of the Tibetan state. By the eighth century, Buddhist lamas ("elders") had built huge fortified lamaseries from which they controlled Tibetan political, economic, and military life, and their armies soon established an empire on the western borders of China. In A.D. 1259, Mongol forces under the command of Kublai Khan defeated the Tibetans. But the great Khan was so impressed by the political, religious, and military systems of the Tibetans that he converted to Buddhism. Forthwith he turned his attention to completing the conquest of China begun by his grandfather, Genghis Khan. Victory complete, he established the Yuan Dynasty and ruled as a

Buddhist over an empire that stretched from the China Sea to the Arabian Desert.

Incidentally, the Mongols were not the first Buddhist emperors of China. During the short-lived Sui Dynasty (A.D. 589–618), northern China was ruled by emperors who effectively made Buddhism the state religion. Wen, the dynasty's founder, compared weapons of war to "offerings of incense and flowers." Buddhists made excellent soldiers, he believed, because of their faith that death in battle would only draw them closer to paradise.

The ups and downs of Buddhism and Hinduism in India also correspond closely to the vicissitudes of armed struggle between states that patronized one or the other nonkilling religions. Buddhism's high point in India came during the reign of Asoka (273–237 B.C.). Having conquered all of India from north to south, Asoka converted to Buddhism and in effect made it the imperial religion. His dynasty came to an end in 185 B.C., when a Hindu general assassinated the reigning Buddhist emperor. Hinduism's restoration was short-lived. One after another, Greeks, Scythians, Bactrians, and Persians launched attacks against Hindu India and in each case celebrated their victories by converting to Buddhism. Hinduism gained ground again with the formation of the Gupta Dynasty under Chandragupta I (A.D. 320), who gave his armies the order to restore Brahmanic authority in every part of India.

Militant Hindu empires also flourished in southern India from the seventh century onward, among them the powerful Chola, whose armed forces raided north to the Ganges Delta and east to Sumatra. Meanwhile, Buddhists in India found themselves increasingly bereft of political and military support, and by A.D. 900 the religion that Gautama had founded and that had been adopted by tens of millions of people in lands as far away as Japan and Korea was driven out of the land of its birth.

What about Christianity? It, too, like Buddhism, was spread at first by peaceful missionaries. People from all social strata were attracted to the new religion, but its communal and charitable aspects made it especially attractive to the laboring poor. Although Christians were willing to "render unto Caesar that which is Caesar's," the Romans found it difficult to separate them from the revolutionaries who were causing so much trouble in the colonies. After all, Christians worshipped a Jew whom the Romans had crucified for complicity in a guerrilla war. Nero struck at the Christians in A.D. 64 and there were additional intermittent waves of persecution for the next 250 years. These pogroms slowed but did not halt the spread of Christianity. Most emperors faced too many bigger threats to sovereignty as a result of constant uprisings and usurpations of power by barbarian generals to bother with sustaining an all-out attack on religious dissidents. After a particularly vicious but ineffectual attempt by Diocletian in A.D. 303 to wipe out the Christians, Rome embarked on a wholly new strategy, that of co-opting Christian beliefs in order to provide or restore a sense of purpose to the Empire. The architect of this new strategy was Emperor Constantine I. In A.D. 312, as he battled with rivals for control over the Empire on the outskirts of Rome, Constantine saw a cross of light superimposed upon the sun with the inscription, "In this sign victory shall be ours." His conversion almost immediately revolutionized the prospects of the new religion. Not only did he stop the persecution of Christians, but he confiscated the treasures and estates of the old Roman gods and goddesses, turned them over to Christian bishops to build new churches (sometimes with the stones of the old temples), and established imperial funds to indemnify Christians for their suffering and for expenses incurred in feeding the poor. Constantine changed the whole legal structure of the Empire to accommodate Christian principles. He permitted celibates to inherit property, prohibited divorce, condemned concubinage, forbade gladiatorial games, and prohibited animal sacrifice. One of Constantine's most important acts was his legalization of bequests to the Church. As Robin Lane Fox points out, this was a particularly sensitive issue "because of the clergy's special presence at the moment of death." In return, the Christian bishops agreed that it was a Christian's obligation to perform military service when the emperor called.

The importance of Rome's contribution to the preservation and propagation of Christianity lay as much in its suppression of rival factions within Christian communities as in its suppression of rival religions. At the time of Constantine's conversion, Christianity was plagued by heresy and torn by doctrinal and jurisdictional disputes. There were the Gnostics, who needed no church to expiate their sins. Basilides, Valentius, Marcion, Montanus—each claimed to be the authentic carrier of the apostolic message. One of Constantine's most significant undertakings, therefore, was to convene the Council of

Nicea in A.D. 325 to adjudicate doctrinal disputes about whether Jesus the Son was one and the same God as the Father. Three hundred bishops attended, setting the precedent for Councils in the fourth, fifth, and sixth centuries that settled issues surrounding the Trinity and Person of Christ without developing permanent schisms fatal to the unity of the Church.

By the end of Constantine's reign, the bulk of the imperial establishment consisted of Christians. His successors continued to introduce severe penalties against any kind of pagan worship, public or private, destroyed most of the remaining temples, barred pagans from civil service, the army, the practice of law, and the teaching professions. Finally, in 529, Justinian ordered all who refused to become Christians to surrender their property and go into exile. The wrath of the new nonkilling imperial religion fell with equal harshness on Judaism and rival nonkilling religions.

Early in the fifth century, the Romans forbade Jews and Samaritans to build synagogues, serve in the government or army, or practice law. They also took similar measures to suppress the alarming spread of Manichaeism, a rival nonkilling religion founded by the third-century A.D. Persian visionary Mani, who regarded himself as the final prophet in the line of Adam, Enoch, Zoroaster, Gautama, and Christ. Alas for Mani, no armies rose to his defense and his splendid ecumenical dream of uniting the nonkilling religions of Europe and Asia has never been fulfilled.

A CHINESE PUZZLE

CONFUCIUS, CHINA'S MOST POPULAR philosopher of ethics and politics, was born in the same century as Gautama and Mahavira. Like his Indian contemporaries, Confucius journeyed from one warring state to another, preaching an "eightfold way" that included love of humankind, benevolence, filial and civic duties, truthfulness, reverence for ancestors and for learning, and peace between states. Confucius may have been the first person to formulate the Golden Rule, at least in its negative form: "What you do not wish done to yourself, do not do to others."

This message of love and peace did not go down easily among the warlords to whom it was principally addressed. Mencius, Confucius's most famous disciple (sometimes likened to Jesus' Paul), went so far as to suggest that fair treatment of ordinary citizens was more important in the scheme of things than the wealth and glory of the sovereign. Said Mencius, "The people are [a state's] most valued possession, the altars of the soil and crops its next, and the prince its least." Mencius may have been the first person in history to condemn warmongers as criminals: "In a battle for the possession of a piece of land those killed will cover the fields; in the siege to take a city those killed will fill the city. This is to lead the land to devour human beings. For such a crime even a death penalty is too light."

And yet Confucius and Mencius were scarcely the most radical of China's early ethical reformers. Confucius's lesser-known contemporary, Mo Tse, advocated principles that bear a startling resemblance to the central ethic of Christianity. Rejecting the need for hierarchy in social life and even the priority of a parent's claim on a child's affection, Mo Tse declared that all humans must love each other equally. "Partiality is to be replaced by Universality." The new way is to be the way of universal love and mutual aid. In fact, in the matter of filial love, so vital to Confucian ethics, it is more essential, argued Mo Tse, to love other people's parents than one's own. For only then can one's own parents be safe from the ill will of others:

> Judging from the whole doctrine of filial piety, it is certain that they desire to have others love their parents. Now, what should I do first in order to attain this? Should I first love others' parents in order that they would love my parents in return, or should I first hate others' parents in order that they would love my parents in return? Of course I should first love others' parents. . . . Hence those who desire to be filial to their own parents . . . had best first love and benefit others' parents.

Confucius and his followers were outraged by Mo Tse's advocacy of universal love, and Mencius, in particular, launched a bitter diatribe against impartiality toward one's parents. To acknowledge the claims of neither father nor emperor to be loved more than others was to "reduce humans to the level of the beasts." The "perverse speakers" who advocate universal impartiality should not be permitted to show themselves anymore. As for universal love applied to relations between superiors and inferiors, Mencius had this to say: "In regard to the inferior creatures, the superior man is kind to them, but not loving. In regard to people in general, he is friendly to them but not affectionate. He is affectionate to his relatives, and friendly to people in general. He is friendly to people in general, and kind to creatures."

Mo Tse's belief in the principle of universal love led him to engage in a lifelong personal struggle to abolish war. Like a modern-day pacifist, Mo Tse tried to show that the motivation for war was greed and that while victory might bring wealth and glory to the few, it was a calamity for the many. As soon as Mo Tse and his disciples received news of impending hostilities, they would rush off to the aggressor state and try to persuade the warlords not to attack. But Mo Tse was not a complete pacifist. He was opposed to unilateral disarmament and his argument in favor of a strong defense has an eerily modern ring to it. Peace could be maintained only if small states stockpiled supplies, kept their outer and inner walls in good repair, and maintained harmonious internal social relationships.

Because of their commitment to a strong defense as a deterrent to war, Mo Tse and his disciples became experts on the military arts and were much sought after by states that wanted to protect themselves from aggressive neighbors.

As I indicated, Confucianists were also strongly critical of warfare. But Moists went further. Sung Tse, a Moist contemporary of Mencius, advocated the avoidance of conflict by, in effect, turning the other cheek: "By showing that to be insulted one is not thereby dishonoured, we may prevent people from struggle. People fight because they all feel they are dishonored by insult. When they discover that to be insulted is no dishonour, they will struggle no more." And this brings me to one of the greatest enigmas of human history. Despite the close parallels between sixth- and fifth-century B.C. Chinese and Indian ethical principles, none of the Chinese reformers can be said to have founded a radically new religion. Their impact on Chinese beliefs about the human soul, life after death, the proper performance of rituals, and the achievement of salvation is virtually undetectable.

Wherever the discourses of the Confucianists touch on matters relating to gods and ancestors, they become shallow, hesitant, and often frankly agnostic. Indeed, in the *Analects* of Confucius, we learn that "the subjects on which the Master did not talk were—extraordinary things, feats of strength, disorder and spiritual beings." When his disciple Chi Lu asked how one should serve the spirits of the dead, Confucius replied, "While you are not able to serve men, how can you serve their spirits?" Chi Lu then ventured to ask about what death was like. "While you do not know life, how can you know about death?" was the answer. On another occasion, someone asked Confucius to explain ancestor sacrifice. Although he was in favor of maintaining such rites, he said he didn't know. "Anyone who knows the explanation can deal with all things under Heaven as easily as I lay this here," he said, putting his finger on the palm of his hand. Overall, Confucius gives the impression of being a rather cold fish in matters religious. His definition of wisdom was "to give oneself earnestly to the duties due to men, and while respecting spiritual beings, to keep aloof from them." Nor did Confucius ever bother to clarify if he thought of "heaven" as an impersonal cosmic force like "nature," or as an animistic personal god who took an interest in human affairs.

True, Mo Tse was far more concerned than Confucius with grounding his ethical principles in the will of a personal god who takes an interest in human affairs. It is heaven that desires righteousness and abominates unrighteousness and it is heaven that wills people to love each other universally. But the main body of Mo Tse's argument for universal love is really based on the pragmatic grounds that impartiality will prevent war and suffering. Nor was Mo Tse breaking with Chinese tradition in postulating a personal god. Inscriptions and texts of the Shang period show that a belief in "Ti" or "Shang Ti" (God on High) formed an important element in Chinese religion long before the sixth century B.C. Scholars generally agree that

> Shang religion was inextricably involved in the genesis and legitimation of the Shang state. It was believed that Ti, the high god, conferred fruitful harvest and divine assistance in battle, that the king's ancestors were able to intercede with Ti and that the king could communicate with his ancestors. Worship of the Shang ancestors, therefore, provided powerful psychological and ideological support for the political dominance of the Shang kings.

So there was really nothing new in Mo Tse's concept of heaven as a personal god except for the ethical content of heaven's will. Entirely absent from Mo Tse's religion are the cosmic marvels, intricate musings, and adoring passions evoked by the existence of supreme beings in the world religions of India and the West. Like Confucius, Mo Tse accepted the need to sacrifice to the dead but he was not quite sure that ghosts and spirits existed (other than in heaven). He took the position that nothing could be lost in performing the rituals of sacrifice since the food was not simply thrown away but eaten (as I have been emphasizing all along), and doesn't everyone enjoy a good feast? In Mo Tse's own words:

> If ghosts and spirits do not exist, it will seem to be a waste of material for the cakes and wine. But such use of it is not just to throw it into the ditch or gully. For the relatives from the clan and friends from the village and district can yet eat and drink it. So, even if there were really no ghosts and spirits, a

sacrifice will yet gather together a party and the participants can enjoy themselves and befriend their neighbors.

This passage shows that Mo Tse understood the practical relationship between food offerings and redistributive feasting 2,500 years before anthropologists such as myself. But in his pragmatic approach to the life and death of the soul, his genius deserted him and he seems to have heeded Confucius's advice to remain respectful but aloof. In any event, if Mo Tse did in fact come close to founding a new religion, it was of no consequence in the subsequent history of Chinese religious life. Starting with the Han Dynasty, Confucianism became the Chinese state's official philosophical and ethical creed, and the teachings of Mo Tse were condemned. Only in recent times have Chinese scholars come to recognize him as Confucius's equal and rescued his memory from an undeserved oblivion.

Is it mere accident that China's great ethical reformers were not charismatic religious leaders, and that down to modern times ancestor worship remained the dominant religion of the Chinese people and the Chinese state? Buddhism was the only universalistic world religion that ever took hold in China, and it did so only by making ancestor worship one of the principal modes of gaining merit on the path to nirvana. Even so, the state feared the spread of this alien religion among the masses, and except for two dynastic interludes to which I alluded a few pages back, Buddhism never replaced ancestor worship as the state religion. Given their freedom and their right to found monasteries and nunneries, Buddhist missionaries easily made converts among the Chinese masses, many of whom were left spiritually unfulfilled by the shamanistic tendencies of Taoism and the arid pragmatics of Confucian ancestor worship. But as Buddhist temples and monasteries multiplied and the number of converts swelled, the state repeatedly intervened to prevent their further spread. Finally in A.D. 845, the T'ang Dynasty launched an all-out effort to destroy Buddhism's material base. The state confiscated millions of acres of land controlled by the monasteries, razed 40,000 shrines and 4,600 temples, and compelled 260,500 monks and nuns to return to productive lay occupations. Chinese Buddhism never recovered from this assault.

Returning to Confucius, Mo Tse, and Mencius, there remains the question of why their ethical vision never became the basis of a spiritualized church, much less of a world religion. Was there something different about the early Chinese states? Was it that they were more culturally homogeneous and more centralized than their counterparts in India and the West and could therefore dispense with the need for a universalistic religion transcending ancestor worship? Or was it something else entirely different? Frankly, I don't know the answer.

THE FUTURE
OF BELIEF
AND
DISBELIEF

*O*UR KIND HAS HAD BELIEFS about animistic beings for at least 35,000 years. Is it likely that these beliefs will disappear as agrarian and preindustrial societies become industrialized and as industrial societies adopt ever-more-complex technologies of production, reproduction, and information processing?

One thing is clear. While atheists are more numerous in some industrial societies than ever before, believers are everywhere more common than social theorists once predicted they would be. Surveys in Western Europe show that on average, about two-thirds of the population believe that some kind of godlike being exists. Among industrial societies, the United States represents one extreme and the Soviet Union the other. A mere 4 percent of Americans tell pollsters that they do not believe in a god or a universal spirit; only 13 percent say that religion is not important in their lives; barely 9 percent believe that God played no role in the creation or evolution of the human species. In contrast, in the Soviet Union, people who say they are nonbelievers constitute a slight majority in the country as a whole. But only 30 percent of Russians, the ethnic group that has received the greatest rewards of the Soviet system, profess a belief in God. Among other ethnic groups, especially in Islamic regions, believers may still be in the majority. Overall, for the country as a whole, 45 percent of the population say they are believers.

The percentage of Soviet believers as compared with the percentage of Western European believers does not seem to be proportionate to the effort the Soviet Union has made to stamp out religion. Soviet state policy has always been predicated on Marx's view that religion is a cheap opiate distributed by ruling groups in order to befuddle the masses. As they acquired a scientific knowledge of natural and human phenomena, people would automatically abandon their superstitions and religious beliefs and practices. Or so Marx thought. To facilitate the growth of atheism, the Soviet state has used its control over school curricula to foster atheistic worldviews since its inception in 1917. It has sponsored organizations like the League of Militant Atheists to ridicule believers and it has mounted special exhibitions at museums to depict the history of religious wars, massacres, and inquisitions. In addition, known believers cannot join the Communist Party and therefore theoretically have been at a competitive disadvantage in gaining admission to the best universities and institutes, finding well-paying jobs, and obtaining decent housing. So why are there still at least 100 million people in the Soviet Union who refuse to identify themselves as unabashed atheists?

The answer may lie partly with the failure of the Soviet system to assure that atheists enjoy standards of living that are significantly better than those enjoyed by believers. For despite all the advantages that are supposed to be given to nonbelievers, Soviet studies show that living standards of believers and nonbelievers differ by only a few percentage points. The believer group has more single women and more retired, handicapped, and rural people, but their standard of living gets a substantial boost from various welfare programs that effectively eliminate the worst extremes of poverty in the Soviet Union. As Gorbachev's glasnost ("openness") campaign has revealed, the Soviet economy has been operating in an extremely inefficient manner as far as the production of consumer amenities is concerned. Given chronic shortages of meat, vegetables, and fruits, an endemic lack of decent housing, and the prevalence of shoddy goods and services, the Soviet system has not been able to reward nonbelievers enough to make up for the psychological costs that atheism incurs.

Traditional Marxist theory of religion is misleading in this regard because it fails to concede that animistic beliefs provide psychological satisfactions that most people are unwilling to forgo without some kind of compensatory benefit. Religion may sometimes function as an opiate but it was used for that purpose long before there were ruling classes. Even in state societies, ruling classes need not be the only beneficiaries. Animism has something for everyone, whether they live in bands and villages, chiefdoms or states, or whether they are capitalists or communists, oppressors or the oppressed. Who does not like to be reassured that life has purpose and meaning and that it does not end with the death of the body?

Why should people give up these pleasant beliefs merely because they use computer-age technologies to earn their living? Belief in God and an afterlife for the soul does not conflict with the efficient performance of most industrial tasks. One can even be a believer in this general sense and excel in the sciences, medicine, and engineering. Problems and conflicts arise only at a much more specific level of belief, as when a geologist must choose between a bit of religious dogma that sets the beginning of the world at no more than 10,000 years ago and radiometric chronologies that span thousands of millions of years, or when biologists must choose between the evolution of species or special creationism; or when M.D.s must choose between curing a blocked intestine with prayer or curing it by surgical intervention. Since most people do not have to make such choices in order to earn their living, animistic worldviews remain more attractive than their opposites, even in high-tech urban civilizations.

Apparently it takes much less institutional pressure to make a nation of believers than a nation of disbelievers. Yet I don't want to give the impression that one can understand the extreme unpopularity of atheism in the United States without noting the existence of such pressures. In the United States, unlike the Soviet Union, both believers and nonbelievers alike are nominally free to proselytize. But atheism in the United States has long been linked with "godless communism" and hence carries with it the stigma of something that is officially associated with America's enemies. People in the United States who condemn or ridicule religion in public or openly proselytize atheistic beliefs run the risk of displeasing employers and supervisors and of being socially ostracized or even of being physically abused in states where fundamentalist creeds predominate. At the same time, despite laws that decree the separation of church and state, the American tax system provides indirect support for religious institutions. Contributions to churches are tax-deductible, and church buildings, real estate, and normal income are tax-exempt. Not without cause do fundamentalists point to the motto of the Great Seal of the United States, "In God We Trust," and to the words of the pledge of allegiance, "One nation under God," as evidence that prayer in public schools could be a constitutionally mandated part of American life.

If I am correct about the linkage between the fear of communism and the fear of atheism in the United States, the end of the cold war could lead to a convergence in the percentages of believers in the United States and the Soviet Union. Were the Soviet Union to grant churches the right to proselytize as part of a movement toward free speech, the number of Soviet believers would surely increase. While if Americans no longer lived in constant fear that godless communists were about to take away their homes and churches, more Americans might feel free to voice their criticism of animistic beliefs and rituals. Something much closer to the Western European pattern of belief and disbelief would then emerge in both countries. Beyond this near-term equivocation, my crystal ball grows almost completely dark. I cannot say more of the long run than that the future of religion will not be determined by the intrinsic value of belief or disbelief, but by the value of belief or disbelief in relation to the specific kinds of political and economic systems to which computer-age societies may eventually give rise. Perhaps it is time, therefore, for us to return to the unfinished business of trying to understand if the selection of our kind's political and economic systems is governed by predictable processes.

DID HISTORY
REPEAT ITSELF?

*S*HORTLY AFTER THE TRANSITION in Sumer, states began to appear in other parts of the world: in the Nile Valley at about 3200 B.C., the Indus Valley in India at about 2200 B.C., in northern China at about 2200 B.C., and in Mexico and Peru at about 300 B.C.

Let us suppose that Sumer had never been settled and that Uruk, Eridu, Ur, and other places had never existed. Would the state and all it stands for in terms of human relationships have emerged anyway, at other places on earth? Because the actual order of appearance of the earliest states seemed to be roughly in proportion to their distance from the Middle East, past generations of archaeologists and historians assumed that the state recurred simply because it had diffused from one region to another. No doubt the emergence of states in Sumer accelerated the process of state formation in neighboring chiefdoms, forcing them to develop centralized state structures in order to survive. But the armies of Sumer never menaced the centers of early state development in Egypt or the Indus Valley, much less in China or the Americas.

How else might the growth of these early states have been influenced by events in Sumer? Perhaps traders familiar with Sumerian statecraft might have transmitted descriptions of Sumer over great distances, the way viruses get passed from one part of the world to another. But why would that information be of any help to a paramount chief seeking permanent hegemony over his followers? The Hawaiian chiefs obviously had the *idea* of kingship and of permanent hereditary classes, for they repeatedly attempted to impose statelike institutions on their followers. It was not for lack of information about Sumer or of any other state that they were unable to take the next step.

Proponents of a single origin for the state confront a curious dilemma. If it was unlikely that chiefdoms could have crossed the threshold to the state more than once, then it must also have been unlikely that other evolutionary events, such as the domestication of plants and animals or the passage from headmen to big men and big men to chiefs, could have happened more than once. Pushed to its extreme, this line of reasoning results in the theoretical stance known as "diffusionism," which, in effect, denies that in the aggregate people think and behave in similar ways under similar conditions, or that history can ever repeat itself.

While diffusionism plausibly accounts for the chronological order in which the first states and empires appeared, it does not plausibly account for the evolutionary order that underlies the appearance of the state in each region. In each region, the first states sit on top of an archaeological sequence that starts with local foragers, passes through plant and animal domestication, increased population density and settlement size, sedentary villages, and warring chiefdoms with monumental public works. If diffusion rather than independent evolutionary processes was responsible for the state everywhere but in Sumer, this recurring sequence would be impossible to explain. For it would imply that only one active center of cultural selection has ever existed, the rest of the world being filled with dullards who remained fixed in their ways until stimulated by successive waves of innovation radiating out of the Middle East. But the greater the distance between innovators and imitators, the more implausible it becomes that the original developmental sequence would be preserved intact as it spread from one region to another.

Since the crucial event in the Middle Eastern sequence leading to the state was the domestication of wild grasses and of sheep and goats, the credibility of diffusionist explanations is closely linked to the question of whether the same complex appears at the base of the evolutionary sequences in the other centers of state development. While this criterion does not rule out diffusion in the case of Egypt and the Indus Valley, it comes close to doing so in the case of China.

Radiometric dating of archaeological sites indicates that in the Huang He (Yellow River) Valley of northern China, people were living in villages and planting two kinds of domesticated millet at least 8,000 years ago. And in southern China, rice, both long-grained and short-grained, was widely cultivated as early as 7,000 years ago. Near Pan-P'o, in the semiarid highlands bordering the upper reaches of the Huang He, villages were planting millet, raising pigs and dogs, burying their dead in well-defined graveyards, making painted pottery, and experimenting with prototypes of the characters used in the Chinese form of writing at about 4000 B.C.

The varieties of millet found in northern China have wild ancestors that grew both in China and Europe. One of the varieties was also domesticated near Argissa, Greece. Could this have been the source of Chinese millet? Not if the time it took other early Neolithic crops to diffuse to China is applicable. Wheat, for example, one of the two basic grains of the Middle Eastern Neolithic period, had no wild progenitors in China. The Chinese began to plant it at about 1300 B.C., over 6,000 years after it was domesticated in the Middle East. If it took wheat 6,000 years to diffuse across Asia, how could millet, a less productive crop, have made the journey to China in fewer than a thousand years? Equally damaging to the diffusionist perspective is the question of why it was millet and not wheat, a more productive crop, that diffused. The theory that millet must have diffused from the Middle East further overlooks the fact that East Asians were themselves able to domesticate plants that were unknown in Europe, especially rice and soybeans, highly nutritious and productive crops that did not diffuse to Europe until recent times. The Chinese were probably equally innovative when it came to farming and to breeding livestock. Wild progenitors of the domesticated pig were present in both China and the Middle East in Paleolithic times and domesticated varieties appear along with the earliest rice grains. Bones found at the same site may be the earliest remains of domesticated water buffalo, another species indigenous to the Far East, which was not part of the Middle Eastern Neolithic complex.

Reviewing the process of state formation in China, K. C. Chang concludes that archaeological evidence supports the existence of chiefdoms marked by distinctions of rank, warfare, specialized handicrafts, and religious specialists in several regions of China at least as far back as 2500 B.C. According to Chang, states appeared during the period known as Hsia, about 2200 B.C. States of imperial dimensions began to emerge 500 years later, the most precocious being Shang, which was centered in the lower Huang He basin, in northern Honan province. Shang possessed wheeled vehicles, horses, cattle, a system of writing, and an advanced knowledge of bronze metallurgy. The capital, near Anyang, was enclosed by a huge earthen wall and had residential districts inhabited by craft specialists. The royal tombs display evidence of human sacrifice. Life in this early dynasty, despite the basically independent origins of Chinese civilization, bore remarkable similarities to the early dynastic period in Mesopotamia and Egypt.

The more distant and mutually isolated any two centers of early state development are, and the fewer domesticated species of plants and animals they share, the less likely it is that the evolution of one was influenced by the evolution of the other. I admit that China and the Middle East are not so isolated from each other by land as to rule out every chance of interaction. Wheat, as I said, did diffuse to China, even though it arrived after Chinese chiefdoms had crossed the threshold to the state. And there is still the remote possibility that domesticated millet had made the same journey at an earlier date. The ideal way to test for independent recurrences of major developmental sequences in cultural selections would be to study the evolution of human societies on distant planets similar to the earth. If the same sequences occurred on each of them, then we would know for certain that history does repeat itself. Most people don't realize it, but in effect, one such planet was actually discovered some time ago. The story has not often been told outside of anthropological circles, but it seems our kind formerly did live in two separate earths that for all practical purposes were out of contact with each other for the whole time that band-and-village societies were evolving into states. After a lapse of about 12,000 years, the inhabitants of one of these earths, traveling in primitive forerunners of spacecraft, managed to locate the other. What they found were civilizations and cultures, distinctive in detail but remarkably similar in structure and levels of organization to their own. History, indeed, had repeated itself on a grand scale.

HOW THE
SECOND
EARTH BEGAN

ℰ *XACTLY WHEN THE SECOND EARTH* was colonized is hard to say. Some archaeologists think it was 20,000 or more years ago; others say not much before 10,000 B.C. How it began is easier to answer: Big-game hunters living in northeastern Siberia followed herds of mastodons, mammoths, caribou, and horses across Beringia, a great shelf of land now under water, that connected Siberia and Alaska during the last Ice Age. Advancing at the rate of ten miles per year, the main wave of migrants reached the tip of South America by 9000 B.C. We know that the original Americans were immigrants to the second earth rather than "natives" because no trace of any australopithecine or presapiens hominids, not even a great ape, living or dead, has ever been found in the Western Hemisphere. Big-game hunters do not carry boats with them, so they must have come by land. Besides, no oceangoing craft had been invented 12,000 years ago, as at that time enough water was still locked up in the polar ice caps for much of Beringia to be dry land. Finally, we know that they came from Asia, rather than from Europe or Africa, because American Indians have more racial features in common with East Asians than with northern Europeans or with Africans.

The view that our kind had already colonized the second earth long before the end of the last Ice Age can be supported with data from a number of ancient sites—a rock shelter in Pennsylvania, hearths in highland Peru, wooden houses in southern Peru, and another rock shelter in northeast Brazil—whose radiometric dates collectively span a period from 33,000 to 13,000 years ago. But many archaeologists remain skeptical, having witnessed numerous previous claims for similar dates fall by the wayside. I don't have to take sides in their argument, because its outcome does not affect the question of whether the immigrants to the second earth invented agriculture and developed chiefdoms and states independently of their first-earth counterparts. The point is, no one claims that the original colonists came as farmers or pastoralists, whether they arrived 30,000 or 12,000 years ago. Furthermore, long after the descendants of the original settlers had fanned out across North and South America and developed states based on agriculture, vast regions as far south as the Amur River on one side of the Bering Strait and California on the other remained populated by foraging peoples rather than by agriculturalists. How could the knowledge of agriculture have been passed along over this vast area where no one planted any crops?

If the practice of agriculture could not have come via Siberia and Alaska, perhaps it came across the Pacific Ocean from Polynesia, or even directly from Indonesia or China on oceangoing canoes or junks blown off course. Or might it not have come directly on boats that were blown across the Atlantic from Europe or Africa? Yes, except for one big problem: First-earth people were completely unfamiliar with second-earth plant foods. They had never seen grains like maize, amaranth, and quinoa; legumes like black beans, string beans, and lima beans; fruits and vegetables like avocados, squash, melons, and tomatoes; root crops like manioc, potatoes, and sweet potatoes; condiments like chili peppers, cacao, and vanilla; and narcotics and stimulants like coca and tobacco. If oceanic voyagers from the first earth had brought agriculture to the second earth, where did all these strange foods come from? Why maize, amaranth, and quinoa instead of wheat, barley, and rice?

The standard diffusionist response has long been that the voyagers didn't bring the crops—they simply brought the knowledge that plants could be domesticated. Whereupon the original settlers fell to work breeding as many native grains and tubers as they could. This theory might have some credibility if the original migrants had taken a few decades or even a few centuries to domesticate their plants, as one would expect if mysterious benefactors from across the seas had suddenly turned on a light bulb inside their heads. But the process of domesticating native American plants went on for thousands of years, during which time second-earth peoples reduced their reliance on hunting and gathering more slowly than the Middle Easterners had done. For example, it took over 2,000 years to turn a grain called teosinte, which still grows wild in Mexico's highlands, into fully domesticated varieties of maize. Before 3000 B.C., maize cobs were less than an inch long and had just a few rows of tiny kernels, which were easily dislodged at harvest time. Two thousand years later the cobs had reached modern dimensions, with their enlarged kernels so firmly fixed to the cob that the plant could no longer propagate itself without human intercession (even boiling does not dislodge the kernels, a trait for which those who enjoy corn on the cob are grateful).

A final refutation of diffusionist explanation of second-earth agriculture is that between 7000 B.C. and 5000 B.C., foragers in the Mexican highlands were already planting small quantities of beans, squash, amaranth, chili peppers, and avocados as seasonal supplements to their wild foods. Since this is a period during which the Chinese were just beginning and Western Europeans and West Africans had not yet begun to adopt a Neolithic way of life, neither transpacific nor transatlantic voyagers could have added anything to what second-earth people already knew. And this is true not only of agriculture, but of the great political transformations that agriculture made possible.

THE EVOLUTION
OF THE
SECOND EARTH

*A*S ON THE FIRST EARTH, changing climates and hunting overkill led the early colonists of the second earth to broaden their diet. In Mexico, this shift had consequences that were different for coastal lowland and interior highland populations. Taking advantage of the rich riverine and marine flora and fauna, people living along the coast of Tabasco, Vera Cruz, and Belize began to live in permanent villages a thousand or more years before they adopted agriculture as their principal means of subsistence. The first chiefdoms on the second earth probably developed among these villages. By contrast, people living in the interior upland did not establish permanent villages until improved varieties of maize became available after 3000 B.C. The difference can be accounted for by the ability of coastal peoples to exploit fish and other concentrated marine sources of animal fats and proteins from permanent dwellings, while the uplanders, despite their head start in domesticating plants, had to be more mobile in order to obtain the dispersed deer, rabbits, gophers, rats, birds, and insects included in their broad spectrum of prey species.

As settlements filled up the best riverine and coastal sites, the lowlanders began to pay more attention to agriculture and added domesticated squash and peppers to their diet. Between 3000 B.C. and 2000 B.C., they added maize, borrowed from the highland centers of domestication. Advanced chiefdoms appeared first in two regions: Tabasco–Vera Cruz, homeland of the Olmec, and Yucatán–Belize, homeland of the Maya.

Olmec chiefs directed big public works including carved stone monuments, earthen platforms, and pyramids. Basalt for nine-foot-high, round, carved heads, monoliths, altars, and tombs had to be transported from quarries fifty miles away. The Olmec located their settlements near natural levees whose rich soil was well suited for planting maize, but they also continued to fish, gather shellfish, and hunt. At about 400 B.C., disaster struck. Parties unknown smashed the monoliths, toppled the stone heads, and defaced and buried the altar stones. What do these desecrations commemorate? Probably rebellions by commoners who were determined to prevent any further concentration of power and who preferred to live without their would-be kings and without access to the levee lands rather than submit to stepped-up demands for labor and taxes.

Maya evolution took a different turn. Shortly after the Olmec collapse, Maya chiefdoms successfully crossed the threshold to states governed from ceremonial centers spaced about one day's walk apart. Each center contained ornamental multiroom buildings set on top of platforms symmetrically grouped around paved plazas. Along each center's main axis, the Maya placed monoliths and statues inscribed with their own system of glyphs and telling the history of the kingdom, great battles won, and other heroic deeds, all with precise dates as reckoned by meticulous astronomical observations. Towering over each center, like the ziggurats of Mesopotamia, were truncated pyramids with stone facing and flights of steps leading to temples at the crests. Most of the population lived dispersed in clusters of houses close to the fields, visiting a center only on market days or to witness important public ceremonies or to donate their labor when summoned by the overlords.

In response to population growth, the Maya switched from cutting and burning to more intensive agricultural techniques. They built drainage canals, mounded the wet soils to create permanent fields, harvested the aquatic plants and animals that flourished in the canals, and grew fruit trees mulched with household wastes. These long-term investments, in combination with widespread destruction of the original forest cover, left the Maya commoners with little opportunity or incentive to flee from their rulers' stepped-up demands for labor and taxes.

After A.D. 800, the Maya heartland underwent an abrupt change. All construction ceased, people stayed away from the centers, and the regional population entered a period of permanent decline. Various lines of evidence suggest that this collapse occurred because the Maya states intensified their agricultural production beyond carrying capacity. Removal of the forest cover, the chief source of trouble, increased the rate of runoff and soil erosion and probably lowered rainfall over the entire Yucatán peninsula. Hillside erosion and lowered rainfall led, in turn, to silting of the basins and drainage ways. Not only did mounding become more difficult and less productive, but the rich aquatic flora and fauna that lived in the drainage canals disappeared. These ecological changes increased competition between the various centers and led to popular discontent. Wars, rebellions, and the disruption of trade routes then brought the classic phase of Maya civilization to its close.

In the Mexican highlands, greater intensifiability and productivity of agricultural systems permitted chiefdoms to evolve into states that were far bigger and more powerful than among the Maya, culminating in political systems of imperial dimensions. The largest states developed in the Basin of Mexico, a region that roughly corresponds to modern-day Mexico City and its far-flung suburbs. Farming villages developed here comparatively late, from 1400 B.C. to 1200 B.C. The first villagers practiced a form of cut-and-burn agriculture on the hillsides, at middle altitudes above the basin floor, where they could obtain a balance between maximum amounts of rainfall and minimum amounts of crop-limiting frosts. With population growth, they were obliged to use the basin's least favorable northern fringe, where rainfall was lowest. It was here, in the valley of Teotihuacán, some twenty-five miles northeast of the center of modern-day Mexico City, that the first imperial state of the second earth evolved.

The founders of Teotihuacán solved the water and frost problem by using permanent springs fed by rain and snow percolating through volcanic soils at high altitudes. By A.D. 500, the urban center of Teotihuacán covered an area of 7.7 square miles and had a population of over 100,000. It was a planned city, as indicated by the grid pattern of avenues and alleys, markets in various districts, and exclusive quarters allotted to craft specialists. In the middle there rose a complex of public buildings and monuments that, by comparison, dwarf those of Tikal, the largest Maya center, and render the Olmec sites puny. The central monument, the so-called Pyramid of the Sun, still figures among the world's largest structures. Measuring 214 feet in height and over 700 feet on a side, it was bigger than the ziggurat of Babylon.

As the city expanded, the demand for fuel and lumber denuded the surrounding mountains. The runoff pattern changed and less water flowed from the springs. Popular discontent and foreign armies probably put an end to the state. In A.D. 750, the city was sacked, set on fire, and abandoned.

But the Basin of Mexico, unlike the Maya heartland, did not become depopulated after the fall of Teotihuacán. New states rose and fell, culminating with the Aztecs, whose capital, Tenochtitlán, was also inhabited by over 100,000 people and whose gardens, causeways, markets, pyramids, and temples were the wonders of their time. Agriculture was even more intensive and productive than at Teotihuacán. Massive flood control, desalinization, and drainage works made it possible to raise crops year round on "floating gardens" (actually, raised mounds built up out of the mud and debris of lakeside lands, interconnected for drainage and transportation by a network of canals).

Despite the productivity of chinampa agriculture, my guess is that the Aztecs could not have avoided the collapse and ruin that was the common fate of their predecessors. Their habit of rounding up defeated armies and marching them off to Tenochtitlán to be sacrificed and eaten is not the stuff out of which long-lasting empires are made and was itself symptomatic of a society deeply troubled by population pressure and environmental depletions. But the Aztecs met a unique fate. In A.D. 1419, they were conquered by a handful of invaders from another world, clad in impenetrable armor and mounted on large animals that had been hunted to extinction and not been seen by second-earth people for 10,000 years.

THE PHARAOHS
OF THE ANDES

*T*HE *"BIG APPLE"* of second-earth civilization was located far to the south of the Aztecs in the high valleys of the Andes Mountains and along the Pacific coast of South America. We know that this additional center of early state-formation was not entirely free of Mexican influence. Maize, for example, almost certainly diffused from north to south. But as agriculturalists, the South Americans were extremely innovative in their own right, and had already domesticated several types of beans and potatoes and a high-altitude grain, quinoa, before they began to plant maize. As domesticators of animals, they outclassed the Aztecs. They used llamas and alpacas—unknown in Mexico—ate the flesh and spun the wool, and they dined on domesticated guinea pigs—also unknown in Mexico—which they raised in their houses as kitchen scavengers.

As in Mesoamerica, the first sedentary villages appeared in coastal locales and preceded the introduction of animal and plant food domesticates. Along the coast of Peru, chiefdoms, responsible for building the first large mounds and masonry monuments at about 2000 B.C., got their nourishment from catches of anchoveta, which school in vast numbers close to shore. Later, with population growth, settlements moved away from the ocean and up the river valleys, where they became dependent on planting maize in irrigated fields. Circumscribed by desert, ocean, and steep Andean slopes, these river-valley chiefdoms began to cross the threshold to the state at about 350 B.C.

Meanwhile, a comparable series of developments involving irrigation agriculture had been unfolding in circumscribed valleys and lake shores of the Andean highlands. Imperial systems evolved when rulers were able to integrate coastal valley states and mountain valley states into a single system. This was first achieved by the Chimu, whose huge mud-walled capital of Chan Chan was located on the coast. The Inca, whose capital, Cuzco, was in the highlands,

484

absorbed the Chimu and created an empire in A.D. 1438 that stretched for 2,000 miles and was inhabited by six million people.

Considering that their only means of keeping records was by tying knots on bundles of strings called *quipus,* Inca methods of statecraft compare favorably with the early imperial systems of the first earth. There were three levels of basic administrative units: villages, districts, and provinces, each with its appointed officials who maintained a chain of command that led directly back to Cuzco. Officials were responsible for law and order, the collection of taxes, and the planning, execution, and conscription of labor for public works. Village lands were also divided into three parts, the largest of which was set aside for the peasant householders, while harvests from the second and third parts were turned over to the priesthood and the state and stored in special granaries. The distribution of these stores was entirely under the control of the central administration. Likewise, when labor power was needed to build roads, bridges, canals, fortresses, or other public works, government recruiters went directly into the villages. Because of the size of the administrative network and the density of population, huge numbers of workers could be placed at the disposal of the Inca engineers. In the construction of Cuzco's fortress of Sacsahuaman, 30,000 people quarried, hauled, and erected huge monoliths, some weighing as much as 200 tons. Labor contingents of this size were rare in medieval Europe, but were common in ancient Egypt, the Middle East, and China.

The Inca emperors were the second earth's pharaohs, firstborn of the firstborn, descendants of the sun god and celestial beings of unparalleled holiness. Gods-on-earth, they enjoyed power and luxury undreamed of by the poor Mehinacu chief in his plaintive daily quest for respect and obedience. Ordinary people could not approach an emperor face to face. His audiences were conducted from behind a screen, and all who approached him did so with a burden on their back. When traveling, he reclined on an ornate palanquin carried by special crews of bearers. An army of sweepers, water carriers, woodcutters, cooks, wardrobemen, treasurers, gardeners, and hunters attended his needs in the palace at Cuzco. If members of this staff gave offense, their entire village could be destroyed.

The emperor ate his meals from gold-and-silver dishes in rooms whose walls were covered with precious metals. His clothing was made of the softest vicuña wool, and he gave away each change of garments to members of the royal family, never wearing the same ones twice. He enjoyed the services of a large number of concubines who were methodically culled from among the empire's most beautiful girls. To conserve the holy line of descent from the god of the sun, his wife had to be his own full or half-sister, as I explained earlier. When he died, his wife, concubines, and many other retainers were strangled during a great drunken dance in order that he suffer no loss of comfort in the afterlife. His body was then eviscerated, wrapped in cloth, and mummified. Women with fans stood in constant attendance upon these mummies, ready to drive away flies and to serve any needs the dead emperor might choose to express.

WHY THE FIRST EARTH CONQUERED THE SECOND

O *N HIS WAY TO* Tenochtitlán after landing in Vera Cruz in 1519, Hernando Cortez traveled through a cultural landscape that was eerily familiar. He passed through cities, towns, and villages that had streets and plazas and houses for the rich and poor; he saw people growing crops in lush, irrigated fields, while others carried baskets of food and craft products such as obsidian knives, well-made pottery, featherwork, and skins and furs. Along the way he met a familiar variety of humble and exalted men and women: potentates, aristocratic merchants, bricklayers, stonemasons, judges, priests, soldiers, slaves. Many were dressed in colorful woven garments and were adorned with exquisite jewelry appropriate to their high rank. And he passed palaces, pyramids, and other stone structures whose bulk, height, and symmetry spoke of great architectural and engineering skills. Yet there were certain things that were part of the everyday world of sixteenth-century Spain that were strangely absent. The people in the fields were using sticks and wooden spades. Where were the plows and oxen to pull them? And there was not so much as a single goat or sheep to be seen anywhere. Nor was there any sign of a cart, wagon, or any wheeled vehicle at all. For arms, the soldiers bore darts and spears that had points made out of stone. They knew nothing of steel swords or blunderbusses. And their ignorance of horses was so total that they initially judged animal and rider to be one and the same creature.

Social life on the two earths had evolved along essentially parallel paths, but the pace of change was definitely slower in the Americas. Aggregate human responses tend to be similar when underlying conditions are similar. But, of course, underlying conditions are seldom exactly alike. The two earths were twins but not identical twins. After the animal extinctions that occurred toward the end of the last Ice Age on the second earth, the regions that were well endowed with domesticable plants became poorly endowed with

488

domesticable animals. Nothing like sheep, goats, pigs, cattle, asses, water buffalo, or horses survived to be penned and fed from agricultural surpluses. True, the ancestors of the Inca had llamas and alpacas to domesticate, but they were fragile creatures, adapted to the highest Andean valleys. They could not be milked like sheep, goats, and cows, nor could they carry heavy loads like asses or horses, nor pull wagons or plows like oxen. Nor were guinea pigs an adequate stand-in for swine. Besides, none of the second-earth animals that were suitable for domestication were native to the highland Mexican region in which the progenitors of maize grew wild. I think this explains why the highland Mexicans retained seminomadic ways of life long after they had begun to domesticate their basic food crops. In the Middle East, sedentary villages could have their plants and their animal fat and protein, too, since both plants and animals were domesticated at the same time. Sedentism increased the productivity of the plant domesticates, which increased the commitment to village life. But in highland Mexico, the need to retain animal food in the diet worked against the abandonment of hunting. Hence, in contrast to the Middle East, the development of villages in highland Mesoamerica did not precede the first phase of cultivation, but followed it after a lapse of several thousand years. This, in turn, delayed the appearance of agricultural chiefdoms in the highlands and the appearance of the first highland states in habitats suitable for imperial growth.

The Mexicans ultimately did domesticate the turkey, the Muscovy duck, the honeybee, and hairless dogs bred for meat, but these species were of no significance in the incipient agricultural phase and never did amount to much in later periods.

Some anthropologists have questioned the idea that the paleo-Indians confronted a poor choice of domesticable species and want to know why they did not domesticate tapirs, peccaries, antelope, or deer. Tapir and peccaries are lowland jungle species adapted to moist habitats and could scarcely have benefitted the people who domesticated maize and amaranth in the arid highland valleys. As for deer and antelope, since no one else has succeeded fully in domesticating them, I do not see why the ancient Mexicans should be expected to have done so. At any rate, they would have made even worse pack, traction, or milk animals than llamas and alpacas.

Not only did the faunal extinctions retard the onset of sedentary agricultural villages on the second earth, but they deprived the second earth of animal-drawn plow agriculture and the ability to develop the full range of agricultural systems that were developed on the first earth. (The Inca actually did use a kind of plow that people pushed and pulled.) Most importantly, perhaps, the lack of traction animals inhibited the development of wheeled vehicles. The Mexicans had no trouble inventing the wheel, but they used it only to make toys for their children. Without traction animals, they had little incentive to build carts. Harnessing people to wagons is not much of an improvement over having them carry cargo on their heads or backs, especially if one includes the cost of building roads that are level enough and wide enough to accommodate a first-earth oxcart. The Inca did build an extensive network of roads, but only for human and llama foot traffic, saving themselves a lot of expense by using steps rather than switchbacks to master steep slopes.

It is a striking fact that the great cities of the second earth were primarily administrative rather than trading centers. Not that they lacked markets, crafts specialists, or merchants, but most trade other than in preciosities consisted of food grown only a short distance outside the city or of items produced within the city itself. Production for export of food or goods in bulk was strictly limited by the absence of carts. Symptomatic of the relative underdevelopment of commercial exchange was the absence of all-purpose money. Except for the limited use of cacao beans by merchant castes in Mexico, the second earth lacked a coin of the realm. The lack of long-distance trade in bulk and the absence of coinage severely inhibited the development of the kinds of commercial classes that played an important role in the development of the classical imperial centers of Eurasia.

Lack of interest in wheels inhibited technological change in many other fields. Without wheels, there could be no pulleys, gears, or cogs, devices that enabled first-earth people to construct machines that milled flour, spun thread, kept time, and helped raise heavy weights, including the anchors and sails on their oceangoing vessels, and that formed the basis of mechanical engineering in the ages of steam and internal combustion engines.

Would second-earth people eventually have developed wheels, cogs, gears, pulleys, and complex machines and gone on to their own industrial revolution? One good reason for answering in the affirmative is that they had taken several crucial steps in the field of metallurgy. Having begun like their first-earth counterparts with cold-hammering of copper sheets, they had gone on to smelting and casting copper, gold, silver, and several alloys, including bronze, which they had just begun to use for knives and maceheads when the first Spaniards arrived with steel weapons and armor. An astonishing achievement of second-earth metallurgical specialists was their independent invention of the casting technique known as the lost-wax method. To make a mold for a desired object, they first made a wax model of it. Then they placed the model in a pit, or form, covered it with tightly packed sand, and poured molten metal onto the model through a small opening at the top. The metal instantly vaporized the wax and filled the resulting space with a metal facsimile of the wax model. A people who had gone so far with metallurgical skills must be credited with the likelihood of being able to go still further, perhaps not as rapidly as on the first earth, but in essentially the same direction. Second earth's invention of writing and numerology and its astronomical and mathematical achievements also argue for an eventual convergence of science and technology in the two worlds. Pre-Columbian Mexican calendars were more accurate than their Egyptian counterpart, and the Maya had mastered a crucial step in mathematics that eluded even the Romans and Greeks—a glyph for a zero quantity to mark the absence of a base number or its exponents. But none of this changes the fact that the first-earth people had gotten a head start. It was they who possessed oceangoing vessels, gunpowder, muskets, steel swords, and the four-legged equivalent of armored tanks. The Inca and Aztec armies fought bravely, but without a glimmer of hope. Unbeknown to either side, their fates had been sealed long before, when first-earth people had turned away from hunting to domesticate sheep and goats and to settle down in agricultural villages, while second-earth people, bereft of domesticable species, continued to favor hunting for another 5,000 years.

CULTURAL
DISCONTENTS
AND THE
KNOWING MIND

THE STORY OF THE SECOND EARTH shows that cultural evolution has not resulted in a chaotic jumble of contradictory and unique events, but in orderly recurrent processes of continuity and change. Rather than produce endlessly diverging varieties of cultures, cultural evolution has resulted in massive parallel and convergent trends. And even as it produced diversity, it did so in orderly ways, in response to knowable restraints imposed by specific habitats on a people's productive and reproductive strategies. The story of the second earth therefore demonstrates the underlying unity of the physical and cultural divisions of our species and the universal applicability of the principles of cultural selection. It refutes currently fashionable attitudes about the uniqueness and noncomparability of each culture. Because cultures everywhere serve the same set of basic human needs, appetites, and drives, people everywhere tend to make similar choices under similar conditions. I find this view of cultural differences to be far more hopeful than the radical relativism of colleagues who believe that it is impossible to transcend cultural differences in the pursuit of knowledge about the human condition. Only if there is a prospect for mutual understanding, apart from one's culture, can we hope for global reconciliation and an end to the threat of mutual destruction.

On a less optimistic note, let me point out that the major processes of cultural evolution do not bear witness to our kind's ability to exert conscious, intelligent control over our species' destiny. This is a paradoxical finding in view of the fact that uniquely among organisms, our brains have "minds" that are aware of the processing of information, the making of choices, the planning of behavior, and the intentional effort to achieve future goals. So it has always seemed obvious that cultural change is a process that people consciously control by making decisions regarding alternative goals. But retrospectively, the decisions our predecessors made and the changes these decisions brought about show that there was a disjunction between

494

the two, and that all the major steps in cultural evolution took place in the absence of anyone's conscious understanding of what was happening.

The people who participated in the transformations that led from foragers to pharaohs made conscious decisions and were as intelligent, alert, and thoughtful as modern generations of our kind. They chose to prolong or delay this or that activity for a day or a season, to hunt or not to hunt a particular species, to break camp or stay put, to nourish or neglect a particular infant, to listen to a headman or ignore him, to raid or not to raid a particular village, to work for one redistributor rather than another, or to plant more yams this year than last. But they never chose to transform foraging bands with egalitarian gender roles, and reciprocal exchange, into sedentary agricultural villages with gender hierarchies and redistributive exchange. No one ever chose to convert patrilocal residence into matrilocal residence or egalitarian forms of redistribution into stratified forms of redistribution, or internal warfare into external warfare. Each great transformation in human history and prehistory occurred as a consequence of conscious decisions, but the conscious decisions were not about great transformations.

Natural resource depletions, which have played crucial roles in cultural evolution, provide strong examples of this unconscious form of consciousness. The Ice Age foragers did not intentionally seek the extinction of mammoths, giant bison, horses, and other big game; the Fore and the Sambia did not intend to turn New Guinea forests into grasslands, nor did the Maya intentionally silt up their drainage canals. Circumscription is another crucial unintended result. The Sumerians did not intend to trap themselves into stratified settlements by creating their lush irrigated habitat in the middle of a desert; nor did the founders of Teotihuacán intend to trap themselves into dependence on their spring-fed irrigation system.

The twentieth century seems a veritable cornucopia of unintended, undesirable, and unanticipated changes. The automobile, intended merely as a machine to help people get from one place to another faster than the horse and buggy, completely changed the settlement patterns and marketing practices of industrial societies. No one intended or foresaw the conversion of farmlands into suburbs, the blighted roadside strips, and the rise of shopping malls as the new center of social life. Nor did anyone foresee the look on people's faces during gridlock, the anxiety and hypertension generated by being stalled for reasons unknown in a ten-mile backup, or the twisted wreckage and blood on the road two hours later. And surely no one intended motorists to take longer to get to work today or to go from one side of town to the other than horse-and-buggy drivers.

Were our parents aware of the industrial buildup of toxic wastes in all of nature's life-sustaining solids, fluids, and gases? As they cleaned and groomed their cars like household pets, did they ever pause to wonder what happens to the excremental vapors engines emit? They expected better living through chemistry and they got it in the form of new fabrics, plastics, and alloys. They didn't expect worse living through chemistry in the form of cancer-promoting dumps and landfills, and rivers, lakes, and oceans brimming with PCBs and contaminated fish. They wanted electricity, but they didn't want the burning of fossil fuels to turn rain into acid that kills trees and poisons mountain lakes. Nor did they want refrigerator gases to strip the sky of the ozone shield against skin cancer, while other industrial emissions threatened to melt the polar ice caps and drown cities under a hundred feet of water.

Twentieth-century political and economic events reveal the same pattern of unintended, unanticipated, and undesirable consequences: a war to end all wars followed by a war to make the world safe for democracy, followed by a world full of military dictatorships. The great revolution to give the working class a communist utopia gave them secret police, overcrowded apartments, and long lines at every store. Not to be outdone, a quarter of a century after the U.S. government declared war on poverty, more homeless Americans beg in the streets than ever before.

Nobody wants poverty, least of all the people who do the begging, but poverty endures. Nobody wants recessions, stock market collapses, or the abandonment of family farms, but these things happen anyway. Large numbers of married mothers began to enter the wage labor force in the 1960s with the intention of supplementing their husbands' income. Thirty years later, the expansion and feminization of the labor force had driven wage rates down, making a second income mandatory to pay for decent housing while decent children became an unaffordable luxury. How were these things decided? Did women ever want the fastest growing form of the family to consist of mother and children living in poverty, with no father present?

Yes, there are some bright spots, as in the eradication and control of smallpox and other epidemic diseases, rising life expectancy, higher consumption standards in parts of Asia, and the removal of trade barriers and the elimination of centuries-old military rivalries in Western Europe. But in other domains, efforts to bring about fundamental change remain spectacularly ineffective. During the 1980s, some of the worst famines in history afflicted large parts of Africa and South Asia, under the very noses of the United Nations and other international agencies. In absolute numbers, more illiterate, impoverished, and chronically malnourished people live in the world at the end of the twentieth century than at the beginning. And in country after country, the rich grow richer while the poor grow poorer. Record numbers of bad loans threaten the solvency of the international banking system with results no one dares to predict. Drugs have ruined more lives, killed more people, caused more thefts, at the end of the twentieth century than ever before in history or prehistory. Death squads, secret police, and the torture of prisoners remain at all-time highs, and ethnic, religious, and racial groups are killing each other on a grander scale than ever: Protestant against Catholic in Northern Ireland, Jew against Palestinian in Israel; Christian against Moslem in Beirut; Shiite against Suni in Saudi Arabia; Hindu against Moslem in India; Sikh against Hindu in the Punjab; Tamil against Ceylonese in Sri Lanka; Hutu against Watutsi in Burundi; black against Afrikaner in South Africa; white against black in America; Armenian against Azerbaijani in the U.S.S.R.; Iraqi against Kurd in Iraq; Basque against Spaniard in Spain.

Did the Wright brothers ever imagine that the miracle of flight could not take place unless passengers submitted themselves to X rays, metal detectors, and body searches? Or that innocent people would be killed for nothing more than sitting in a sidewalk café, dancing in a nightclub, waiting at an airline ticket counter, or relaxing on a cruise ship? Guerrilla attacks and full-scale wars abound: Iraq versus Iran; Lebanon versus Israel; contras versus Sandinistas; Argentina versus Britain; the United States versus Granada; Ethiopia versus Eritrea; Vietnam versus Cambodia; the Soviet Union versus

Afghanistan—not to mention guerrilla movements in Angola, Mozambique, Namibia, Ecuador, and the Philippines. As one of these conflicts ends, another begins: Nothing warrants the hope that the rate of carnage is about to slacken. Virtually every industrial power, east or west, is manufacturing and selling the latest weapons, short of nuclear bombs, to dozens of countries that fear or hate each other.

In the light of all these unintended calamities, I wonder if we are any closer to conscious control over cultural evolution than our ancestors at the dawn of the Stone Age. Like them, we are busy making decisions, but are we making decisions about the great transformations that must be made if our kind is to survive?

WILL OUR KIND
SURVIVE?

*W*ILL NATURE'S EXPERIMENT with mind and culture end in nuclear war? No one knows the answer, but there are many reasons for pessimism. Enough nuclear weapons are stockpiled to permanently kill off the entire human species and much of the animal and plant world as we know it. Military strategists believe that this capability will never have to be used because the Soviet Union will not attack Western Europe or the United States, either with nuclear or conventional weapons, as long as it knows that a nuclear exchange will annihilate both sides. What alarms me most is the acquiescence of ordinary citizens and their elected officials to the idea that our kind has to learn to live with the threat of mutual annihilation because it is the cheapest and best way of reducing the danger that one nuclear power will attack another. By what set of practical, moral, or ethical principles is it allowable for a small number of experts to wager the future of our species on the gamble that nuclear weapons will never be used? This bet has been made entirely without the consent of most of the people who will die if the strategists have bet wrong. Even the citizens of the superpowers have never directly voted on whether they are willing to risk global annihilation as the price of maintaining peace through a nuclear deterrent.

In evolutionary perspective, the crisis we confront is inextricably the crisis of the state as a predatory form of political organization, born, nurtured, and spread by the sword. If so, it seems highly likely that our kind will not survive the next century or even half-century unless we transcend the state's insatiable demands for sovereignty and hegemony. And the only way to do this may very well be to transcend the state itself by consciously creating new means of maintaining law and order on a global basis and by submerging the sovereignty of existing states within a global federation whose members agree to disarm, except for local and regional police forces equipped with conventional weapons.

500

What are the prospects that cultural evolution will be deflected from a suicidal trajectory? Global peace seems much less probable than global war, given the reputation of hawks as hard-headed realists and of doves as impractical dreamers. But the paths of cultural evolution have not left our kind totally bereft of a practical basis for transcending the state. Satellite transmissions and jumbo jets have prepared the way for local and regional populations to be kept informed about events in distant parts of the globe, a necessary condition if we are to develop a sense of world community to replace or take precedence over traditional forms of nationalism, ethnocentrism, racism, and sectarianism. Advances in transportation and telecommunications also make a global parliament technically more feasible at the end than at the beginning of the twentieth century. Using the same technological advances, business and commerce have become increasingly global in scope and increasingly opposed to national barriers to the free flow of goods and services. Consider, further, that the largest and most successful corporations maintain executive offices and production facilities in a dozen countries. Active promoters of global interests and perspectives, transnational corporations, when not in the business of manufacturing weapons, can be counted on to support further efforts to transcend the state.

Finally, studies of the rate of consolidation of sovereign political units from prehistoric times to the present offer some encouragement for those who believe the state must be surpassed if our kind is to survive. Robert Carneiro, of the American Museum of Natural History, estimates that the number of autonomous political units in the world was at its height at about 1000 B.C. At that time, there were perhaps as many as 500,000 separate bands, villages, and chiefdoms. As states and empires expanded worldwide, the number of autonomous units fell to 200,000 by A.D. 500. Between A.D. 500 and the present, the process accelerated and there was a further reduction to fewer than 200 units. In Germany alone, where in 1648 there had been 900 sovereign states, there are now only two. By extending the curve that connects successive reductions in the number of sovereign units, Carneiro found that after A.D. 2300, there will be only one state for the entire globe. Unfortunately, as Carneiro points out, the principal means for reducing the number of autonomous units has always been warfare. Therefore, he envisions the reduction from some small number to one as a consequence of a final war that the world must somehow manage to survive. Since I take it as a virtual certainty that our kind will not survive another global war, our only hope is to find peaceful ways to complete the trend toward unity.

In striving for the preservation of mind and culture on earth, it is vital that we obtain a clearer understanding of the limits placed upon us by nature. Yet we must recognize the significance of cultural takeoff and the great difference between biological and cultural evolution. We must rid ourselves of the notion that we are an innately aggressive species for whom war is inevitable. As the evidence shows, we must reject, as unscientific, claims that there are superior and inferior races and that the hierarchical divisions within and between societies are the consequences of natural selection rather than of a long process of cultural evolution. We must recognize the degree to which we are not yet in control of cultural selection and we must struggle to gain control over it through objective studies of the human condition and the recurrent processes of history.

NOTES AND REFERENCES

IN THE BEGINNING (2–3)
Darwin 1871:3. *Bipedalism:* Lovejoy 1988; Lewin 1988c; Marzke, Longhill, and Rasmussen 1988. *Knuckle-walking and other terrestrial gaits:* Jolly 1985:47–51; Tuttle 1969.

THE BIRTH OF A CHIMERA (6–7)
Darwin 1871. *Pithecanthropus:* Day 1986:337ff.

THE RISE AND FALL OF DAWSON'S DAWN MAN (10–11)
Piltdown hoax: Weiner 1955; Blinderman 1986.

LUCY IN THE SKY WITH DIAMONDS (14–16)
Australopithecus: Dart 1925; Broom and Schepers 1946; Johanson and White 1979. *Afarensis and L.S.D.:* Johanson and Edey 1981:18. *Afarensis:* Day 1986:251ff. See Zihlman and Lowenstein 1985 for size differences among afarensis. *On dates:* Boaz 1988; Ward and Hill 1987. *Footprints:* M. Leakey 1979; White and Suwa 1987.

THE TREE OF LIFE (18–19)
Hominid ancestry: Ciochon 1985; Fleagle et al. 1986; Kinzey 1987; Simons 1985; Miyamoto, Slightom, and Goodman 1987. *Molecular dating:* Sarich 1974; Lewin 1987a. *Conflict over:* Lewin 1987e, 1988a, 1988b. *Gap between 14 and 4 mya:* Simons 1985; Pilbeam 1985; Hill and Ward 1988.

THE ENIGMA OF THE LITTLE HANDY MAN (22–23)
Discovery of H. habilis: L. Leakey, Tobias, and Napier 1964; L. Leakey and Goodall 1969. *Small female habilis:* Johanson 1987; Lewin 1987c. *Omo dates:* Toth and Schick 1986:22. *Hadar tools:* J. Harris 1983.

THE DAWN OF TECHNOLOGY (26–30)
Vultures: Van Lawick-Goodall 1968. *Mammals:* Beck 1980. *Gombe chimps:* Van Lawick-Goodall 1986. *Quote, page 27:* McGrew 1977:278. *Ivory Coast chimps:* Boesch and Boesch 1984. *More nutcracking:* Whitesides 1985. *Throwing things:* Teliki 1981. *Cleaning teeth:* McGrew and Tutin 1973; Menzel, Savage-Rumbaugh, and Lawson 1985. *Other chimps:* Nishida 1973. *Mechanical leopard:* Kortlant 1967.

TOOLS FOR WHAT? (32–33)
See McGrew 1987 for comparison between chimp tool-using behavior and tool use among simple human foragers.

MEAT (36–38)
On monkeys and insects: Redford et al. n.d. *Baboons:* Hamilton 1987; Harding 1975. *Babies as chimp food:* Nishida and Kawanaka 1985. *Chimp hunting style:* Boesch and Boesch 1989; Teliki 1981:332. *Gombe hunting totals:* Van Lawick-Goodall 1986:304–305. *Worzle's tantrum:* ibid.:373–374.

AFRICAN GENESIS REVISITED (40–41)
Chimps fighting big cats: Hiraiwa-Hasegawa et al. 1986; Ardrey 1961. *Bone tools:* Dart and Craig 1959. *Hyenas:* Brain 1981.

KNAPPER, BUTCHER, SCAVENGER, HUNTER (44–46)
Australopithecines as knappers: Lewin 1988d. Toth and Schick 1986. *Scavenging versus hunting:* Lewin 1984; Shipman 1986; Bunn anad Kroll 1986; Blumenschine 1987; Binford 1988; Bunn and Kroll 1986. See also O'Connell, Hawkes, and Jones 1988; Stahl 1984.

THE ENIGMA OF H. ERECTUS (48–50)
Erectus tool functions: G. Isaac 1984:12. *Brain size:* Beals, Smith, and Dodd 1984. *Fire controversy:* Binford and Stone 1986; S. James 1989; Lanpo 1989. *Evolutionary stasis:* Holt 1987; Eldredge and Tattersall 1982; Gould and Eldredge 1977.

HEAT, HAIR, SWEAT, AND MARATHONS (52–56)
Fialkowski 1986, 1987. *Human runners:* Carrier 1984; Devine 1985. *Tarahumara quote:* Devine 1985:555. *Nganasan quote:* ibid.:559. *Sweat and hair:* Newman 1970; Robertshaw 1985; Kushlare 1985. Cf. Ebliny 1985. *Erectus stature:* Trinkhaus 1983. *Bergman's rule:* Weiss and Mann 1985:489–492.

THE BRAIN BEGINS TO THINK (58–59)
Parallel processing: Gibson 1989; C. Smith 1985. *Combat dolphins:* Booth 1988; Eagan 1989; Ridgway 1989. See also Jerison 1973.

RUDIMENTARY CULTURES (62–64)
Termiting: Van Lawick-Goodall 1986; McGrew 1977:282. *Mahale chimps:* Nishida 1973. *Kyoto monkeys:* Itani 1961; Itani and Nishimura 1973; Miyadi 1967.

LINGUISTIC TAKEOFF (66–69)
Quotes: Bickerton 1981:15, 19.

PRIMITIVE LANGUAGES? (72–73)
Plant words: Witowski and Brown 1978. *Limb words:* Witowski and Brown 1985. Sapir 1921:234.

APE-SIGNS (76–79)
Dragging branches: Ingmanson 1989. *Chimp talk:* Van Lawick-Goodall 1986. *Viki:* Hill 1978. *Washoe:* Gardner and Gardner 1971, 1973. *Sarah:* Premack 1971, 1976. *Lana:* Rambaugh 1977. *Lucy and Loulis:* Fouts and Fouts 1985. *Koko:* Patterson 1981. *Doubters:* Terrace 1981; Sebeok and Umiker-Sebeok 1980. *Videotapes:* Reiss 1985; Dehavenon 1977. *Brain and language:* Bradshaw 1988:631.

THE TRIUMPH OF SOUND (82–84)
Darwin quote: P. Lieberman 1985:663. *Pharynx and larynx:* P. Lieberman 1984; Crelin 1987; Laitman 1985. *Origin of language:* S. Parker 1985; Marshack 1976. But see Liberman and Mattingly 1989.

ON BEING NEANDERTAL (86–89)
Species question: Lewin 1989b. *Neandertal anatomy:* Stringer 1984:68; Mellars and Stringer 1989; Jacobs 1985. *Neandertal burials:* Gargett 1989a, 1989b; Chase and Dibble 1987. *Language:* P. Lieberman 1985; Laitman 1985. But see Arensberg et al. 1989. *Symbolism:* Mellars 1989; Marshack 1989. *Flowers:* Solecki 1971. *Language and complex behavior:* B. F. Skinner 1984. See also Trinkhaus 1986.

NEANDERTAL'S FATE AND THE ORIGIN OF OUR KIND (92–94)
Klasies River Mouth: Singer and Wymer 1982. *Qafzeh:* Valladas et al. 1988. *Out of Africa:* Stringer and Andrews 1988a, 1988b; Stringer 1984, 1988. Cann et al. 1987; Lewin 1987a, 1987c, 1987e, 1988a, 1988b. *Multiregional alternative:* Wolpoff 1988a, 1988b; Spuhler 1988. *Neandertal cultures compared with sapiens cultures:* White 1982; Binford 1982. *Basically middle Paleolithic technology of early sapiens in Middle East:* Mellars 1989:370. Cf. Brooks and Yellen 1989.

CULTURE OVERSHADOWING (96–99)
Animal figurines: Mellars 1989:363. *Venus statues:* Fagan 1983. *Beads:* Soffer 1985:457. *Upper Paleolithic:* Gamble 1986. *Paleolithic art:* Conkey 1983. Jochim 1983; Pfeiffer 1982. *Wish list:* Rice and Patterson 1986. *Intichiuma:* Spencer and Gillin 1968:170ff. *Paintings and plaques:* Marshack 1985. Cf. Davidson and Noble 1989. For Randall White see Lewin 1989a.

ANCESTORS (102–104)
Genealogical passions: Shoumatoff 1985:253. Haley 1976. *For fallacy of deep genealogies:* Wachter 1980. *Genes and Jews:* Montagu 1974:362ff.

HOW OLD ARE THE RACES? (106–110)
Bundle of traits: Molnar 1983. *Brazilian races:* M. Harris 1970. *Blood groups and clines:* Birdsell

1972:435ff. *PTC:* Weiss and Mann 1985. *Adaptiveness of blood groups:* Molnar 1983:172ff.; Cavalli-Sforza et al. 1988. *Criticism:* O'Grady et al. 1989.

HOW OUR SKINS GOT THEIR COLOR (112–114)

Skin: Montagna 1985. *Skin cancer:* Ariel 1981. *Melanin and radiation:* Malkenson and Keane 1983. *Rickets and osteomalacia:* Molnar 1983:162ff. *Infant foreskin:* Webb, Kline, and Holick 1988. *Cattle herders:* Bogucki 1987. *Rate of change of skin color genes:* Ammerman and Cavalli-Sforza 1984.

WHY AFRICA LAGS (116–119)

Huxley 1901. Kroeber 1948:202. See M. Harris 1958 for a case study of colonialism's effects in Africa. *Japan and Indonesia:* Geertz 1963. Cf. B. White 1983.

DO THE RACES DIFFER IN INTELLIGENCE? (122–123)

Racial I.Q.: Jensen 1969. *Twins:* Kamin 1974. Hirsch 1981:36. *Critiques of raciological paradigms:* Lewontin, Rose, and Kamin 1984; Montagu 1974; Goleman 1988.

A DIFFERENT KIND OF SELECTION (126–128)

For more on general principles of cultural selection see M. Harris 1979.

TO BREATHE (130–131)

Russel et al. 1987:44

TO DRINK (134–135)

Liquid diet: Russel et al. 1987:41. *Thirst:* Rolls et al. 1986.

TO EAT (138–139)

Warsaw ghetto: Winick 1979:14ff.; Fliederbaum 1979. *More on starvation:* Keys 1950; Aubert and Frapa 1985; Young and Scrimshaw 1971; Sorokin 1975.

WHY WE EAT TOO MUCH (142–143)

Keys 1950. *Foodstat:* Martin and Mullen 1987. National Center for Health Statistics 1987:6.

WHY WE FEAST (146–148)

Metabolic adaptations: Waterlow 1986; Sims and Danforth 1987; Miller and Parsonage 1975; Dreon et al. 1988. *African hungry seasons—Bemba:* Richards 1939; *elsewhere:* Jenike 1989. *Chronic shortages:* Konner 1983:369; Speth 1987. *Hypoplasias and Harris (no relative) lines:* Goodman, Thomas, Swedlund, and Armelagos 1988. Key parts of this section were anticipated in Konner 1982.

WHY WE GET FAT (150–151)

Tikal: Haviland 1967. *English schoolboys:* Harris and Ross 1987:76.

INNATE TASTES (154–157)

Essential nutrients: L. Lieberman 1987:225. *Infant aversions:* Steiner 1979; Cowart 1981. *Peppers:* Rozin and Schiller 1980. *Sugar:* Mintz 1985:15. *Salt:* Denton 1982. *Yanomami salt aversion:* Kenneth Good, personal communication.

ACQUIRED TASTES (160–163)

Reduced flatus: Rozin and Schiller 1980. *Insects:* Dufour 1986. *Cows:* Vaidyanathan, Nair, and Harris 1982.

ONE FOR THE GENES (166–168)

See M. Harris 1985:130–153, 253–254 for full account.

SEXUAL PLEASURE (170–172)

Sex drive: Cicala 1965; Singer and Toates 1987; Efron 1985. *Varieties of sexual practice:* Gregerson 1982; W. Williams 1986. *Brain stimulation:* Valenstein 1973; Routtenberg 1980. *Septum stimulation:* Rancour-Laferriere 1985. *Epilepsy and orgasm:* Remillard et al. 1983. *Endorphins:* Davis 1984. *Endorphin test:* Goldstein and Hansteen 1977. See also Changeux 1985; Heath 1964; Persky 1987.

CARNAL IGNORANCE (174–178)
Human reproductive physiology: Keeton 1972:311. *Other species:* Forsyth 1986. *Primate patterns:* Jolly 1985. *Great apes:* Graham 1981. *Gorillas:* Fossey 1982. *Chimps:* Van Lawick-Goodall 1986. *Sperm competition:* Small 1988; R. Smith 1984. *Testes:* Harcourt et al. 1981. *Pygmy chimps:* Savage-Rumbaugh and Wilkerson 1978; Susman 1984. *Genital-genital rubbing:* Thompson-Handler, Malenky, and Badrian 1984:355. Badrian and Badrian 1984; Karoda 1984.

AND NOW FOR SOMETHING COMPLETELY DIFFERENT (180–183)
Thompson-Handler, Malenky, and Badrian 1984. *Human sperm:* Small 1988:87; Kurland 1988:90. *Sperm count changes:* W. James 1980. *Sexual thoughts:* Shanor 1978. *Sex for food:* Karoda 1984:317.

WHY WOMEN HAVE PERENNIALLY ENLARGED BREASTS (186–188)
Morris 1967. *Breasts and reproductive success:* Mascia-Lees, Relethford, and Sorger 1986. Cant 1981. *Pygmy chimps:* Badrian and Badrian 1984:336. Lessa 1966:78.

GIVING AND TAKING (190–191)
For the relationship between the evolution of systems of exchange and the evolution of political systems see sections beginning with "Was There Life Before Chiefs?"

HOW MANY MATES? (194–196)
For monogamy and home base: Lovejoy 1981; Silk 1987. *Against:* Zihlman 1981. *De facto polyandry:* Sharff 1980, 1981. *Marriage pattern database:* Murdock 1937. *Causes of changing family patterns:* M. Harris 1981:77ff.

GENES AGAINST INCEST? (198–201)
Royalty: Bixler 1981, 1982. Hopkins 1980. Westermark 1894. *Effects in large populations:* Adams and Neil 1967. *In small populations:* Livingstone 1969. *Taiwan adoption:* Wolf and Huang 1980. *Kibbutz:* Shepher 1983. *Refutation:* Hartung 1985.

THE MYTH OF THE GREAT TABOO (204–207)
Tylor 1888:267. *On alliances, peace, and war:* Tefft 1975; Kang 1979; Podolefsky 1984; Leavitt 1989; Hayden 1987. *Weakening of taboo:* Y. Cohen 1978; Leavitt 1989.

THE MYTH OF THE PROCREATIVE IMPERATIVE (210–214)
Devereux 1967. *Infanticide, direct and indirect:* Divale and Harris 1976; Scrimshaw 1983. *Brazil:* Scheper-Hughes 1984, 1987; Birdsell 1972:356. *China:* Dickeman 1975. *India:* Nag, White, and Peet 1978; Miller 1981, 1987a; Krishnaji 1987. *Europe:* M. Harris 1977:183–184. *Quote, page 213:* Langer 1972:98. *Japan:* Hanley 1977:182; Hanley and Yamamura 1977; G. W. Skinner 1987. See also Mull and Mull 1987.

HOW MANY CHILDREN? (216–221)
Gregor 1985:167. B. White 1976, 1982. Cain 1977. See M. Harris and Ross 1987 and Weil 1986 for cost/benefit approach. B. Miller 1981, 1987a; G. W. Skinner 1987. Mamdani 1973. *Return to Manupur:* Nag and Kak 1984. Sharff 1980, 1981. See also Hayden 1986.

REPRODUCTIVE FAILURE (224–227)
Vining 1985. *Rajput quote:* B. Miller 1981:53. See Dickeman 1975 and Daly and Wilson 1978 for sociobiological approach.

THE NEED TO BE LOVED (230–233)
Harlow 1960, 1964. Konner 1982:292–293.

WHY HOMOSEXUALITY? (236–237)
Fay, Turner, Klassen, and Gagnon 1989. Herdt 1988. See Whitman and Mathy 1986 for obligatory homophilia.

MALE WITH MALE (240–245)
Greeks: Dover 1980. *Azande:* Evans-Pritchard 1970. *Sambia:* Herdt 1984a, 1984b. *More on Greeks:* Bentham 1978. *Brazil:* Fry 1986. *Not-men:* Callendar and Kochem 1986. *Berdache:* D. Greenberg 1986; W. Williams 1985. *Hijras:* Nanda 1986. *Laws against nonreproductive sex:* Bullough 1976.

506

FEMALE WITH FEMALE (248–250)
Dahomey: Herskovits 1938. Blackwood 1986:13–14. Lockard 1986. Sankar 1986. Gay 1986.

SPERM VERSUS EGG? (252–255)
E. O. Wilson 1978:125. Barash 1977. Cf. Kitchen 1985. *Primate female sexuality:* Small 1988. *Human female sexuality suppressed:* Hrdy 1981. *For a history of female prostitution:* Bullough and Bullough 1978.

STOLEN PLEASURES (258–261)
Malinowski 1929:488–489. See Weiner 1976, 1986 for Malinowski's androcentrism. Mead 1928:51. *Affair table:* Gregor 1985:36. *Quote:* ibid.:36. *San quotes:* Shostak 1981: 271, 288.

ARE MEN MORE AGGRESSIVE THAN WOMEN? (264–266)
Castrated monkeys: A. P. Wilson 1969. *Castrated prisoners:* Bremer 1959. *For Bagoas: Encyclopaedia Britannica,* vol. 2. *For Cheng Ho:* Goodrich 1976:174ff. *Monkey testosterone levels:* Rose et al. 1975; Mason et al. 1969. *Rank and testosterone:* Bernstein et al. 1983:551. *Wrestlers:* Elias 1981. *War:* Mazur 1983. *Surgery:* Fausto-Sterling 1985:147. *Quote:* Bernstein et al. 1983:558–559. *Jobs and testosterone:* Purifoy and Koopmans 1980. But see Konner 1988 and Mazur 1983.

OF TOMBOY GIRLS AND PENIS-AT-TWELVE BOYS (268–270)
Money and Ehrhardt 1972; Imperato-McGinley et al. 1974. Imperato-McGinley et al. 1979. Reinisch and Karow 1977. I have followed the critiques offered by Bleier 1984 and Fausto-Sterling 1985. See Richards, Bernal, and Brackbill 1976 for circumcision effects.

MIND, MATH, AND THE SENSES (272–275)
Benbow and Stanley 1983. *Discouraged girls:* Haven 1972; Tobias 1978. *Quotes, page 273:* Bleier 1984:104. *Hearing:* M. Baker 1987:6ff. *Taste:* ibid.:13.

SEX, HUNTING, AND DEADLY FORCE (278–281)
Male specialty: Murdock 1937. *Height:* Gray and Wolfe 1980:442. *Strength:* Percival and Quinkert 1987:136. *Track-and-field data:* Boehm, Benagh, Smith, and Matthews 1987. Cf. Drinkwater 1986. *Agta:* Estioko-Griffin and Griffin 1981, 1985. Leacock 1975, 1981. *Quote:* Leacock 1983:116. *Quote:* Turnbull 1982:153. *Quote:* Shostak 1981:246. *Male edge:* Begler 1978. *Mbuti quotes:* Turnbull 1965:127, 287, 271. Lee 1979:453. *Twenty-two killings:* ibid.:382. *Spunky women:* ibid.:377. *Not afraid to die:* Shostak 1981:307.

FEMALE WARRIORS? (284–285)
Quote: Hayden, Deal, Cannon, and Casey 1986. See Goldman 1982 for various accounts of guerrillas and uniformed female soldiers.

WAR AND SEXISM (288–293)
Raiding: Lee 1979:382. Thomas 1959. *F.B.I.:* Knauft 1987:458. *Queensland raiding:* D. Harris 1987:374. *Lumholtz quotes:* ibid.:375, 377. Warner 1958:91. Cf. Gale 1974. See Hayden, Deal, Cannon, and Casey 1986 for correlation between warfare and women's status among foragers. *Yanomami:* Chagnon 1974, 1983. *Yanomami mothers:* Lizot 1985:74. *Wounded monkey:* ibid.:153. *Prisoner:* ibid.:155. *Male deaths:* Chagnon 1988, 1989. Shapiro 1971. *Gender in New Guinea:* Gelber 1986. *Nama:* Read 1984. Langness 1967. *New brides shot in thigh:* Langness 1974. *Unyielding power:* Feil 1987:201. *Punishment:* ibid.:203. *Sambia:* Herdt:1984a, 1984b, 1987. *Warfare:* Fiel 1987:69. *Homicide rate:* Knauft 1987:458.

WHY WAR? (296–300)
For cultural causes: Robarchek and Dentan 1987. *Spoils of war:* Meggitt 1977. Ember and Ember 1988. Divale and Harris 1976, 1978. Leavitt 1977. See Waal 1983, 1988 for social control of violence in nonhuman primates.

MEAT, NUTS, AND CANNIBALS (302–304)
On problems with nuts: Ford 1979. *!Kung subsistence and health:* Konner 1982:370–376. Pennington and Harpending 1988. *Prolonged lactation:* Frisch 1984. *Queensland food supply:* D. Harris 1987; Jones and Bowler 1980. *Cannibalism:* ibid.:368ff. *Relation between food hunger and cannibalism:* Morren 1986:54–55; Lindenbaum 1979.

507

A DISSERTATION ON FATTY MEAT (306–307)
Preference for meat: Abrams 1987; Harris 1985:19–46. *Saving protein:* L. Lieberman 1987. *Calories from fat and the creation of fat:* Dreon et al. 1988; Brody 1988.

GAME WARS? (310–312)
Good 1987. *Reproductive success:* Chagnon 1988. Chagnon and Hames 1979. *Refutation:* M. Harris 1984; Baksh 1985. Cf. Vickers 1988. See also Sponsel 1986.

HUNGRY PAPUANS (314–315)
See Ember 1982 for positive correlation between ecological stress and New Guinea warfare. *Forest to grasslands:* Sorenson 1972. *Malnutrition:* Dennet and Connell 1988:272. *Gahuka-Gama:* Read 1982, 1984. *Bena Bena:* Langness 1977:263. See also Buchbinder 1977 and Rappaport 1987: 468–470. *Maggots:* Lindenbaum 1979:20.

WHERE WOMEN RULE THE ROOST (318–321)
See Divale 1974 for theory of matrilocality and external warfare. Whyte 1978:130 fails to consider this theory in rejecting a correlation between warfare and female subordination. Cf. Hayden, Deal, Cannon, and Casey 1986:458. *Iroquois warfare:* Gramby 1977. *Iroquois matrons:* Brown 1975. Trigger 1978. *Feminine nature:* Di Leonardo 1985; Salter 1980; Pierson 1987. *Tupinamba:* Staden 1929. See M. Harris 1985:211ff. for accounts of Iroquois torture of prisoners of war.

WOMEN UP, WOMEN DOWN (324–326)
Subsistence and male control: Schlegel and Barry 1986:147. *Significance of bride-price:* Schlegel and Eloul 1988:301; Bossen 1988. *Significance of dowry:* Kaplan 1984. *Evolution of stratified societies:* Carneiro 1981, 1988. *Women in West Africa:* Hart 1985:263; Sudarkasa 1973. Herskovits 1938. *Sitting on a man:* Van Allen 1972. *Ijesa and Ondo:* Awe 1977. *India:* B. Miller 1981, 1987b. *Burnings:* Sharma 1983; Crossette 1989. *African widows:* Potash 1986. See also Sanday 1981 and Schlegel 1977.

HOES, PLOWS, AND COMPUTERS (328–331)
Hoes and plows: Goody 1976; Maclachlan 1983:98ff. *Southeast Asia and Indonesia:* Tanner 1974; Bacdayan 1977; Potter 1977; Peletz 1987.

WHY DO WOMEN LIVE LONGER THAN MEN? (334–337)
Size of gap, fetal mortality, and X-linked diseases: Holden 1987; Metropolitan Life Insurance Company 1988a, 1988b. I have relied on Waldron 1976, 1982 for most of the data and arguments in this section. *For reverse longevity gap in India:* Karkal 1987.

THE HIDDEN COST OF MACHISMO (340–341)
U.S. Surgeon General's 1989 Report; Miller and Gerstein 1983.

WAS THERE LIFE BEFORE CHIEFS? (344–347)
Hobbes 1960:64. R. Gould 1982:76. *Quote:* Dentan 1968:49. *"Much meat":* Lee 1969a:62. *Sharing food:* Lee 1969b:58

HOW TO BE A HEADMAN (350–351)
All headmen here: Lee 1979:348. *Mehinacu:* Gregor 1969:88–89. Dentan 1968:68.

COPING WITH FREELOADERS (354–355)
Land ownership: Speck 1915. Leacock 1975; Knight 1974. *!Kung land tenure:* Lee 1979:335ff. *For shamanic control:* Dole 1966; Knauft 1987:456.

FROM HEADMAN TO BIG MAN (358–360)
Basic ideas about redistribution: Polanyi 1957; Sahlins 1963. *Australian camps:* McKnight 1986. *Mumis:* Oliver 1955. *Soni:* Hogbin 1964:66.

THE BIRTH OF THE GREAT PROVIDERS (362–363)
Kwakiutl big men: B. Isaac 1988:11. *Kwakiutl productivity:* Mitchell and Donald 1988. *Complex hunter-gatherers:* Reitz 1988; Price and Brown 1985; Testart 1982, 1988; Hayden, Eldridge, Eldridge, and Cannon 1985; Woodburn 1982a.

WHY WE CRAVE PRESTIGE (366–368)
Quote: Veblen 1934:110. *Narrow waist:* ibid.:149. *Toasted king:* ibid.:43.

WHY WE CONSUME CONSPICUOUSLY (370–372)
Forsyth 1986:40. *Quote from Tso Ch'iu-ming:* Chang 1983:100.

WHY YUPPIES? (374–376)
Hutton 1963:205. Duran 1964.

FROM BIG MAN TO CHIEF (378–380)
Trobriand chiefs: Malinowski 1935; Brunton 1975.

POWER: WAS IT SEIZED OR GIVEN? (382–385)
Mumis at war: Oliver 1955:411, 399. *Wonderful times:* ibid.: 415. *Kwakiutl warfare:* Ferguson 1984; Coupland 1988. *Conflict versus consensus view of the state:* R. Cohen and Service 1978; R. Cohen 1984; Haas 1982. *Violence in advanced chiefdoms and early states of Europe:* M. Green 1986; Kristiansen 1982. *Vedic India:* Lincoln 1981. *Jericho:* Kenyon 1981. *Egypt:* Hoffman 1979:290–291. *Maya:* Webster 1985; Marcus 1983. *Quote:* Gilman 1981. *Riposte:* Lethwaite 1981:14. See also Gibson and Geselowitz 1987.

ON THE THRESHOLD OF THE STATE (388–390)
Circumscription: Carneiro 1970, 1988. *Chiefdoms:* Carneiro 1981; Roosevelt 1987. *Previous bigmanship:* R. Green 1986:53. *Hawaii:* R. Green 1986; Hommon 1986; Kirch 1984; Earle 1987, 1989. *Rats:* Malo 1951:195.

THE FIRST STATES (392–395)
Faunal extinctions: Martin 1984. *Broad spectrum:* M. Cohen 1977; Unger-Hamilton 1989. *Natufians:* Henry 1985. *Origin of agriculture:* Rindos 1984. *Domestication of animals:* Moore 1985. *Çatal Hüyük:* Mellaart 1967, 1975. *Precocious Neolithic:* Stevens 1986; Voigt 1986. *Sumer:* Fagan 1983. *Succession of empires:* Garraty and Gay 1972; Pareti 1965.

WHY WE BECAME RELIGIOUS (398–401)
Mana: Codrington 1891. Tylor 1871. *Other definitions of religion:* Wax 1984. *Buddhism's gods:* Pardue 1967; Johnson 1988. *Plural souls:* Rivière 1987. *Afterlife:* Van Baaren 1987. See also Lester 1975. *Minimal elaboration of afterlife among some hunter-gatherers:* Woodburn 1982b.

THE EVOLUTION OF THE SPIRIT WORLD (404–407)
Creator gods: Sullivan 1987. *Totemism:* Wagner 1987. *Washo:* Downs 1966:59. *Dusun:* T. Williams 1965:43. *Witchetty-grub men:* Spencer and Gillin: 1968:170. *Pork and ancestors:* Rappaport 1987. *Dobuans:* Fortune 1965.

THE BASIC ANIMISTIC RITUALS (410–412)
Eskimo: Rasmussen 1929; Wallace 1966. *Crow:* Lowie 1948. *Shamans:* Winkelman 1986; Harner 1982.

DIVINE EXCHANGES (414–416)
Benedict 1938:632. *Gilgamesh:* Tigay 1982:225. Genesis 8:21. "The dependence of the gods upon man for food is an axiom of Mesopotamian religious thought" (Tigay 1982:229).

MEAT OFFERINGS (418–420)
East Africa: Lincoln 1981:13ff. *Yasna:* ibid.:157. *Quote:* ibid.:68. *Solomon's party:* Kings 9:64. *Assurnasirpal:* Fagan 1983:298.

HUMAN SACRIFICE (422–425)
Tophets: Stager and Wolff 1984. *Carthage:* ibid.:32. Herodotus 1954:290. *Celts:* M. Green 1986. *Shang oracle bones:* K. Chang 1980:229. *Hsiao-t'un:* ibid.:194. *Eastern Chou:* Xequin 1985:176. *Qin:* ibid.:252.

THE GODS WHO WOULD NOT EAT PEOPLE (428–430)
Occurrence of cannibalism: M. Harris 1985:199ff. Also see references above for "Meat, Nuts, and Cannibals." *Merry England:* Gordon-Grube 1988. *Cannibalism as subsistence:* Dornstreich and Morren 1974. *Fontebregona:* Villa et al. 1986. *Prisoners of war:* Gelb 1973.

THE GODS WHO ATE PEOPLE (430–436)
Fate of Aztec captives: Hassig 1988:118–121. Sahagún 1951. Duran 1964. *Critic:* Ortiz de Montellano 1983. *Gorbachev:* Gumbel 1988.

THE NONKILLING RELIGIONS (438–441)
Confronting the killing religions: Hardy 1988. *Zoroastrianism:* Gnoli 1987. *Jainism and Buddhism:* Hardy 1988; Eliade 1982; Pareti 1965; Garraty and Gay 1972.

THE ORIGIN OF NONKILLING RELIGIONS (444–446)
India: Lincoln 1981; Bose 1961. *Christianity:* Brandon 1968a, 1968b.

HOW THE NONKILLING RELIGIONS SPREAD (448–452)
Pareti 1965; Garraty and Gay 1972. *Buddhism:* Pardue 1967; Johnson 1988; Eliade 1982. *Christianity:* Fox 1987. *Quote:* ibid.:624. *Church schisms:* Pagels 1981. *Manichaeism:* Davies 1987.

A CHINESE PUZZLE (454–459)
Confucius 1960:301. *Mencius:* Dobson 1963:182. *Warmongers:* quoted in Mei 1934: 100. *Mo Tse quotes:* Mei 1934:89, 92. *Sungtse quote:* ibid.:101. *Confucian disinterest in afterlife:* Wechsler 1985:124. *High god:* Loewe 1982:127. *Quote on Shang:* Keightly 1978:212. *Mo Tse on food offerings:* Mei 1934:152. *Buddhism in T'ang:* Pardue 1967:178.

THE FUTURE OF BELIEF AND DISBELIEF (462–465)
U.S. believers: Gilbert 1988. *Soviet believers:* Fletcher 1981:212. *Low rate of belief in France and England:* Hastings and Hastings 1988:468–477.

DID HISTORY REPEAT ITSELF? (468–471)
Proponents of diffusionism: Perry 1923; E. G. Smith 1933. *Chinese millet:* Zhiman 1988:757. Te-Tzu Chang 1983:78. K. Chang 1980, 1983, 1984; Pearson 1983. See also Needham et al. 1986 for Chinese inventiveness.

HOW THE SECOND EARTH BEGAN (474–476)
Bering Straits: Fladmark 1986. *Siberian cultures:* Yi and Clark 1983. *Rate of advance:* Greenberg, Turner, and Zegura 1986; Turner 1989. *Early dates:* Bryan 1985; Dillehay 1984; Guidon 1985. Cf. Dinacauze 1984; Haynes 1988; *agriculture:* R. Ford 1979. *Maize:* Beadle 1981. *Chronology:* MacNeish 1978.

THE EVOLUTION OF THE SECOND EARTH (478–481)
Olmec: Coe 1968. *Maya:* Marcus 1983, 1984; Hammond 1982. *Maya collapse:* Webster 1985; Tainter 1988:152–178. *Teotihuacán:* Sanders, Santley, and Parsons 1979; Sanders and Webster 1988; Kurtz 1987. *Aztecs:* Fagan 1984; Hassig 1985, 1988. N. Davies 1983. Fagan 1984.

THE PHARAOHS OF THE ANDES (484–486)
Chan Chan: Mosely 1982. *Inca:* Mason 1957; C. Morris 1976; D'Altroy and Earle 1985.

WHY THE FIRST EARTH CONQUERED THE SECOND (488–491)
Cortés 1971. Hassig 1988. Fagan 1984. *Potential animal domesticates:* Hunn 1982. *Metallurgy:* Hosler 1988. *Administrative centers:* Sanders and Webster 1988.

CULTURAL DISCONTENTS AND THE KNOWING MIND (494–498)
See M. Harris 1981 for additional unintended consequences of hyperindustrialization.

WILL OUR KIND SURVIVE? (500–502)
Hawks and doves: Ferguson 1984:12. Carneiro 1978.

BIBLIOGRAPHY

Abrams, H. L. 1987. "The Preference for Animal Protein and Fat: A Cross-Cultural Survey." In *Food and Evolution: Toward a Theory of Human Food Habits,* ed. Marvin Harris and Eric Ross, 207–223. Philadelphia: Temple University Press.

Adams, M., and J. V. Neil. 1967. "The Children of Incest." *Pediatrics* 40:55–62.

Ammerman, A. J., and L. L. Cavalli-Sforza. 1984. *The Neolithic Transition and the Genetics of Population in Europe.* Princeton: Princeton University Press.

Ardrey, Robert. 1961. *African Genesis: A Personal Investigation into the Animal Origins and Nature of Man.* New York: Atheneum.

Arensburg, B., et al. 1989. "A Middle Paleolithic Human Hyoid Bone." *Nature* 338:758–760.

Ariel, I. 1981. *Malignant Melanoma.* New York: Appleton-Century-Crofts.

Aubert, Claude, and Pierre Frapa. 1985. *Hunger and Health.* Emmaus, Penn.: Rodale Press.

Awe, Bolanlie. 1977. "The Iyalode in Traditional Yoruba Political System." In *Sexual Stratification: A Cross-Cultural View,* ed. Alice Schlegel, 144–160. New York: Columbia University Press.

Bacdayan, Albert S. 1977. "Mechanistic Cooperation and Sexual Equality Among the Western Bontoc." In *Sexual Stratification: A Cross-Cultural View,* ed. Alice Schlegel, 270–291. New York: Columbia University Press.

Badrian, A., and N. Badrian. 1984. "Social Organization of *Pan paniscus* in the Lomako Forest, Zaire." In *The Pygmy Chimpanzee,* ed. R. Susman, 325–346. New York: Plenum Press.

Baker, Mary Anne. 1987. "Sensory Functioning." In *Sex Differences in Human Performance,* ed. M. Baker, 5–36. New York: John Wiley & Sons.

Baker, Susan. 1980. "Psychosexual Differentiation in the Human." *Biology of Reproduction* 22:66–72.

Baksh, Michael. 1985. "Faunal Food as a 'Limiting Factor' on Amazonian Cultural Behavior: A Machiguenga Example." *Research in Economic Anthropology* 7:145–175.

Barash, David P. 1977. *Sociology and Behavior.* New York: Elsevier.

Bartram, William. 1958. *Travels of William Bartram.* New Haven: Yale University Press.

Beadle, G. 1981. "The Ancestor of Corn." *Scientific American* 242(1):96–103.

Beals, K., C. Smith, and S. Dodd. 1984. "Brain Size: Cranial Morphology, Climate and Time Machines." *Current Anthropology* 25:301–330.

Beck, Benjamin. 1980. *Animal Tool Behavior: The Use and Manufacture of Tools by Animals.* New York: Garland Publishing.

Begler, Elsie. 1978. "Sex, Status and Authority in Egalitarian Society." *American Anthropologist* 80:389–405.

Benbow, C. P., and J. C. Stanley. 1983. "Sex Differences in Mathematical Reasoning Ability: More Facts." *Science* 222:1029–1031.

Benedict, Ruth. 1934. *Patterns of Culture.* Boston: Houghton Mifflin.

———. 1938. "Religion." In *General Anthropology,* ed. F. Boas, 627–665. Boston: D. C. Heath.

Bentham, Jeremy. 1978. "Offenses Against One's Self: Pederasty." *Journal of Homosexuality* 3:389–405.

Bernstein, Irwin, et al. 1983. "The Introduction of Hormones, Behavior, and Social Context in Non-Human Primates." In *Hormones and Aggressive Behavior,* ed. Bruce Svare, 535–561. New York: Plenum Press.

Bickerton, Derek. 1981. *Roots of Language.* Ann Arbor: Karoma Publishers.

———. 1984. "The Language Biogram Hypothesis." *Behavioral and Brain Sciences* 7:173–221.

Binford, Lewis R. 1982. "Comment on R. White: Rethinking the Middle/Upper Paleolithic." *Current Anthropology* 23:177–181.

———. 1988. "Fact and Fiction About the *Zinjanthropus* Floor: Data, Arguments and Interpretations." *Current Anthropology* 29:123–151.

Binford, Lewis R., and Nancy Stone. 1986. "Zhoukoudian: A Closer Look." *Current Anthropology* 27:453–475.

Birdsell, J. B. 1972. *An Introduction to the New Physical Anthropology.* New York: Rand McNally.

Bixler, Ray. 1981. "Incest Avoidance as a Function of Environment and Heredity." *Current Anthropology* 22:639–654.

———. 1982. "Comment on the Incidence and Purpose of Royal Sibling Incest." *American Ethnologist* 9:580–582.

Blackwood, Evelyn. 1986. "Breaking the Mirror: The Construction of Lesbianism and the Anthropological Discourse on Homosexuality." In *Anthropology and Homosexual Behavior,* ed. Evelyn Blackwood, 1–18. New York: Haworth Press.

Bleier, Ruth. 1984. *Science and Gender: A Critique of Biology and Its Theories of Women.* New York: Pergamon Press.

Blinderman, Charles. 1986. *The Piltdown Inquest.* Buffalo, N.Y.: Prometheus Books.

Blumenschine, Robert. 1987. "Characteristics of an Early Hominid Scavenging Niche." *Current Anthropology* 28:383–407.

Boaz, Noel T. 1988. "Status of *Australopithecus afarensis.*" *Yearbook of Physical Anthropology* 31:85–113.

Boehm, David, J. Benagh, C. Smith, and P. Matthews, eds. 1987. *Guinness Sports Record Book 1987–1988.* New York: Sterling Publishing Co.

Boesch, Christophe, and Hedwige Boesch. 1984. "Mental Map in Wild Chimpanzees: An Analysis of Hammer Transports for Nut Cracking." *Primates* 25(2):169–170.

———. 1989. "Hunting Behavior of Wild Chimpanzees in the Tai National Park." *American Journal of Physical Anthropology* 78:547–573.

Bogucki, Peter. 1987. "The Establishment of Agrarian Communities on the North European Plain." *Current Anthropology* 28:1–24.

Booth, William. 1988. "The Social Lives of Dolphins." *Science* 240:1273–1274.

Bose, A. N. 1961. *The Social and Rural Economy of Northern India, 600 B.C.–200 A.D.* Calcutta: Mukhopodhya.

Bossen, Laurel. 1988. "Toward a Theory of Marriage: The Economic Anthropology of Marriage Transactions." *Ethnology* 27:127–144.

Bourguignon, Erika. 1980. "Comparisons and Implications: What Have We Learned?" In *A World of Women: Anthropological Studies of Women in the Societies of the World,* ed. Erika Bourguignon et al., 321–342. New York: Praeger Scientific.

Bradshaw, John. 1988. "The Evolution of Human Lateral Asymmetries: New Evidence and Second Thoughts." *Journal of Human Evolution* 17:615–637.

Braidwood, Linda, and R. Braidwood. 1986. "Prelude to the Appearance of Village-Farming Communities in Southwestern Asia." In *Ancient Anatolia: Aspects of Change and Cultural Development,* ed. J. V. Canby et al., 3–11. Madison, Wis.: University of Wisconsin Press.

Brain, C. K. 1981. *The Hunters or the Hunted.* Chicago: University of Chicago Press.

Brandon, S. 1968a. *Jesus and the Zealots.* New York: Charles Scribner's Sons.

———. 1968b. *The Trial of Jesus of Nazareth.* London: B. T. Batsford.

Bremer, J. 1959. *Asexualization*. New York: Macmillan.

Brody, Jane E. 1988. "It's Not Just the Calories, It's Their Source." *New York Times*, July 12, C3.

Brooks, A. S., and J. E. Yellen. 1989. "An Archaeological Perspective on the African Origins of Modern Humans." *American Journal of Physical Anthropology* 78:197.

Broom, R., and G. W. H. Schepers. 1946. "The Southern African Ape-Men, the Australopithecinae." *Transvaal Museum Memoires* 2:1–272.

Brown, Judith K. 1975. "Iroquois Women: An Ethnohistoric Note." In *Toward an Anthropology of Women*, ed. Rayna Reiter, 235–251. New York: Monthly Review Press.

Brunton, Ron. 1975. "Why Do the Trobriands Have Chiefs?" *Man* 13:1–22.

Bryan, Allan, ed. 1985. *New Evidence for the Pleistocene Peopling of the Americas*. Orono, Maine: Center for the Study of Early Man.

Buchbinder, G. 1977. "Nutritional Stress and Post-Contact Population Decline Among the Maring of New Guinea." In *Malnutrition, Behavior and Social Organization*, ed. L. S. Greene, 109–141. New York: Academic Press.

Bullough, Verne. 1976. *Sex, Society, and History*. New York: Science History.

Bullough, Verne, and Bonnie Bullough. 1978. *Prostitution: An Illustrated and Social History*. New York: Crown.

Bunn, H. T., and E. M. Kroll. 1986. "Systematic Butchery by Plio/Pleistocene Hominids at Olduvai Gorge, Tanzania. *Current Anthropology* 27:431–452.

———. 1988. Reply to Binford 1988. *Current Anthropology* 29:135.

Cain, Meade. 1977. "The Economic Activities of Children in a Village in Bangladesh." *Population and Development Review* 3:201–227.

Callender, Charles, and Lee Kochems. 1986. "Men and Not-Men: Male Gender-Mixing Statuses and Homosexuality." In *Anthropology and Homosexual Behavior*, ed. Evelyn Blackwood, 165–178. New York: Haworth Press.

Campbell, Bernard. 1985. *Human Evolution: An Introduction to Man's Adaptation*. Hawthorne, N.Y.: Aldine de Gruyter.

Cann, R., et al. 1987. "Mitochondrial DNA and Human Evolution." *Nature* 352:31–36.

Cant, J. G. 1981. "Hypothesis for Evolution of Human Breasts and Buttocks." *American Nutritionist* 117:199–204.

Carneiro, Robert. 1970. "A Theory of the Origin of the State." *Science* 169:733–738.

———. 1978. "Political Expansion as an Expression of the Principle of Competitive Exclusion." In *Origins of the State*, ed. R. Cohen and E. Service, 205–223. Philadelphia: ISHI.

———. 1981. "Chiefdom: Precursor of the State." In *The Transition of Statehood in the New World*, ed. Grant Jones and Robert Kautz, 37–75. New York: Cambridge University Press.

———. 1988. "The Circumscription Theory: Challenge and Response." *American Behavioral Scientist* 31:497–511.

Carrier, David. 1984. "The Energetic Paradox of Human Running and Hominid Evolution." *Current Anthropology* 25:483–495.

Cavalli-Sforza, L. L., et al. 1988. "Reconstruction of Human Evolution: Bringing Together Genetic, Archaeological, and Linguistic Data." *Proceedings of the National Academy of Sciences* 85:6002–6011.

Chagnon, Napoleon A. 1968. *The Fierce People*. New York: Holt, Rinehart and Winston.

———. 1974. *Studying the Yanomamo*. New York: Holt, Rinehart and Winston.

———. 1983. *Yanomamo: The Fierce People*. 3rd edition. New York: Holt, Rinehart and Winston.

513

————. 1988. "Life Histories, Blood Revenge, and Warfare in a Tribal Population." *Science* 239:985–992.

————. 1989. Letter to the editor. *Anthropology Newsletter* 30(1):24.

Chagnon, Napoleon, and R. Hames. 1979. "Protein Deficiency and Tribal Warfare in Amazonia: New Data." *Science* 203:910–913.

Chang, K. C. 1980. *Shang Civilization.* New Haven: Yale University Press.

————. 1983. *Art, Myth, and Ritual: The Path to Political Authority in Ancient China.* Cambridge, Mass.: Harvard University Press.

————. 1984. "China." *American Antiquity.* 49:754–756.

Chang, Te-Tzu. 1983. "The Origins and Early Culture of the Cereal Grains and Food Legumes." In *The Origins of Chinese Civilization,* ed. David Keightley, 65–94. Berkeley: University of California Press.

Changeux, Jean-Paul. 1985. *Neuronal Man: The Biology of Mind.* Translated by Laurence Garey. New York: Oxford University Press.

Chase, P., and H. Dibble. 1987. "Middle Paleolithic Symbolism." *Journal of Anthropological Archaeology* 6:263–296.

Cicala, George. 1965. *Animal Drives: An Enduring Problem in Psychology.* Princeton: Van Nostrand.

Ciochon, Russel. 1985. "Hominoid Cladistics and the Ancestry of Modern Apes and Humans." In *Primate Evolution and Human Origins,* ed. R. L. Ciochon and J. G. Fleagle, 345–362. Menlo Park, Calif.: Benjamin/Cummings.

Codrington, R. 1891. *The Melanesians.* Oxford: Clarendon Press.

Coe, M. 1968. *America's First Civilization.* New York: American Heritage.

Cohen, Mark. 1977. *The Food Crisis in Prehistory.* New Haven: Yale University Press.

Cohen, Mark, and George Armelagos, eds. 1984. *Paleopathology and the Origin of Agriculture.* New York: Academic Press.

Cohen, Ronald. 1984. "Warfare and State Formation: Wars Make States and States Make Wars." In *Warfare, Culture and Environment,* ed. Brian Ferguson, 329–355. Orlando, Fla.: Academic Press.

Cohen, Ronald, and Elman Service, eds. 1978. *Origins of the State.* Philadelphia: ISHI.

Cohen, Yehudi. 1978. "The Disappearance of the Incest Taboo." *Human Nature* 1:72–78.

Confucius. 1960. *Confucian Analects,* ed. James Legge. Hong Kong: Hong Kong University Press.

Conkey, M. W. 1983. "On the Origins of Paleolithic Art: A Review and Some Critical Thoughts." In *The Mousterian Legacy.* BAR S164, ed. E. Trinkaus, 201–227. Oxford: British Archaeological Reports.

Cortés, Hernán. 1971. *Letters from Mexico.* New York: Grossman.

Coupland, Gary. 1988. "Prehistoric Economic and Social Change in the Tsimshian Area." In *The Prehistoric Economics of the Pacific Northwest Coast,* ed. Barry Isaac, 211–243. Greenwich, Conn.: JAI Press.

Cowart, B. 1981. "Development of Taste Perception in Humans." *Psychological Bulletin* 90:43–73.

Crelin, E. S. 1987. *The Human Vocal Tract.* New York: Vantage.

Crossette, Barbara. 1989. "India Studying the 'Accidental' Deaths of Hindu Wives." *New York Times,* Jan. 15, 4.

D'Altroy, T., and T. K. Earle. 1985. "Staple Finance, Wealth Finance, and Storage in the Inka Political Economy." *Current Anthropology* 26:187–206.

Daly, Martin, and Margo Wilson. 1978. *Sex Evolution and Behavior: Adaptations for Reproduction.* North Scituate, Mass.: Duxbury Press.

Dart, Raymond A. 1925. *"Australopithecus africanus:* The Man-Ape of South Africa." *Nature* 115:195–199.

Dart, Raymond, and D. Craig. 1959. *Adventures with the Missing Link.* New York: Viking.

Darwin, Charles. 1871. *The Descent of Man.* London: J. Murray.

Davidson, Iain, and William Noble. 1989. "The Archaeology of Perception: Traces of Depiction and Language." *Current Anthropology* 30:125–155.

Davies, J. G. 1987. "Manicheism." In *The Encyclopedia of Religion,* vol. 9, 161–171. New York: Macmillan and Free Press.

Davies, N. 1983. *The Ancient Kingdoms of Mexico.* New York: Penguin.

Davis, Joel. 1984. *Endorphins: New Waves in Brain Chemistry.* Garden City, N.Y.: Dial Press.

Day, Michael. 1986. *Guide to Fossil Man.* 4th edition. Chicago: University of Chicago Press.

Dehavenon, A. L. 1977. *Rank Ordered Behavior in Four Urban Families: A Comparative Video-Analysis of Patterns of Superordination in Two Black Families.* Ph.D. dissertation, Columbia University.

Dennet, G., and J. Connell. 1988. "Acculturation and Health in the Highlands of Papua New Guinea." *Current Anthropology* 29:273–299.

Dentan, Robert. 1968. *The Semai: A Non-Violent People of Malaya.* New York: Holt, Rinehart and Winston.

Denton, D. A. 1982. *The Hunger for Salt.* New York: Springer-Verlag.

Devereux, George. 1967. "A Typological Study of Abortion in 350 Primitive, Ancient, and Pre-Industrial Societies." In *Abortion in America,* ed. H. Rosen, 95–152. Boston: Beacon Press.

Devine, John. 1985. "The Versatility of Human Locomotion." *American Anthropologist* 87:550–570.

Dickeman, M. 1975. "Demographic Consequences of Infanticide in Man." *Annual Review of Ecology and Systematics* 6:100–137.

Di Leonardo, Micaela. 1985. "Morals, Mothers and Militarism: Anti-Militarism and Feminist Theory." *Feminist Studies* 11(3):599–617.

Dillehay, T. D. 1984. "A Late Ice Age Settlement in Southern Chile." *Scientific American* 25(4):547–550.

Dinacauze, D. 1984. "An Archaeological Evaluation of the Case for Pre-Clovis Occupations." *Advances in World Archaeological Theory* 3:275–323.

Divale, William. 1974. "Migration, External Warfare, and Matrilocal Residence." *Behavior Science Research* 9(1):75–133.

Divale, William, and Marvin Harris. 1976. "Population, Warfare and the Male Supremacist Complex." *American Anthropologist* 78:521–538.

———. 1978. "The Male Supremacist Complex: Discovery of a Cultural Invention." *American Anthropologist* 80:668–671.

Dixon, A. F. 1983. "Observation on the Evolution and Behavioral Significance of 'Sexual Skin' in Female Primates." *Advances in the Study of Behavior* 13:63–106.

Dobson, W. 1963. *Mencius: A New Translation Arranged and Annotated for the General Reader.* Toronto: University of Toronto Press.

Dole, Gertrude. 1966. "Anarchy Without Chaos." In *Political Anthropology,* ed. M. J. Swartz, V. Turner, and A. Tuden, 73–88. Chicago: Aldine.

Dornstreich, M., and G. Morren. 1974. "Does New Guinea Cannibalism Have Nutritional Value?" *Human Ecology* 2:1–12.

Dover, K. J. 1980. *Greek Homosexuality.* New York: Vintage.

Downs, James F. 1966. *The Two Worlds of the Washo: An Indian Tribe of California and Nevada.* New York: Holt, Rinehart and Winston.

515

Dreon, Darlene M., et al. 1988. "Dietary Fat: Carbohydrate Ratio and Obesity in Middle-Aged Men." *American Journal of Clinical Nutrition* 47:995–1000.

Drinkwater, Barbara L. 1986. *Female Endurance Athletes.* Champaign, Ill.: Human Kinetics Publishers, Inc.

Dufour, Darna. 1986. "Insects as Food: A Case Study from the Northwest Amazon." *American Anthropologist* 89:383–397.

Duran, Diego. 1964. *The Aztecs: The History of the Indies of New Spain.* New York: Orion Press.

Eagan, Timothy. 1989. "Navy Unmoved by Critics, Presses Plan for Dolphins to Guard Subs." *New York Times,* April 9, 1.

Earle, Timothy. 1987. "Chiefdoms in Archaeological Perspective." *Annual Review of Anthropology* 16:279–308.

———. 1989. "The Evolution of Chiefdoms." *Current Anthropology* 30:84–88.

Ebliny, J. 1985. "The Mythological Evolution of Nudity." *Journal of Human Evolution* 14:33–41.

Efron, Arthur. 1985. *The Sexual Body: An Interdisciplinary Perspective.* New York: Institute of Mind and Behavior.

Ehrhardt, Anke A. 1975. "Prenatal Hormonal Exposure and Psychosexual Differentiation." In *Topics in Psychoendocrinology,* ed. Edward Sachar, 67–82. New York: Grune & Stratton.

———. 1985. "The Psychology of Gender." In *Gender and the Life Course.* ed. Alice S. Rossi, 81–95. Hawthorne, N.Y.: Aldine de Gruyter.

Ehrhardt, Anke A., and H.F.L. Meyer-Bahlburg. 1981. "Effects of Prenatal Sex Hormones on Gender-Related Behavior." *Science* 211:1312–1318.

Eldredge, Niles, and Ian Tattersall. 1982. *The Myths of Human Evolution.* New York: Columbia University Press.

Eliade, Mircea. 1982. *A History of Religious Ideas: From Gautama Buddha to the Triumph of Christianity.* Translated from the French by Willard R. Trask. Chicago: University of Chicago Press.

Eliade, Mircea, ed. 1987. *The Encyclopedia of Religion.* New York: Macmillan and Free Press.

Elias, Michael. 1981. "Serum Cortisol, Testosterone, and Testosterone-Binding Globulin Responses to Competitive Fighting in Human Males." *Aggressive Behavior* 76:215–224.

Ember, Melvin. 1982. "Statistical Evidence for an Ecological Explanation of Warfare." *American Anthropologist* 84:645–649.

Ember, Melvin, and Carol Ember. 1988. "Fear of Disasters as an Engine of History: Resource Crisis, Warfare and Interpersonal Aggression." Paper read at the multidisciplinary conference "What Is the Engine of History?" at Texas A&M University, Oct. 27–29, 1988.

Estioko-Griffin, Agnes, and P. B. Griffin. 1981. "Woman the Hunter: The Agata." In *Woman the Gatherer,* ed. Frances Dahlberg, 121–151. New Haven: Yale University Press.

———. 1985. "Women Hunters: The Implications for Pleistocene Prehistory and Contemporary Ethnography." In *Women in Asia and the Pacific,* ed. M. Goodman, 61–81. Honolulu: University of Hawaii Press.

Evans-Pritchard, E. E. 1970. "Sexual Inversion Among the Azande." *American Anthropologist* 72:1428–1434.

Fagan, Brian. 1983. *People of the Earth: An Introduction to World Prehistory.* Boston: Little, Brown.

———. 1984. *The Aztecs.* New York: W. H. Freeman.

Fausto-Sterling, Ann. 1985. *Myths of Gender: Biological Theory of Women and Men.* New York: Basic Books.

Fay, Robert, Charles Turner, Albert Klassen, and John Gagnon. 1989. "Prevalence and Patterns of Same-Gender Sexual Contact Among Men." *Science* 243:338–348.

Feil, Daryl. 1987. *The Evolution of Highland Papua New Guinea Societies.* New York: Cambridge University Press.

Ferguson, Brian R. 1984a. "Introduction: Studying War." In *Warfare, Culture and Environment,* ed. Brian Ferguson, 1–61, Orlando, Fla.: Academic Press.

———. 1984b. "A Reexamination of the Causes of Northwest Coast Warfare." In *Warfare, Culture, and Environment,* ed. Brian Ferguson, 267–328. Orlando, Fla.: Academic Press.

———. n.d. "Game Wars: Ecology and Conflict in Amazonia." Unpublished paper.

Fialkowski, Konrad. 1986. "A Mechanism for the Origin of the Human Brain: A Hypothesis." *Current Anthropology* 27:288–290.

———. 1987. "On the Origins of the Human Brain: Preadaptation vs. Adaptation." *Current Anthropology* 28:540–543.

Field, Tiffany. 1987. "Interaction and Attachment in Normal and Atypical Infants." *Journal of Consulting and Clinical Psychology* 55:853–890.

Fladmark, Knut. 1986. "Getting One's Berings." *Natural History,* Nov., 8ff.

Fleagle, John G., et al. 1986. "Age of the Earliest African Anthropoids." *Science* 234:1247–1249.

Fletcher, William. 1981. *Soviet Believers: The Religious Sector of the Population.* Lawrence, Kans.: The Regents Press of Kansas.

Fliederbaum, Julian, et al. 1979. "Clinical Aspects of Hunger and Disease in Adults." In *Hunger Disease: Studies by the Jewish Physicians in the Warsaw Ghetto.* ed. Myron Winick, 11–36. New York: John Wiley & Sons.

Ford, C. S., and F. A. Beach. 1951. *Patterns of Sexual Behavior.* New York: Harper & Row, Publishers.

Ford, R. 1979. "Gathering and Gardening: Trends and Consequences of Hopewell Subsistence Strategies." In *Hopewell Archaeology: The Chillicothe Conference,* ed. D. S. Brose and N. Greber, 234–238. Kent, Ohio: Kent State University Press.

Forsyth, Adrian. 1986. *A Natural History of Sex.* New York: Charles Scribner's Sons.

Fortune, Reo. 1965. *Manus Religion.* Lincoln, Neb.: University of Nebraska Press.

Fossey, D. 1982. "Reproduction Among Free-living Mountain Gorillas." *American Journal of Primatology, Supplement* I:97–104.

Fouts, R., and D. Fouts. 1985. "Signs of Conversation in Chimpanzees." In *Sign Language of the Great Apes,* ed. B. Gardner, R. Gardner, and T. van Cantforts. New York: State University of New York Press.

Fox, Robin L. 1987. *Pagans and Christians.* San Francisco: Harper & Row, Publishers.

Frisch, R. 1984. "Body Fat, Puberty and Fertility." *Science* 199:22–30.

Fry, Peter. 1986. "Male Homosexual and Spirit Possession in Brazil." In *Anthropology and Homosexual Behavior,* ed. Evelyn Blackwood, 137–153. New York: Haworth Press.

Gale, F., ed. 1974. "Women's Role in Aboriginal Society." Australian Aboriginal Studies, no. 36. Canberra: ANU Press.

Gamble, C. 1986. *The Paleolithic Settlement of Europe.* New York: Cambridge University Press.

Gardner, B. T., and R. A. Gardner. 1971. "Two-Way Communication with a Chimpanzee." In *Behavior of Non-Human Primates.* Vol. 4, ed. A. Schrier and F. Stollnitz, 117–184. New York: Academic Press.

———. 1973. "Early Signs of Language in Child and Chimpanzee." *Science* 187:752–753.

Gargett, Robert. 1989a. "Grave Shortcomings: The Argument for Neandertal Burial." *Current Anthropology* 30:157–190.

———. 1989b. "Reply." *Current Anthropology* 30:326–330.

Garraty, John, and Peter Gay, eds. 1972. *The Columbia History of the World.* New York: Harper & Row, Publishers.

Gay, Judith. 1986. " 'Mummies and Babies' and Friends and Lovers in Lesotho." In *Anthropology and Homosexual Behavior,* ed. Evelyn Blackwood, 97–116. New York: Haworth Press.

Geertz, C. 1963. *Agricultural Involution.* Berkeley: University of California Press.

Gelb, I. 1973. "Prisoners of War in Early Mesopotamia." *Journal of Near Eastern Studies* 32:70–98.

Gelber, M. 1986. *Gender and Society in New Guinea Highlands: An Anthropological Perspective on Antagonism Toward Women.* Boulder, Colo.: Westview Press.

Gibson, K. R. 1989. "Brain Size Revisited: Implications of Parallel Distributed Processing Models of Brain Function." *American Journal of Physical Anthropology* 78:228.

Gibson, O. Blair, and Michael N. Geselowitz. 1987. *Tribe and Polity in Late Prehistoric Europe: Demography, Production, and Exchange in the Evolution of Complex Social Systems.* New York: Plenum Press.

Gilbert, Dennis A. 1988. *Compendium of American Public Opinion.* New York: Facts on File Publications.

Gilman, A. 1981. "The Development of Stratification in Bronze Age Europe." *Current Anthropology* 22:1–23.

Gnoli, Gherardo. 1987. "Zoroastrianism." In *The Encyclopedia of Religion,* vol. 9, 579–582. New York: Macmillan and Free Press.

Goldman, Nancy L., ed. 1982. *Female Soldiers—Combatants or Noncombatants? Historical and Contemporary Perspectives.* Westport, Conn.: Greenwood Press.

Goldstein, A., and Ralph Hansteen. 1977. "Evidence Against Involvement of Endorphins in Sexual Arousal and Orgasm in Man." *Archives of General Psychiatry* 34:1179–1180.

Goleman, Daniel. 1988. "An Emerging Theory on Blacks' I.Q. Scores." *New York Times,* April 10, 22–24.

Good, Kenneth. 1987. "Limiting Factors in Amazonian Ecology." In *Food and Evolution: Toward a Theory of Human Food Habits,* ed. M. Harris and E. Ross, 407–426. Philadelphia: Temple University Press.

Goodman, Alan H., R. B. Thomas, A. C. Swedlund, and G. Armelagos. 1988. "Biocultural Perspectives on Stress in Prehistoric, Historical, and Contemporary Population Research." *Yearbook of Physical Anthropology* 31:169–202.

Goodrich, Carrington, ed. 1976. *Dictionary of Ming Biography.* New York: Columbia University Press.

Goody, Jack. 1973. "Bridewealth and Dowry in Africa and Eurasia." In *Bridewealth and Dowry,* ed. Jack Goody and S. J. Tambiah. Cambridge: Cambridge University Press.

———. 1976. *Production and Reproduction.* New York: Cambridge University Press.

Gordon-Grube, Karen. 1988. "Anthropophagy in Post-Renaissance Europe: The Tradition of Medieval Cannibalism." *American Anthropologist* 90:405–409.

Gould, Richard. 1982. "To Have and Not to Have: The Ecology of Sharing Among Hunter-Gatherers." In *Resource Managers: North American and Australian Hunter-Gatherers,* ed. Nancy Williams and Eugene Hunn, 69–91. Boulder, Colo.: Westview Press.

Gould, Stephen. 1988. "A Novel Notion of Neanderthal." *Natural History,* June, 16–21.

Gould, Stephen, and Niles Eldredge. 1977. "Punctuated Equlibria: The Tempo and Mode of Evolution Revisited." *Paleobiology* 3:115–151.

Graham, B., ed. 1981. *Reproductive Biology of the Great Apes.* New York: Academic Press.

Gramby, R. 1977. "Deerskins and Hunting Territories: Competition for a Scarce Resource of the Northeastern Woodlands." *American Antiquity* 42:601–605.

Gray, Patrick, and Linda Wolfe. 1980. "Height and Sexual Dimorphism and Stature Among Human Societies." *American Journal of Physical Anthropology* 53:441–456.

Green, Miranda. 1986. *The Gods of the Celts.* Totowa, N.J.: Barnes and Noble.

Green, R. C. 1986. "The Ancestral Polynesian Settlement Pattern." In *Island Societies,* ed. Patrick Kirch, 50–54. New York: Cambridge University Press.

Greenberg, David. 1986. "Why Was the Berdache Ridiculed?" In *Anthropology and Homosexual Behavior,* ed. Evelyn Blackwood, 179–189. New York: Haworth Press.

Greenberg, Joseph C., Christy Turner, and S. Zegura. 1986. "The Settlement of the Americas: A Comparison of the Linguistic, Dental and Genetic Evidence." *Current Anthropology* 27:477–497.

Greenberg, Joseph C., and respondents. 1987. "Language in the Americas: A Review." *Current Anthropology* 28:647.

Gregerson, Edgar. 1982. *Sexual Practices: The Story of Human Sexuality.* London: Mitchell Beazley.

Gregor, Thomas. 1969. *Social Relations in a Small Society: A Study of the Mehinacu Indians of Central Brazil.* Ph.D. dissertation, Columbia University.

———. 1985. *Anxious Pleasures: The Sexual Lives of an Amazonian People.* Chicago: University of Chicago Press.

Guidon, Niede. 1985. "Las Unidades Culturales de São Paemundo Nonato—Sudeste del Estado de Piaui-Brazil." In *New Evidence for the Pleistocene Peopling of the Americas,* ed. Alan Bryan, 157–171. Orono, Maine: Center for the Study of Man.

Gumbel, Peter. 1988. "Down on the Farm: Soviets Try Once More to Straighten Out Old Agricultural Mess." *Wall Street Journal,* Dec. 2, 1.

Haas, Jonathan. 1982. *The Evolution of the Prehistoric State.* New York: Columbia University Press.

Haley, Alex. 1976. *Roots.* Garden City, N.Y.: Doubleday.

Hamilton, William. 1987. "Omnivorous Primate Diets and Human Over-Consumption of Meat." In *Food and Evolution: Toward a Theory of Human Food Habits,* ed. M. Harris and E. Ross, 117–132. Philadelphia: Temple University Press.

Hammond, N. 1982. *Ancient Maya Civilization.* New Brunswick, N.J.: Rutgers University Press.

Hanley, Susan. 1977. "The Influence of Economic and Social Variables on Marriage and Fertility in 18th and 19th Century Japanese Villages." In *Population Patterns in the Past,* ed. R. Lee et al., 165–200. Boulder, Colo.: Westview Press.

Hanley, Susan, and Kozo Yamamura. 1977. *Economic and Demographic Change in Preindustrial Japan, 1600–1868.* Princeton: Princeton University Press.

Harcourt, A., et al. 1981. "Testes Weight, Body Weight, and Breeding Systems in Primates." *Nature* 293:55–57.

Harding, Robert. 1975. "Meat Eating and Hunting in Baboons." In *Socioecology and Psychology of Primates,* ed. R. H. Tuttle, 245–257. The Hague: Mouton.

Hardy, Freidhelm. 1988. "The Renouncer Traditions." In *The World's Religions,* ed. Steward Sutherland et al., 582–603. Boston: G. K. Hall.

Harlow, Harry. 1960. "Primary Affection Patterns in Primates." *American Journal of Ortho-Psychiatry.* 30:676–684.

———. 1964. "Early Deprivation and Later Behavior in the Monkey." In *Unfinished Tasks in the Behavioral Sciences,* ed. A. Abrams et al., 154–173. Baltimore: Williams and Wilkins.

Harner, Michael. 1982. *The Way of the Shaman: A Guide to Power and Healing.* New York: Bantam Books.

519

Harris, David. 1987. "Aboriginal Subsistence in a Tropical Rain Forest Environment: Food Procurement, Cannibalism and Population Regulation in Northeastern Australia." In *Food and Evolution: Toward a Theory of Human Food Habits,* ed. M. Harris and E. Ross, 357–385. Philadelphia: Temple University Press.

Harris, J. W. 1983. "Cultural Beginnings: Plio-Pleistocene Archaeological Occurrences from the Afar." In *African Archaeological Review,* ed. N. David, 3–31. Cambridge: Cambridge University Press.

Harris, Marvin. 1958. *Portugal's African Wards.* New York: American Committee on Africa.

———. 1970. "Referential Ambiguity in the Calculus of Brazilian Racial Identity." *Southwestern Journal of Anthropology* 26:1–14.

———. 1977. *Cannibals and Kings: The Origins of Cultures.* New York: Random House.

———. 1979. *Cultural Materialism: The Struggle for a Science of Culture.* New York: Random House.

———. 1981. *America Now: The Anthropology of a Changing Culture.* New York: Simon and Schuster.

———. 1984. "Animal Capture and Yanomami Warfare: Retrospect and New Evidence." *Journal of Anthropological Research* 40:183–201.

———. 1985. *Good to Eat: Riddles of Food and Culture.* New York: Simon and Schuster.

Harris, Marvin, and Eric Ross. 1987. *Death, Sex and Fertility: Population Regulation in Pre-Industrial Societies.* New York: Columbia University Press.

Hart, Keith. 1985. "The Social Anthropology of West Africa." *The Annual Review of Anthropology* 14:243–272.

Hartung, John. 1985. Review of *Incest: A Biosocial View,* by J. Shepher. *American Journal of Physical Anthropology* 67:169–171.

Hassig, Ross. 1985. *Trade, Tribute, and Transportation: The Sixteenth-Century Political Economy of the Valley of Mexico.* Norman, Okla.: University of Oklahoma Press.

———. 1988. *Aztec Warfare.* Norman, Okla.: University of Oklahoma Press.

Hastings, Elizabeth, and Philip Hastings. 1988. *Index to International Public Opinion, 1986–1987.* New York: Greenwood Press.

Haven, E. W. 1972. "Factors Associated with the Selection of Advanced Academic Mathematical Courses by Girls in High School." Research Bulletin 72-12. Princeton: Educational Testing Service.

Haviland, W. 1967. "Stature at Tikal." *American Antiquity* 32:326–335.

Hayden, Brian. 1986. "Resources, Rivalry and Reproduction: The Influence of Basic Resource Characteristics on Reproductive Behavior." In *Culture and Reproduction: An Anthropological Critique of Demographic Transition Theory,* ed. W. P. Handwerker, 176–195. Boulder, Colo.: Westview Press.

———. 1987. "Alliances and Ritual Ecstasy: Human Responses to Resource Stress." *Journal for the Scientific Study of Religion* 26:81–91.

Hayden, Brian, M. Deal, A. Cannon, and J. Casey. 1986. "Ecological Determinants of Women's Status Among Hunter/Gatherers." *Human Evolution* 1(5):449–474.

Hayden, Brian, M. Eldridge, A. Eldridge, and A. Cannon. 1985. "Complex Hunter-Gatherers in Interior British Columbia." In *Prehistoric Hunter-Gatherers: The Emergence of Cultural Complexity,* ed. D. Price and J. Brown, 181–199. New York: Academic Press.

Haynes, C. Vance, Jr. 1988. "Geofacts and Fancy." *Natural History,* Feb., 4–12.

Heath, R. G., ed. 1964. *The Role of Pleasure in Behavior.* New York: Harper & Row, Publishers.

Henry, Donald. 1985. "Preagricultural Sedentism: The Natufian Example." In *Prehistoric Hunter-Gatherers: The Emergence of Cultural Complexity,* ed. D. Price and J. Brown, 365–381. New York: Academic Press.

Herdt, Gilbert. 1984a. "Ritualized Homosexual Behavior in the Male Cults of Melanesia 1862–1983: An Introduction." In *Ritualized Homosexuality in Melanesia,* ed. Gilbert Herdt, 1–81. Berkeley: University of California Press.

———. 1984b. "Semen Transactions in Sambia Cultures." In *Ritualized Homosexuality in Melanesia,* ed. Gilbert Herdt, 167–210. Berkeley: University of California Press.

———. 1987. *The Sambia: Ritual and Custom in New Guinea.* New York: Holt, Rinehart and Winston.

———. 1988. "Cross-Cultural Forms of Homosexuality and the Concept of Gay." *Psychiatric Annals* 19(1):37–39.

Herodotus. 1954. *The Histories.* New York: Penguin.

Herskovits, Melville. 1938. *Dahomey: An Ancient West African Kingdom.* 2 vols. Evanston, Ill.: Northwestern University Press.

Hill, Andrew, and Steven Ward. 1988. "Origin of the Hominidae: The Record of African Large Hominoid Evolution Between 14 My and 4 My." *Yearbook of Physical Anthropology* 31:49–83.

Hill, Jane. 1978. "Apes and Language." *Annual Review of Anthropology* 7:89–112.

Hiraiwa-Hasegawa, M., et al. 1986. "Aggression Toward Large Carnivores by Wild Chimpanzees of Mahale Mountains National Park, Tanzania." *Folia Primatologica* 47(1):8–13.

Hirsch, Jerry. 1981. "To Unfrock the Charlatans." *Sage Race Relations Abstracts* 6:1–67.

Hobbes, Thomas. 1960. *Leviathan.* Oxford: Basil Blackwell.

Hoffman, M. A. 1979. *Egypt Before the Pharaohs.* New York: Alfred A. Knopf.

Hogbin, H. I. 1964. *A Guadalcanal Society: The Kaoka Speakers.* New York: Holt, Rinehart and Winston.

Holden, Constance. 1987. "Why Do Women Live Longer Than Men?" *Science* 238:158–160.

Holt, B. M. 1987. "An Analysis of Rates of Change in *Homo erectus* Based on a Cladistic Definition." Paper presented at the Annual Meeting of American Association of Physical Anthropologists.

Hommon, Robert. 1986. "Social Evolution in Ancient Hawai'i." In *Island Societies: Archaeological Approaches to Evolution and Transformation,* ed. Patrick Kirch, 55–69. New York: Cambridge University Press.

Hopkins, Keith. 1980. "Brother-Sister Marriage in Ancient Egypt." *Comparative Studies in Society and History* 22:303–354.

Hosler, Dorothy. 1988. "Ancient West Mexican Metallurgy: South and Central American Origins and West Mexican Transformations." *American Anthropologist* 90:832–835.

Hrdy, Sarah. 1981. *The Woman That Never Evolved.* Cambridge, Mass.: Harvard University Press.

Hunn, Eugene. 1982. "Did the Aztec Lack Potential Animal Domesticates?" *American Ethnologist* 9:578–579.

Hutton, J. H. 1963. *Caste in India: Its Nature, Function, and Origins.* New York: Oxford University Press.

Huxley, Thomas. 1901. "Emancipation—Black and White." In *Science and Education.* New York: Collier.

Imperato-McGinley, Julianne, et al. 1974. "Steroid 5-Alpha-Reductase Deficiency in Man: An Inherited Form of Male Pseudohermaphroditism." *Science* 186:1213–1215.

———. 1979. "Androgens and the Evolution of the Male Gender-Identity among Male Pseudohermaphrodites with 5-Alpha-Reductase Deficiency." *New England Journal of Medicine* 300(22):1233–1237.

Ingmanson, E. J. 1989. "Branch Dragging by Pygmy Chimpanzees at Wamba, Zaire: The

521

Use of Objects to Facilitate Social Communication in the Wild." *American Journal of Physical Anthropology* 78:244.

Isaac, Barry. 1988. "Introduction." In *Prehistoric Economies of the Pacific Northwest Coast*, ed. Barry Isaac, 1–16. Greenwich, Conn.: JAI Press.

Isaac, Glynn. 1984. "The Archaeology of Human Origins: Studies of the Lower Pleistocene in East Africa." *Advances in World Archaeology* 3:1–87.

Itani, J. 1961. "The Society of Japanese Monkeys." *Japan Quarterly* 8:421–430.

Itani, J., and A. Nishimura. 1973. "The Study of Infra-Human Culture in Japan." In *Preindustrial Primate Behavior*, ed. E. W. Menzell, 26–50. Basel: S. Karjer.

Jacobs, Kenneth. 1985. "Climate and the Hominid Post-Cranial Skeleton in Wurm and Early Holocene Europe." *Current Anthropology* 26:512–514.

James, Steven R. 1989. "Hominid Use of Fire in the Lower and Middle Pleistocene: A Review of the Evidence." *Current Anthropology* 31:1–26.

James, W. H. 1980. "Secular Trends in Reported Sperm Counts." *Andrologia* 12:381–388.

Jenike, M. R. 1989. "Seasonal Hunger Among Tropical Africans: The Lese Case." *American Journal of Physical Anthropology* 78:247.

Jensen, A. 1969. "How Much Can We Boost I.Q. and Scholastic Achievement?" *Harvard Educational Review* 29:1–123.

Jerison, H. J. 1973. *Evolution of the Brain and Intelligence.* New York: Academic Press.

Jochim, Michael. 1983. "Paleolithic Cave Art in Ecological Perspective." In *Hunter-Gatherer Economy in Prehistory: A European Perspective*, ed. G. Bailey, 212–219. New York: Cambridge University Press.

Johanson, Donald. 1987. "New Partial Skeleton of *Homo habilis* from Olduvai Gorge, Tanzania." *Nature* 327:205–209.

Johanson, Donald, and Maitland Edey. 1981. *Lucy: The Beginnings of Humankind.* New York: Warner.

Johanson, Donald, and T. D. White. 1979. "A Systematic Assessment of Early African Hominids." *Science* 203:321–330.

Johnson, Allen, and Timothy Earle. 1987. *The Evolution of Human Society: From Foraging Group to Agrarian State.* Stanford: Stanford University Press.

Johnson, W. J. 1988. "Theravada Buddhism in South-East Asia." In *The World's Religions*, ed. Steward Sutherland et al., 726–738. Boston: G. K. Hall.

Jolly, Alison. 1985. *The Evolution of Primate Behavior.* 2nd edition. New York: Macmillan.

Jones, R., and J. Bowler. 1980. "Struggle for the Savanna: Northern Australia in Ecological and Prehistoric Perspective." In *Northern Australia: Options and Implications*, ed. R. Jones, Canberra: Research School of Pacific Studies.

Kamin, L. J. 1974. *The Science and Politics of I.Q.* New York: Halstead Press.

Kang, Elizabeth. 1979. "Exogamy and Peace Relations of Social Units: A Cross-Cultural Test." *Ethnology* 18:85–99.

Kaplan, Marion. 1984. *The Marriage Bargain: Women and Dowries in European History.* New York: Haworth Press and the Institute for Research in History.

Karkal, Malini. 1987. "Differentials in Mortality by Sex." *Economic and Political Weekly* 22(32):1343–1347.

Karoda, S. 1984. "Interaction over Food Among Pygmy Chimpanzees." In *The Pygmy Chimpanzee*, ed. R. L. Susman, 301–324. New York: Plenum Press.

Keeton, William. 1972. *Biological Science.* New York: W. W. Norton.

Keightley, David N. 1978. "The Religious Commitment: Shang Theology and the Genesis of Chinese Political Culture." *History of Religions* 17:211–225.

Kenyon, K. 1981. *Excavations at Jericho.* London: British School of Archaeology in Jerusalem.

Keys, Ancel. 1950. *The Biology of Human Starvation*. Minneapolis: University of Minnesota Press.

Kinzey, Warren G. 1987. *The Evolution of Human Behavior: Primate Models*. Albany: State University of New York Press.

Kirch, Patrick. 1984. *The Evolution of the Polynesian Chiefdoms*. New York: Cambridge University Press.

Kitchen, Philip. 1985. *Vaulting Ambition: Sociobiology and the Quest for Human Nature*. Cambridge, Mass.: M.I.T. Press.

Knauft, Bruce. 1987. "Reconsidering Violence in Simple Societies: Homicide Among the Gebusi of New Guinea." *Current Anthropology* 28:457–500.

Knight, Rolf. 1974. "Grey Owl's Return: Cultural Ecology and Canadian Indigenous Peoples." *Reviews in Anthropology* 1:349–359.

Konner, Melvin. 1982. *The Tangled Wing*. New York: Holt, Rinehart and Winston.

———. 1988. "The Aggressors." *New York Times Magazine*, Aug. 14, 33–34.

Kortlant, A. 1967. "Experimentation with Chimpanzees in the Wild." In *Progress in Primatology*, ed. D. Starck, R. Schneider, and H. Kuhns, 119–139. New York: Plenum Press.

Krishnaji, N. 1987. "Poverty and Sex Ratio: Some Data and Speculations." *Economic and Political Weekly* 22(23):892–897.

Kristiansen, Kristian. 1982. "The Formation of Tribal Systems in Later European Prehistory: Northern Europe 400–500 B.C." In *Theory and Explanation in Archaeology*, ed. Colin Renfrew, M. Rowlands, and B. Segraves, 241–280. New York: Academic Press.

Kroeber, Alfred L. 1948. *Anthropology*. New York: Harcourt Brace.

Kurland, Jeffery. 1988. "Comments on Small." *Current Anthropology* 29:89–90.

Kurtz, Donald. 1987. "The Economics of Urbanization and State Formation at Teotihuacan." *Current Anthropology* 28:329–353.

Kushlare, J. A. 1985. "Vestian Hypothesis of Human Hair Reduction." *Journal of Human Evolution* 14:29–32.

Laitman, Jeffrey. 1985. "Evolution of the Hominid Upper Respiratory Tract: The Fossil Evidence." In *Hominid Evolution: Past, Present and Future*, ed. P. Tabias, 281–286. New York: Alan R. Liss.

Langer, W. 1972. "Checks on Population Growth." *Scientific American* 226(2):92–99.

Langness, L. L. 1967. "Sexual Antagonism in the New Guinea Highlands: A Bene Bene Example." *Oceania* 37:161–177.

———. 1974. "Ritual, Power, and Male Dominance." *Ethos* 2:189–212.

———. 1977. "Ritual Power and Male Domination in the New Guinea Highlands." In *The Anthropology of Power*, ed. R. Fogelson and R. Adams, 3–22. New York: Academic Press.

Langness, L. L., and Terence E. Hays, eds. 1987. *Anthropology in the High Valleys: Essays on the New Guinea Highlands in Honor of Kenneth E. Read*. Novato, Calif.: Chandler & Sharp.

Lanpo, Jia. 1989. "On Problems of the Beijing-Man Site: A Critique of New Implications." *Current Anthropology* 30:200–204.

Leacock, Eleanor Burke. 1975. "The Montagnais-Naskapi Band." In *Cultural Ecology: Readings on the Canadian Indians and Eskimos*, ed. B. Cox, 81–100. Toronto: McClelland and Stewart.

———. 1981. *The Myth of Male Dominance: Collected Articles of Women Cross-Culturally*. New York: Monthly Review Press.

———. 1983. "Ideologies of Male Dominance as Divide and Rule Politics: An Anthropologist's View." In *Woman's Nature*, ed. Marian Lowe and Ruth Hubbard, 111–121. New York: Pergamon Press.

Leakey, L.S.B., P. V. Tobias, and J. R. Napier. 1964. "A New Species of the Genus *Homo* from Olduvai Gorge." *Nature* 202:7–9.

Leakey, L.S.B., and V. M. Goodall. 1969. *Unveiling Man's Origins*. Cambridge, Mass.: Schenkman.

Leakey, Mary. 1979. "Footprints Frozen in Time." *National Geographic* 155:446–457.

Leavitt, Gregory. 1977. "The Frequency of Warfare: An Evolutionary Perspective." *Sociological Inquiry* 47(1):49–58.

————. 1989. "Disappearance of the Incest Taboo." *American Anthropologist* 91:116–131.

Lee, Richard. 1969a. "Eating Christmas in the Kalahari." *Natural History*, Dec., 14–22, 60–63.

————. 1969b. "!Kung Bushman Subsistence: An Input-Output Analysis." In *Environment and Cultural Behavior*, ed. A. P. Vayda, 47–79. Garden City, N.Y.: Natural History Press.

————. 1979. *The !Kung San: Men and Women in a Foraging Society*. Cambridge: Cambridge University Press.

Lessa, William. 1966. *Ulithi: A Micronesian Design for Living*. New York: Holt, Rinehart and Winston.

Lester, David. 1975. "The Fear of Death in Primitive Societies." *Behavior Science Research* 10:229–232.

Lethwaite, James. 1981. "Comment on Gilman 1981." *Current Anthropology* 22:14.

Lewin, Roger. 1984. "Man the Scavenger." *Science* 224:861–862.

————. 1987a. "Africa: Cradle of Modern Humans." *Science* 237:1292–1295.

————. 1987b. "Domino Effect Invoked in Ice Age Extinctions." *Science* 238:1509–1510.

————. 1987c. "The Earliest 'Humans' Were More Like Apes." *Science* 236:1061–1063.

————. 1987d. "My Close Cousin the Chimpanzee." *Science* 238:273–275.

————. 1987e. "The Unmasking of the Mitochondrial Eve." *Science* 238:24–26.

————. 1988a. "Conflict over DNA Clock Results." *Science* 241:1598–2000.

————. 1988b. "DNA Clock Conflict Continues." *Science* 241:1756–1759.

————. 1988c. "Hip Joints: Clues to Bipedalism." *Science* 241:1433.

————. 1988d. "A New Tool Maker in the Hominid Record?" *Science* 240:724–725.

————. 1988e. "New Views Emerge on Hunters and Gatherers." *Science* 240:1146–1148.

————. 1988f. "A Revolution of Ideas in Agricultural Origins." *Science* 240:984–986.

————. 1989a. "Ice Age Art Toppled." *Science* 243:1435.

————. 1989b. "Species Questions in Modern Human Origins." *Science* 243:1666–1667.

Lewontin, R., S. Rose, and L. Kamin. 1984. *Not in Our Genes: Biology, Ideology and Human Nature*. New York: Pantheon.

Liberman, Alvin M., and Ignatius G. Mattingly. 1989. "A Specialization for Speech Perception." *Science* 243:489–494.

Lieberman, Leslie. 1987. "Biocultural Consequences of Animals Versus Plants As Sources of Fat, and Other Nutrients." In *Food and Evolution: Toward a Theory of Human Food Habits*, ed. M. Harris and E. Ross, 225–258. Philadelphia: Temple University Press.

Lieberman, Philip. 1984. *The Biology and Evolution of Language*. Cambridge, Mass.: Harvard University Press.

————. 1985. "On the Evolution of Human Syntactic Ability. Its Pre-adaptive Bases— Motor Control and Speech." *Journal of Human Evolution* 14:657–668.

Lincoln, Bruce. 1981. *Priests, Warriors, and Cattle: A Study in the Ecology of Religions*. Berkeley: University of California Press.

Lindenbaum, Shirley. 1979. *Kuru Sorcery: Disease and Danger in the New Guinea Highlands.* Palo Alto, Calif.: Mayfield.

Livingstone, F. 1969. "Genetics, Ecology, and the Origins of Incest and Exogamy." *Current Anthropology* 10:45–62.

Lizot, Jaques. 1977. "Population, Resources and Warfare Among the Yanomamo." *Man* 12:497–517.

———. 1979. "On Food Taboos and Amazon Cultural Ecology." *Current Anthropology* 20:150–151.

———. 1985. *Tales of the Yanomami: Daily Life in the Venezuelan Forest.* New York: Cambridge University Press.

Lockard, Denyse. 1986. "The Lesbian Community: An Anthropological Approach." In *Anthropology and Homosexual Behavior,* ed. Evelyn Blackwood, 83–96. New York: Haworth Press.

Loewe, Michael. 1982. *Chinese Ideas of Life and Death: Faith, Myth and Reason in the Han Period (202 B.C.–A.D. 220).* London: George Allen & Unwin Ltd.

Lovejoy, Owen C. 1981. "The Origin of Man." *Science* 211:341–350.

———. 1988. "Evolution of Human Walking." *Scientific American* 259(5):118–125.

Lowie, Robert. 1948. *Primitive Religion.* New York: Liveright.

McGrew, W. C. 1977. "Socialization and Object Manipulation of Wild Chimpanzees." In *Primate Bio-Social Development,* ed. Susan Chevalier-Skolinkoff and Frank Poirier, 261–288. New York: Garland Publishing.

———. 1987. "Tools to Get Food: The Subsistence of Tansmanian Aborigines and Tanzanian Chimpanzees Compared." *Journal of Anthropological Research* 43:247–258.

McGrew, W. C., and C. E. Tutin. 1973. "Chimpanzee Tool Use in Dental Grooming." *Nature* 241:477–478.

McKnight, David. 1986. "Fighting in an Australian Supercamp." In *The Anthropology of Violence,* ed. David Riches, 136–163. New York: Basil Blackwell.

Maclachlan, Morgan. 1983. *Why They Did Not Starve: Biocultural Adaptation in a South Indian Village.* Philadelphia: Institute for the Study of Human Issues.

MacNeish, R. 1978. *The Science of Archaeology?* Belmont, Calif.: Duxbury Press.

Maddin, Robert, ed. 1988. *The Beginning of the Use of Metal and Alloys.* Cambridge, Mass.: M.I.T. Press.

Malinowski, Bronislaw. 1929. *The Sexual Life of Savages.* New York: Harcourt Brace and World.

———. 1935. *Coral Gardens and Their Magic.* London: George Allen & Unwin Ltd.

Malkenson, Frederich, and J. Keane. 1983. "Radiobiology of the Skin." In *Biochemistry and Physiology of the Skin,* ed. Lowell Goldsmith, 769–814. New York: Oxford University Press.

Malo, D. 1951. *Hawaiian Antiquities.* Bishop Museum Special Publication 2, Special Edition. Translated from the Hawai'ian by Dr. N. B. Emerson. Honolulu: B. P. Bishop Museum Press.

Mamdani, M. 1973. *The Myth of Population Control.* New York: Monthly Review Press.

Marcus, Joyce. 1983. "Lowland Maya Archaeology at the Crossroads." *American Antiquity* 48:454–488.

———. 1984. Reply to Hammond and Andrews. *American Antiquity* 49:829–833.

Marshack, Alexander. 1976. "Some Implications of the Paleolithic: Symbolic Evidence for the Origin of Language." *Current Anthropology* 17:274–282.

———. 1985. *Hierarchical Evolution of the Human Capacity: The Paleolithic Evidence.* New York: American Museum of Natural History.

————. 1989. "The Evolution of the Human Capacity: The Symbolic Evidence." *Yearbook of Physical Anthropology*. In press.

Marshall, Donald. 1971. "Sexual Behavior on Mangaia." In *Human Sexual Behavior,* ed. D. Marshall and R. Suggs, 103–162. Englewood Cliffs, N.J.: Prentice-Hall.

Martin, Paul. 1984. "Prehistoric Overkill: The Global Model." In *Quaternary Extinctions: A Prehistoric Revolution,* ed. P. S. Martin and R. Klein, 354–403. Tucson: University of Arizona Press.

Martin, Roy, and Barbara Mullen. 1987. "Control of Food Intake: Mechanisms and Consequences." *Nutrition Today,* Sept./Oct., 4–10.

Marzke, Mary, J. Longhill, and S. Rasmussen. 1988. "Gluteus Maximus Muscle Function and the Origin of Hominid Bipedality." *American Journal of Physical Anthropology* 77:519–528.

Mascia-Lees, Frances E., John Relethford, and Tom Sorger. 1986. "Evolutionary Perspectives on Permanent Breast Enlargement in Human Females." *American Anthropologist* 88:423–428.

Mason, J. A. 1957. *The Ancient Civilizations of Peru.* London: Penguin.

Mason, J. W., et al. 1969. "Urinary Androsterone, Etiocholanolone, and Dehydroepiandrosterone Responses to 72-Hour Avoidance Sessions in the Monkey." *Osychosomatic Medicine* 30:710–720.

Mazur, Allan. 1983. "Hormones, Aggression, and Dominance in Hawaii." In *Hormones and Aggressive Behavior,* ed. Bruce Svare, 563–576. New York: Plenum Press.

Mead, Margaret. 1928. *Coming of Age in Samoa.* New York: American Museum of Natural History.

Meggitt, Mervyn. 1977. *Blood Is Their Argument: Warfare Among the Mae Enga Tribesmen of the New Guinea Highlands.* Palo Alto, Calif.: Mayfield.

Mei, Yi-Pao. 1934. *Motse, the Neglected Rival of Confucius.* London: Arthur Probsthain.

Mellaart, James. 1967. *Çatal Hüyük: A Neolithic Town in Anatolia.* New York: McGraw-Hill.

————. 1975. *The Earliest Civilizations in the Near East.* London: Thames and Hudson.

Mellars, Paul. 1985. "The Ecological Basis of Social Complexity in the Upper Paleolithic of Southwestern France." In *Prehistoric Hunter-Gatherers: The Emergence of Cultural Complexity,* ed. D. Price and J. Brown, 271–297. New York: Academic Press.

————. 1989. "Major Issues in the Emergence of Modern Humans." *Current Anthropology* 30:349–385.

Mellars, P., and C. Stringer, eds. 1989. *The Human Revolution: Behavioral and Biological Perspectives on the Origins of Modern Humans.* Edinburgh: Edinburgh University Press.

Mencius. 1970. *The Works of Mencius.* Translated by James Legge. New York: Dover.

Menzel, E. W., Jr., E. S. Savage-Rumbaugh, and J. Lawson. 1985. "Chimpanzee (*Pan troglodytes*) Spatial Problem Solving with the Use of Mirrors and Televised Equivalents of Mirrors." *Journal of Comparative Psychology* 99:211–217.

Metropolitan Life Insurance Company. 1988a. "Women's Longevity Advantage Declines." *Statistical Bulletin* 69(1):18–23.

————. 1988b. "New Longevity Record in the United States." *Statistical Bulletin* 69(3):10–15.

Miller, Barbara. 1981. *The Endangered Sex: Neglect of Female Children in Rural North India.* Ithaca, N.Y.: Cornell University Press.

————. 1987a. "Female Infanticide and Child Neglect in Rural North India." In *Child Survival,* ed. Nancy Scheper-Hughes, 95–112. Boston: D. Reidel.

————. 1987b. "Wife-beating in India: Variations on a Theme." Paper read at the Annual Meetings of the American Anthropological Association, Nov. 1987.

526

Miller, D., and S. Parsonage. 1975. "Resistance to Slimming: Adaptation or Illusion?" *Lancet,* April 5, 773–775.

Miller, G. H., and D. R. Gerstein. 1983. *Public Health Reports* 98:343–352.

Mintz, Sydney. 1985. *Sweetness and Power.* New York: Viking Penguin.

Mitchell, D., and L. Donald. 1988. "Archaeology and the Study of Northwest Coast Economies." In *Prehistoric Economies of the Pacific Northwest Coast,* ed. Barry Isaac, 293–351. Greenwich, Conn.: JAI Press.

Miyadi, D. 1967. "Differences in Social Behavior Among Japanese Macaque Troops." In *Progress in Primatology,* ed. D. Starck, R. Schneider, and H. Kuhn. Stuttgart: Gustav Fischer.

Miyamoto, Michael, Jerry Slightom, and Morris Goodman. 1987. "Phylogenetic Relations of Human and African Apes from DNA Sequences." *Science* 238:369–373.

Molnar, S. 1983. *Human Variation: Races, Types, and Ethnic Groups.* Englewood Cliffs, N.J.: Prentice-Hall.

Money, J., and A. Ehrhardt. 1972. *Man and Woman, Boy and Girl.* Baltimore: Johns Hopkins University Press.

Montagna, W. 1985. "The Evolution of Human Skin." *Journal of Human Evolution* 14:3–22.

Montagu, Ashley. 1974. *Man's Most Dangerous Myth: The Fallacy of Race.* New York: Oxford University Press.

Moore, A. 1985. "The Development of Neolithic Societies in the Near East." *Advances in World Archaeology* 4:1–69.

Morren, George. 1984. "Warfare in the Highland Fringe of New Guinea: The Case of the Mountain O.K." In *Warfare, Culture and Environment,* ed. Brian Ferguson, 169–208. Orlando, Fla.: Academic Press.

———. 1986a. "No Need to Doubt Cannibalism in New Guinea," letter to the editor. *New York Times,* Aug. 3.

———. 1986b. *The Miyanmin: Human Ecology of a Papua New Guinea Society.* Ann Arbor: UMI Research Press.

Morris, C. 1976. "Master Design of the Inca." *Natural History,* Oct., 58–67.

Morris, Desmond. 1967. *The Naked Ape: A Zoologist's Study of the Human Animal.* New York: McGraw-Hill.

Morrison, David C. 1988. "Marine Mammals Join the Navy." *Science* 242:1503–1504.

Mosely, M. 1982. *Chan Chan: Andean Desert City.* Albuquerque: University of New Mexico Press.

Mo Tse. *See* Mei, Yi-Pao.

Mull, Dorothy, and J. Dennis Mull. 1987. "Infanticide Among the Tarahumara of the Mexican Sierra Madre." In *Child Survival,* ed. Nancy Scheper-Hughes, 113–132. Boston: D. Reidel.

Murdock, George. 1937. "Comparative Data on the Division of Labor by Sex." *Social Forces* 15:551–553.

———. 1967. *Ethnographic Atlas.* Pittsburgh: University of Pittsburgh Press.

Nag, Moni, Benjamin White, and Robert Peet. 1978. "An Anthropological Approach to the Study of the Economic Value of Children in Java and Nepal." *Current Anthropology* 19:239–306.

Nag, Moni, and N. Kak. 1984. "Demographic Transition in the Punjab Village." *Population and Development Review* 10:661–678.

Nanda, Serena. 1986. "The Hijras of India: Cultural and Individual Dimensions of an Institutionalized Third Gender Role." In *Anthropology and Homosexual Behavior,* ed. Evelyn Blackwood, 35–54. New York: Haworth Press.

National Center for Health Statistics. 1987. Publication (PHS) 87-1688. Hyattsville, Md.

Needham, Joseph, et al. 1986. *Science and Civilization in China*. Vol. 5, *Military Technology: The Gunpowder Epic*. Cambridge: Cambridge University Press.

Newman, R. W. 1970. "Why Is Man Such a Sweaty, Thirsty, Naked Animal?" *Human Biology* 42:12–27.

Nishida, Toshisada. 1973. "The Ant-Gathering Behavior by the Use of Tools Among Wild Chimpanzees of the Mahale Mountains." *Journal of Human Evolution* 2:357–370.

Nishida, Toshisada, and Kenji Kawanaka. 1985. "Within-Group Cannibalism by Adult Male Chimpanzees." *Primates* 2(3):274–284.

O'Connell, James F., Kristen Hawkes, and Nicholas Blurton Jones. 1988. "Hadza Scavenging: Implications for Plio/Pleistocene Hominid Subsistence." *Current Anthropology* 29:356–363.

O'Grady, Richard T., et al. 1989. "Genes and Tongues," letter to the editor. *Science* 243:1651.

Oliver, Douglas. 1955. *A Solomon Island Society: Kinship and Leadership Among the Sivai of Bougainville*. Cambridge, Mass.: Harvard University Press.

Ortiz de Montellano, B. R. 1983. "Counting Skulls: Comment on the Aztec Cannibalism Theory of Harner-Harris." *American Anthropologist* 85:403–406.

Pagels, Elaine. 1981. *The Gnostic Gospels*. New York: Vintage Books.

Pardue, Peter. 1967. "Buddhism." *Encyclopedia of the Social Sciences*, 165–184. New York: Crowell, Collier and Macmillan.

Pareti, Luigi. 1965. *The Ancient World: 1200 B.C. to A.D. 500: History of Mankind*. New York: Harper & Row, Publishers.

Parker, Sue. 1985. "A Social-Technological Model for the Evolution of Language." *Current Anthropology* 26:617–639.

Parker, S., and H. Parker. 1979. "The Myth of Male Superiority: Rise and Demise." *American Anthropologist* 81:289–309.

Patterson, Francine. 1981. *The Education of Koko*. New York: Holt, Rinehart and Winston.

Pearson, Richard. 1983. "The Ch'ing-lien-kang Culture and the Chinese Neolithic." In *The Origins of Chinese Civilization*, ed. David Keightley, 119–145. Berkeley: University of California Press.

Peletz, Michael G. 1987. "Female Heirship and the Autonomy of Women in Negeri Sembilan, West Malaysia." In *Research in Economic Anthropology: A Research Annual*. Vol. 8, ed. Barry L. Isaac, 61–101. Greenwich, Conn.: JAI Press.

Pennington, Renee, and Henry Harpending. 1988. "Fitness and Fertility Among Kalahari !Kung." *American Journal of Physical Anthropology* 77:303–319.

Percival, L., and K. Quinkert. 1987. "Anthropometric Factors." In *Sex Differences in Human Performance*, ed. Mary Baker, 121–139. New York: John Wiley & Sons.

Perry, W. J. 1923. *Children of the Sun*. London: Methuen.

Persky, Harold. 1987. *Psychoendocrinology of Human Sexual Behavior*. New York: Praeger.

Pfeiffer, John F. 1982. *The Creative Explosion: An Enquiry into the Origins of Art and Religion*. New York: Harper & Row, Publishers.

Pierson, Ruth R. 1987. " 'Did Your Mother Wear Army Boots?' Feminist Theory and Women's Relation to War, Peace and Revolution." In *Images of Women in Peace and War: Cross-Cultural and Historical Perspectives*, ed. Sharon Macdonald, P. Holden, and S. Ardener, 205–227. Madison, Wis.: University of Wisconsin Press.

Pilbeam, David. 1985. "Patterns of Hominoid Evolution." In *Ancestors: The Hard Evidence*, ed. Eric Delson, 51–59. New York: Alan R. Liss.

Podolefsky, Aaron. 1984. "Contemporary Warfare in the New Guinea Highlands." *Ethnology* 23:73–87.

Polanyi, Karl. 1957. "The Economy as Instituted Process." In *Trade and Markets in the Early*

Empires, ed. K. Polanyi, C. Arensberg, and H. Pearson, 243–270. New York: Free Press.

Potash, Betty. 1986. "Widows in Africa: An Introduction." In *Widows in African Societies: Choices and Constraints,* ed. Betty Potash, 1–43. Stanford: Stanford University Press.

Potter, Sulamith. 1977. *Family Life in a Northern Thai Village: A Study in the Structural Significance of Women.* Berkeley: University of California Press.

Premack, David. 1971. "On the Assessment of Language Competence in the Chimpanzee." In *The Behavior of Nonhuman Primates.* Vol. 4, ed. A. M. Schrier and F. Stollnitz, 185–228. New York: Academic Press.

———. 1976. *Intelligence in Ape and Man.* Hillsdale, N.J.: Earlbaum.

———. 1983. "The Codes of Man and Beast." *The Behavioral and Brain Sciences* 6:125–167.

Price, Douglas, and James Brown, eds. 1985. *Prehistoric Hunter-Gatherers: The Emergence of Cultural Complexity.* New York: Academic Press.

Purifoy, F. E., and L. H. Koopmans. 1980. "Androstenedione, T and Free T Concentrations in Women of Various Occupations." *Social Biology* 26:179–188.

Rambaugh, D. M. 1977. *Language Learning by a Chimpanzee: The Lana Project.* New York: Academic Press.

Rancour-Laferriere, D. 1985. *Signs of the Flesh: An Essay on the Evolution of Hominid Sexuality.* Berlin: Mouton de Gruyter.

Rappaport, Roy. 1987. *Pigs for the Ancestors: Ritual in the Ecology of a New Guinea People.* 2nd edition. New Haven: Yale University Press.

Rasmussen, Knud. 1929. *The Intellectual Culture of the Iglulik Eskimo. Report of the Fifth Thule Expedition.* Copenhagen: Glydendal.

Read, K. 1982. "Male-Female Relationships Among the Gahuku-Gama: 1950 and 1981." *Social Analysis* 12:66–78.

———. 1984. "The Nama Cult Recalled." In *Ritualized Homosexuality in Melanesia,* ed. G. Herdt, 211–247. Berkeley: University of California Press.

Redford, Kent, et al. n.d. "The Relationship Between Foraging and Insectivory in Primates." Unpublished paper.

Reinisch, June, and W. G. Karow. 1977. "Prenatal Exposure to Synthetic Progestin and Estrogens: Effects on Human Development." *Archives of Sexual Behavior* 6:257–288.

Reiss, Nira. 1985. *Speech Acts Taxonomy as a Tool for Ethnographic Description: An Analysis Based on Videotapes of Continuous Behavior in Two New York Households.* Philadelphia: John Benjamins.

Reitz, Elizabeth. 1988. "Faunal Remains from Paloma, an Archaic Site in Peru." *American Anthropologist* 88:311–322.

Remillard, G. M., et al. 1983. "Sexual Manifestations Predominate in a Woman with Temporal Lobe Epilepsy: A Finding Suggesting Sexual Dimorphism in the Human Brain." *Neurology* 33:3–30.

Rice, Patricia, and A. Patterson. 1986. "Validating the Cave Art—Archaeofaunal Relationship in Cantabrian Spain." *American Anthropologist* 88:658–667.

Richards, Audrey. 1939. *Land, Labour, and Diet in Northern Rhodesia.* London.

Richards, M., J. Bernal, and Y. Brackbill. 1976. "Early Behavioral Differences: Gender or Circumcision?" *Developmental Psychology* 9:89–95.

Ridgway, Sam. 1989. "Navy Marine Mammals." *Science* 243:875.

Rindos, David. 1984. *The Origins of Agriculture: An Evolutionary Perspective.* Orlando, Fla.: Academic Press.

Rivière, C. 1987. "Soul: Concepts in Primitive Religions." In *The Encyclopedia of Religion,* 426–430. New York: Macmillan and Free Press.

Robarchek, Clayton A., and Robert Knox Dentan. 1987. "Blood Drunkenness and the

Bloodthirsty Semai: Unmaking Another Anthropological Myth." *American Anthropologist* 89:356–365.

Robertshaw, David. 1985. "Sweat and Heat Exchange in Man and Other Mammals." *Journal of Human Evolution* 14:63–73.

Rolls, Barbara, et al. 1986. "Human Thirst: The Control of Water Intake in Healthy Men." In *The Physiology of Thirst and Sodium Appetite,* ed. G. de Caro, A. Epstein, and M. Massi, 521–526. New York: Plenum Press.

Roosevelt, Anna. 1987. "Chiefdoms in the Amazon and Orinoco." In *Chiefdoms in the Americas,* ed. R. Drennan and C. Uribe, 153–185. Lanham, Md.: University Press of America.

Rose, Robert M., et al. 1975. "Androgens and Aggression: A Review of Recent Findings in Primates." In *Primate Aggression, Territoriality and Xenophobia,* ed. Ralph Holloway, 275–305. New York: Academic Press.

Rotberg, Robert, and Theodore Rabb. 1985. *Hunger and History: The Impact of Changing Food Production and Consumption Patterns on Society.* New York: Cambridge University Press.

Routtenberg, Aryeh. 1980. *Biology of Reinforcement: Facets of Brain-Stimulation Reward.* New York: Academic Press.

Rozin, P., and D. Schiller. 1980. "The Nature and Acquisition of a Preference for Chili Peppers by Humans." *Motivation and Emotion* 4:77–101.

Russel, A., et al., eds. 1987. *The Guinness Book of World Records.* New York: Bantam Books.

Sahagún, Bernadino de. 1951. *General History of the Things of New Spain: The Ceremonies.* Salt Lake City: University of Utah Press.

Sahlins, M. 1963. "Poor Man, Rich Man, Big Man, Chief." *Comparative Studies in Society and History* 5:285–303.

Salter, Mary Jo. 1980. "Annie, Don't Get Your Gun." *Atlantic,* June, 83–86.

Sanday, Peggy. 1981. *Female Power and Male Dominance: On the Origins of Sexual Inequality.* New York: Cambridge University Press.

Sanders, William, R. Santley, and J. Parsons. 1979. *The Basin of Mexico: Ecological Processes in the Evolution of a Civilization.* New York: Academic Press.

Sanders, William, and David Webster. 1988. "The Mesoamerican Urban Tradition." *American Anthropologist* 90:521–546.

Sankar, Andrea. 1986. "Sisters and Brothers, Lovers and Enemies: Marriage Resistance in Southern Kuangtung." In *Anthropology and Homosexual Behavior,* ed. Evelyn Blackwood, 69–81. New York: Haworth Press.

Sapir, Edward. 1921. *Language: An Introduction to the Study of Speech.* New York: Harcourt Brace.

Sarich, Vincent. 1974. "Just How Old Is the Hominid Line?" *Yearbook of Physical Anthropology* 17:98–112.

Savage-Rumbaugh, Sue, and Beverly Wilkerson. 1978. "Socio-sexual Behavior in *Pan paniscus* and *Pan troglodytes:* A Comparative Study." *Journal of Human Evolution* 7:327–344.

Scheper-Hughes, Nancy. 1984. "Infant Mortality and Infant Care: Cultural and Economic Constraints on Nurturing in Northwest Brazil." *Social Science and Medicine* 19(5):535–546.

———. 1987. "Culture, Scarcity, and Maternal Thinking: Mother Love and Child Death in Northeast Brazil." In *Child Survival,* ed. Nancy Scheper-Hughes, 187–208. Boston: D. Reidel.

Schlegel, Alice, ed. 1977. *Sexual Stratification: A Cross-Cultural View.* New York: Columbia University Press.

Schlegel, Alice, and Herbert Barry III. 1986. "The Cultural Consequences of Female Contribution to Subsistence." *American Anthropologist* 88:142–150.

Schlegel, Alice, and R. Eloul. 1988. "Marriage Transactions: Labor, Property and Status." *American Anthropologist* 90:291–309.

Scott, Joan, and Louis Tilley. 1975. "Women's Work and Family in Nineteenth Century Europe." *Comparative Studies in Society and History* 17:36–64.

Scrimshaw, Susan. 1983. "Infanticide as Deliberate Fertility Regulation." In *Determinants of Fertility in Developing Nations: Supply and Demand for Children,* ed. R. Bulatao and R. Lee, 245–266. New York: Academic Press.

Sebeok, T., and J. Umiker-Sebeok. 1980. *Speaking of Apes.* New York: Plenum Press.

Shanor, K. 1978. *The Shanor Study: The Sexual Sensitivity of the American Male.* New York: Dial Press.

Shapiro, Judith. 1971. *Sex Roles and Social Structure Among the Yanomamo Indians.* Ph.D. dissertation, Columbia University.

Sharff, Jagna. 1980. *Life on Dolittle Street: How Poor People Purchase Immortality.* Final report, Hispanic Study Project No. 9, Department of Anthropology, Columbia University.

———. 1981. "Free Enterprise and the Ghetto Family." *Psychology Today,* March, 40–48.

Sharma, Ursula. 1983. "Dowry in North India: Its Consequences for Women." In *Women and Property, Women as Property,* ed. Renee Hirschon, 62–74. London: Croom Helm.

Shepher, J. 1983. *Incest: A Biosocial View.* New York: Academic Press.

Shipman, Pat. 1986. "Scavenging or Hunting in Early Hominids: Theoretical Framework and Tests." *American Anthropologist* 88:27–43.

Shostak, Marjorie. 1981. *Nisa: The Life and Words of a !Kung Woman.* Cambridge, Mass.: Harvard University Press.

Shoumatoff, Alex. 1985. *The Mountain of Names: A History of the Human Family.* New York: Simon and Schuster.

Silk, Joan. 1987. "Primatological Perspectives on Gender Hierarchies." Paper prepared for symposium no. 103, Wenner-Gren Foundation for Anthropological Research, an International Symposium, "Gender Hierarchies," Jan. 10–18, 1987.

Simons, Elwyn L. 1985. "Origins and Characteristics of the First Hominids." In *Ancestors: The Hard Evidence,* ed. Eric Delson, 37–41. New York: Alan R. Liss.

Sims, E., and E. Danforth. 1987. "Expenditure and Storage of Energy in Man." *Journal of Clinical Investigation* 79:1019–1025.

Singer, Barry, and Frederick Toates. 1987. "Sexual Motivation." *The Journal of Sex Research* 23(4):481–501.

Singer, R., and J. Wymer. 1982. *The Middle Stone Age at Klasies River Mouth in South Africa.* Chicago: University of Chicago Press.

Skinner, B. F. 1984. "An Operant Analysis of Problem Solving." *The Behavioral and Brain Sciences* 7:583–613.

Skinner, G. William. 1987. "Gender and Power in Japanese Families: Consequences for Reproductive Behavior and Longevity." Paper prepared for symposium no. 103, Wenner-Gren Foundation for Anthropological Research, an International Symposium, "Gender Hierarchies," Jan. 10–18, 1987.

Small, Meredith F. 1988. "Female Primate Sexual Behavior and Conception." *Current Anthropology* 29:81–100.

Smith, Curtis. 1985. *Ancestral Voices: Language and the Evolution of Human Consciousness.* Englewood Cliffs, N.J.: Prentice-Hall.

Smith, E. G. 1933. *The Diffusion of Culture.* London: Watts.

Smith, Robert L. 1984. "Human Sperm Competition." In *Sperm Competition and the Evolution of Animal Mating Systems,* 602–652. New York: Academic Press.

Soffer, Olga. 1985. *Upper Paleolithic of the Central Russian Plain.* Orlando, Fla.: Academic Press.

Solecki, Ralph. 1971. *Shanidar: The First Flower People*. New York: Alfred A. Knopf.

Sorenson, R. 1972. "Socio-Ecological Change Among the Fore of New Guinea." *Current Anthropology* 15:67–72.

Sorokin, Pitirim. 1975. *Hunger as a Factor in Human Affairs*. Gainesville, Fla.: University Presses of Florida.

Speck, Frank. 1915. "The Family Hunting Band as the Basis of the Algonkian Organization." *American Anthropologist* 17:289–305.

Spencer, B., and F. Gillen. 1968. *The Native Tribes of Central Australia*. New York: Dover.

Speth, J. 1987. "Early Hominid Subsistence Strategies in Seasonal Habitats." *Journal of Archaeological Science* 14:13–29.

Sponsel, Leslie. 1986. "Amazon Ecology and Adaptation." *Annual Review of Anthropology* 15:67–97.

Spuhler, J. N. 1988. "Evolution of Mitochondrial DNA in Monkeys, Apes and Humans." *Yearbook of Physical Anthropology* 31:15–48.

Staden, Hans. 1929. *The True History of His Captivity*. (Original edition, 1557.) New York: Robert McBride.

Stager, Lawrence, and Samuel Wolff. 1984. "Child Sacrifice at Carthage—Religious Rite or Population Control?" *Biblical Archaeology Review* 10:30–51.

Stahl, Ann. 1984. "Hominid Dietary Selection Before Fire." *Current Anthropology* 25:151–168.

Steiner, J. 1979. "Human Facial Expression in Response to Taste and Smell Stimulation." *Advances in Child Development and Behavior* 13:257–295.

Stevens, William. 1986. "Prehistoric Society: A New Picture Emerges." *New York Times*. Dec. 16, 17, 22.

Stringer, Chris B. 1984. "Human Adaptation and Biological Adaptation in the Pleistocene." In *Hominid Evolution and Community Ecology*, ed. R. Foley, 53–83. Orlando, Fla.: Academic Press.

———. 1988. "The Dates of Eden." *Nature* 331:565–566.

Stringer, Chris B., and Peter Andrews. 1988a. "Genetic and Fossil Evidence for the Origins of Modern Humans." *Science* 239:1263–1268.

———. 1988b. Response to Wolpoff's letter. *Science* 241:773–774.

Sudarkasa, N. 1973. *Where Women Work: A Study of Yoruba Women in the Marketplace and in the Home*. Ann Arbor: University of Michigan Museum.

Sullivan, Lawrence. 1987. "Supreme Beings." In *The Encyclopedia of Religion*. vol. 14, 166–181. New York: Macmillan and Free Press.

Susman, Randall, ed. 1984. *The Pygmy Chimpanzee: Evolutionary Biology and Behavior*. New York: Plenum Press.

———. 1987. "Pygmy Chimpanzees and Common Chimpanzees: Models for the Behavioral Ecology of the Earliest Hominid." In *The Evolution of Human Behavior: Primate Models*. ed. G. Warren and G. Kinzey, 72–86. Albany: State University of New York Press.

———. 1988. "Hand of *Paranthropus robustus* from Member 1, Swartkrans: Fossil Evidence for Tool Behavior." *Science* 240:781–784.

Tainter, J. 1988. *The Collapse of Complex Societies*. New York: Cambridge University Press.

Tanner, Nancy. 1974. "Matrifocality in Indonesia and Africa and Among Black Americans." In *Woman, Culture and Nature*, ed. Michelle Z. Rosaldo and Louise Lamphere, 129–156. Stanford: Stanford University Press.

———. 1983. "Hunters, Gatherers, and Sex Roles in Space and Time." *American Anthropologist* 85:335–341.

Tefft, Stanton. 1975. "Warfare Regulation: A Cross-Cultural Test of Hypotheses." In *War:*

Its Causes and Correlates, ed. Martin Nettleship et al., 693–712. Hawthorne, N.Y.: Mouton de Gruyter.

Teliki, G. 1981. "The Omnivorous Diet and Eclectic Feeding Habits of Chimpanzees in Gombe National Park, Tanzania." In *Omnivorous Primates: Gathering and Hunting in Human Evolution,* ed. G. Teleki and S. O. Harding, 305–343. New York: Columbia University Press.

Terrace, Herbert. 1981. *Nim: A Chimpanzee Who Learned Sign Language.* New York: Washington Square Press.

Tertullian. 1984. Quoted in Lawrence Stager and Samuel Wolff, "Child Sacrifice at Carthage —Religious Rite or Population Control?" *Biblical Archeology Review* 10:30–51.

Testart, Alain. 1982. "The Significance of Food-Storage Among Hunter-Gatherers: Residence Patterns, Population Densities and Social Inequalities." *Current Anthropology* 23:523–537.

———. 1988. "Some Major Problems in the Social Anthropology of Hunter-Gatherers." *Current Anthropology* 29:1–31.

Thomas, Elizabeth. 1959. *The Harmless People.* New York: Alfred A. Knopf.

Thompson-Handler, Nancy, Richard K. Malenky, and N. Badrian. 1984. "Sexual Behavior of *Pan paniscus* Under Natural Conditions in the Lomako Forest." In *The Pygmy Chimpanzee,* ed. R. Susman, 347–368. New York: Plenum Press.

Tigay, J. 1982. *The Evolution of the Gilgamesh Epic.* Philadelphia: University of Pennsylvania Press.

Tobias, Sheila. 1978. *Overcoming Math Anxiety.* New York: Norton.

Toth, Nicholas, and K. Schick. 1986. "The First Million Years: The Archaeology of Protohuman Culture." *Archaeology Method and Theory* 9:1–96.

Trigger, Bruce. 1978. "Iroquois Matriliny." *Pennsylvania Archaeologist* 48:55–65.

Trinkaus, E. 1983. "Neanderthal Postcrania and the Adaptive Shift to Modern Humans." In *The Mousterian Legacy: Human Biocultural Change in the Upper Pleistocene.* BAR S164, ed. E. Trinkhaus, 165–200. Oxford: British Archaeological Reports.

———. 1986. "The Neanderthals and Modern Human Origins." *Annual Review of Anthropology* 15:193–218.

Turnbull, Colin M. 1965. *Wayward Servants: The Two Worlds of the African Pygmies.* Garden City, N.Y.: The Natural History Press.

———. 1982. "The Ritualization of Potential Conflict Between the Sexes Among the Mbuti." In *Politics and History in Band Societies,* ed. Eleanor Leacock and Richard Lee, 133–155. Cambridge: Cambridge University Press.

Turner, Christy, II. 1989. "Teeth and Prehistory in Asia." *Scientific American* 260(2):88–96.

Tuttle, Russell. 1969. "Knuckle-Walking and the Problem of Human Origins." *Science* 166:953–961.

Tylor, Edward R. 1871. *Primitive Culture.* London: J. Murray.

———. 1888. "On a Method of Investigating the Development of Institutions; Applied to Laws of Marriage and Descent." *Journal of the Royal Anthropological Institute* 18:245–269.

Unger-Hamilton, Romana. 1989. "The Epi-Paleolithic Southern Levant and the Origin of Cultivation." *Current Anthropology* 30:88–103.

Vaidyanathan, A., N. Nair, and M. Harris. 1982. "Bovine Sex and Age Ratios in India." *Current Anthropology* 23:365–383.

Valenstein, Elliot S. 1973. *Brain Control: A Critical Examination of Brain Stimulation and Psychosurgery.* New York: John Wiley & Sons.

Valladas, H., et al. 1988. "Thermoluminescence Dating of Mousterian 'Proto–Cro Magnon' Remains from Israel and the Origin of Modern Man." *Nature* 331:614–616.

Van Allen, J. 1972. "Sitting on a Man: Colonialism and the Lost Political Institutions of Igbo Women." *Canadian Journal of African Studies* 6(2):165–182.

Van Baaren, Thomas P. 1987. "Afterlife: Geographies of Death." In *The Encyclopedia of Religion*, vol. 1, 107–120. New York: Macmillan and Free Press.

Van Lawick-Goodall, Jane. 1968. "Tool-Using Bird: The Egyptian Vulture." *National Geographic* 133:630–641.

————. 1986. *The Chimpanzees of Gombe*. Cambridge, Mass.: Harvard University Press.

Veblen, Thorstein. 1934. *Theory of the Leisure Class*. New York: Modern Library.

Vickers, William. 1988. "Game Depletion Hypothesis of Amazonian Adaptation: Data from a Native Community." *Science* 239:1521–1522.

Villa, Paola, et al. 1986. "Cannibalism in the Neolithic." *Science* 233:431–437.

Vining, Daniel. 1985. "Social Versus Reproductive Success: The Central Theoretical Problems of Sociobiology." *Behavioral and Brain Sciences* 9:167–216.

Voigt, Mary. 1986. Review of T. Young, P. Smith, and I. Mortensen, eds., *The Hilly Flanks and Beyond*. *Paleorient* 12(1):52–53.

Waal, Frans de. 1983. *Chimpanzee Politics*. New York: Harper & Row, Publishers.

————. 1988. *Peacemaking Among Primates*. Cambridge, Mass.: Harvard University Press.

Wachter, K. 1980. "Ancestors at the Norman Conquest." In *Genealogical Demography*. ed. B. Dyke and W. Morrill, 85–93. New York: Academic Press.

Wagner, Roy. 1987. "Totemism." In *The Encyclopedia of Religion*, vol. 14, 573–576. New York: Macmillan and Free Press.

Waldron, Ingrid. 1976. "Why Do Women Live Longer Than Men?" *Social Science and Medicine* 10:349–362.

————. 1982. "An Analysis of Causes of Sex Differences in Mortality and Morbidity." In *The Fundamental Connection Between Nature and Nurture*, ed. W. R. Grove and G. R. Carpenter, 69–116, Lexington, Mass.: Lexington Books.

Wallace, A. 1966. *Religion: An Anthropological View*. New York: Random House.

————. 1976. "Why Do Women Live Longer Than Men?" *Social Science and Medicine* 10:349–362.

Ward, Steven, and Andrew Hill. 1987. "Pliocene Hominid Partial Mandible from Tabarin, Baringo, Kenya." *American Journal of Physical Anthropology* 72:21–37.

Warner, W. L. 1958. *A Black Civilization*. New York: Harper & Row, Publishers.

Waterlow, J. C. 1986. "Metabolic Adaptation to Low Intakes of Energy and Protein." *Annual Review of Nutrition* 6:495.

Wax, Murray. 1984. "Religion as Universal: Tribulations of an Anthropological Enterprise." *Zygon* 19(1):5–20.

Webb, A. R., L. Kline, and M. F. Holick. 1988. "Influence of Season and Latitude on the Cutaneous Synthesis of Vitamin D3: Exposure to Winter Sunlight in Boston and Edmonton Will Not Promote Vitamin D3 Synthesis in Human Skin." *Journal of Clinical Endocrinology and Metabolism* 67(2):373–377.

Webster, David. 1985. "Surplus, Labor, and Stress in Late Classic Maya Society." *Journal of Anthropological Research* 41:375–399.

Wechsler, Howard. 1985. *Offerings of Jade and Silk: Ritual and Symbol in the Legitimation of the T'ang Dynasty*. New Haven: Yale University Press.

Weil, Peter. 1986. "Agricultural Intensification and Fertility in Gambia (West Africa)." In *Culture and Reproduction: An Anthropological Critique of Demographic Transition Theory*, ed. W. P. Handwerker, 294–320. Boulder, Colo.: Westview Press.

Weiner, Annette. 1976. *Women of Value, Men of Renown*. Austin, Tex.: University of Texas Press.

————. 1986. "Forgotten Wealth: Cloth and Woman's Production in the Pacific." In *Woman's Work,* ed. E. Leacock, H. Safa, and J. Weiner, 96–110. South Hadley, Mass.: Bergin and Garvey.

Weiner, Joseph. 1955. *The Piltdown Forgery.* London: Oxford University Press.

Weiss, M., and A. Mann. 1985. *Human Biology and Behavior.* Boston: Little, Brown.

Westermark, E. 1894. *The History of Human Marriage.* New York: Macmillan.

White, Benjamin. 1976. "Production and Reproduction in a Javanese Village." Ph.D. dissertation, Columbia University.

————. 1982. "Child Labour and Population Growth in Rural Asia." *Development and Change* 13:587–610.

————. 1983. *"Agricultural Involution" and Its Critics: Twenty Years After Clifford Geertz.* The Hague: Institute of Social Studies.

White, Douglas, and M. Burton. 1988. "Causes of Polygyny: Ecology, Economy, Kinship, and Warfare." *American Anthropologist* 90:871–887.

White, Douglas, M. Burton, and M. Dow. 1981. "Sexual Division of Labor in African Agriculture: A Network Autocorrelation Analysis." *American Anthropologist* 83:824–849.

White, Randall. 1982. "Rethinking the Middle/Upper Paleolithic Transition." *Current Anthropology* 23:169–192.

White, Tim, and Gen Suwa. 1987. "Hominid Footprints at Laetoli: Facts and Interpretations." *American Journal of Physical Anthropology* 72(4):485–514.

Whitesides, George. 1985. "Nut Cracking by Wild Chimpanzees in Sierra Leone, West Africa." *Primates* 26:91–94.

Whitman, Frederick, and Robin Mathy. 1986. *Male Homosexuality in Four Societies: Brazil, Guatemala, the Philippines, and the United States.* New York: Praeger.

Whyte, Martin King. 1978. *The Status of Women in Preindustrial Societies.* Princeton: Princeton University Press.

Williams, Thomas. 1965. *The Dusun: A North Borneo Society.* New York: Holt, Rinehart and Winston.

Williams, Walter. 1985. "Persistence and Change in the Berdache Tradition Among Contemporary Lakota Indians." In *Anthropology and Homosexual Behavior,* ed. Evelyn Blackwood, 191–205. New York: Haworth Press.

————. 1986. *The Spirit and the Flesh: Sexual Diversity in American Indian Culture.* Boston: Beacon Press.

Wilson, A. P. 1969. "Behavior of Agonadal Free-Ranging Rhesus Monkeys." *American Journal of Physical Anthropology* 31:261.

Wilson, E. O. 1978. *Human Nature.* Cambridge, Mass.: Harvard University Press.

Winick, Myron, ed. 1979. *Hunger Disease: Studies by the Jewish Physicians in the Warsaw Ghetto.* New York: John Wiley & Sons.

Winkelman, Michael J. 1986. "Magico-Religious Practitioner Types and Socioeconomic Conditions." *Behavior Science Research* 20:17–46.

Witowski, Stanley, and Cecil A. Brown. 1978. "Lexical Universals." *Annual Review of Anthropology* 7:427–451.

————. 1985. "Climate, Clothing, and Body-Part Nomenclature." *Ethnology* 24:197–214.

Wolf, A. P., and C. S. Huang. 1980. *Marriage and Adoption in China, 1845–1945.* Stanford: Stanford University Press.

Wolpoff, M. H., et al. 1988a. "Modern Human Origins." *Science* 241:772.

————. 1988b. "Multiregional Evolution: The Fossil Alternatives to Eden." In *The Origins and Dispersal of Modern Humans: Behavioral and Biological Perspectives,* ed. C. B. Stringer and P. Mellars. Chicago: University of Chicago Press.

Woodburn, James. 1982a. "Egalitarian Societies." *Man* 17:431–451.

———. 1982b. "Social Dimension of Death in Four African Hunting and Gathering Societies." In *Death and the Regeneration of Life,* ed. Maurice Block and Jonathan Parry, 187–210. New York: Cambridge University Press.

Xequin, Li. 1985. *Eastern Zhou and Qin Civilizations.* New Haven: Yale University Press.

Yi, Seonbok, and G. A. Clark. 1983. "Observations on the Lower Paleolithic of Northeast Asia." *Current Anthropology* 24:181–202.

Young, V. R., and N. S. Scrimshaw. 1971. "The Physiology of Starvation." *Scientific American* 225:14–21.

Zhiman, A. 1988. "Archaeological Research on Neolithic China." *Current Anthropology* 29:753–759.

Zihlman, Adrienne. 1981. "Women as Shapers of the Human Adaptation." In *Woman the Gatherer,* ed. F. Dahlberg, 74–120. New Haven: Yale University Press.

Zihlman, Adrienne, and J. Lowenstein. 1985. "*Australopithecus afarensis:* Two Sexes or Two Species?" In *Hominid Evolution: Past, Present and Future,* ed. Philip Tobias, 213–220. New York: Alan R. Liss.

Zottola, George. 1972. *El hambre, la sed y los hombres.* Barcelona: Editorial Bruguera.

Zvelebil, M., ed. 1986. *Hunters in Transition: Mesolithic Societies of Eurasia and Their Transition to Farming.* New York: Cambridge University Press.

INDEX

Egalitarianism, 345–47, 354–55, 367–68; leaders, 366; redistribution, 358–60
Eggs (ova), human, 174–75
Egypt, ancient: incest, 198–99; souls, 400; warfare, 384
Ehrhardt, Anke, 268
Elephants, 26
Ember, Carol and Melvin, 297
Empires, 406
Emulation, 367–68, 374–75
Endorphins, 171–72
Enkephalin, 171
Environment: and family organization, 196; and racial traits, 108–9
Erect posture, 2, 16
Eskimos, 87, 113, 147, 350, 410
Estrogen, and heart disease, 335
Ethiopia, 15, 23, 44
Ethnic descent, 103–4
Eucharist, 441
Eunuchism, 264–65
Europe, infanticide, 213
Evanthropus Dawsoni, 10
Evaporation, cooling by, 54
Exchanges, 190–91, 345–47, 358–60, 370; and family formation, 195–96; and human sacrifice, 425; marriage patterns, 204–5; religious, 414–16
Extramarital sex, 259–61
Eyesight, sex differences, 275

Fallopian tubes, 174
Families, 191, 194–96, 224–25; and incest, 206; number of children, 216–21; and sexual orientation, 250
Famines, 497
Fang people, souls, 401
Fangs (teeth), 3
Fat, 146, 187; in meat, 306–7
Father-daughter incest, 199, 206
Feasts: ancestor-worship, 406; competitive, 359, 362; redistributive, 358–60, 420; seasonal, 147, 148
Feet: bound, 188; and upright posture, 2
Feil, Daryl, 292
Female-headed households, 195, 253
Female heat, 175
Female homosexuality, 248–50; pygmy chimpanzees, 177–78
Female infanticide, 213, 225–27, 303, 310–12, 314–15; warfare and, 297–98
Female sexuality, 252–53; and male dominance, 255, 258–61
Female warriors, 284–85
Fermented milk products, 167
Fialkowski, Konrad, 50, 52–56, 58, 59
Field, Tiffany, 231
Fire, 48–49; and air quality, 130
Fish, tool use, 26
Fluorine dating of fossils, 11

Flutes, prehistoric, 97
Fontebregona Cave, France, 429
Food, 135, 138–39, 146; gifts to chiefs, 379–80; and human sacrifice, 425; male supremacy and, 289; overeating, 142–43; and population pressure, 299, 302; preferences, 160–63, 166–68; production, 134, 139; religious exchange, 415–16; sex in exchange for, 182–83, 190–91; shortages, 146–47; sources, and tool use, 32–33; storage, 378; and warfare, 296–97
Foraging societies, 204, 278–81, 362; nonegalitarian, 363; polygynous, 194
Fore people, 495; food habits, 315
Forsyth, Adrian, 371–72
Foundling hospitals, 213–14
Fouts, Roger, 78
Fox, Robin Lane, 451
France, archaeological finds, 94
Freeloaders, 355
Freud, Sigmund, 174
Funeral rites, Neandertal, 88

Gabon, Fang people, 401
Gahuka-Gama people, birth control, 314
Ganges Valley, Vedic period, 444–45
Gardner, Allen and Beatrice, 77
Gautama Siddhartha, 439–40
Gay community, 244–45, 249–50
Gelada baboons, 176, 186
Gender differences, 252–55, 278–81
Gender roles: in chiefdoms, 324–25; in foraging societies, 280, 289–90; and mathematical ability, 273
Genealogies, 102–4
General History of the Things of New Spain, Sahagún, 432–33
Genes, defective, 335
Genetic analysis techniques, 18–19
Genetic programming, 62
Genetic theories of incest-avoidance, 199–201
Genetic traits, racial, 106–10
Genghis Khan, 449
Genito-genital rubbing, 177–78
Gezer, human sacrifice, 422
Ghetto women, reproduction rates, 220
Gilgamesh, 415
Gillman, Antonio, 384
Glaciations, Neandertals and, 86–87
Global peace, 501–2
Gnostics, 451
Goiter, and PTC tasting, 109
Gombe National Park, Tanzania, chimpanzees, 27–28, 32, 37, 63
Gona, Ethiopia, stone tools, 23
Good, Kenneth, 307, 310–11
Goods, exchange of, 190
Gorbachev, Mikhail, 436
Gordon-Grube, Karen, 428
Gorillas, 2; mating habits, 176–77
Gould, Richard, 345

Jews, 104; religion, 440–41
Jívaro people, 400
Johanson, Donald, 15
Johns Hopkins University talent search, sex
    differences, 272–73
Jordan, Neolithic settlements, 394
Josiah, king of Israel, 423
Julius Caesar, 419
Jungles, animal life, 310
Justinian, emperor of Rome, 452

Kalahari Desert, 53, 302. *See also* !Kung
    people
Kamehameha I, king of Hawaii, 390
Kaoka people, 360, 363
Karnataka, India, agriculture, 329
Karoda, Sueshi, 182
Kasakati Forest, chimpanzees, 28
Kenya, 15–16, 48; baboon studies, 37
Kerala, India, 329
Keys, Anselm, 142
Kibbutz, marriage patterns, 201
Kings (Old Testament books), 422
Klasies River Mouth, 92–93
Konner, Melvin, *The Tangled Wing,* 231–32
Koobi Fora, Kenya, 48–49
Kroeber, Alfred, 117
Kublai Khan, 449–50
!Kung people, 279–81, 288, 302–3, 345–46,
    350, 354; extramarital sex, 261; female
    homosexuality, 249
Kwakiutl Indians, 72, 362–63, 383

Labor force, women in, 496
Labrador, foraging culture, 279
Lactase, 166–67
Lactation, extended, 302–3
Lactose, 155, 166–67
Laetoli, Tanzania, 15–16
Lana (chimpanzee), 78
Language, 66, 72–73, 79, 82–84, 191
Larynx, 77, 82
Leacock, Eleanor, 279, 280
Leadership, 347, 350–51, 362, 366, 438
Leakey, Louis, 22–23
Leakey, Mary, 15
Learned behavior, 62–64
Leavitt, Gregory, 299
Lee, Richard, 280–81, 288, 345–46,
    350
Legs, length, 16
Leisure class, 367–68
Lessa, William, 188
Levirate, 326
Levites, 419–20
Leviticus (Old Testament book), 419
Lieberman, Philip, 83
Life expectancy, 334–37, 497
Lincoln, Bruce, 419
Linnaeus, Carolus, 6

Livestock. *See* Animal husbandry
Living standards, 497
Lizot, Jacques, 290–91
Llamas, 484, 489
Long-distance running, brains and, 52–53
Long-distance warfare, 319–21
Lost-wax method of casting, 491
Loulis (chimpanzee), 78–79
Love, need for, 230–33, 366
Luck concept, 399
Lucy (chimpanzee), 78
Lucy (hominid), 15
Lumholtz, Carl, 289
Lungs, evolution of, 58

Macaques, cultures, 63
McCarthy, Joseph, 242
Machismo, and life expectancy, 340–41
Maclachlan, Morgan D., 329
MacLaine, Shirley, 412
Macumba cults, 243
Mae Enga people, warfare, 296–97
Maggots, as food, 315
Maghzaliyah, 393
Mahabarata, 445
Mahale Mountains, chimpanzees, 63
Mahale National Park, chimpanzees, 41
Mahavira, 439
Maidu Indians, religion, 404
Maize, 475–76, 478, 484
Malaysia: Semai people, 345, 351; Semang
    people, 404
Male dominance, 205; and female behavior, 255,
    258–61; and warfare, 288–93, 297–98. *See
    also* Men
Male homosexuality, 240–45
Malinowski, Bronislaw, 258, 378, 383
Malnutrition, 299; and teeth, 147–48
Malo, David, 389, 390
Mamadi, Mahmood, 219
Mana, 399
Mangaia Island, sexuality, 259
Manichaeism, 452
Manupur, India, 219
Marathon runners, 195, 278
Marital fidelity, 259–60
Marriage, 194–96, 204–5, 318–19; between
    women, 325. *See also* Incest
Marshack, Alexander, 87, 98
Marx, Karl, and religion, 462–63
Massai people, 418
Masturbation, 181
Mathematical ability, 272–73, 330
Mathematics, Mayan, 491
Matrilocality, 319–21
Maya people, 384, 478, 479–80, 495; class
    structure, 151; mathematics, 491
Mazdaism, 438–39
Mbuti people, 279, 280
Mead, Margaret, 258

ABOUT THE AUTHOR

One of the best known of contemporary anthropologists, Marvin Harris has devoted his career to asking big questions about the human condition and answering them authoritatively in clear, down-to-earth prose. In an age of specialists who choose to communicate only within small circles, Harris stands out as an unrepentant generalist interested in the global processes that account for human origins and the evolution of human cultures. His sixteen previous books, which have been translated into fifteen languages, include best-sellers such as *Cows, Pigs, Wars and Witches* and *Cannibals and Kings* as well as a widely used introductory college textbook, *Culture, People, Nature,* now in its fifth edition. After receiving his doctorate, he taught in the Department of Anthropology at Columbia University, served as chairman there, and carried out research in Brazil, Mozambique, Ecuador, India, and East Harlem. In 1981 he accepted the position of graduate research professor of anthropology at the University of Florida in Gainesville and is currently the chair of the General Anthropology Division of the American Anthropological Association. He does most of his writing at a summer cottage on Cranberry Island, Maine. The manuscript for *Our Kind,* like those of all his books, was handwritten, but he vows to switch to a word processor for his next project because it is getting too hard to find decent yellow pads.